12/6

HENRIK IBSEN

Also by Michael Meyer

Play
The Ortolan

Biography
Henrik Ibsen
The Making of a Dramatist 1828–1864

Translations of Ibsen
Brand
John Gabriel Borkman
The Lady from the Sea
When We Dead Awaken
Little Eyolf
The Master Builder
Hedda Gabler
The Wild Duck
Ghosts
The Pillars of Society
Peer Gynt
An Enemy of the People
The Pretenders
A Doll's House
Rosmersholm

Translations of Strindberg
The Plays, Volume One
(The Father, Miss Julie, Creditors,
The Stronger, Playing with Fire,
Erik the Fourteenth, Storm, The
Ghost Sonata)

Ibsen in 1878, aged 50. *'Confused, yet striving for clarity.'*

Michael Meyer

HENRIK IBSEN

The Farewell to Poetry 1864–1882

Rupert Hart-Davis   London

Granada Publishing Limited
First published in Great Britain 1971
by Rupert Hart-Davis Ltd
3 Upper James Street London W1R 4BP

ISBN 246 64001 4
Printed in Great Britain by C. Tinling & Co. Ltd
London and Prescot

Note

All translations of passages from languages
other than English are original, unless
otherwise indicated.

For Michael and Rose Elliot

Contents

List of Illustrations

❧ Acknowledgements

My thanks are due to Mr Tancred Ibsen for granting me access to his grandfather's unpublished account books; to Faber & Faber Ltd for permission to quote James Joyce's *Epilogue to Ibsen's* Ghosts, and to Little, Brown and Company for permission to quote the passage on pp. 319-20 from J. J. Robbins's translation of Konstantin Stanislavsky's *My Life in Art*. I must repeat the acknowledgement paid in my first volume of a particular debt to Halvdan Koht's *Henrik Ibsen: eit diktarliv*, and to the Centenary Edition of Ibsen's works edited by Koht, Francis Bull and Didrik Arup Seip, especially the introductions to the various volumes by those three scholars. In discussing Ibsen's work I have used some material previously printed in my introductions to my translations of the plays, published by Rupert Hart-Davis Ltd. My debts to other sources are acknowledged in the footnotes and bibliography.

I should also like to thank Mr Øyvind Anker and his staff at the University Library, Oslo, and the staffs of the University Library of Stockholm, the Royal Library of Stockholm, the library of University College, London, the British Museum and the British Drama League, for much courteous and patient assistance.

I am grateful to the following for permission to reproduce the various paintings, caricatures, photographs and manuscripts used in the illustrations: Nationalmuséet, Stockholm (Severin Falkman's drawing of Carl Snoilsky); Drottningholms Teatermuseum, Stockholm (still from 1883 production of *Ghosts*); Det. Kgl. Bibliotek, Copenhagen (photographs of Laura Kieler and Clemens Petersen); Gyldendalske Boghandel—Nordisk Forlag, Copenhagen (photographs of Georg Brandes, Frederik Hegel and Hans Christian Andersen); Municipal Gallery of Modern Art, Dublin (Max Beerbohm's caricature, 'Henrik Ibsen receiving Mr William Archer in audience'). All other illustrations are reproduced by kind courtesy of Universitetsbiblioteket, Oslo, and Gyldenal Norsk Forlag, Oslo.

ACKNOWLEDGEMENTS

Works which appear repeatedly in the footnotes have been given the following short titles after their first appearance:

C.E.—Centenary Edition of Ibsen's Works (Henrik Ibsen, *Samlede verker, hundreårsutgave*), I–XXI, ed. Halvdan Koht, Francis Bull and Didrik Arup Seip (Oslo, 1928–1958).

Koht—Halvdan Koht, *Henrik Ibsen: eit diktarliv*, I–II (revised edition, Oslo 1954).

Brandes Brevveksling—*Georg og Edvard Brandes Brevveksling med nordiske Forfattere og Videnskabsmænd*, ed. Morten Borup, Francis Bull and John Landquist, I–VIII (Copenhagen, 1939–1942).

All translations of passages from languages other than English are by myself, except where otherwise indicated.

M.M.

'Anyone who wishes to understand me fully must know Norway. The spectacular but severe landscape which people have around them in the north, and the lonely, shut-off life—the houses often lie miles from each other—force them not to bother about other people, but only their own concerns, so that they become reflective and serious, they brood and doubt and often despair. In Norway every second man is a philosopher. And those dark winters, with the thick mists outside—ah, they long for the sun!'

Ibsen in conversation, quoted by Felix Philippi, *Mein Verkehr mit Henrik Ibsen*, in *Neue Freie Presse* (Vienna), *27 October 1902*.

HENRIK IBSEN

PART ONE
ITALIAN SPRING

ONE

❧ The New Michelangelo

(1864–1866)

THE ITALY which greeted Ibsen in the summer of 1864 was a country rejoicing in new-found unification and liberty. Here, if nowhere else in Europe, the hopes of 1848, that year of revolutions and disillusionments, had at last been fulfilled. In 1859, five years before Ibsen's arrival, Napoleon III had helped the Italians to drive their Austrian overlords out of Milan and Lombardy; and although, to the anger of his allies, he had then made peace with the young Emperor Franz Josef and left him in possession of Venice, the fires of rebellion had been ignited. One by one the little kingdoms of Modena, Parma and Tuscany had risen against and ejected their tyrants. In 1860 Garibaldi had liberated Sicily, taken Naples, and been dissuaded from marching on Rome only by the fear of provoking a clash with Napoleon; after which, in surely the most remarkable gesture that any conqueror has made, he had accepted the sovereignty of the young King Victor Emmanuel of Piedmont-Sardinia and sailed away with a little borrowed money to a life of hard work, poverty and meditation on the island of Caprera. So Rome, when Ibsen entered it that June, was still an independent state under the once liberal but now reactionary Pope Pius IX, garrisoned and protected by French troops. It and Venice were the only parts of Italy that remained outside the new kingdom, of which Florence was the capital, and into which they, too, were to find themselves incorporated within four years.

Rome, which then contained some two hundred thousand inhabitants, was, more than Paris, the cynosure of contemporary writers and artists, and to Scandinavians, especially, it was the promised city. Its influence had been a decisive turning-point in the lives of Oehlenschläger, Thorvaldsen, Hans Andersen, Ole Bull and many others, as it was to be in Ibsen's. An Englishman who was a boy there at the time remembered Rome in the eighteen-sixties as 'changed but little from the Rome of the eighteenth century . . . still lit at night by oil-lamps, with streets mostly innocent of sidewalks, but gay with the coloured hoods of the wine-carts and the coaches of the Cardinals with their big black horses and red trappings . . . Only the uniforms of the French army of occupation struck a rather anomalous note.'[1] The old ghetto still existed near the Cenci Palace, though its walls had been pulled down in 1848. Another Englishman visiting the city in 1866–1887 noted the narrowness of the streets ('there are few, if any, in which three friends can walk arm in arm'); even the Corso was 'a very long, narrow and dirty lane with many turnings'.[2] Compared with Florence, it was an evil-smelling city. 'The streets of Rome, the houses of Rome—to the very palaces and museums—reek with such horrible odours that you are very soon led to conjecture that the ever-quoted malaria from the Pontine Marshes has been made responsible for a great deal of which it is quite innocent, and that one of the chief predisposing causes of the Roman fever is the inconceivable filthiness of the people and their dwellings.'[3] George Augustus Sala was not exaggerating, for Ibsen later recalled how 'the inhabitants were permitted to perform their necessary functions, for want of other arrangements, in the courtyards of the ancient palaces'.[4] Nor did the method of supplying dairy products contribute to the general cleanliness, for the streets in the early mornings were commonly full of goats which would be milked outside any restaurant that needed that luxury, and were even led up two or three flights of stairs to individual customers.[5]

Up to five years previously, visitors from the north had travelled the final stages of their journey by coach, keeping a sharp watch for bandits, and had ridden romantically in through the Porta del Popolo; but in 1861 the railway had been completed, so that Ibsen arrived soberly by train—doubtless to his relief, for the bandits still flourished, and tourists unwise enough to stray outside the city after dark were liable to be kidnapped and held to ransom.

Ibsen lost no time in acquainting himself with the Norwegian consul, a hook-nosed old Holstein Jew named Johan Bravo. Born in the previous century, he had lived in Rome since 1827 and was to prove a good friend and counsellor to Ibsen over the next two decades. Early on the morning of 19 June, presumably the day of or the day after Ibsen's arrival, Bravo took him along to the Circolo Scandinavico, or Scandinavian Club, a lively meeting-place with impressive quarters in the Palazzo Correa, which had been built into the remains of the Mausoleum of Augustus. Bravo's young secretary, Lorentz Dietrichson, was librarian of the Club, and lodged there; he was in bed when

---

[1] Sir Rennell Rodd, *Rome of the Renaissance and Today* (London, 1932), p. 24.
[2] George Augustus Sala, *Rome and Venice, with Other Wanderings in Italy* (London, 1869), pp. 443 and 446.
[3] *Ibid.*, p. 448.
[4] John Paulsen, *Samliv med Ibsen, 2en Samling* (Copenhagen & Christiania, 1913), p. 111.
[5] Lorentz Dietrichson, *Svundne tider.* (Christiania, 1894–1917), III, p. 29.

his visitors arrived, but Bravo roused him from it with a series of oaths and commanded him to take the newcomer on a tour of the city.

Dietrichson, who at thirty was six years younger than Ibsen, had been a childhood friend of Suzannah in Bergen, and had known Ibsen slightly in Christiania. After studying at the University, he had worked for a while under Paul Botten Hansen on *Illustreret Nyhedsblad*, and had then lectured for two years on Scandinavian literature at Upsala University. There he had scandalised the Swedes by denouncing their modern poets as sterile and backward-looking and, worse, by bidding them turn to the tougher and more realistic work being produced in Norway by such as Ibsen and Bjørnson. He had now been in Rome for two years, studying art history, a subject in which he was later to become professor at Christiania University, and he proved an excellent and sympathetic guide. It was a fine, hot Sunday, and, after witnessing High Mass at St Peter's—almost the only recorded instance of Ibsen attending a church service, other than a wedding or funeral—they walked to the Forum and examined its ruins. Then they crossed the Tiber into the working-class quarter of the Trastevere and climbed the Janiculum Hill, where Garibaldi had made his stand for the republic against the Papal troops in 1849, and whence they enjoyed a magnificent panoramic view of the city. On the way down, they passed the oak-tree where Tasso was reputed to have found the inspiration for his epic *Jerusalem* and, when evening came, sat down to dine in a little garden restaurant by the Tiber named Fornarina, after the baker's daughter of that name whom Raphael loved and whom he was reputed to have first seen there.

Forty years later, Dietrichson recalled in his florid style the impression that Ibsen had made on him that first evening in Rome. He found him, to his surprise, 'quite another person than the withdrawn and bitter man I had left three years earlier. He had of course been deeply shaken by the latest events in Scandinavia, and expressed himself with burning indignation on the deceitful policies which had been adopted towards Denmark and how, with suppressed anger, he had seen the Prussians enter Berlin with their trophies from the Schleswig campaign. But at the same time it was as though, on his arrival into *la bella Italia* and *la Roma eterna*, he had put all this behind him, and now wished only to live as intensively as possible for his writing . . . Now he was able to laugh at all the dust which *Love's Comedy* had raised, and which had embittered his life in Norway—now he was able doubly to rejoice in the ten [*sic*] full houses which *The Pretenders* had achieved before he had left. And when the sun went down and we felt the gentle air of the Italian evening shimmer through the little garden where we sat beneath the vine leaves in our pergola with a *foglietta* of Roman wine before us—while the natives of Trastevere came to enjoy the cool of the river flowing beneath the garden wall, and the small dwarf improvised to his mandolin beneath the vines that hung out over the river—while the lamps burned on the garden tables and the lights on the far bank in the Palazzo Farnese and around the great and ancient city mirrored themselves in the water—yes, then, for a moment, we were two young men happy in the certainty that life was rich and beautiful and that its finest fruits were beckoning to us from the future . . . With the aid of our *fogliette* we built our dream-castles in the little garden, and when night fell we wandered home in the soft Mediterranean moonlight.'[1]

Ibsen spent the next few days in further sight-seeing, spending much time, as befitted a painter, in the museums and galleries, where, as we shall see, he formed impressions quite out of fashion with prevalent taste. Yet while he wandered the streets and hills of Rome, unembarrassed by the smells and enjoying the unaccustomed heat in which, like so many Scandinavians, he was always to revel, the indignation which was so inescapable a part of his character seethed unabated; and it was not long before it found expression. The Scandinavian community was about to break up and go into the countryside to avoid the worst of the summer heat, and they held a farewell party at Raphael's Vigne on the Aquiline Hill, on the then still completely rural Via Merulana between S. Maria Maggiore and the Lateran. Dietrichson describes the scene, 'on an open loggia, where we ate our frugal dinner and drank a glass of wine under the sky. It was the first evening for some while that Ibsen had spent among Scandinavians, and he began to speak of the painful and disturbing impressions of recent events in the war which he had received on his journey. Gradually, and almost imperceptibly, his talk took on the character of an improvised speech; all the bitterness which had so long been stored up within him, all the fiery indignation and passion for the Scandinavian cause which he had bottled up for so long, found an outlet. His voice began to ring, and in the evening dusk one saw only his burning eyes. When he had finished, no one cried Bravo or raised his glass, but I think we all felt that that evening the Marseillaise of the North had rung out into the Roman night air.'[2] According to another listener, Ibsen concluded his speech by banging on the table 'so that all the wine-glasses rattled', and vowing that 'never should his son set foot on Norwegian soil before Norway had expiated the wrong that she had done to Denmark'.[3]

Dietrichson and his family had taken a villa at Genzano on Lake Nemi, and

[1] Dietrichson, I, pp. 330, 333–334.

[2] *Ibid.*, pp. 334–335.

[3] Halvdan Koht, *Henrik Ibsen: eit diktarliv* (revised edition, Oslo, 1954), I, p. 236, quoting the Danish painter Frederik Lund.

Ibsen decided to join them there. After watching the illumination of St Peter's and the fireworks on Monte Pincio on St Peter's and St Paul's Day, 29 June, he rode out to Genzano with the Finnish sculptor Walter Runeburg (son of the famous poet J. L. Runeburg) and took lodgings with the village *caffettiere*, who leased them a room in the billiards saloon. To protect himself against the sun Ibsen had purchased a broad-brimmed soft hat with a sky-blue lining, which earned him among the locals the nickname of *capellone* (big hat). 'Here', records Dietrichson, 'we spent the summer in a delightful *far niente*.'[1]

Also living at Genzano that summer was a Norwegian lady named Lina Bruun, with her artist son Peter and her daughter Thea, both suffering from tuberculosis, from which they were both to die within eighteen months. Her other son Christopher, a theological student, had accompanied them to Rome the previous year, but had returned north to fight with the Danes against their Prussian invaders; he was to become a lifelong friend of Ibsen, and was to provide one of the chief inspirations for his next play. Ibsen saw a good deal of Lina, Thea and Peter Bruun at Genzano, and on 4 July Lina wrote to Christopher conveying her distaste for their new acquaintance. Ibsen, she wrote, aroused 'evil feelings' in her; five days previously (i.e., within twenty-four hours of Ibsen's arrival), they had had a set-to; his genius, she explained, needed something to censure and chastise, and he had continually to be seeking targets for his wrath. However, they got on better than she had anticipated. On 5 August she wrote again to Christopher about Ibsen: 'So dual a character it is difficult to imagine. To meet day by day he is the most sociable, cheerful and friendly man you could conceive.' But sometimes, she added, his eyes glitter cruelly, and then all he wants is to play the devil. She added a note on his drinking habits. 'He likes to take a glass of wine, because it heightens his animal spirits, and, since they are already lively, it is easy to get a false impression . . . But when he is writing, he drinks tea.'[2] Ibsen assured Lina Bruun that if Christopher fell in the war he would raise a memorial to him in poetry. Christopher Bruun did not fall, but returned to point the finger of judgment at Ibsen, who raised a poetic memorial to him none the less.

Dietrichson tells how Ibsen and he spent their days in Genzano. 'In the morning we worked. At noon we gathered to eat in a wine cellar, literally a cellar, an almost pitch-dark room filled with *vinfoustager* and a huge basket containing a bitch with her litter. There was only one tiny window and when, as frequently happened, one of the village donkeys stopped outside to scratch itself against the wall, Ibsen or one of us had to run out and chase it away so

---

[1] Dietrichson, I, p. 336.
[2] Francis Bull, *Nordisk kunsterliv i Rom* (Oslo, 1960), pp. 163–164.

that we could see to eat.' In the afternoon they lay reading or chatting under
the trees on one of the hills overlooking Lake Nemi. 'I remember especially',
writes Dietrichson, 'that one day I was lying there reading Ammianus Marcel-
linus's account of Julian the Apostate's campaigns, and Ibsen became much
interested in this. We began to talk of Julian, and I know that the idea of
writing about this subject took root in his mind that day. At any rate, when I
had finished reading, he said he hoped no one would write about it before he
did. . . . Towards evening we either walked across the hill to Lake Nemi or
descended to the lake, strolled along it and climbed up to Nemi through the
bushes. There, many an evening, we good friends emptied a glass of Nemi
wine on a pretty verandah with a splendid view across the lake, the village of
Genzano, the *campagna* and the sea, or inside in the little *locanda* where the cat
rubbed itself against the foot of the old woman at her spinning-wheel and Pius
IX smiled benignly down on us from a fearful painting on the wall, while the
tiny Roman lamp was lit and the landscape outside with its lake, woods and
campagna grew dim in the magic dusk of evening, which swiftly turned into
the blackest night. And as we walked home we would usually meet the natives
singing as they moved from Madonna portrait to Madonna portrait with their
devout songs in the warm, dark summer night, while the lamps gleamed in the
niches of the saints along the roadside and at street corners.'[1]

One day they heard that the Pope, whom Ibsen had not yet seen, was to pass
in formal procession through the nearby village of Castelgandolfo on his way
to his summer residence there, and they decided to go over and have a look at
him. 'We acquired two donkeys', relates Dietrichson, 'and rode cheerfully off.
As we approached the village we saw that its single long street was filled with
people waiting to watch the procession and receive his blessing; they thronged
the street on either side . . . We had no choice but to ride with as good a face
as we could muster through the town gate and, like two *matti inglesi*, run the
gauntlet of the laughing lines of people. For a few moments all went well, but
then the donkeys broke into a violent gallop, and suddenly first one of them,
then the other, were flat on their bellies in the middle of the street with us
standing above them. The jubilation was immense. At that moment, the papal
procession arrived. The donkeys were dragged out of the way, braying and
protesting, and the Pope made his entry undisturbed by the Norwegian poet
and his squire; nor did he withhold from us the blessing which he extended to
his loyal disciples.'[2] Which was just as well, for Pius IX was supposed to have
the evil eye; to counter which many a peasant would hold a finger pointed
towards him, in the cover of his pocket.

---

[1] Dietrichson, I, pp. 336–337.
[2] *Ibid.*, p. 337.

That summer at Genzano Ibsen began to write a play in prose;[1] but he encountered a block, technical or psychological, and set to rework it as a long epic poem. This was the work whose theme had been growing in him 'like a foetus' ever since that day in April when he had seen the Danish cannon captured at Dybbøl drawn in triumph through the Berlin streets and spat on by the watching crowds. He composed this poem in eight-line stanzas of rhymed pentameters, and clearly planned it as an indictment of his countrymen for their lassitude and materialism, as particularly manifested in their non-assistance of the Danes. The opening section, 'To The Accomplices', states the theme:

> My people, my fair land, my northern home . . .
> I'll sing you a sad song. Perhaps my last
> As Norway's bard. For no bard sings again
> Who has bemoaned the passing of his people.
> And the sickness has begun. I see a corpse
> Huge as a giant's, poisoning field and fjord.
> Deck it with Norway's flags and sink it deep . . .
> What is dead can't be lied back to life.
> What is dead must go down into the dark.
> The dead have only one task; to provide
> Soil and nourishment for the new-sown seed.

Section Two shows two boys lying on a Norwegian hillside. One is 'the kind that looks bright-eyed upon the world'; the other 'faces north, his back towards the sun'. The former, looking down into the valley, speaks of his happy home; the other speaks of his, and tells how, when his father died, he had dreamed he had seen his mother creep in and strike her husband's corpse. Soon after this point the section breaks off, apparently unfinished. Section Three, entitled 'Across The Mountain', shows the happier of the two boys, Ejnar, now a painter, with his fiancée, Agnes, taking farewell of friends at a betrothal feast in the mountains. As they leave, they meet the 'northward-facing' boy, Koll (later altered to Brand), who is now a priest. From this point until the fragment ends, the action closely corresponds to that of the play which Ibsen was shortly to write. Brand denounces Ejnar's lazy and self-indulgent hedonism as typical of their countrymen, continues alone on his way and comes to the village where he was born. As he looks down into the valley with its cramped church, a crazed peasant girl sees him, says: 'Come to my church', and leads him up the mountain to a huge natural cave hollowed into the rock

---

[1] So states Martin Schneekloth in his diary for 6 February 1867, printed in Peter Schindler's moving memoir of Schneekloth, *En Ungdom* (Copenhagen, 1942), pp. 120–122.

which local people call the 'Ice Church'. Brand ponders the contrast between this awe-inspiring God-made church and the mean building below. He descends to the village, where there is famine. The Mayor is doling out meagre rations to the people; he appeals to Brand to give food or money, but Brand tells them that the famine is God's judgment on them for their materialism and lack of spirituality. The poem breaks off in the middle of his sermon.

It measures, to this point, just over two hundred stanzas, or sixteen hundred lines. With its splendidly Byronic opening denouncing his compatriots, its fine descriptions of natural scenery and the powerful rhetoric of Brand's condemnation of Ejnar and, later, of the villagers, it was certainly the most powerful and exciting poem that Ibsen had yet written. Yet it made painful progress; he was at one of those critical stages in a writer's career when he realises, slowly and unwillingly, that he is writing in the wrong medium. The composition of these two hundred stanzas took him over a year before he finally abandoned the work in its epic form and began to rewrite it as dialogue.

Meanwhile, as a distraction during that summer of 1864, he composed three short poems, all in something approaching his best manner. *In Time Of Dybbøl* tells how, on the ship from Norway to Denmark the previous spring, the passengers had begun to talk of the Dano-Prussian war, and one old lady had said with a calm smile: 'I do not fear for my son.' Ibsen admired her courage until he learned the reason for it; her son was a soldier in the Norwegian army, and so stood in no danger of being involved in the fighting. *The Power Of Memory* describes how an animal trainer teaches a bear to dance; he ties it in a copper which he heats, and then, as it begins to burn the bear's feet, plays a tune on his barrel organ. The bear dances with pain; afterwards, by association, it dances whenever that tune is played. So, continues the poem, I too must dance whenever I hear the tune that reminds me of the time when 'more than my skin was burned'. The final verse runs:

> Whenever I hear an echo from that time
> It is as though I were bound in a burning copper.
> It pierces me like a needle under my nails
> And makes me dance in verse.

The third poem was a lyric of twelve lines entitled *Gone*, and is traditionally supposed to have been written for Thea Bruun:

> We followed the last
> Guest to the gate.
> The night wind stole
> The syllables of farewell.

The garden and house
Where sweetest sounds
Had drugged my senses
Lay deserted.

It was but a feast
Before the black night.
She was but a guest.
And now she is gone.

That July, Ibsen received in Genzano a letter from Richard Petersen, the chairman of the Christiania Theatre who, six years earlier, had publicly denounced him as 'a playwright of gigantic insignificance', inviting him to become the theatre's artistic director. The post had been offered to Bjørnson, but he had demanded powers which the board regarded as too sweeping. The temptation to Ibsen must have been considerable for, cheap as life was in Italy, his grant was insufficient to provide him with more than the barest necessities. But he had had enough of the 'daily abortion' of running a theatre, and Italy had given him a peace which he had not previously known and was not prepared to surrender. He declined the offer.

In September Ibsen returned, like the other Scandinavians, to Rome, and on the 16th of that month he wrote a long and revealing letter to Bjørnson in Christiania, the first we have from his hand since his arrival in Italy. Bjørnson had learned of the Christiania Theatre's offer to Ibsen, and, not unreasonably, had written to Dietrichson asking for clarification. Ibsen, to whom Dietrichson had passed on the message, explained that Petersen had assured him that negotiations with Bjørnson had broken down, and had urged: 'since *you* would not take the job, I *must* . . . I rejected the offer, rejected it totally and unreservedly, and without implying that any change of circumstances could ever alter my position . . . So you see, my dear Bjørnson, that in this matter you have done me an injustice by nurturing the mistrust which is apparent in your letter to Dietrichson . . . I cannot, though, deny that I can think of an explanation for this mistrust, and that I blame you less than myself for it.' He then allowed himself a rare moment of self-revelation, which has been quoted earlier but bears repeating in its original context. 'I know I have the fault that I cannot make close contact with people who demand that one should give oneself freely and unreservedly. I am rather like the bard in *The Pretenders*, I can never bring myself to strip completely, I have the feeling that, where personal relationships are concerned, I can give only false expression to what I feel deep down inside, to my true self, and that is why I prefer to shut it up within me,

and why we have sometimes stood as it were observing each other from a
distance.' The letter continues:

> *Please accept my thanks for all the beauty I have drunk in on my journey; I can tell*
> *you, it has done me good. Here in Rome especially much has been revealed to me;*
> *though I can't yet get to terms with classical art, I don't really understand its relevance*
> *to our time, I lack the illusion and, above all, the sense of personal and individual*
> *expression in the subject as in the artist, and I cannot help often seeing (as yet, anyway)*
> *mere conventions where others postulate laws. It seems to me that the classical plastic*
> *works of art are, like our heroic ballads, the products of their age rather than of this or*
> *that master; which may perhaps be a reason why so many of our modern sculptors fail*
> *when they persist, today, in trying to create heroic ballads in clay and marble. Michel-*
> *angelo, Bernini and his school I understand better; those fellows had the courage to*
> *commit a madness now and then. The architecture has impressed me more, but neither*
> *the classical style nor its later offsprings attract me as much as the Gothic; to me, the*
> *cathedral in Milan is the most overwhelming thing I can imagine in this field; the man*
> *who could conceive such a work must have been capable, in his spare moments, of*
> *creating a moon and tossing it into the heavens. I know you won't agree with much of*
> *what I have loosely indicated here, but I think it is consistent with my general stand-*
> *point, and that my appreciation of art will develop along these lines.*
>
> *Here in Rome there is blessed peace for writing; I am now working on a longish*
> *poem, and am planning a tragedy,* Julian the Apostate, *a task which I embrace with*
> *inordinate enthusiasm and which I think will bring me joy. My wife and small son will*
> *be coming here this autumn; I hope you approve of this arrangement . . . Dietrichson*
> *will be leaving Rome in the New Year, and I shall be taking over his job* [as librarian
> of the Scandinavian Club], *which will mean free furnished lodgings and a small*
> *salary too; I can live a year in Rome on 400 specie-dollars* [£100].
>
> *Political events at home have grieved me sadly, and have much clouded my happiness.*
> *So it was all lies and dreams. These recent happenings will have a considerable effect*
> *on me. We must now draw a line through our ancient history; the Norwegians of today*
> *clearly have no more connection with their past than the Greek pirates have with the*
> *race that sailed to Troy and fought beside the gods . . .*

Ibsen's first reaction to classical art is interesting in that it closely reflects his
feelings about drama—the need to get away from the generalised and the heroic
towards the human and the individual. The ancient Greek statues must have
seemed to him like the characters in Oehlenschläger's plays, devoid of personality; he preferred, as Shelley had done half a century earlier, the Roman
busts, which portrayed recognisable human beings. For the same reason, he was
disappointed in the paintings of Raphael, whom his fellow-Scandinavians
idolised. In Michelangelo, on the other hand, then fashionably regarded as

extravagant and barbaric, rather as Shakespeare had been during the previous century, he must have recognised a kindred spirit, one of those bleak and lonely artists who tower above their age like a snow-capped mountain, as Dante, Milton and Wordsworth had done, and as Ibsen himself was to do. During his visit to Florence on his journey south, Ibsen can scarcely have missed seeing Michelangelo's unfinished statues, then in the Boboli Gardens (now in the Accademia di Belle Arti), and those mighty figures straining to free themselves from the imprisoning marble must have seemed to Ibsen a mirror of his own struggle as an artist. In the plays to come, from *Brand* to *When We Dead Awaken*, he was to create similar gigantic and tormented prisoners. Michelangelo, more than any writer, was to be Ibsen's master; the one was to create in words what the other had created in stone. Ibsen's equally unfashionable admiration of the Gothic (Milan Cathedral) and the Baroque (Bernini) was also logical in the man who was shortly to write *Peer Gynt*.

When Suzannah and Sigurd arrived Ibsen moved into an apartment at 55 Via Capo le Case, a house (now demolished) on the corner of the Via Due Macelli. The hoped-for librarianship, with its free lodgings, did not materialise, and they remained in the Via Capo le Case until they left Rome four years later. Dietrichson relates that for several days before the arrival of his wife and son Ibsen was 'restless with excitement', and that when they finally met, an occasion at which Dietrichson was present, few words were exchanged, but no one could have doubted that 'these two highly individual people belonged intensely to one another. And I said to myself: "She and no one else is the wife for him; the only one. Only someone like her, with her strong, masculine love of truth and her deep, feminine devotion, can guide him to fulfilment." '[1]

By October Ibsen had exhausted his grant, and only a timely draft of 100 specie-dollars (£25) from Bjørnson, tireless as ever in whipping up money for worthy causes, saw him through the last ten weeks of the year. He was earning nothing, and his expenses in Rome came to 40 scudi (40 specie-dollars, £10) a month.[2] Bjørnson's letter of 5 October enclosing the money contained a few home truths:

'Your whole life has been such that the sun never reached it, and under such circumstances plants absorb more water than light and acquire more mud than colour. What you lacked was affection, love, a calm view of essentials. Now, God be praised, you have all that, and we shall have the fruits! . . . There are many goblins in your head which I think you ought to placate. But, as I'm sure I have often told you, they are a dangerous army to have around; they're like the Praetorians and mediaeval mercenaries; after routing their enemies, they

---

[1] Dietrichson, IV, p. 398.
[2] Letter to Bjørnson, 28 January 1865.

turn on their masters and plunder them ... I understand your admiration for the Gothic; but you'll see it differently when you get home ... As regards classical art, I think you'll soon perceive the individualism behind the convention; but it's true, our senses have to be attuned first ... Here ... the theatre has stood empty for six weeks and is expected to go bankrupt, which would be the best thing for everyone ... I enclose 100 specie-dollars. When you want more, you must tell me.'[1]

Ibsen did not acknowledge this gift for two months, a delay which seems ungracious even for him. To make matters worse, his letter went astray and was never delivered.

Ibsen led a gregarious life that autumn and winter in Rome, as indeed he was to do during the whole of his stay there. Yet he limited himself singularly to his fellow-Scandinavians; he does not seem, now or later, to have made any Italian friends; nor did he meet any of the foreign celebrities living there, such as Franz Liszt, or the aged English consul Joseph Severn, in whose arms John Keats had died nearly half a century before. He became a regular habitué of the Scandinavian Club, which had an excellent library; it had just received a big grant of books from the University library in Christiania, and possessed six thousand volumes. The register shows that Ibsen borrowed, amongst others, the following books during these four years in Rome—and although the list gives no positive clue to his reading, since most were probably taken out for Suzannah, a far more avid reader than he, at least we can be sure that she would have discussed them with him: 1864, Becker's *World History*, and several volumes of Goethe, including *Wilhelm Meister*. 1865, more Goethe, including *Faust*; several of Scott's novels, including *The Heart of Midlothian*, *Waverley* and *The Bride of Lammermoor*; Dante's *The Divine Comedy*, in Danish (in May, re-borrowed in October); two volumes of Goldoni's comedies, and Garibaldi's autobiography. 1866, Aristophanes's *The Birds*, a book about Euripides by Christian Wilster, novels by Georges Sand, Dickens, Dumas and Maria Edgeworth, and *Faust* again. 1867, more Goethe, Eckermann's *Conversations with Goethe*, two volumes of Shakespeare, *Don Quixote* and *David Copperfield*. He also at various times borrowed several volumes of Ludvig Holberg's plays.[2]

---

[1] Bjørnstjerne Bjørnson, *Gro-tid* (*brev fra aarene, 1857–1870*), ed. Halvdan Koht (Christiania, 1912), II, pp. 142–146.

[2] Cf. Øyvind Anker, *Ibsen og den skandinaviska forening i Rom* (*Edda*, 1956), and CE, XIX, pp. 130–134.

Ibsen seems to have visited Italian theatres at least occasionally during this stay, for in 1877 he remarked to Didrik Grønvold that Italian actresses swooned realistically 'whereas in Norway in his time actresses always swooned according to fixed rules, always on the left of the stage and always with a handkerchief in their left hand'. (Cf. Didrik Grønvold, *Diktere og musikere*, Oslo, 1945, p. 16).

Ibsen's name appears frequently in the Club's suggestion book, demanding that the lamps be cleaned, that a packet of glue be removed from the pedestal of a bust of a dancer, that 'the dancer's big left toe be restored', that a map of the papal state be procured and hung, and that the newspaper *Osservatore Romano* be provided. On 6 December he was elected a member of the newspaper committee; on 20 January 1865 he proposed 'That Germans be not permitted entry into the Club', a motion which was rejected at an extraordinary general meeting on 6 February with only two votes in its favour; and on 13 February he was put in charge of the library accounts (why he was not, as he had hoped, appointed librarian is not clear). He was invited to serve on the general committee, but refused, explaining: 'I must belong to the opposition'.[1] He was not the most clubbable of members. One of his fellows recalled how, in his 'single suit of shabby leek-green cloth, he used to stalk sullenly up and down . . . not speaking a word to anyone until supper-time, when he would empty a flask of thin red wine and slowly brighten up, not into geniality exactly, but into loquacity, and dart the scathing bolts of his sarcasm ruthlessly in all directions'.[2] One day, finding in an illustrated magazine a portrait of Count Manderström, the Swedish Foreign Minister and an advocate of non-intervention, he drew a halter round the Count's neck; when, at the next meeting of the Club, the offender was challenged to reveal himself, Ibsen silently rose from his chair.[3]

He often dined with his fellow Scandinavians at an *osteria*—the 'Cucina Tedesca', or 'Deutsche Küche', a very humble place at the junction of the Via Felice and the Via del Tritone, which in addition to the usual Italian dishes served sauerkraut and pancakes; 'Lepre', on the corner of the Via Condotti and the Via Mario dei Fiori, where the wine waiter, Marco, had been a famous bandit; 'Mangani', outside the Porta Pia; and, especially, 'Il Genio' in the Due Macelli. The wine waiter here, Evangelista, had been one of Garibaldi's thousand, and they had a table permanently reserved for them in the far left-hand corner. A meal with half a *foglietta* of wine at any of these places cost 1½ paolo, or about 60 øre (6d.); or you could buy your own food from shops and stalls, washing your vegetables in the nearest fountain, and the *osteria* would provide salt, pepper and oil, and, most important, wine, and cook what needed to be cooked. A Danish acquaintance of Ibsen who came to Rome the following

---

[1] Though when the committee decided to revise the rules, Ibsen 'moved, with statesman-like dexterity, behind the chairs, dropping a word here and there which seemed to have its effect'. (Fr. G. Knudtzon, *Ungdomsdage*, Copenhagen, 1927, p. 165).

[2] Edmund Gosse, *Two Visits to Denmark, 1872, 1874* (London, 1911), pp. 174–175, quoting the Danish writer Christian Molbech.

[3] Kristofer Janson, *Hvad jeg har oplevet* (Christiania, 1915), p. 77.

year, describes one such shopping expedition in detail. 'You saw a *pizzicarolo* and went in and bought a sardine—1 soldo[1]—or, better still, tunnyfish (3 or 4 soldi)—and cheese (1 or 2 soldi). Then the butcher, who for 5 soldi would sell you a veal chop, and the greengrocer, where you could get a lettuce head for 1 soldo. At the entrance to the *osteria* sat a man crying: "*Uova dure! Uova toste! Un soldo l'uno!*", so you bought an egg. Another man would be sitting in the doorway working a machine, specially designed for the purpose, which, disagreeable as it sounds, treated artichokes with lard so that they absorbed it completely. He cried: "*Carciofi romani!*", and sold you one for a soldo. Then you entered the front room of the *osteria*. Behind a counter stood a handsome, blonde, Junoesque creature. You gave her your salad to prepare and your chop to fry. To the right a door led into a larger room, where a long room table was reserved for the Scandinavians. You ordered "*mezza foglietta, bianco*" ... With the wine arrived two glazed clay plates, one bearing the fried chop, the other the salad; also a tin fork, its thin teeth splayed in all directions, a knife, and a napkin of unbleached linen. You now had a splendid dinner: *entrée*, sardine or tunnyfish; *pièce de resistance*, chop with salad, including egg; vegetable, artichoke; and, finally, cheese—stracchino, gorgonzola or parmigiano. The preparations of the salad cost 1 soldo, the frying of the chop the same, and the wine 6–7 soldi.'[2] They usually dined between seven and eight, and took their coffee at the century-old Café Greco in the Via Condotti, as Oehlenschläger, Thorvaldsen and Hans Andersen had done, smoking long pipes or bad papal cigars.

As always, Ibsen took many long walks, alone or in the company of Suzannah and Sigurd, the latter often carried upon Walter Runeburg's shoulders, 'walks', recalled Dietrichson, 'that usually ended in some rustic *osteria* on the Ponte Molle or in the Moletta at the foot of the Palatine Hill'.[3] Among the other writers and artists whose acquaintance he now made were the shy and lonely Jens Adolph Jerichau, the leading sculptor in Denmark since Thorvaldsen's death; the Danish painter Carl Bloch (whom Bjørnson, a few years earlier, had described in a letter to his wife as 'big, handsome, childlike, lazy, nice');[4] and, most importantly, the young Swedish poet Carl Snoilsky, who had arrived in Rome that September and with whom Ibsen was later to enjoy a close friendship. Aged twenty-three, and in appearance not unlike Robert

---

[1] A soldo was worth about one halfpenny.

[2] Knudtzon, pp. 125–126. Extra information from Dietrichson, III, pp. 29 ff.

[3] Dietrichson, I, p. 343.

[4] Bjørnson, *Breve til Karoline, 1858–1907*, ed. Dagny Bjørnson-Sautreau (Oslo, 1957), p. 49.

Louis Stevenson, Snoilsky had already won himself a reputation as one of the most gifted poets in Scandinavia, and as a romantic and successful lover.

Bloch, Snoilsky and Walter Runeburg were all ten or so years younger than Ibsen who, living up to his Learned Holland nickname of Gert Westphaler, the talkative barber, would sit at the centre of the table as they dined, wearing his broad-brimmed hat and leading the discussions in Socratean vein, pressing the arguments of the others to their often uncomfortable conclusions, challenging and bantering. Once when someone, galled by this insistent cross-examination, declared that the truth was as clear as that two and two make four, Ibsen asked whether one could in fact be sure that two and two would make four on, say, Jupiter? One question to which he obsessively returned was how far an artist ought to reject the demands of society and live according to his own creed and morality; he enjoyed citing the example of the English poet Thomas Chatterton, who had starved to death, swallowing (according to legend) even his doorkey, rather than take an ordinary breadwinning job. Ibsen declared that Chatterton had been right, and that he himself would choose the same course; it is ironical to reflect that, unknown to him, his friends in Christiania were at this time trying unsuccessfully to get him an assistant librarianship and, of all things, a post in the customs, the latter of which professions a writer of Ibsen's own temperament and stature on the other side of the world, Herman Melville, was shortly to embrace (and to remain in for nineteen years). Snoilsky remembered Ibsen at these dinners, 'the lightning flashing from beneath the enormous hat'.[1]

The topic which obsessed him most, however, was still the old question of the Dano-Prussian war, and the failure of Norway and Sweden to help their neighbour. Again and again in his letters and recorded utterances he returns to the subject. 'The significant and decisive thing for me', he wrote to Magdalene Thoresen (3 December 1865) 'has been that I have got far enough away from our country to see the hollowness behind all the self-created lies in our so-called public life ... How often do we not hear people in Norway speak with intense complacency of our Norwegian "good sense", which really means nothing but a tepidity of spirit which makes it impossible for those honest souls to commit a madness [the phrase is the one he had used in praise of Michelangelo and Bernini] ... Down here, I assure you, it is different!' In a Norwegian paper he had read of a boy who had cut off a finger to avoid military service. 'I know mothers in Piedmont, in Genoa, Novara, Alessandria, who took their fourteen

---

[1] *Til Henrik Ibsen*, a poem contributed by Snoilsky to the *festskrift* for Ibsen's seventieth birthday: *Henrik Ibsen: festskrift i anledning af hans 70de fødselsdag*, ed. Gerhard Gran (Bergen, 1898), pp. 5–7.

year old sons from school that they might join Garibaldi's adventure in Palermo;
it was not so much a question of liberating their country as of realising an idea.
How many of our politicians do you suppose will do likewise when the
Russians invade Finnmark? . . . I was in Berlin at the time of the triumphal
entry, I saw the people spit on the cannon from Dybbøl, and it was to me a
sign that history will spit in the eyes of Sweden and Norway for their part in
that affair. Here in Rome I find every kind of spiritual squalidity among the
Scandinavians. What do you think of the fact that during the war Danish men
and women sat on Sundays among the Germans in the chapel of the Prussian
Embassy and listened piously while the Prussian priest prayed from his pulpit
for victory for the Prussian armies in their just war against the enemy? But I
have raged and scourged, believe me; for down here, I fear nothing; at home
I was afraid when I stood in that clammy crowd and sensed their ugly smiles
behind me . . . I had to get away from all that swinishness up there to become
cleansed. Up there I could never achieve any coherent inner life; so that I was
one thing in my work and another outside it; and so that my work, too, never
achieved any real entity.'

Yet as Ibsen mocked his fellow-Scandinavians for their cowardice under the
Italian sky, there was one man who did not quail before his onslaughts, and
whose presence must have nagged Ibsen like a Banquo; the young theological
student Christopher Bruun, newly returned to Rome that autumn from the
Danish war, having made the journey through Europe on foot. At a meeting
of the Christiania Students' Union three days before Ibsen left Norway, which
Ibsen did not attend, being otherwise occupied with his Learned Holland
friends, Bruun had exhorted his fellow-countrymen to volunteer with him
and thereby 'testify by action that idealism, truth and justice are not mere
subjects for speeches on festive occasions, but things for which a man should
be prepared to live, fight and, if necessary, die'.[1] He had been much disillusioned
with the Danish army, finding little idealism or patriotism, but mainly a desire
to return safely home; on one occasion he had been warned not to shoot lest
he 'irritate the enemy'. He had signed off from the war, and had arrived in
Rome a deeply disappointed man, very different from the idealist who had
set forth from Christiania.[2] One day when Ibsen brought the Danish war up
for discussion Bruun asked him why, if he felt so strongly, he had not volun-
teered. 'We poets have other tasks to perform', Ibsen replied; but a doubt
remained in his mind. He wondered whether he had been right to compromise;

---

[1] Francis Bull, *Henrik Ibsen* in *Norsk litteratur-historie*, ed. Francis Bull, Frederik Paasche,
A. H. Winsnes and Philip Houm, IV (Oslo, 1960), p. 344.

[2] Cf. Eivind Berggrav and Francis Bull, *Ibsens sjelelige krise* (Oslo, 1937), pp. 37 ff.

and with this doubt was linked another. Was he right to believe so inflexibly in his calling and thus, in all probability, condemn his wife and child to continued poverty?

So this breakaway year of 1864 ended in a mood of, if possible, more than usual doubt. The New Year was ushered in by a buoyant letter from Bjørnson who, notwithstanding his earlier protestations, had finally accepted the directorship of the Christiania Theatre and had forgiven Ibsen the latter's apparent failure to acknowledge his previous letter and draft. 'How often I long for you, Ibsen!' he declared (19 January), surely almost the only time anyone felt or said that. 'I always do when I am parted from you, even when you were in Bergen and I was here—but when we meet, things go wrong. Why? . . . Stay down there as long as you can, and go to Naples and Sorrento as soon as you can manage after Easter.' He added a suggestion which was to have far-reaching and beneficial consequences for Ibsen. 'Let me put you under Hegel's wing! He'll gladly send you an advance, which I shall guarantee on your behalf.'[1]

Frederik Hegel, the first great Scandinavian publisher, had been born the illegitimate son of a servant-girl by her employer's son, Frederik V. Mansa, later to become a well-known doctor and medical historian. One of Mansa's patients was a certain Jacob Deichmann, the head of a small Copenhagen publishing house named Gyldendal, and at Mansa's suggestion Deichmann took Hegel into his employ when the latter was fifteen. In 1850, at the age of thirty-three, Hegel became head of the firm, and within fifteen years had transformed it from its modest beginnings into the distinguished house which it has since remained. Bjørnson had lately become one of his authors, and had found him a wise and generous counsellor; an opinion which Ibsen, after an unfortunate preliminary misunderstanding, was permanently to share. His association with Hegel, on whose advice he came to rely not merely in literary but also in financial matters, was to give him that feeling of trust in his publisher which can be, as it was with Ibsen, such a stabilising influence on an author's career.

This last letter of Bjørnson crossed with one which Ibsen wrote to him on 28 January confirming Bjørnson's prediction that his senses would gradually become attuned to classical art and sculpture. Ibsen confessed that its beauty

grows more and more on me, as you said it would. It comes in flashes, but a single flash throws light over whole vistas. Do you remember the 'Tragic Muse' which stands outside the hall in the Rotunda in the Vatican? No sculpture here has yet been such a revelation to me. I may even say that it is through this that I have understood what

---

[1] *Gro-tid*, II, pp. 150–151.

Greek tragedy was. That indescribably calm, noble and exalted joy in the expression of the face, the richly laurelled head containing within it something supernaturally luxuriant and bacchantic, those eyes that look both inwards and at the same time through and far beyond the object of their gaze—such was Greek tragedy. The statue of Demosthenes in the Lateran, the Faun in the Villa Borghese and the Faun (of Praxiteles) in the Vatican (bracchio nuovo), have also opened great windows for me into Greek life and the Greek character, and have enabled me to understand what imperishability in beauty really is. Pray heaven I may be able to use this understanding for my own work. Michelangelo's Moses in S. Pietro in Vincoli I had not seen when I last wrote to you; but I had read about it and built up an expectation which has not quite been fulfilled—however, I have only seen it once.

How glorious the landscape is down here; in both forms and colours there is an indescribable harmony. I often spend half the day lying out among the graves on the Via Latina or the old Via Appia, and think it an idleness but no waste of time. Caracalla's Baths are another place which holds some special attraction for me . . .

On 25 March he applied to the Royal Norwegian Society for Knowledge at Trondhjem for a grant of 500 specie-dollars (£125) to extend his stay in Italy, explaining that he was 'preparing a long dramatic work based on material from Roman history'. Bjørnson, who had himself received a grant from them, supported Ibsen's application with an ingenious letter (21 April) to the Society, pleading that 'a poetical work does not, indeed, strictly come under the heading of knowledge, but . . . the circumstances under which it springs into existence, and the sum of experience, knowledge and mood from which it is born, demand a very special protection. If this is not forthcoming, the wine ferments—and Henrik Ibsen has always been particularly vulnerable to this danger' (not perhaps the happiest of metaphors to use about one who was well known recently to have been an alcoholic). 'His work', concluded Bjørnson's letter, 'is more strictly akin to knowledge than my own, since he has a greater talent than I for abstract thought.'[1] But the application arrived too late, the Society having already made all its allocations for the next six months.

That spring of 1865 Ibsen struggled with three projects: *Brand* (as an epic poem), *Emperor and Galilean* (as a prose drama), and another epic poem set against the background of a Seventeenth of May celebration in Norway. He read Dietrichson a song from the latter poem which, however, he abandoned, and rewrote four years later as a prose play, *The League of Youth*. The other two projects, likewise, made painful progress. The relaxing atmosphere of Rome, 'its ideal peace, the carefree companionship of the artistic world, an existence comparable only to that of Shakespeare's *As You Like It*', as he was later to des-

---

[1] *Gro-tid*, II, pp. 159–161.

cribe it,[1] was totally different to the conditions which had stimulated his writing in Norway, and it took time for him to assimilate it. *Emperor and Galilean* he was already finding too big a theme to fit into the span of a normal play. 'Why can't one write a drama in ten acts?' he asked Dietrichson one day. 'I can't find room in five.'[2] *Emperor and Galilean* was in fact to occupy ten acts and to take him eight more years to complete; the malaise of contemporary Europe, and of Norway in particular, obsessed him too much for him to concentrate on the problems of Julian the Apostate. The subject uppermost in his mind, as with those two other exiles half a century later, James Joyce and D. H. Lawrence, was the narrowness and complacency of his fellow-countrymen, with their failure to support the Danes as the indelible symbol. Yet his own failure to have acted may have been responsible for the block which he now, as a writer, experienced.

On Good Friday, 14 April, John Wilkes Booth fired a pistol into a box at Ford's Theatre in Washington, and the event roused Ibsen to compose a striking poem, one indeed of his finest, *The Murder of Abraham Lincoln*. Characteristically, he directed his indignation not, like the rest of the world, at Booth, but at what he regarded as the hypocrisy of human reaction. Why such anger now? he asks. Was this worse than the Prussian action at Dybbøl, the Russian rape of Poland, England's bombardment of Copenhagen in 1801 and 1807? These broken promises and betrayals have 'manured the soil of history'; could anyone expect a sweeter harvest? But, the poem ends, I shall not cry woe over every poisoned blossom that opens on time's tree. Let the worm gnaw; there can be no rebirth till the skull is clean. Let the mockery of our system be exposed. Nemesis will the sooner sit in judgment on our hypocrisy.

The same month (the letter is undated) Bjørnson wrote that he was thinking of reviving the Norwegian Theatre in Møllergaden and running it in harness with the Christiania Theatre, and asked Ibsen to come home in six or twelve months to help him with them. 'I am willing to share the salary, the work and the responsibility with you. Let me know.'[3] He promised also to write to Consul Bravo and ask him to advance Ibsen 50 specie-dollars (£12) to see him over the next month. One wonders how Ibsen would have survived that first year and a half in Italy without Bjørnson.

In late June Ibsen left Rome for the countryside, this time to Ariccia, fifteen miles to the south-east in the Alban mountains. Ariccia was, and still is, an

---

[1] Letter to Peter Hansen, 28 October 1870.

[2] Dietrichson, I, p. 339.

[3] *Gro-tid*, II, pp. 156–159.

idyllic little town, containing several fine works by Bernini, including the main piazza, its two fountains and the magnificent Chigi Palace. The Ibsens lived, as Suzannah later described it to her daughter-in-law, 'not just humbly, but like paupers . . . Sigurd can tell you how he used to go each afternoon and buy three soldi-worth of bread and three soldi-worth of Caceotto cheese; this, with half a carafe of red wine, was our dinner.'[1] The work continued to go painfully, and he needed all the encouragement that Bjørnson could give him:

Copenhagen, 25 July 1865.

Why the Devil don't you write? You don't need to frank them . . . From Trondhjem a provisional No, i.e. you applied too late as always, they had made their allocations, but I've spoken to one of them, written again, and something'll happen soon, so don't lose heart if it comes a bit late . . .

Your prospects now are:

What you can earn yourself
What I can raise (*very* little)
300 from Trondhjem Society (am of course asking 500)
400 from Storthing [the Norwegian Parliament]
A performance at the theatre (if Dunker agrees)
Whatever you get when you come home from the theatre or the University library (I'm trying to get you something there whether you like it or not) . . .

But the problem is, you need money *now* . . . Can't you start sending the MS for printing? Then you can ask a bigger advance. If you can't do that yet I'll have to resort to murder . . . Don't lose heart, don't lose faith in your friends, or in your admirers—but, my dear Ibsen, why all these gloomy words? Hasn't everything gone splendidly for you (a few misfortunes apart, which were a bit your own fault partly) since you came to Christiania [!]— you are now regarded as one of the leading poets in Scandinavia, respected, your work eagerly anticipated, you are in Italy, you are liked down there (I hear that from Bloch), you have a handsome and assured future (assured both by the State and by your own dramatic talent), you have young people around you, and you have me!

Your most affectionate
Bjørnstjerne

P.S. Stay in Rome and Italy till everything is settled here, the Storthing, Trondhjem, maybe the library or the theatre too, if you'd prefer that. If

---

[1] Bergliot Ibsen, *De tre* (Oslo, 1948), p. 29.

you'd like to *run* the theatre, that too, I'll soon have had enough. But my
advice is: don't, or at most for a limited period like me . . . I'll tell them it's
a question of money or life—'A poet is dying!' Though you won't b——
die, you're tough, brave, lazy—such people never die.[1]

But by the time this letter reached Ibsen, the longed-for breakthrough had
come. Ibsen described it in his reply to Bjørnson:

Ariccia, 12 September 1865

My dear Bjørnson!

*Your letter and the draft from Hegel came at a good time. Thank you, my dear,
blessed friend, for both! But affectionate and kind as your letter was—indeed, all the
more therefore—I have read it with self-reproach because of the worry and anxiety you
have endured on my account. Thank you for this too! It all adds up to one thing, by
far the most important thing for me and for my calling in life—the fact that I have
met and really found you—this I can never repay except by a devotion which neither
my friends nor your enemies will ever be able to alter. I know you will understand that
it is not Bjørnson the fund-raiser whom I have in mind. Well, more of this when we
meet; now I can speak openly to you, I could never do so before. Everything is going
well for me now, and has really been so the whole time, except for isolated periods when
I didn't know which way to turn, not only as regards money, but because my work
would not progress. Then one day I went into St Peter's—I had gone into Rome on
some business—and suddenly everything I wanted to say appeared to me in a strong and
clear light. Now I have thrown overboard the work with which I had been torturing
myself for a year without getting anywhere, and in the middle of July I started working
on something new which has been making such progress as no other work of mine has
ever done. New, I mean, in the sense that I only then began to write it, but the matter
and mood have been weighing on me like a nightmare ever since those many distasteful happenings at home which forced me to look into myself and our life there and
think seriously about things which had previously passed me by and about which I
didn't seriously bother. It is a dramatic poem, of serious content; contemporary theme;
five acts in rhymed verse (but no Love's Comedy). The fourth act is almost finished, and
I feel I shall be able to complete the fifth in a week. I work both morning and afternoon,
which I have never been able to do before. It is blessedly peaceful out here; no one I
know; I read nothing but the Bible—it is powerful and strong!*

*If I were to name the most important result of my coming here, I should say that it
was that I have rid myself of that aesthetic attitude, that forcing of oneself into isolation
and self-sufficiency, that formerly held sway over me. Aestheticism in this sense now
seems to me as great a curse to writing as theology is to religion. You have never been
troubled by aestheticism in this sense, you have never looked at things through the*

---

[1] *Gro-tid*, II, pp. 166–169.

hollow of your hand. Is it not an indescribable joy to be able to write? But it carries with it a great responsibility, and I now have sufficient earnestness to realise this and be stern with myself. A Copenhagen aesthete once said when I was there: 'Whatever else one may feel about him, Christ was the most interesting phenomenon in the history of the world.' The aesthete relished him as the gourmet relishes the sight of an oyster. I have always had the strength not to become that kind of cartilaginous animal, but God knows what all those spiritual asses might not have made of me if they had had me to themselves, and what prevented them from having me, my dear Bjørnson, was you . . .

You say the Storthing will approve my grant. Do you think so? I have a suspicion that my new work will not dispose the members more charitably towards me, but may God punish me if, for that reason, I cut a single line, whatever those pygmy souls may feel. Let me rather be a beggar all my life. If I cannot be myself in what I write, then my work would be nothing but lies and humbug, and our country has had enough of that without handing out grants for more . . .

I don't think the theatre could stage my play—if I were on the board I would have to vote against it. But if you can use it that's another matter; it's dramatic all right; but whether it is performable on other grounds you must judge for yourself . . .

Our warmest regards to you and yours,

Your affectionate
Henr: Ibsen.

The new version of Brand was in the form of a poetic drama and, as the above letter indicates, he wrote it at an extraordinary speed. We do not know the exact date of his visit to St Peter's, but even if it took place within a week of his leaving Rome it means that he composed nearly three and a half thousand lines of rhymed octosyllabics in, at the most, ten weeks, a rate of fifty lines a day, and it is a measure of his new-found confidence that he was expecting to complete the fifth act in a week. In the end it took him longer, for it extended to seventeen hundred lines, or one-third of the play, but he wrote it at the same rate, finishing it in a little over a month.

Dietrichson has described Ibsen's working routine at Ariccia. 'He liked to rise at 4 a.m. and take a stroll in the wood or the great Chigi park before the day grew hot. As the sun rose higher in the heavens he sat down at his desk, where he would work more or less uninterruptedly until the day ended; and in the evening he liked to sit and enjoy the cool on the big flight of steps in front of the church.'[1] 'I was', Ibsen wrote to Bjørnson the following March, 'despite my poverty and tribulation, so indescribably happy, I felt such a crusading joy within me, that I do not know the thing I would have lacked the

---

[1] Dietrichson, I, p. 345.

courage to tilt at.' On another occasion he used a less Bunyanian image to describe his mood of that summer. 'At the time I was writing *Brand* I had on my table a scorpion in an empty beer glass. From time to time the brute would ail; then I would throw a piece of ripe fruit in to it, on which it would cast itself in a rage and eject its poison into it; then it was well again.'[1] Ibsen's euphoria and venom both found vent; the play is at the same time an exultation and an indictment.

Brand marks an extraordinary leap forward in Ibsen's development as a dramatist, and the chief reason is clear. He was not writing for performance, and was thus able to work uninhibited by the limitations of practical staging (and we have seen how severe these, in the middle of the nineteenth century, were). He wrote it, as Alfred de Musset and Turgenev had written their plays (even *A Month in the Country*), and as Thomas Hardy was to write *The Dynasts*, to be read, and so was able to include, *inter alia*, a storm at sea and an avalanche. But there are other reasons for the immensity of *Brand* compared with any of his previous works. The distance and relaxation which he had found in Italy offered ideal circumstances for the expression of that *saeva indignatio* from which his poetry welled; and his first sight of Italian renaissance art and, more particularly, sculpture and architecture, especially that of Michelangelo, had given him a new standard at which to aim. His former masters, one must remember, had been Oehlenschläger, Holberg, Heiberg, the sagas and ballads, and Shakespeare glimpsed through the mist of dull translation; now he had Michelangelo. It is significant that his revelation of how the play should shape itself had come to him in St Peter's, under Michelangelo's dome. *Brand* is a mighty cathedral of a play, and Brand's God, 'young and strong like Hercules', is an exact description of Christ as painted by Michelangelo in the Sistine Chapel. The same taste that disparaged Michelangelo and Milan Cathedral and admired Raphael dominated Scandinavian taste in drama; it was the dogma of aestheticism which Heiberg had laid down and which no critic had yet authoritatively challenged, though Georg Brandes was shortly to do so. No wonder Ibsen had told Bjørnson that he regarded the ridding of himself of this aestheticism as the most important result of his coming to Italy. Michelangelo, Bernini and the unknown architect of Milan Cathedral had what Ibsen recognised as 'the courage to commit a madness now and then', and *Brand* is the direct result of their influence. Its power is not static but dynamic; each scene, superb in itself, moves irresistibly on to the next, culminating in what is arguably the greatest final act that any dramatist had written since *King Lear*.

The story of the play is that of the epic which Ibsen had left unfinished,

---

[1] Letter to Peter Hansen, 28 October 1870.

lopped of its introductory section about the boys on the hillside, and carried
to its terrifyingly logical conclusion. Brand, the young priest, walking in the
mountains, meets (as in the poem) his old schoolfriend Ejnar with the latter's
fiancée Agnes. He denounces their materialistic hedonism in words that
uninhibitedly reflected Ibsen's opinion of his countrymen:

> You separate
> Faith from doctrine. You do not want
> To live your faith. For that you need a God
> Who'll keep one eye shut. That God is getting feeble
> Like the generation that worships him.
> Mine is a storm where yours is a gentle wind,
> Inflexible where yours is deaf, all-loving
> Not all-doting. And he is young
> And strong like Hercules. His is the voice
> That spoke in thunder when he stood
> Bright before Moses in the burning bush.
> A giant before the dwarf of dwarfs. In the valley
> Of Gideon he stayed the sun, and worked
> Miracles without number—and would work
> Them still, if people were not dead, like you . . .

EJNAR (*waves him away*): Turn the world upside down.
     I still have faith in my God.
BRAND: Good. But paint him
     With crutches. I go to lay him in his grave.

Brand goes on his way and meets the mad girl Gerd, who is pursued in her
imagination by a hawk that is for ever diving and clawing at her. She tries to
lead him to her Ice Church among the peaks:

> Come with me!
> Up there, cataract and avalanche sing Mass.
> The wind preaches along the wall of the glacier
> And the hawk can't get in. He swoops down
> On to the Black Peak and sits there
> On my church steeple like an ugly weathercock.

He descends instead to the village where he was born, which is gripped by
famine, and tells the people that their plight is God's judgment on their lack
of faith. Agnes, inspired by his words, and by his courage in sailing across the

storm-tossed fjord to shrive a dying man, leaves Ejnar and joins him. Brand
warns her what life with him will mean:

> Young woman, think carefully before you decide.
> Locked between mountains, shadowed by crag and peak,
> Shut in the twilight of this ravine
> My life will flow like a sad October evening.

AGNES: The darkness no longer frightens me. A star
> Pierces through the night.

BRAND: Remember, I am stern
> In my demands. I require All or Nothing.
> No half-measures. There is no forgiveness
> For failure. It may not be enough
> To offer your life. Your death may be required also.

EJNAR: Stop this mad game, leave this man of dark law.
> Live the life you know you can.

BRAND: Choose. You stand at the parting of the ways.

She marries Brand, and he remains in the village as priest. They have a child
who, the doctor, warns them, will die if they stay in this cold place which
'the sun never warms'. Brand sees this as a temptation to abandon his calling;
he stays and the child dies; as a result, Agnes dies too. Then Brand sees his
whole life as a failure, and leads the villagers up into the mountains to find God
(as Lammers the revivalist had done with the people of Skien). There they
lose heart, revile and, finally, stone him. Abandoned, he is joined by the mad
girl Gerd who, seeing the blood on him, thinks he is the Saviour and kneels
down and worships him.

GERD: Priest, you're limping. Your foot's hurt.
> How did that happen?

BRAND: The people hunted me.

GERD (*goes closer*): Your forehead is red.

BRAND: The people stoned me.

GERD: Your voice used to be clear as song.
> Now it creaks like leaves in autumn.

BRAND: Everything—everyone—

GERD: What?

BRAND: Betrayed me.

GERD (*stares at him*): Ah! Now I know who you are!
> I thought you were the priest.
> Fie upon him and all the others!
> You're the Big Man. The Biggest of all.

BRAND: I used to think I was.

GERD: Let me see your hands.

BRAND: My hands?

GERD: They're scarred with nails. There's blood in your hair.
The thorn's teeth have cut your forehead.
You've been on the cross. My father told me
It happened long ago and far away.
But now I see he was deceiving me.
I know you. You're the Saviour Man!

BRAND: Get away from me!

GERD: Shall I fall down at your feet and pray?

BRAND: Go!

GERD: You gave the blood that will save us all.
There are nail holes in your hands. You are the Chosen One.
You are the Greatest of all.

BRAND: I am the meanest thing that crawls on earth.

As the sun rises, Brand sees that they are standing in the Ice Church, symbol of the cold and grandiose emptiness of his life. Gerd fires her rifle at the imaginary hawk which she still thinks pursues her, and this brings down the Ice Church in an avalanche, killing them both. As it engulfs them, Brand cries in despair:

> Answer me, God, in the moment of death!
> If not by will, how shall Man be redeemed?

And a voice replies through the thunder:

> He is the God of love.

The character of Brand himself, while probably owing something to hearsay memories of Lammers at Skien,[1] was, by Ibsen's own admission, largely based on Christopher Bruun, whose deep religious feeling, distrust of the established Church and contempt for compromise, had made so profound an impression on Ibsen during the past months in Rome. Bishop Eivind Berggrav, who knew Bruun well, wrote of him that 'behind Bruun's cold mask burned an intense

---

[1] So Ibsen told both William Archer (*Ibsen as I Knew Him*, *Monthly Review*, June 1906, p. 8), and Henrik Jæger (Midbøe, p. 147). Arnt Delhi, Ibsen's masseur during his last years, says that Ibsen denied this (interview in *Aftenposten*, 14 March 1928); but Ibsen often contradicted himself, and his earlier assurances seem the more trustworthy; Delhi knew him only when he was very old and had been weakened by strokes. He told both Jæger and Delhi that Thea Bruun had been the part-original of Agnes.

flame, and also great goodness', but that he '*appeared* hard and cold . . . He could not find the right harmony between loving and chastising . . . This was Bruun's tragedy, an unholy gulf between the warmth of the love that was in him and the coldness of his character; they should have balanced and harmonised each other, but could not be reconciled.'[1] Another friend of Bruun tells that Bruun himself admitted that his greatest defect was his inability to love.[2] Ibsen, however, confessed that he had put a good deal of himself into the part. 'Brand', he once remarked, 'is myself in my best moments.'[3] He later told George Brandes that he could as easily have made Brand a sculptor or a politician, or even Galileo—'except that then of course he would have had to have held strongly to his beliefs, and not pretended that the earth stood still'.[4] It is also worth noting that in the spring of 1865, when he was wrestling with *Brand*, Ibsen had found 'joy and strength'[5] in reading Bjørnson's play *Mary Stuart in Scotland*, one of the central characters of which is the Calvinist preacher John Knox, a figure with whom Brand had much in common.

Another historical figure who probably contributed to the portrait of Brand was Garibaldi, who, when he led the last forlorn hope out of Rome in 1849 to continue his resistance in the Italian mountains, had said to his followers: 'I offer neither pay, nor quarters, nor provisions. I offer hunger, thirst, forced marches, battle and death'—words markedly similar to those used by Brand to his parishioners on the mountain in Act Five—and, as has been stated, we know that Ibsen borrowed Garibaldi's autobiography from the Scandinavian Club library during the year he wrote *Brand*.

Agnes he based at least partly on Bruun's sister Thea, the pretty girl whom he had known in Genzano and who had by now returned to Norway to die. She is perhaps the most tenderly drawn of all Ibsen's heroines. Walter Runeburg, the gay young Finnish sculptor who loved Thea, is traditionally supposed to have been the original of Ejnar who, one suspects, also represented Ibsen's idea of himself in his worst moments, aestheticism pushed to its extreme, like the hero of *On the Heights*. The idea for Gerd probably came from a half-mad peasant girl he had met at Hellesylt on his folk-lore trip in 1862; and a hard old peasant woman whom he heard of at Graffer on the same trip may have contributed towards the portrait of Brand's mother. Many of the descriptions of natural scenery stem from that journey; amongst other things, he had heard of a priest who earlier that year had been killed by an avalanche.

---

[1] Berggrav and Bull, pp. 37 ff.
[2] *Ibid.*, p. 39.
[3] Letter to Peter Hansen, 28 October 1870.
[4] Letter to Georg Brandes, 26 June 1869.
[5] Letter to Bjørnson, 12 September 1865.

Ibsen wrote the play in rhymed four-beat verse, using both iambics ($\cup$–) and trochees (–$\cup$), iambics mainly for colloquial or argumentative dialogue, trochees for scenes of passion, poetry or vision. 'I wanted a metre', he told William Archer, 'in which I could career where I would, as on horseback,'[1] and he achieved a marvellous flexibility, moving without incongruity between colloquialism and high poetry. Archer perceptively observed of *Brand* that it contained 'the prophetic fire of Carlyle fused with the genial verve and intellectual athleticism of Browning, and expressed by aid of a dramatic facility to parallel which we must go two centuries backwards'.

A great deal has been written about the symbolism of *Brand*, and the different significances that might be attached to the hawk, the Ice Church, and so on. Dr Arne Duve, in his stimulating book *Symbolikken i Henrik Ibsens skuespill*, suggests that the hawk represents the life of the emotions, or love, and that it is Brand's fear of the powers of life and light that make him, in Act Five, dismiss the hawk contemptuously as 'the spirit of compromise'. The Ice Church, thinks Dr Duve, represents the opposite of the hawk, the negation of love. Gerd, like Brand, fears and distrusts love (like him, she is the child of a loveless marriage), and Brand's negation of love finally leads him, too, to the terrible citadel of the Ice Church; what Ibsen, thirty years later in *John Gabriel Borkman*, was to term 'the coldness of the heart'. The Ice Church finally killed Brand, just as the coldness of the heart killed John Gabriel Borkman. Mr Michael Elliott, who directed the justly celebrated production of *Brand* in 1959 in London, has expressed the view that the hawk represents nothing as specific as love but rather, in a general way, 'whatever one rejects', just as Room 101 in George Orwell's *1984* contained 'the worst thing in the world', whatever that might be for each individual. I agree with this theory, and believe that the Ice Church stands for the false citadel that each of us builds in his own imagination as a refuge from his particular hawk.

On 30 September, while he was still engaged on Act Five of *Brand*, Ibsen returned to Rome. Thence, in the beginning of November, he posted off his fair copy of the first four acts to his new publisher Frederik Hegel in Copenhagen, promising that the remainder of the play would shortly follow. There now ensued an extraordinary chapter of misunderstandings.

Bjørnson, in recommending Ibsen to Hegel earlier in the year, had informed him that Ibsen's next work was to be a 'play set in the time of Christian IV' (i.e., the drama about Magnus Heineson). Hegel, on receipt of the parcel containing the first four acts of *Brand*, assumed it to be the play Bjørnson had spoken of and, anxious to get it out in time for the Christmas sales, somewhat

---

[1] William Archer, *Ibsen as I Knew Him*, p. 7.

rashly sent it straight to the printers without bothering to read it. At the same time he wrote to Ibsen promising to have the play published by Christmas provided he received the rest of the manuscript before the end of the month and offering to print 1,250 copies against an honorarium of 30 Danish riks-dollars (£3) per signature of sixteen pages, which worked out at just over £50 for the edition. Ibsen immediately accepted this offer and posted the remaining pages on 15 November, the day after he received Hegel's letter. Only when the proofs began to appear from the press did Hegel discover that he was going to publish, not a drama of Danish history, but an immense dramatic poem indicting the modern Norwegian attitude towards almost everything in life. He thereupon (23 November) wrote nervously to Ibsen expressing the fear that '*possibly*, despite its many beauties, it may not be comprehended by the mass of readers, and the demand may not be such as to justify printing so large an impression as 1,250 copies. I hasten therefore to inform you that I propose to print half that number, viz. 625 copies, and accordingly offer 15 riksdollars (£1.50) per signature . . . I sincerely hope, for your sake, that my fears may prove groundless.' He added that should Ibsen not feel able to accept these terms, and prefer to offer the book to another publisher, 'I shall, despite the value I place on becoming your publisher, and despite the fact that much of the book is already printed, be willing to with-draw.'

Ibsen was deeply disappointed at this information. However, he could not afford to be grand, and on 2 December he replied accepting Hegel's conditions. But this letter got lost in the post, with the result that Christmas and the New Year came and went, and *Brand* remained one-third unprinted. In February Hegel wrote a puzzled note to Bjørnson: 'I don't understand Ibsen. I should be very sad if I have unwittingly offended him.'[1] At the beginning of March he wrote again to Bjørnson: 'It is strange that Ibsen has sent me no word. But now we are already into March, and in all conscience I dare not let his book stand unpublished any longer. I shall issue it in a week, and shall print in accordance with the terms originally agreed.'

Meanwhile, as can be imagined, Ibsen in Rome was getting more and more worried at the non-appearance of his play, searching the Danish newspapers as they arrived, a week late, in the hope of seeing a review, or at least an advertisement. On 4 March he wrote a very depressed letter to Bjørnson: 'You call Hegel a high-minded man, and so does Fru Thoresen . . . I have had a thousand difficulties with him, and have agreed to everything so as to have my book out by Christmas, but it hasn't appeared . . . You can well imagine

---

[1] L. C. Nielsen, *Frederik V. Hegel: et Mindeskrift* (Copenhagen, 1909), I, p. 218.

my state of mind, eaten up with worry and tension, waiting for the book and maybe all manner of controversies, attacks, etc., arising from it, unable to start work on a new project which I have in my head waiting to be written. Well, enough of that. Dear Bjørnson, I feel that I am, by some huge and inexorable fate, cut off from both God and man . . . There is nothing so enervating as this accursed waiting. Well, it can only be temporary, I must and shall conquer some day. If Fate has so willed it as to set me in this world and make me the man I am, she must accept the consequences. But no more of this . . . You are the only friend I have. You do not know what it means to have only one friend . . . P.S. I am availing myself of your offer not to frank my mail. I do this from necessity, not from choice.'

Three days later he wrote to Hegel beseeching him for news of Brand and asking him to send the balance of his fee 'to be regarded as an advance on future works, should there be no second edition . . . My new work', he added rather pathetically, 'is a historical drama from the early years of Christian IV and is being written with a view to performance. I also have material for a collection of poems . . . Please debit the postage of this letter to my account with you.'

Brand was published in Copenhagen on 15 March 1866, but Ibsen did not hear of this until the actual day of its appearance, when he received a letter from Hegel dated 5 March which at last put him in the picture. 'I hope', he replied on 16 March, 'that all misunderstandings are now dispelled, and that in the future I may have the honour and pleasure of being associated with you as an author, just as it is my intention to associate myself as closely as possible with Denmark. Norwegians and Swedes have a terrible debt of blood to expiate with you, and I feel it is my calling to use the talents which God has given me to wake my compatriots from their sloth and make them realise what are the important issues in life.'

In the event, the miseries and frustrations of this winter were soon forgotten, for Hegel's fears as to the reception of Brand proved totally false. Throughout Scandinavia it created an immediate and widespread sensation. As he was so often to do in the future, Ibsen had touched his contemporaries on their most sensitive spot; the movement towards liberalism and individualism was just approaching its climax, and the call to follow one's private conscience, avoid compromise and 'be oneself' answered a general and unspoken need. Brand established Ibsen in Scandinavia as the pioneer of revolt against dead thought and tradition. It had the same explosive effect in Norway, Sweden and Denmark which, eleven years later, The Pillars of Society was to have on German audiences and, later still, A Doll's House on thinking people throughout the western world.

To modern readers *Brand* is a mighty, Lear-like poetic tragedy of a lonely, misguided and tormented spirit. To the Scandinavia of 1866 it was before all else a gauntlet thrown down to authority, an attack on complacency and conventionality, whether in the field of religion, of patriotism or of human relationships. Orthodox Christianity, as preached by the established church, was of course a prime target (in this respect, the play did for Scandinavians what the new scientific teaching and Bible criticism were doing in England), but unthinking humanism, as represented by Ejnar and to some extent by the Mayor, also came under fire. Truth, the play stressed, was something which every man must find out for himself, and every woman too. One could no longer accept the sum of human wisdom garnered through the ages. Another target important to his contemporaries, and one which, again, Ibsen was further to indict in so many of his later plays, was the narrowness of small community life, that parochialism which still besets the Scandinavian countries more than their bigger neighbours, and which no writer had so eloquently condemned before. Finally, the character of Brand himself—narrow, intolerant, harsh to his wife and child as to his flock and himself—was a new kind of hero, new at any rate since *Coriolanus*, and as unfamiliar and refreshing to readers in the eighteen-sixties as another kind of anti-hero was to be to European theatre audiences ninety years later.

Illustreret Nyhedsblad of 29 April 1866 quoted *Morgenbladet*'s Copenhagen correspondent on the book's reception in Denmark: 'Of the new literary works that have lately appeared, *Brand* takes a pre-eminence which few poetic works have previously been able to claim. It is read with the greatest interest, its praise is in all men's mouths and its powerful words in all men's thoughts.' Paul Botten Hansen added an editorial comment: 'That this picture is not exaggerated is confirmed by private information from Denmark. Wherever people meet, the talk is only of *Brand* . . . The interest in *Brand* has also led men of letters to read Ibsen's earlier works, such as *Love's Comedy*, and they have marvelled greatly that such a book managed to create so little effect up here as to pass virtually unnoticed.' In Sweden it was the same. The poet Gustaf af Geijerstam recalled: 'It would be vain for me to attempt to describe the passion with which we young men read and discussed the great poet.' The reading of Ibsen, he explains, became a bond of unity between friends and lovers. 'No more sacred gift could be offered to anyone than *Brand*.'[1] Axel Lundegård remembered how the play had 'hypnotised us all with its rigorous pietism . . . That dark fanatic who set out to slay the obsolete God of the time has been the

---

[1] Gustaf af Geijerstam, *Två minnen om Ibsen*, in *Ord och Bild* (Stockholm, 1898), pp. 116–117.

D

pennant-bearer of our younger generation.'[1] And August Strindberg, who was seventeen when *Brand* appeared and twenty when he read it belatedly in 1869 (and wrote a play that year, *The Freethinker*, which bears evident signs of its influence), described it as 'the voice of a Savonarola'.[2]

So controversial a work naturally excited some opposition. The disciples of J. L. Heiberg's doctrine of aestheticism found it contrary to their beliefs (though Heiberg's widow sent Ibsen a letter of admiration), and Clemens Petersen, while finding much to praise in it ('This remarkable poem . . .' began his front-page review in *Fædrelandet*), declared that so violently committed a work 'could not be called poetry'.[3] 'He is no poet', Petersen wrote privately to Bjørnson that March, 'but a critic. His imagination breeds reflection, not human beings; he can perceive ideas, but not create them . . . *Brand* . . . is essentially criticism, and not poetry'[4]—a statement typical of the aesthetic viewpoint which was always to find Ibsen's work unsatisfying. Similarly: 'The Devil is in that man,' wrote the Danish art historian Julius Lange of Ibsen when he met him in Rome a couple of years later. 'If I had the curing of him, I'd prescribe Greek literature or art, first in small doeses so he wouldn't spit them out, then in larger and larger quantities until his sense of form and purpose was restored to health.'[5] Lange defined the quality that offended him as 'spiritual overstrain', reminding one of early critical reaction in England to Shelley and Keats.

It is curious for a modern reader to find Ibsen condemned as a romantic. Yet this reaction against the supposed extravagances of *Brand* was echoed by the man who most of all might have been expected to welcome them, the young Georg Brandes. But Brandes, in 1866, was only twenty-four, and had not yet found himself as a critic; he, too, was still under the sway of that 'aesthetic' attitude towards life and literature which Ibsen was congratulating

---

[1] Axel Lundegård, *Röde Prinsen* (Stockholm, 1889), p. 219.

[2] August Strindberg, *Den litterära reaktionen i Sverige sedan 1865*, a lecture given in Paris on 25 November 1885 and printed in the Copenhagen monthly, *Tilskueren*, in May 1886 (p. 393).

[3] Ibsen had written to Petersen on 4 December 1865 expressing the hope that Petersen would review *Brand* when it appeared: 'Your criticism will have a decisive effect on how my compatriots receive the book . . . Should you have anything to say to me for which you cannot find space in your review, which I await confidently and with anticipation, I should be most grateful for a few lines. I have an intolerably oppressive sensation of standing alone.' There is no record of whether Petersen bothered to send Ibsen a letter—probably not, judging from his remarks to Bjørnson.

[4] Kari Hamre, *Clemens Petersen og hans forhold til norsk litteratur i aarene 1856–1869* (Oslo, 1945), pp. 160–161.

[5] *Brev fra Julius Lange*, ed. P. Købke (Copenhagen, 1902), pp. 29–30.

himself on having escaped from.[1] Brandes's response to *Brand* was confused. He admired the work as literature but disapproved of it on doctrinaire grounds; he believed that poetry should move and calm the reader, not inflame or disturb him. 'One cannot but admire', he wrote in the Danish newspaper *Dagbladet* on 23 May 1866, 'the versifying skill and command of language which enable him to compose so long a poem from start to finish in short lines of sometimes triple or even quadruple rhymes . . . but . . . they rush forward at a speed so impetuous that the Muse might almost be wearing the red shoes of Andersen's story; one stumbles now on a tastelessness of language, now on an ill-chosen image, now on an expression which imperfectly clothes the thought; and one's only consolation is that one very quickly finds one's feet again . . . As in general his pen flows too freely, so too does his indignation.' Brandes also found the characters (Brand himself, and even Gerd) inconsistent; he seems, like so many contemporary critics of Ibsen, to have been unable to accept that a character could be divided. And yet, he admitted, 'it is a poem which will leave no reader cold. Every receptive and unblunted mind must feel, on closing the book, a penetrating, nay, an overwhelming impression of having stood face to face with a great and indignant genius, before whose piercing glance weakness feels compelled to cast down its eyes. What makes the impression less definite, namely, the fact that this master-mind is not quite clear and transparent, renders it, on the other hand, all the more fascinating.'[2]

'From the critics in Norway', Ibsen wrote to Bjørnson on 4 March, 'I expect no understanding. I know they will attack me.' He was right. By far the most vehement opposition to *Brand* came from his fellow-countrymen.

---

[1] Brandes's attention had first been drawn to Ibsen works in 1863-4, probably through Clemens Petersen's not very understanding reviews in *Fædrelandet* of *Love's Comedy* and *The Pretenders* and Carl Rosenberg's more sympathetic article on *The Pretenders* in *Dansk Maanedsskrift*, February 1864. He really got to know Ibsen as a dramatist in November 1864 when, according to his diary, he read five of the plays in five days, admiring especially *The Pretenders*, which he thought 'magnificent, remarkable'. Ibsen, on his side, first became interested in Brandes early in 1866 through a mutual friend in Rome, Ludvig David, as we know from the latter's letters to Brandes. When David died in tragic circumstances that March Ibsen wrote to Brandes informing him of the details—the first direct contact between the two. But at that time he knew of Brandes as a writer only through the latter's polemics against Professor Rasmus Neilsen (on the question of faith in a scientific age) which had appeared in *Fædrelandet*. Brandes had not yet published any literary criticism except a reprint of some lectures on Paludan-Muller. Eighteen months later he was to write a much more favourable consideration of *Brand* in *Dansk Maanedsskrift*, November 1867. (Cf. Henning Fenger, *Ibsen og Georg Brandes indtil 1872*, in *Edda*, 1964, pp. 169–208, and Francis Bull's introduction to *Georg og Edvard Brandes Brevveksling med nordiske Forfattere og Videnskabsmænd*, IV (Copenhagen, 1939), pp. XXVI ff.)

[2] William Archer's translation.

Professor M. J. Monrad, by now well behind the times, wrote four long articles in *Morgenbladet* to prove that the play was both morally and politically misguided, asserting that in fact the only true form of self-sacrifice lay in compromise. Nor did he approve of it on aesthetic grounds. 'The author', he declared (5 April 1866), 'has not spared his colours, and they are perhaps in some places employed with a trifle too much boldness'; and he could not understand why 'a man who knows so well how to achieve the pure music of language chooses to employ such discords.' A priest named O. T. Krohg attacked the play later in *Morgenbladet* (nr. 324) as immoral; amazingly for one of his profession, he thought that when Agnes, in the boat, says: 'We are three on board', (meaning, of course, God), it signified that she was pregnant with Ejnar's child, and protested, equally surprisingly, that it was against Christian ethics that Brand, knowing this, should marry her. Johan Vibe in *Norge* dismissed it as 'brilliant lunacy'.

Bjørnson detested it for what seemed to him its nihilism. 'I'll tell you my opinion of Henrik Ibsen's *Brand*', he wrote to Clemens Petersen on 30 March, a fortnight after the play's publication. 'It is no poem, and Ibsen is not really a poet. He has been, for he has possessed the talent to a great degree, if only he wouldn't destroy it by doubt and sophistry . . . The truths come out fighting, screaming, racketing, *à la* Kierkegaard, but are elementary enough; they've never had any flesh and blood of their own . . . The whole thing's no more than an abstract experiment . . . The book so bored me that I still haven't been able to read it properly through, I've skimmed to the end, unable to manage more than a few pages a day. Apart from everything else, it's so badly constructed . . . The book is only . . . a furious outburst against religion . . . Grant that he's achieved the sensationalism which seems to be his only goal (you can't call this a crusade), but I beg you, help us to go on building and working for a healthy society . . . What *is* Ibsen? First in *Catiline* he imitates Victor Hugo or whoever it was, then Hertz, then the sagas and me, then Paludan-Muller and Byron—then off he hops of a sudden to the negative philosophy of the Germans and comes back with their dregs . . . That any poet should help such charlatans [i.e., negative philosophers] I never thought possible in so positive a people as that of Scandinavia.' Bjørnson was not unique among authors in confusing his own limitations with that of a work that repelled him.[1]

Yet even in Norway such condemnation was not universal. There were

---

[1] Though, to give him his due, he recanted his condemnation twelve years later. 'I understand *Brand* better now', he wrote to Georg Brandes on 29 April 1878. 'I didn't understand it before. You'll see, that book will come again! For the first time I am deeply grateful to Ibsen for it.' (*Gro-tid*, II, pp. 189–192.)

men and women, especially among the young, for whom *Brand* said things that had long needed saying. An anonymous correspondent (possibly the young philosopher G. V. Lyng) replied to Monrad's criticisms in *Morgenbladet* pointing out that Ibsen had not put Brand forward as a model of conduct but as a tragic and misguided figure striving blindly for truth. 'The poem', he declared, 'has had a powerful and elevating effect on hundreds of our countrymen.' Ditmar Meidell in *Aftenbladet* (7 April 1866), while doubting the dramatic merits of the play,[1] praised it highly as literature, admiring 'the sonorous tone and beauty which one expects from an Ibsen poem. Here and there the language is marred by violent word-formations, just as the expression is now and then bold to the point of looseness. Nevertheless, despite these and other weaknesses which one might note, it is distinguished by such daring imagination and such strength of execution that one may safely assert, not merely that it is its talented author's most significant work, but that it will claim for itself a lasting and influential place in our national literature.' And Ibsen's old friend Vinje, although as a fervent nationalist he was upset by some of the hits at the Norwegian character, compared it favourably with the much more fashionable plays of Bjørnson. 'Ibsen's bright knife with its cutting edge', he wrote in *Dølen* (8 April), 'is more to my taste than Bjørnson's bland smile. Ibsen can cast bolts of lightning, and in *Brand* there are many . . . And Ibsen knows better how to construct a play.' He concluded by declaring *Brand* to be 'a satirical masterpiece, comparable with Pope's *Dunciad* . . . It is acid, biting, witty and poetic.'

Brand was, in short, discussed and debated as no previous book had ever been in Scandinavia—including Kierkegaard, for *Brand* was written in more accessible and less abstract language. Sermons were preached about it; more importantly for Ibsen, it sold. Within two months Hegel ordered a reprint of five hundred copies; a third edition followed in August, and a fourth in December. Yet nobody dared to stage it. Act Four was performed at the Christiania Theatre on 26 June 1867 (after an amateur performance at the Students' Union), and was successful enough to take its place in the general repertory; but it was to be nineteen years before the play was presented in its entirety. But Ibsen, who had not written it for the theatre, cannot have been surprised or disappointed at this.

Together with the critical and popular success of the book came relief from financial worry. Bjørnson, despite his feelings about *Brand*, had not relaxed his

---

[1] 'This poem can only be called dramatic insofar as it is written in the form of dialogue . . . The thread which runs through the main personage's various utterances and holds them together is sometimes so thinly spun that, at a first reading at least, it is difficult to follow . . . The play on which the curtain here rises belongs only to the theatre of the imagination.'

efforts to raise Ibsen money; indeed, he decided with his usual naïvety that a sense of security was the most likely thing to give Ibsen 'that clear and moving view of life which alone makes a man a poet'.[1] He asked Riddervold, the minister in charge of the ecclesiastical department which administered grants to authors, to give Ibsen the same civil list pension which he himself had received; but Riddervold, perhaps remembering *Love's Comedy*, refused. Undeterred, Bjørnson approached friends in the Storthing, and together they collected twenty-eight signatures to a motion demanding that a pension be allotted 'which, by assuring Ibsen of future means, will surely honour and reward us as much as it will him'.

The sponsors of this motion were not sanguine as to its chances, but by good fortune Riddervold fell ill and his place in charge of the ecclesiastical department was taken by another parliamentarian, Frederik Stang, who let it be known that he would treat any application relating to Ibsen sympathetically. On 19 April Ibsen's friend Michael Birkeland, now the state archivist, sent Stang a formal plea on Ibsen's behalf signed by three others of the Learned Holland circle, O. A. Bachke, Jakob Løkke and Paul Botten Hansen. This was approved within two days and forwarded to the King in Stockholm for ratification. Birkeland had already telegraphed Ibsen advising him to write personally to the King, and on 15 April, four days before Birkeland formally handed his appeal to Stang, Ibsen posted his petition to Carl XV. 'I am', he wrote, 'not fighting for a sinecure existence, but for the calling which I inflexibly believe and know that God has given me—the calling which I believe to be the most important for a Norwegian, namely, to wake the people and make them think big . . . It rests in Your Majesty's royal hands whether I must remain silent and bow to the bitterest deprivation that can wound a man's soul—the deprivation of having to abandon one's calling in life, of having to yield when I know I have been granted the spiritual armoury to fight; and this would be tenfold grievous to me; for to this day I have never yielded.'

His request was modest; for an annual pension of 400 specie-dollars (£100). On 12 May this proposal was put before the Storthing and was approved with only four dissentient votes. A few days earlier the Trondhjem Society for Knowledge had allotted him a single grant of 100 specie-dollars (£25), and on 28 July the government gave him a new travel stipend of 350 specie-dollars (£87)—a total of 850 specie-dollars (£212). The first edition of *Brand* had brought him 200 specie-dollars (£50), so that he, who for the past year had lived on loans, now found himself with over £260 to his credit, a sum so far in excess of his modest requirements that on 21 May he wrote Hegel that he

---

[1] *Gro-tid*, II, p. 193.

did not need to avail himself of the latter's offer of an advance on the second edition.

A letter which Ibsen addressed to Michael Birkeland on 4 May thanking him for organising the petition expresses the euphoria which he now felt. 'I had not expected', he wrote, 'that my book would be so favourably received. I have been sent many expressions of admiration and good will from Denmark ... also various invitations, etc., which make me happy, since I am thinking of making Copenhagen my future home ... I have such a lust for work, such strength, that I could strangle bears. I went round wrestling with that play of mine for a year before it took shape, but once I had it I wrote from morning till evening and finished it in under three months. About Rome it's impossible to write, especially when one knows it inside out as I do. I have wandered through most of the Papal State at various times, on foot with a knapsack on my back. The brigand situation isn't as dangerous as people at home imagine ... Inwardly I think I am in certain respects much changed; yet I feel I am more myself then ever before. Outwardly I've grown thin, which I shall prove with a photograph.'

This new security and euphoria found visible expression. During the months of nervous waiting for the publication of *Brand* he had, as in those months of despair in Christiania, neglected his dress and appearance, and walked around with untrimmed beard, shoes worn to their uppers and holes in his solitary leek-green coat. When the Norwegian colony in Rome held a vote for the worst-dressed member among them, they elected Ibsen *nem. con.*[1] The first thing he did when he learned of the money that was coming to him was to reform his dress to the smartness for which he had been noted in Bergen. One day in that May of 1866 he set out with friends on a walking tour in the mountains around Rome, but at the first *osteria* at which they halted a mood came over him, he decided to go no further, and they proceeded without him, leaving him unkempt, shaggy and silent over a *foglietta* of wine. When they returned a few days later they found him elegantly clothed, shod and barbered —a description to which a photograph taken that year, probably identical to the one promised to Birkeland, bears witness. Another piece of evidence exists in the form of a clothes list written in Ibsen's hand on the back of a letter to him from Consul Bravo:[2]

8 shirts	16 scudi
8 pairs socks	3
1 pair boots	3

[1] Bergliot Ibsen, p. 33.
[2] In the possession of Mr Tancred Ibsen. (1 scudo = 1 specie-dollar = 25p).

2 woollen vests	3
1 frock coat	14
2 waistcoats	4
1 pr. black trousers	6
1 pr. coloured ditto	6
1 overcoat	14
1 hat	3
2 cravats	1
cuff-links	3
watch	10
lorgnette	2
	——
	88 scudi

His son Sigurd later remembered that when the £50 for *Brand* arrived, his parents were so overwhelmed by the 'enormous sum' that they did not know what they would do with it all.[1] And Kristofer Janson (later to be the part-original of Hjalmar Ekdal) records that, finding himself short of money that summer, he asked Ibsen for a loan, and Ibsen opened a drawer, took out a sock and gave Janson some silver from it, explaining that 'this was the fruits of *Brand*, and that he was so well off that he had been able to put some in the bank'.[2]

In such a mood Ibsen felt disinclined to rest on his newly-won laurels. 'I will let you know shortly which work I shall be embarking on next', he wrote to Hegel on 21 May. 'I feel more and more inclined to get down in earnest to *Emperor Julian*, which I have been thinking about for two years.' Magnus Heineson, the sixteenth-century freebooter, had been pushed into the background. But as things turned out the Emperor Julian was to join him there. A new and hitherto unmeditated theme began to preoccupy Ibsen's mind.

---

[1] Bergliot Ibsen, p. 33.
[2] Janson, p. 75.

TWO

🐝 Peer Gynt

(1866–1868)

EARLY IN JUNE 1866 Ibsen left Rome to spend the summer in Frascati, a few miles to the south-east. 'I live out here among the mountains, see no newspapers and know nothing of what is happening outside', he wrote to Hegel on 9 June. 'It is miraculously beautiful.' A week later, he who had written so many letters begging for help, received one himself. Edvard Grieg, not yet twenty-three, had spent five months in Rome that winter and spring; like Ibsen, he claimed, and was proud of, Scottish ancestry, which in his case was less remote, his grandfather having emigrated after the battle of Culloden in 1746. Ibsen and Grieg had got on well (they had even considered collaborating on an operatic version of *Olaf Liljekrans*), and now, on 10 June, Grieg wrote to Ibsen from Christiania asking him to recommend him for the job of *kapellmeister* at the Christiania Theatre. Would Ibsen drop a line to the artistic director, Bjørnson, who had not answered Grieg's application of six weeks previously? 'He may not be able to stand me, I may be being stupid about the matter, but I hope you will be able to put things right . . . I have read your splendid *Brand*, it's a strange thing about truth, people can take it in poetry, it doesn't go too near the knuckle, whereas in plain prose, as Kierkegaard has said, it's too close, too cheeky. How else explain the tremendous furore *Brand* has created, the huge numbers who daily gulp it down?'[1] Ibsen tried to help, but Grieg never got the job; instead, he became *kapellmeister* at the Philharmonien. But he remained grateful for Ibsen's assistance and encouragement ('Don't say your whole future depends on this', Ibsen wrote to him on 24 August. 'No, my dear Grieg, your future will be bigger and better than a musical directorship'), and a decade later their friendship was to ripen into a successful, if mutually incomprehending partnership.

Ibsen enjoyed Frascati. 'We live in an old palace of the nobility, the Palazzo Gratiosi, inexpensively and in splendour', he wrote to Paul Botten Hansen on 22 July. 'Frascati lies below ancient Tusculum where, as you know, Cicero had

---

[1] Grieg's letter was first published in Bergliot Ibsen, pp. 57–58.

his great villa and wrote his Tusculan letters; the ruins of the villa are still standing; his little theatre, probably the same as what he called his *schola*, where he used to give lectures to a chosen circle of guests, remains almost intact. It is indescribably beautiful to sit up here of an evening, 2,000 feet above sea level, with a view far out over the Mediterranean, the *campagna* and Rome; eastwards the whole mountainous Sabine country, with the Apennines, and southwards the Volscian mountains rising on the Neapolitan frontier. From the windows of my study I can see in the farthest distance Mount Soracte towering in solitary splendour across the limitless plain. In short, whichever way one turns it is as if one were surveying the battlefield where the Goddess of History staged her greatest events. Soon, now, I shall write in earnest; I am still wrestling with the material, but soon, I know, I shall have the beast under me, and then the rest will glide forwards of its own volition.' He was still undecided whether to stay away from Norway. 'When I shall return I can't say; I am already known, and feel at home, here; but I must go back some time. I can live on my pension here, since life is very cheap, and the climate suits us all well.'

Whether the 'beast' referred to was *Emperor and Galilean* or the old Magnus Heinesson project we do not know, but whichever it was it continued to resist him, and on 22 August he had to tell Hegel that he was doubtful whether it would be ready by the autumn, suggesting instead a re-issue of *Love's Comedy* 'as a Christmas book', and hopefully observing, as a bait, that 'it may be regarded as a forerunner of *Brand*'. Hegel accepted the idea, and Ibsen spent the next five weeks revising the play and removing some of the more specifically Norwegian words so as to make it more palatable to Danish readers (and thereby, it has been suggested, indirectly indicating his contempt for the campaign in his own country to purge the Norwegian language of its foreign influences, a campaign which he was shortly to castigate in a more outspoken and vehement fashion).

In the first week in October he returned to Rome; and his financial position was now so secure that he was able to ask Hegel (5 October) 'not to send me the honorarium for *Love's Comedy* when it falls due, but to hold it over till next summer, or such time as I shall need more than serves my ordinary purposes'. He was planning to use this money, he informed Michael Birkeland the same day, 'to pay a visit next summer to Paris, and then to Greece'—the latter perhaps to gather background material for *Emperor and Galilean*, part of which is set there (though as things turned out, when the summer arrived he found himself writing a different play, and he never to the end of his life visited Greece, a country which would surely have excited him). He also decided to risk a little gentle speculation and requested Hegel to buy him some tickets for the Copenhagen lottery: 'I hold no hope of winning, but there is an excitement in it which I enjoy.' He was in fact to win two small prizes within the year.

The following month came disagreeable news; a Christiania solicitor named Nandrup, who had lent Ibsen money in 1862, had obtained a warrant of distraint on such few of Ibsen's possessions as remained in Norway, and had sold them by auction. 'I don't', he wrote to Bjørnson,[1] 'mourn the loss of my furniture, etc., but to know that my private letters, papers, drafts, etc. may be in anyone's hands is a most vexatious thought, not to speak of the loss of many things which had a more than material value for me. You were not told the truth when they said the auction was held because I had not surrendered possession of my lodgings; it was because Nandrup, from the time I left, was discourteously rebuffed at Dunker's[2] office—I won't bother you with the details.' In the same letter he hinted for the first time that his stay in the south might be more than temporary. 'In a year or two I plan to come north, but scarcely further than Copenhagen. If I can now and then make a summer trip to Norway, I think that will be the best arrangement.'

On 2 November he told Hegel he was still meditating the Magnus Heinesson play, but added a rider: 'Whether this work will be the *first* I shall complete I am not yet certain. I have a couple of other themes in my head; but this very division of interest means that none of them has yet sufficiently matured; however, I feel sure this will soon happen, and hope to be able to send you the completed manuscript during the spring.' As the three themes jostled for precedence in his head that November and December, he completed his revisions for *Love's Comedy* and, painfully, composed the foreword.

That December a young Dane named Frederik G. Knudtzon, later to become a distinguished publisher, visited Rome, and his memoirs, published long after his death, give a vivid picture of Ibsen in his new role of established author in exile, a picture which interestingly contrasts with that left by Lorentz Dietrichson of those first eighteen months of struggling poverty. Recalling that Ibsen once described these years as his '*Sturm-und-Drang* period',[3] Knudtzon continues: 'There was so much conflict within him that he could never appear a harmonious person. His high ideals, his extraordinary narrow-mindedness in

---

[1] This letter, uncharacteristically undated by Ibsen, was originally dated October by Halvdan Koht in the Centenary Edition of Ibsen's works; but Koht later (*CE*, XIX, p. 487) re-dated it November, on the evidence of an item in Ibsen's account books.

[2] Bernhard Dunker, who had several times helped Ibsen with money, was acting as his lawyer in Norway.

[3] Letter to Lorentz Dietrichson, 2 March 1871.

social matters, his joy in Italy and in art, his residue of bitterness towards
Norway, the financial difficulties which he had only recently overcome, and
his secret need to keep a strict discipline—all this and much more that simmered
within him meant that he was liable to explode to this side or that, and he
moved among the Scandinavians like a lion of whom most of them were
terrified. There was a *noli me tangere* quality about his personality, as about
his dress; a long, buttoned tail coat, an elegant cravat—everything impeccable.
The previous year, I was told, he had walked around with holes under his
arms, as though indifferent to such trivia.'[1]

The character of the Scandinavian Club had changed somewhat during the
past year; several of the livelier members, including Bruun and Snoilsky, had
returned home, and memories of the Danish war had receded. Even Ibsen
seemed to have got a good deal of it out of his system with *Brand*. A few days
after Knudtzon's arrival in Rome he attended a Christmas party at the Club
with Ibsen present, and leaves a pleasant record of the occasion. 'It was the
custom for every guest to bring a little gift for the Christmas tree. When the
dance round the tree was finished, the gifts were shared out, so that everyone
went home with something other than what he had brought . . . We ate rice
porridge, and duck had to serve for the goose we would have enjoyed at
home . . . In the absence of a fir, a laurel had to serve as Christmas tree.'[2]
Then Consul Bravo, the badness of whose Danish was a perpetual source of
joy to the members, rose as he had done for years to propose the health of
'the three Norwegian kingdoms'. What he meant was the three Scandinavian
kingdoms, but he had (surprisingly, considering his position as consul) never
mastered the difference between *nordisk* (Scandinavian) and *norsk* (Norwegian),
and it had long been agreed that no one should spoil this annual delight by
telling him.[3]

During the dinner, however, there was trouble. The new arrivals included
Kristofer Janson, the young novelist to whom Ibsen had lent money from his
sock. Janson was a fervent devotee of the *landsmaal* movement, of which Ibsen
was an equally fervent opponent, and he announced to the gathering that after
the meal he proposed to read one of his stories in *landsmaal* aloud; at which
Ibsen declared that if Janson did this he, Ibsen, would leave. Janson saved the

---

[1] Knudtzon, pp. 161–162.

[2] *Ibid.*, p. 127.

[3] 'He talked no language quite correctly', recalled Bjørn Bjørnson of Bravo. 'He was,
as it were, born a foreigner'. Bjørn's father used him as the model for Harald Gille in his
play *Sigurd Slembe*. Bravo prided himself greatly on the perfection of his teeth, and once
put Johanne Luise Heiberg's fingers into his mouth to feel them, which much offended
her. (Bjørn Bjørnson, *Fra barndommens dage*, Christiania, 1922, pp. 201–202).

situation by reciting a poem by Bjørnson, not, one might think, the most tactful alternative, but one that passed off without ado.[1]

Knudtzon gives several further examples of Ibsen's pepperiness that winter. One evening in the Club some well-meaning member proposed a toast to the two members who had chosen the food and wine, Ibsen and an old Danish painter named Lars Hansen. 'Hansen rose, ready to drink. But Ibsen suddenly stood up, stamped his foot and said: 'No one is going to drink my health as a member of the food committee.'[2] On another occasion a Swedish nobleman, Count von Rosen, entered the Club with an effeminate young guest whom he introduced as Herr Sverdrup. When the two had left, Jerichau the sculptor remarked that the guest was evidently a girl. Most of the members, writes Knudtzon, thought this a fair joke, but 'Ibsen felt deeply offended on behalf of the fair sex . . . He declared to all and sundry that the Scandinavian Club should not tolerate such behaviour; ladies were not admitted into the Club except on special occasions; Rosen and Sverdrup should be banned. Ibsen felt that the insult touched him most deeply as a *paterfamilias*—he was worried more on Fru Ibsen's account than on that of the Scandinavian ladies in general. He lived at that time in a state of permanent anxiety at not being sufficiently appreciated *qua familie.*'[3] It transpired that Rosen's companion was indeed a girl, named Emma Toll, and Ibsen started a campaign to get her and Rosen excluded, writing letter after letter to Consul Bravo, and then to a Docent Landmanson who was acting on Rosen's behalf. Landmanson diplomatically managed to delay the explosion until Rosen and Emma had left Rome, and Ibsen was very annoyed with the Norwegians and Danes for their lack of co-operation.

Then the German Club in Rome decided to hold a banquet, and told Dietrichson's successor as librarian at the Scandinavian Club, Otto Mourier, that any of their members who wished to come would be welcome. Mourier wrote letters to the four Scandinavian families which contained young ladies who would need to bring dresses suitable for dancing, and informed the rest of the members by means of a notice on the Club board. 'Every sensible person', comments Knudtzon, 'had to agree that Mourier had acted correctly and with discretion. But there was one member who felt otherwise and regarded himself as having been disgracefully insulted, and that was Henrik Ibsen. Mourier's failure to send him and his wife a special invitation like the other four families had been an insult to his house, and he attacked the unfortunate librarian with

---

[1] Knudtzon, pp. 128–129.
[2] *Ibid.*, p. 166.
[3] *Ibid.*, p. 168.

reproaches and accusations—more, he demanded that he be dismissed from his post. Ibsen's anger and vehemence could hardly have found a more inappropriate target than Mourier, who was everyone's favourite . . . It naturally followed that Ibsen's violent attack on him and his absurd demand that he be dismissed resulted in everyone rallying to Mourier's defence, and the most active of these was Vilhelm Bergsøe [a Danish novelist of whom Ibsen was to see a good deal more that year]. Bergsøe pleaded Mourier's case against Ibsen before us, and easily outmanoeuvred his more heavily armed adversary. His task was simple, for Fru Ibsen, who was not in her first youth and was, besides, very stout, could scarcely be thought of as a *baldame*, and to have issued her with a special invitation might almost have been taken for a saucy jest. Ibsen's defeat was absolute.'

Knudtzon continues: 'Most people must wonder that Ibsen could have become so furious and have felt so deeply insulted over so comparatively trivial a matter. But this was Ibsen's most vulnerable point: not receiving sufficient respect as a *paterfamilias*. Ever since his youth in Bergen and Christiania he had felt most painfully that he was not accepted in the best society, and until this was put right, during his visit to Copenhagen in 1870,[1] this remained a tender point with him—he longed not to be excluded from what was best in high society. The visit to Fru Heiberg and his *Rhymed Letter* to her[2] reveal his enjoyment and gratitude for some of the happiest moments of his life.'[3]

These memoirs of Knudtzon are the earliest record we have of a trait which Ibsen appears to have developed after achieving fame, and which was to remain his most unappealing characteristic. Throughout the rest of his life he maintained a monarchical sensitivity in matters of protocol; we shall find many further examples. Amazingly for one who so despised convention, and who was to bring such enlightenment to his contemporaries, he was, in his contacts with other human beings, to remain always a *nouveau riche* (or anyway a *nouveau* well-to-do, for his capital was never to exceed eleven thousand pounds) of the most aggressive and hypersensitive kind. The root lay deeper in time than Knudtzon knew, in his father's bankruptcy and the rumours of his own illegitimacy, those twin themes which haunt his plays so obsessively. Kristofer Janson noted: 'As long as one took care not to touch on those old and hated memories, Ibsen was friendly and amiable. But [he adds, and it is a point which others were to make] you had to be alone with him.'[4]

---

[1] More correctly, his visit to Stockholm in 1869.
[2] See p. 145 below.
[3] Knudtzon, pp. 213–220.
[4] Janson, p. 75.

Ibsen spent the last weeks of 1866 completing his foreword[1] to the new edition of *Love's Comedy*, which he posted to Hegel on 5 January 1867, complaining that 'these few lines have caused me a bigger headache than the whole play. I have rewritten it innumerable times and finally settled for the first version.' He had, though, more important news. 'At last I can tell you that my new work is well under way and will, if nothing untoward happens, be ready early in the summer. It will be a long dramatic poem, having as its principal a part-legendary, part-fictional character from Norwegian folk-lore during *recent* times. It will bear no resemblance to *Brand*, and will contain no direct polemics or anything of that kind. I have long been pondering the theme;[2] now I have the whole plan worked out and on paper, and have begun the first act. It grows as I work on it and I am confident that you will be satisfied with the result. Please keep this secret for the time being.'

This new play was *Peer Gynt*; though, if we are to believe the dates inscribed by Ibsen on his manuscript, he did not in fact begin it until 14 January, nine days after his letter to Hegel. He had a tendency, not unique among authors, to tell white lies to his publisher. He composed it, as he had composed *Brand*, in rhymed verse, but of a far greater variety, in both octosyllabics and decasyllabics, not merely iambic ($\cup$ –) and trochaic (– $\cup$), but dactylic (– $\cup\cup$) and anapaestic ($\cup\cup$ –) too, and even, for those interested in these things, in amphibrachs ($\cup$ – $\cup$). He completed Act One in six weeks, on 25 February. Six days later, on 3 March, he started on Act Two. On 8 March he wrote Hegel what must have been another slight untruth, that he had 'now reached the middle of the second act', adding: 'it will comprise five [acts] and as far as I can calculate will occupy about 250 pages. If you wish, I shall be able to send you the manuscript as early as July.'

The play continued to make good progress, for on 27 March he was able to tell Hegel that he had finished Act Two. Then there was something of a hold-up, for by 2 May he had no further progress to report than that 'the plan for the rest of the play is completely clarified and worked out. Here in Rome', he added, 'I scarcely think I shall be able to manage any more on it; for I feel a restlessness in my blood and, still more, the need for greater isolation.'

A week after Ibsen wrote this letter, the 'restlessness' to which he referred manifested itself in an unpleasant incident which showed him at his ugliest.

---

[1] See *Henrik Ibsen: The Making of a Dramatist*, pp. 224–225.

[2] As early as 16 March 1866, the day after the publication of *Brand*, he had written to Anton Klubien: 'This summer I shall go to Sorrento, where I plan to write a new play; I must be near the sea to get the right air into it.' And as things turned out, thanks to an earthquake, he did write the last two acts of *Peer Gynt* there. This letter is not in the Centenary Edition and was first printed in *Ibsen-Årbok 1953* (Skien, 1953), p. 100.

Knudtzon tells that on 10 May the Scandinavians were having a party at an *osteria*, and a young painter named August Lorange, who suffered from tuberculosis (he was to die of it eight years later) was helping old Lars Hansen to add up the bill. 'Ibsen suddenly stood up and began a speech which gradually turned into a brutal attack on Lorange. He was irritated partly because Lorange was helping to add up the bill, partly because he was generally hostile to the young man both as an artist and as a person; he was a poor painter, very untalented and unstable. He was (thus Ibsen concluded his speech) "not worthy to walk on two feet, but ought to crawl on four". We were all left speechless at such an attack on an unoffending and defenceless man, an unfortunate consumptive who had enough to contend with without being banged on the head by Ibsen. But then Vilhelm Bissen[1] intervened and told Ibsen it was wrong to suggest that Lorange had interfered about the bill, since he himself had heard Hansen ask Lorange to help him. Ibsen became a little calmer; but the insult to Lorange had been delivered and could not be withdrawn. And the worst of the matter was that most of what Ibsen had said about Lorange both as an artist and as a person was true—though clearly it should not have been said so brutally, least of all to an unfortunate invalid. When Ibsen had been silent for a while, he rose again, and now, after the storm, the gentleness in his nature found expression. He proposed a toast to a young man who was an example of the best kind of artist, Ludvig Abelin Schou [a Danish painter]. In handsome and well-chosen words he praised Schou's talent, his truthfulness and industry, and we emptied our glasses to his future.'

When the party broke up, several of the diners went off with Lorange to console him, and Ibsen, Knudtzon and a journalist named Jørgen Meincke were the last to rise. 'But alas! It now became apparent that Ibsen could not steer his own course. So Jørgen took him by the right arm and I by the left, and we started on our way home. This afternoon walk with the great poet was not of the shortest. On the road a few remarks passed, but not many. At Ibsen's door I asked him to give me his key so that I could let him in. This he did; but when we made to accompany him up the stairs to his apartment he resisted violently. Beyond doubt Ibsen's brain was functioning much better than his legs. He pondered, made up his mind and gravely expressed his thanks to us.'[2]

Ibsen was evidently (there are other witnesses to the fact) one of that not uncommon tribe who, when drunk, become cruel, lose the use of their legs, yet remain mentally clear. It was not until Ibsen attempted to walk that

---

[1] A sculptor who executed a bust of Ibsen around this time—as did Walter Runeberg. The two worked simultaneously in Bissen's studio.

[2] Knudtzon, pp. 172 ff.

Knudtzon realised he was drunk; perhaps that was why he remained at table till most of the others had left.

Eleven days after this incident, on 21 May, Ibsen left Rome with Suzannah and Sigurd for the island of Ischia, where he lived for three months in the little town of Casamicciola on the northern side of the island, near the extinct volcano of Epomeo. The weather was exceptionally hot, even for the natives, but Ibsen seemed to revel in it; he completed Act Three in as little as two and a half weeks, on 2 July. Vilhelm Bergsøe was his companion throughout his stay, and noted his routine. He rose early, took a walk, drank coffee and wrote from ten till two. Then he had a siesta and, in the late afternoon, read through what he had written and fair-copied it. For relaxation he went on long, silent walks with Bergsøe, often saying nothing. He wrote, as the speed of his composition confirms, at intense pressure; he told Bergsøe that he felt 'like a rearing stallion about to leap',[1] and later recalled to William Archer that his head was so full of verses that he would sometimes rise in his nightshirt to write them down—though, as so often happens in such cases, these sometimes turned out in the morning to be 'the veriest nonsense'.[2]

In the beginning of July the sirocco arrived, and lasted ten days, tearing the roofs off houses, scattering the chairs and tables, and leaving, when it departed, the air filled with a fine yellow dust through which the sun glowed dully, casting no rays. They scattered ice on the stone floor to give a little cool as it melted, but Ibsen continued to work uninterruptedly. One day, while walking with Bergsøe, Ibsen suddenly asked: 'Can one put a man on the stage running around with a casting-ladle?' 'Yes, why not?' 'But it will have to be a big ladle —big enough to recast human beings in.' 'It'll look rather strange,' Bergsøe ventured, to which Ibsen replied: 'Yes, I think so too, but I don't think the play's for acting.'[3]

Bergsøe's portrait of Ibsen during these months on Ischia is vivid and detailed. He cites several examples of that physical cowardice which has already been remarked. 'He had a curious fear of anything that might bring death or misadventure. This fear was not grounded in the thought of losing his life, but in a terror lest he might not achieve the artistic goal he had set himself.'[4] Once Bergsøe took him to a crevasse named *valle del tamburro*. 'As one penetrates more deeply the crevasse changes character, the vegetation becomes sparse, the walls narrow, the light fades and . . . finally one has to walk on the big

---

[1] Vilhelm Bergsøe, *Henrik Ibsen paa Ischia og 'Fra Piazza del Popolo'* (Copenhagen, 1907), p. 160.

[2] William Archer, *Ibsen as I Knew Him*, p. 18.

[3] Bergsøe, p. 212.

[4] This anecdote and those which follow are from Bergsøe, pp. 159–179.

E

stones that lie in the hot water. When we reached this point Ibsen exclaimed in alarm: "Where are you taking me, do you want me inside the mountain? I won't go any further. It might close over us." When I said this was impossible he cried: "But a rock might fall and crush us! I want to get out, I want to go home!" Ignoring my assurances, he hastened off, and that afternoon I saw him no more.'

A similar thing happened when they climbed Punto Imperatore, a hill with a fine view over the sea. 'The last part of the way I had almost to drag Ibsen with me, for he repeatedly asserted that the cliff might fall, and when I objected that we were in proportion to the cliff as a fly to a tower he made the curious observation that even a fly could bring down a tower if it were on the point of falling.' Unable to persuade him further, Bergsøe climbed along to the cliff's edge and surveyed the view. 'Now and then I seemed to hear Ibsen's voice, but because of the roar of the sea I could not distinguish what he was saying. When I finally turned round, I saw him lying with his face to the ground, clasping a rock with both hands. "You will kill me!" he cried furiously. "Why didn't you come when I called? I shall never go on one of your so-called nature walks again!"'

Even now their troubles were not over, for on their way down they found their path barred by a large dog. 'There is a dog', said Ibsen, and stopped. Bergsøe assured him that it had no hostile intentions. 'You cannot know', replied Ibsen. 'I am not going near it.' Bergsøe said there was no danger as long as Ibsen did not appear afraid. 'I am not afraid', said Ibsen angrily, but moved over to the other side. 'So we walked briskly towards the dog, which stood there calmly enough; but just as we were about to pass it Ibsen made a movement as though about to break into a run, and immediately the dog jumped at him and bit him in the hand. A well-aimed blow from my stick sent it yelping off, but Ibsen went as white as a corpse and stared at his hand. I looked at it and found only a tiny scratch, but Ibsen cried: "The dog is mad, it must be shot, otherwise I shall go mad too." In vain I explained to him that there was no evidence that the dog was mad, and that it was a groundless superstition that a human being could catch hydrophobia if, long after biting him, a dog developed the disease. He was foaming with rage, and it was several days before his fear departed.'

Bergsøe noted (as Knudtzon did) Ibsen's habit of interlarding his conversation with phrases from Holberg, especially from *Jeppe of the Hill*—'*Hej, Jakob Skomager! Er Du opstaaen? Lukk op, Jakob! Hej, Jakob Skomager, nu ska vi mare have os en Dram!*' ('Ho, Jacob Cobbler! Are you up? Open up, Jacob! Ho, Jacob Cobbler, let's have a dram!')—and the meticulous care with which he recorded even the smallest purchases. Once he bought two cheap local cigars, took out his notebook and carefully wrote down their price. ' "Do you make a note of things like that?" I asked in amazement. "Yes", he replied, "I have to keep a very careful account of my expenses now I am married. I didn't when I was young." [1] Sometimes he would behave in an unexpectedly school-boy fashion. When a copy of *Fædrelandet* arrived with a hostile criticism of Bergsøe's work in it, Ibsen astonished the townspeople by rolling it into a trumpet and hooting it as he trotted across the square. On the subject of his mother country he was very haughty. 'I shall not go back to Norway', he told Bergsøe, 'until Norway calls me.'

At the beginning of August the sirocco returned even worse than before, and the temperature rose to no less than 37° Reaumur, or 115° Fahrenheit (46° Centigrade), making it almost impossible to breathe. Nevertheless on 8 August Ibsen was able to write to Hegel: 'I have today sent you, via Consul-General Danchertsen in Naples, the manuscript of the first three acts of my new work, entitled *Peer Gynt*, a dramatic poem. This section will come to around 120 printed pages, and the remainder will add up to about the same. I hope to be able to send you Act Four towards the end of the month, and the rest not long afterwards. In case it should interest you, Peer Gynt was a real person who lived in Gudbrandsdalen, probably around the end of the last century or the beginning of this. His name is still famous among the people up there, but not much more is known about his life than what is to be found in Asbjørnsen's *Norwegian Fairy Tales* (in the section entitled *Stories from the Mountain*). So I haven't had much on which to base my poem, but that has meant that I have had all the more freedom with which to work on it.'

On the night of 14 August there was a slight earthquake on Ischia. The next day Ibsen and Bergsøe walked down to the church in Casamicciola, where a crack had opened in the tower broad enough for a man's hand to enter. Ibsen put his hand in the crack, looked at it, looked at Bergsøe and left the island next day for Sorrento on the mainland.[2] Here he remained for two months, writing the last two acts. There was no earthquake to trouble him, but in nearby Naples there was an outbreak of cholera, and at one time he thought Suzannah had caught it; but this fear proved to be unfounded. We do not know when he began the long fourth (African) act, but he completed it on 15 September and posted the fair copy to Hegel three days later, adding: 'If the

---

[1] Similarly, John Paulsen saw the accounts Ibsen had kept at Ariccia while working on *Brand*, and noted that one item read: 'Bought an orange, 1 bajoc [halfpenny]. To a beggar, 1 bajoc. A glass of lemonade, 2 bajoc.' (Paulsen, *Samliv med Ibsen*, II, Copenhagen and Christiania, 1913, p. 221).

[2] For once Ibsen's fears were to prove not altogether groundless. Sixteen years later Casamicciola was destroyed by an earthquake.

printing of the *dramatis personae* could be delayed until I have sent you the rest
of the play, I should be grateful, since I might possibly wish to add a few
minor ones; but this isn't important.' The next day, 19 September, he began
the great final act, which he completed, amazingly, in twenty-five days on
14 October—over a thousand lines of rhymed verse, at the rate of forty a day.
Four days later he posted the fair copy of this to Hegel—'and may luck attend
it!'

They spent a week relaxing in Sorrento; then, towards the end of the
month, left for Pompeii, where they stayed two days. From there they moved
on to Naples, now free of the cholera. Bergsøe tried to persuade Ibsen to take
a trip with him in a fishing boat to Capri, but Ibsen refused. 'I won't go out
with these Neapolitans. If there's a storm they lie flat in the boat and pray to
the Virgin Mary instead of reefing the sails.' Bergsøe adds, however, that
Ibsen's fear in this context was, again, not without foundation, since a boat
with a young girl in it had recently overturned in the bay—whereupon the
fisherman swam ashore and the young girl was found drowned the following
evening.[1]

At the end of October they set out from Naples for Rome. But politics intervened; a week previously Garibaldi had invaded the Papal State, fighting was
in full progress, the railway was cut, and the Ibsens and Bergsøe found themselves stuck at San Germano, a few miles short of the Papal frontier. For a
professed champion of liberty, Ibsen showed a disappointing lack of enthusiasm
for his hero's cause, very different from his mood of two years earlier. 'Damn
all war!' he wrote to Consul Bravo in Rome from San Germano on 4 November, two days after Garibaldi had been defeated at Mentana by the French and
Papal forces. 'We have been sitting here, a few miles from the Papal frontier,
since Wednesday, in the continued but as yet vain hope of being able to proceed to Rome.'[2] At length, on 8 November, the trains started running again
and he was able to return.

Rome presented a strangely changed appearance. 'The corso', writes Bergsøe,
'was almost empty, and the few people I met were foreigners. Many of the
great palazzos seemed deserted, there was quiet in the small streets, and instead
of the conversing groups usually to be found on the Piazza Colonna one now
saw bivouacking soldiers, their rifles piled in pyramids, guarded by sentry

---

[1] Bergsøe, p. 248.

[2] Edmund Gosse (*Ibsen*, London, 1907, p. 121) rightly observes that in his attitude of
passive appreciation Ibsen resembled Walter Savage Landor rather than those other
illustrious exiles such as Stendhal, Lamartine, Ruskin and the Brownings, who had 'spent
nights of insomnia dreaming of Italian liberty'. Landor had died in Florence three months
after Ibsen's first arrival in Rome.

posts at each corner of the square. Patrols moved ceaselessly through the streets; but when the French bugles sounded, the Romans stared at the red-breeched troops with a mixture of hatred and contempt, remembering that it had been a French general who had defeated Garibaldi at Mentana.' At night 'numerous patrols roamed in long grey coats and with rifles over their shoulders. When an Orsini bomb exploded they placed themselves back to back and fired at random in all directions, regardless of where the shots might land.'[1]

On 14 November 1867, six days after Ibsen had returned to Rome and less than four weeks after Hegel had received the final section of the manuscript (why were publishers so much quicker then?), *Peer Gynt* appeared in the Scandinavian bookshops. Ibsen was delighted at its being out in time to catch the Christmas sales. 'Let us hope the critics will be kind to us', he wrote to Hegel on 23 November. 'I think the book will be much read in Norway.'

Peer Gynt, however—the tale of a man the exact opposite of Brand, a compromiser who thinks only of himself, shuns work and suffering, and (it is hinted) typifies the most common Norwegian failings—gained a mixed reception in Scandinavia. The first omens were good; Hegel sent word that the first edition of 1,250 copies had sold out almost at once, and that a second edition of 2,000 was in the press. Three days after publication Bjørnson, that most patriotic of poets who more than most might have been expected to take offence at the fun poked at Norwegian nationalism, especially since Peer was the exact opposite of Bjørnson's own romanticised peasant heroes, wrote Ibsen a letter full of admiration: 'I love your spleen, I love the courage with which it has armed you, I love your strength, I love your recklessness—oh, it turned all my thoughts to laughter, like the smell of the sea after the closed air of a sickroom,' and ending: 'This is a love letter, and nothing else . . . *Peer Gynt* is magnificent, Ibsen! Only Norwegians can see how good it is!'[2] He reviewed the book in *Norsk Folkeblad* on 23 November, describing it as 'a satire on Norwegian egotism, narrowness and self-sufficiency, so executed as to have made me not only again and again laugh till I was sore, but again and again give thanks to the author in my heart, as I do here in public',[3] and dispraising nothing but the over-exuberance of detail and certain aspects of the versification. He especially admired the threadballs scene.

F. Bætzmann wrote a long and favourable review in *Aftenbladet* (30 November and 4 December), noting that 'the kind of free dramatic writing to which

---

[1] Bergsøe, pp. 271–272. Felice Orsini had tried to assassinate Napoleon III by throwing a bomb (made in Birmingham) at his carriage in 1858, and had been executed.

[2] *Gro-tid*, II, pp. 244–246.

[3] William Archer's translation.

Peer Gynt belongs . . . [means] that the author need not bother about the many cramping considerations to which one must pay regard when writing for stage performance'. He complained, however, that the 'happy' ending was banal, 'and a little absurd', questioned whether 'the genre in which (in *Love's Comedy*, *Brand* and *Peer Gynt*) Ibsen has shown increasing mastery is really a good genre and answers to the demands which our society and age make of literature', and concluded by expressing the hope that 'as eminent a talent as Ibsen's might give us less of polemics and nihilism and more that is beautiful and aesthetically satisfying than he has in his last three wide-ranging dramas'. An anonymous reviewer in *Morgenbladet* (29 November), although complaining that the play stopped before the end of Act Four [!] and that Act Five was stationary and therefore dramatically bad, ended by praising it as 'a work which takes a very pre-eminent place in our literature . . . giving the most striking evidence of the originality of [Ibsen's] views and the strength and depth of his imagination . . . an expression of a great spirit's battle for truth and beauty in life'.

So far, so good; but the most influential critic in Scandinavia was Clemens Petersen, and his long notice in *Fædrelandet* (30 November), though granting the play some merits and admitting its 'often surprising brilliance', ultimately rejected it on doctrinaire philosophical grounds. The article, a formidable specimen of woolly-mindedness and dogmaticism, condemned *Peer Gynt* as lacking in idealism, objected that the characters were not fully rounded or alive and that the play contained 'riddles which are insoluble because they are empty', dismissed Peer's identification of the Sphinx with the Boyg as 'an intellectual swindle', and ended by categorising the play as political journalism, declaring that 'it is not poetry, because in the transmutation of reality into art it fails to meet the demands of either art or reality'.

Hostility to *Peer Gynt*, it gradually became apparent, was widespread. Hans Andersen hated it. 'Ibsen is repellent to him', wrote Edvard Grieg to Bjørnson, 'and *Peer Gynt* the worst that he has read.' Camilla Collett, the pioneer of women's independence in Norway, was offended by the passivity of Solveig's character, declaring that a more forceful female would have shown Peer the error of his ways much earlier. Kristofer Janson, in *Aftenbladet*, denounced the attack (through the character of Huhu) on the language reformers, of whom he was one. A reviewer in *Nordisk Tidskrift* thought the play had 'too much thought'; another, in the Danish newspaper *Berlingske Tidende*, thought it 'not truly aesthetic'. Even Georg Brandes, in his notice in *Dagbladet* on 16 December, shared in the condemnation. While granting Ibsen's 'incredible gift for versification' and 'wonderful command of language', he found the theme and its treatment ethically offensive. 'What great and noble powers are wasted on this thankless material! . . . It would be unjust to deny that the book contains great beauties, or that it tells us all, and Norwegians in particular, some important truths; but beauties and truths are of far less value than Beauty and Truth in the singular, and Ibsen's poem is neither beautiful nor true. Contempt for humanity and self-hatred make a bad foundation on which to build a poetic work. What an unlovely and distorting view of life this is! What acrid pleasure can a poet find in thus sullying human nature?'[1] And in a second review, in *Illustreret Tidende* on 29 December, Brandes complained: 'The more polemical and tendentious Ibsen's satire, the greater is the danger of its proving short-lived . . . There is a lack of harmony and to some extent of clarity . . . In conclusion, one wishes that this man would give himself time and peace to work out particulars which have not flowed perfectly from his pen and which he has all too carelessly allowed to stand.'

On 30 December *Morgenbladet* printed a letter from its Copenhagen correspondent summarising critical reaction in Denmark: 'The verdict on this remarkable work, which was at first uncertain and much divided, now seems more or less agreed that a writer of such great gifts, mastery of form and intellectual depth, ought to abandon the moralising and polemising in which he has indulged in his latest works and serve with a larger sense of beauty and discrimination the Muse of Poetry who has elected to bless him with her patronage.'

Petersen's review, from which Ibsen had hoped so much, drove him into a fury, not merely because it was hostile (Brandes's was almost equally so), but because it represented just that kind of pompous mental rigidity which he most detested and which he was to spend his life castigating. He received a copy of the notice just as he had composed a letter of thanks to Bjørnson for the latter's praise of the play, and was so enraged that he tore this letter up and wrote another. His redrafted letter reveals that manic side of his character which he rarely allowed to appear in his writing but which, as we have seen, not infrequently emerged in social intercourse. 'Dear Bjørnson', he wrote on 9 December. 'What is this curse that at every juncture interposes itself between us? It is as though the Devil came in person to cast his shadow over us . . . An hour ago, I read Hr Clemens Petersen's review in *Fædrelandet* . . . If I were in Copenhagen and anyone stood as near to me as Clemens Petersen does to you, I would have struck him senseless before allowing him to commit so calculated an offence against Truth and Justice . . . My book *is* poetry; and if it isn't, it

---

[1] Archer's translation. It is much to Ibsen's credit that he did not let these adverse reviews spoil the friendship which was shortly to develop between him and Brandes. He recognised the difference in quality between Brandes's mind and Petersen's. Brandes was later to recant his condemnation of *Peer Gynt*, except concerning Act Four.

will become such. The conception of poetry in our country, in Norway, shall shape itself according to this book . . . However, I am glad that this injustice has been flung at me; it is a sign of divine aid and dispensation; anger increases my strength. If there is to be war, then let there be war! If I am not a poet, what have I to lose? I shall try my hand as a photographer. I shall deal with my contemporaries up there, each and all of them, one by one, as I have dealt with these language reformers; I shall not spare the child in its mother's womb, nor any thought nor feeling that may have motivated the actions of any man who shall merit the honour of being my victim . . . Do you know that all my life I have turned my back on my parents, on my whole family, because I could not bear to continue a relationship based on imperfect understanding?'

He did not post the letter at once, but added a postscript the following day: 'I have slept on these words and read them again in cold blood. The mood they express is that of yesterday; I shall send them, nevertheless.' After another hysterical outburst ('Do not underrate my friends and supporters in Norway; the party whose paper has allowed its pages to carry an injustice against me shall realise that I do not stand alone . . . My enemies shall learn that if I cannot build I have at least strength enough to destroy'), he ended on a scarcely appeasing note: 'I reproach you merely with inactivity. It was not good of you to permit, by doing nothing, such an attempt to be made in my absence to put my reputation under the auctioneer's hammer.'

Bjørnson accepted this abuse calmly, and wrote Ibsen a letter (16 December) of splendid generosity and exhortation, begging him to 'be just towards us and have faith in yourself'. He told Ibsen that he had misread Petersen's article and (which was scarcely true) that Petersen had disliked it only from a philosophical standpoint; added that 'they are thinking of "decorating" us— shouldn't we reject this?' (a question which was to remain a lifelong bone of contention between them), and ended by summarising the critical reaction to the play. 'Don't rely too much on Brandes, there's something misleading about anyone who doesn't believe in God . . . Brandes has written in Dagbladet about Peer Gynt, like Petersen, but more severely . . . Erik Bøgh has written excellently, wittily, full of praise . . . Bætzmann cleverly in Aftenbladet . . . Petersen was here just now; he wants to answer you himself; expect a letter which will be plain-spoken but will do it decently.'[1]

Bjørnson's letter, which ran to 3,500 words, reached Ibsen on Christmas Day, and so mollified him that in his reply, of 28 December, he actually asked Bjørnson to give Petersen his regards. But his old feeling of resentment soon

---

[1] Gro-tid, II, pp. 256–267.

returned, and it was to be ten years before he wrote to Bjørnson again. After his first outburst of fury, Ibsen accepted the criticisms calmly. 'How goes it with *Peer Gynt?*' he asked Hegel on 24 February 1868. 'In Sweden, as far as I can tell from the newspaper reviews, it has been very well received; but has it sold accordingly? In Norway I gather the book has caused a great rumpus; which bothers me not in the least; but both there and in Denmark, people have discovered much more satire than I intended. Why can't people read the thing as a work of fiction? That is how I wrote it. The satirical sections are pretty isolated. But if, as seems to be the case, the Modern Norwegian recognises himself in Peer Gynt, that is those good gentlemen's own funeral.'

Suprisingly, in view of the controversy surrounding it, *Peer Gynt* did not sell particularly well; the second edition, printed immediately after publication, was not exhausted until 1874, by which time *Brand* had entered its seventh edition. It was nine years before anyone staged it, and thirteen years before Ibsen received a request for translation rights.

Like *Brand*, Alfred de Musset's comedies, Turgenev's *A Month in the Country* and (probably, for Büchner's exact intention regarding his plays is unknown) *Woyzeck* and *Danton's Death*, *Peer Gynt* was written with no thought of performance; and the consequent rejection of the accepted limitations of stagecraft proved, as with *Brand*, tremendously liberating. It was not merely that Ibsen felt free to move uninhibitedly in time and space (*Peer Gynt* contains forty scenes). He had done that in *Brand*. More importantly, he felt free to ignore other frontiers, the frontiers between reality and fantasy, between (as we should now say) the conscious and the unconscious. Nobody, one hopes, any longer takes the last act of *Peer Gynt* at its face value, as the return of an old man to his youthful love; such an ending would have been, for Ibsen, most untypically banal and sentimental, two adjectives which recur frequently in contemporary criticisms of it. Whether one regards Peer as having died in the madhouse at the end of Act Four, or in the shipwreck at the beginning of Act Five, we must surely take that fifth act as representing either the unreeling of his past life in his mind at the moment of death or (which is perhaps the same thing) as the wandering of his soul in purgatory, '*limbo patrum*, nigh to hell'. Viewed thus, the last hour of the play is Peer's life seen in a distorting mirror, just as the troll scene in Act Three is the wedding party and Peer's hopes and fears concerning it dreamed by a drunken and concussed man: the desirable yet (once he has got her) repulsive girl, the wrathful vengeance-seeking father, the conflict between lust and conscience. To present *Peer* on a purely realistic level, as still, alas, occasionally happens, is to reduce it to an amiable and confused pantomime with a facile ending, an interpretation to which Grieg's music, for all its intrinsic merits, has lent authority. Ibsen was not Freud's darling playwright, and Joyce's, for nothing; he understood, as few of their predecessors did, the power of the unconscious, the truth behind dreams and nightmares, the higher reality of what most of his contemporaries dismissed as unreality; and *Peer Gynt* may be regarded as the first prolonged exploration, whether deliberate or unconscious, of this field, to which, nearly twenty years later, he was to return with such effect in *Rosmersholm, The Lady from the Sea,* and the powerful and, to his contemporaries, scarcely intelligible plays which followed. *Peer Gynt* is the direct ancestor of Strindberg's *A Dream Play*. But at the time of its appearance, as Ibsen complained, it was regarded mainly as a satire.

Yet in one sense at least Ibsen's critics came nearer the truth than some of the play's later admirers. They were right to find it disturbing, discordant and offensive. It is one of the most upsetting and uncomfortable plays ever written. Trolls, properly understood, are not mere goblins but, as Professor Francis Bull has written: 'the evil forces of Nature . . . embodying and symbolising those powers of evil, hidden in the soul of man, which may at times suppress his conscious will and dominate his actions . . . By ever pandering to his evil instincts and desires they have come to be really his rulers—mysterious powers that make him afraid of himself.'[1] This is what *Peer Gynt* is really about—the struggle between the divine purpose and our undermining passions and egocentricities, between man's deeper self and his animal, or troll, self; in Stekel's phrase 'how the soul, oppressed by the primal passions, struggles to escape the hell of the instincts'.[2] The Boyg, the Greenclad One, and the Strange Passenger are, like the Thin Person, lackeys of the Enemy; as is Peer himself, apart from the image of him which Solveig keeps

> With the mark of destiny on his brow
> As he sprang forth in the mind of God.

The Strange Passenger has been the subject of several extraordinary theories. Mr Michael Elliott, who directed the 1962 production of the play at the Old Vic, suggests, and I agree, that he represents, like the hawk in *Brand*, the thing that destroys you because you reject and exclude it, and that the turning-point in Peer's quest for salvation is that moment of despair when he sees the star fall, because the moment of despair is the moment of hope.

---

[1] Taylorian Lecture at Oxford, 1954, published in the catalogue to the Oslo University Library Ibsen memorial exhibition of 1956 (p. 12).

[2] Wilhelm Stekel, 'Analytic Notes on *Peer Gynt*' in *Compulsion and Doubt* (London, 1950), II, pp. 599–600.

Ibsen himself thought *Peer Gynt* too Norwegian ever to be appreciated abroad, much as Synge felt about *The Playboy of the Western World* (a character who has much in common with Peer, as the styles of the two plays have much in common, with their ebullient rhythms and extravagant imagery). 'Of all my books', Ibsen wrote to a would-be German translator, Ludwig Passarge (19 May 1880), 'I regard *Peer Gynt* as the least likely to be understood outside Scandinavia . . . You know the people and the personalities one finds up there. But is not all this necessary if one is to find any real flavour in the poem?' Ibsen's doubts were to prove unfounded, for *Peer Gynt* has become the best known of his works outside, as well as inside Scandinavia. Peer himself has everywhere been accepted as a national prototype; a Japanese critic has described him as 'typically Japanese'[1]; as Bernard Shaw wrote: 'The universality of Ibsen makes his plays come home to all nations.'[2]

In a later letter (16 June 1880) to Passarge, who, despite the warning, had translated the play, Ibsen made it clear, if any confirmation were needed, that *Peer Gynt* is a self-analysis. Referring specifically to this play, he stated: 'Everything that I have written is most minutely connected with what I have lived through, if not personally experienced; every new work has had for me the object of serving as a process of spiritual liberation and catharsis; for every man shares the responsibility and the guilt of the society to which he belongs. That is why I once inscribed in a copy of one of my books the following dedicatory lines:

> To live is to war with trolls in heart and soul.
> To write is to sit in judgment on oneself.[3]

If, as Ibsen once remarked, Brand was 'myself, in my best moments', Peer was the other side of the medallion.

Ibsen's letters from Rome during the last months of 1867 show him toying with the idea of returning to Scandinavia. Several times he hints that Copenhagen may be the answer; Norway still seemed out of the question. 'I can never make out how you endure it up there', he wrote to Magdalene Thoresen

---

[1] Bull, *Taylorian Lecture, 1954*, p. 23.

[2] *Saturday Review*, 22 November 1896. But there is some evidence that Ibsen in later years rather took against *Peer Gynt*. P. G. la Chesnais tells that, to a French visitor who began to praise the play in 1900, Ibsen replied (I quote la Chesnais's version; Ibsen would not have said it in French): '*Bah! Une œuvre de jeunesse! Ce fut mon Manfred. Qui sait s'il n'a pas persisté en moi un byronien attardé?*' (*Œuvres complètes, traduites par* P. G. la Chesnais, Paris, 1914–1945, VIII, p. 94).

[3] William Archer's translation.

on 15 October. 'Life up there, as I now see it, seems boring beyond description. It bores the soul from one's body, it bores the marrow from one's will; that's the damnable thing about petty surroundings, they make a man's soul petty!' And in his last letter to Bjørnson on 28 December he had said: 'Where we shall spend next winter, I don't know. I only know it won't be in Norway. If I went home now, one of two things would happen. Either I'd make an enemy of everyone within a month, or I'd bury my head in the sand again and become a lie to myself and others.' After warning Bjørnson not to continue in theatre management ('Working in the theatre is, for a writer, a daily repeated abortion . . .'), he exhorted him: 'No, come abroad, *carissimo!* Both because distance gives one a broader perspective, and because one is out of people's sight.' In a similar mood at this time he told Frederik Knudtzon: 'One should live down here and rule them all.'[1]

But his son was now eight, and there was his schooling to consider; for all his hatred of Norway, Ibsen was unwilling that Sigurd should be educated as a foreigner. He did not know enough Italian, anyway, to go to an ordinary local school, and such foreign schools as there were in Rome at this time could not take a child who was fluent only in Norwegian; so on 24 February 1868 we find Ibsen asking Hegel to send him 'a geography book, a general world history, an arithmetic book and books containing the elements of religious instruction, all suitable for an eight year old child . . . My little boy has read a lot, especially history (both general and biblical), but as yet quite unsystematically, and it must not continue so.' By the spring he was beginning to accept that, if for this reason only, he would have to return to Norway. 'What it will be like to live outside Italy, and above all what it will be like to live in Christiania', he wrote to Magdalene Thoresen on 31 March, 'I can scarcely imagine. However, I suppose I shall have to. But one will have to isolate oneself totally up there (I shall, anyway), if I am not to make an enemy of everyone . . . The best that could happen to our country would be a great national calamity. If one can't survive that one has no right to live. I have witnessed sacrifices down here which make me draw comparisons from which our country does not emerge with honour.'

Early in 1868 Ibsen had resumed work on *Emperor and Galilean*, but after *Brand* and *Peer Gynt* he found himself wanting to write for the theatre again, as opposed to the printed page, and on 28 February he told Hegel: 'My next work will probably be a play for the stage, and I hope it will not be long before I begin to work seriously on it.' Another plan had occurred to him. 'I have been thinking of making a collection of my various unpublished poems, but

[1] Knudtzon, pp. 165–166.

I can't do that down here, as they must be ferreted out of various newspapers, etc. But some time I shall have to come north again, and I suppose make a detour to Christiania, in which case I could start things moving.'

That spring, Ibsen seems to have been in an unusually prickly mood. His marriage may have entered upon a difficult phase. Martin Schneekloth, a young Dane whom Ibsen found sympathetic and who, like so many of those young Scandinavians in Rome, was shortly to die of consumption, noted in his diary, which was to remain unpublished for three-quarters of a century:

> 'To find that one does not really love the woman one has married, that one's requirements for a happy co-existence are so opposed to one's wife's that no reconciliation is possible, must be a desperate situation for a man, and that is Ibsen's. He is a domineering character, egocentric and un-bending, with a passionate masculinity and a curious admixture of personal cowardice, compulsively idealistic yet totally indifferent to expressing these ideals in his daily life, restlessly questing, confused, yet striving for clarity. *She* is unwomanly, tactless, *but* a stable, hard character, a mixture of intelligence and stupidity, not deficient in feeling but lacking humility and feminine love. They cannot find peace through love, so they wage war on each other, ruthlessly, coldly, and yet she loves him, if only through their son, their poor son, whose fate is the saddest that could befall any child, to see divided what should be reconciled in him. Whose is the fault if not the man's? He took her from her father's house, led her out into the strange world, and, instead of devoting his life to finding some form of reconciliation he gives all his mind and passion to a demonic pursuit of literary fame. It is disturbing to hear him describe his plans to send his wife and child home so that he may work in peace abroad. He lacks the courage to pursue his career without abandoning his domestic responsibilities, to face up to the consequences of his ambition, to work incessantly to give her life fulfilment, to suffer and strive to educate his son. Thus he, who so loudly and brilliantly condemns the cravenness of our age, who in mighty poems proclaims the strength of human will, is himself a craven, a vacil-lating weakling.'

This formidable indictment is reinforced by a later entry for the same month:

> 'Does Ibsen love his wife? I don't know, but she loves him, but is not happy in her love. Ibsen himself is so obsessed with his work that the proverb "humanity first, art second" has practically been reversed. I think his love for his wife has long vanished, and been replaced by a mood of resignation, if such is possible in so restless a character. His crime now is

that he cannot discipline himself to correct the situation, but rather asserts his moody and despotic nature over both her and their poor, spiritually warped, terrified son.'[1]

Schneekloth might almost have been prophetically describing the marriages of the Master Builder, John Gabriel Borkman, or Arnold and Maja Rubek in *When We Dead Awaken*; and the theme of at any rate the last two plays is indeed 'humanity first, art [or ambition] second'. Yet Schneekloth's account, though probably accurate, gives only half the picture, the surface half which so many other acquaintances of the Ibsens were to record. Unlike Solness, Borkman and Rubek, Ibsen was dependent on and devoted to his wife, as the statements of their son and daughter-in-law, and the frequent references in his own letters, show. Ibsen was, like Milton, Dickens, Tolstoy, Dostoevsky, Shelley, Carlyle, D. H. Lawrence and Joyce (to say nothing of numberless great painters and composers) monstrously egocentric and frequently cruel; yet if he had survived Suzannah and recorded his private thoughts about her, it is difficult to imagine that they would have greatly differed from those of Thomas Carlyle about his Jane, another couple whom their contemporaries supposed to live in a state of permanent mutual torment.

Frederik Knudtzon recounts an anecdote from this spring of 1868 which vividly illustrates the duality in Ibsen's nature, and the suddenness with which he would switch from one mood to another. One Sunday afternoon, while accompanying the sculptor Frederik Stramboe to the latter's studio, Knudtzon saw Ibsen on the other pavement in the Via Felice, together with Lars Hansen and the Norwegian sculptor Fladager.

'As soon as Ibsen caught sight of us he crossed the street towards us and cried: "*Ih, mare,*[2] Knudtzon! You must come out with us to La Baracca." "But I've promised Stramboe I'd go to his studio." That could be done tomorrow, said Ibsen; we must join him; it would be a delightful walk. So we turned round, introduced ourselves to his companions and joined them. It soon became apparent that Ibsen had been lunching with them and had come straight from the table. We arrived at the Piazza Barberina. There were several cabs there, and Ibsen made straight for them. As he seized on the first, Fru Ibsen announced that she would not accompany us. Ibsen protested at this, but she maintained that she would not come. "Get up into the cab!" thundered Ibsen with all his might, if somewhat

---

[1] Schindler, pp. 120–122.

[2] An exclamation much used by Jeppe of the Hill in Holberg's play of that name, roughly equivalent to 'What cheer?'

indistinctly. It was very disagreeable for the four of us to listen to. But the moment the words were out of his mouth Fru Ibsen climbed up and took her seat in the cab. Ibsen and Fladager followed, we three others jumped hastily into another cab, and the two vehicles rolled off. After a quarter of an hour we trundled into the spacious courtyard of La Baracca, with its splendid view towards the blue Alban mountains. Our little Sunday symposium was about to begin; but the violent scene in the Piazza Barberina had undeniably given us the feeling that there was thunder in the air.

'Under the great tree where we usually sat there was ample room. I came first to the table, and as the Bodega simultaneously presented himself I ordered *un mezzo*, but Ibsen was just behind me, and when he heard my order he shouted in a leave-this-to-me voice: *"Due mezzi!"* This meant three *mezzi*, i.e. six *fogliette*, which if equally divided would mean a whole *foglietta* each . . . However, we drank and chatted and the wine effected a considerable change in the atmosphere. Ibsen seemed from the start to have some worm of indignation in the depths of his soul, an indignation which grew as the tempo heightened under the influence of the wine and the general euphoria increased. This indignation weighed on him and demanded an outlet. It may have been connected with Ibsen's sense of responsibility and calling as a poet; he once told me he saw his ideal of a poet in the Old Testament prophets. Perhaps . . . his prophetic indignation had built up until it could find vent only through an explosion.

'However, as we sat under the great tree looking now at each other, now at the blue Alban mountains, everything still went agreeably. I think we emptied most of the three *mezzi*, and as darkness fell we prepared to leave. But now the same happened as the previous year; Ibsen's brain was found to be functioning better than his legs. Had we been wise we would have sent for a carriage. But we failed to take that precaution. We moved off, Fru Ibsen going ahead with old Hansen and Fladager. Ibsen followed some distance behind, with Stramboe and myself on either side; we kept a good hold of him under the arms and started to walk slowly and carefully. But when we had come about a third of the way, something on the other side of the road caught Ibsen's attention. Behind an iron gate in a wall surrounding one of the big villas we saw a huge dog, which barked angrily at us. Ibsen quickened his pace—he had to go over to it, in other words *we* had to go over, and soon the three of us were standing at the gate. Ibsen had a stick in his hand, which he now began to poke at the dog, one of those gigantic brutes that resemble small lions. It came closer, and Ibsen poked and struck at it, trying in every way to madden it, and succeeding. It rushed at the gate, Ibsen prodded and struck it anew, and

worked it into such a rage that without doubt, had not the solid iron gate
stood between it and us, it would have torn us apart. This, I realised, was
the explosion of violence which resulted from the enjoyment of the wine,
and which had been the cause of the attack on Lorange. But it lasted
longer. Ibsen must have stood teasing the dog for six to eight minutes.
At length he grew bored with the sport. Then his eye chanced on two
Italian children who, attracted by the furious barking, were standing by
his side, two enchanting children in national dress with fresh, red cheeks,
a sight in complete contrast to the raging dog. Ibsen looked down at them,
and with an astonishing glow of kindness and gentleness in his eyes took
between two of his fingers a little pinch of each child's cheek, and
released it—a gesture of love that was expressive both of human kindness
and the need to protect. It was an *adagio* after the storm, like the speech to
Ludvig Abelin Schou after the outburst against Lorange. Now both his
prophetic indignation and his benevolence had found expression, and we
continued on our way.'[1]

People still occasionally write about Ibsen as though he was a figure of Olym-
pian calm and detachment. It cannot be over-emphasised that, while his
writing was indeed detached, in the sense of being supremely objective, it was
a detachment born of a fearful discipline exercised over a manic depressive
temperament. Ibsen never spoke more truly than when he likened himself to
an Old Testament prophet. Isaiah, dressed in a tall hat and morning coat,
would surely have looked and talked like Ibsen.[2]

On 9 May 1868 Ibsen, Suzannah and Sigurd left Rome, 'to spend the
summer', as he informed Hegel on 27 April, 'in Northern Italy or the Tyrol',
probably with the intention of proceeding to Christiania in the autumn. For
the time being, at any rate, on account of Sigurd's schooling, they had put
Italy behind them. They spent eight days in Florence, two in Bologna, eight
in Venice and eight in Botzen (now Bolzano) in the Tyrol. In the middle of
June, riding in an old-fashioned coach with the postilion blowing his bugle,
they reached the little Bavarian resort of Berchtesgaden, where they settled
for the summer (and to which they were frequently to return). 'I don't know
if you are familiar with this place', Ibsen wrote to Consul Bravo on 22 June.
'If not, it is worth discovering. It is the most beautiful country I have seen

---

[1] Knudtzon, pp. 215–218.
[2] The Swedish writer Ola Hansson once remarked that Ibsen always had 'something of
Moses on Sinai with the tablets of the law in his hand'. (Quoted by Paulsen, *Samliv med
Ibsen*, II, p. 233).

north of the Alps, cheap, easy of access, pleasant in every way . . . I have started a new work, which I hope to complete here . . . When we shall return to our home in Rome is still uncertain; but some time we shall come back, or anyway I shall, life and health permitting.' On 28 July he wrote to Hegel: 'We shall spend the winter in Munich and Dresden, and shall then probably come home. I have not yet got down seriously to anything big, but I shall soon . . . The landscape here is splendid, but the weather changeable; I miss my beloved Italy in more respects than one.' He visited Salzburg, and in August spent eight days walking to Gastein and back. By this time, his new play was beginning to mature in his mind. 'My new dramatic work (written for the theatre, and wholly realistic, influenced no doubt by the heavy German air) occupies all my thoughts', he told Hegel on 20 August.

At the end of August they left Berchtesgaden and proceeded to Munich. They stayed there a month, in an apartment at Maximilianplatz 13, 'the whole time under a blessedly Italian sky, rejoicing in the city's wonderful art treasures and in the local populace's hatred of all things Prussian'.[1] In the first days of October they arrived in Dresden, where they were to spend the next six and a half years.

---

[1] Letter to Hegel, 22 September 1868.

F

PART TWO
GERMAN SEED-TIME

THREE

Dresden: The League of Youth (1868–1869)

A CENTURY EARLIER the poet Johann Gottfried von Herder, fresh from introducing the young Goethe to the beauties of Shakespeare and Gothic architecture, had described Dresden as 'the German Florence', and the compliment, if not strictly accurate, was still reasonably deserved. Surrounded by blue hills, and traversed by the curving Elbe with its ancient bridges and terraces, the city greeted the traveller with a picturesque skyline of green copper roofs, spires and cupolas. In 1868 Dresden was still, despite the bombardment it had suffered in 1760, largely of the seventeenth and eighteenth century, with many fine mediaeval buildings in the Altstadt or Old Town, which Canaletto had so admired. It was a favourite resort of foreigners, partly for the splendour of its art collections and historic buildings, and partly, for those with children, on account of the famed excellence of its educational facilities—an important consideration, as we have seen, for Ibsen, whose movements in Europe over the next decade and a half were largely to be dictated by the needs of his son.

He took furnished lodgings in a small two-roomed apartment on the first floor at An der Frauenkirche 6, shown in contemporary photographs as a pleasant, tall house, and settled down to complete his plans for his new play. On 10 October, less than a week after his arrival, he asked Hegel to send him regular copies of the newspaper *Dagbladet*, 'not to satisfy an idle curiosity for news . . . but because I shall thereby be drawn more closely and intensively into life in Norway, and thus feel strengthened for my work'. He was determined to make his play nothing if not realistic.

He began his first draft on 21 October, and completed Act One in five days. On the last of the month he was able to report happily to Hegel that 'the play makes swift progress. All this summer I have been turning it over in my mind without actually writing; now the whole draft is ready and on paper, Act One is finished, Act Two will be in a week, and I hope the whole play will be completed by the end of the year. It will be in prose, and written entirely with the stage in mind. The title of the play is *The League of Youth*, or *Our Lord*

& Co.; a comedy in five acts. It deals with frictions and currents in modern life. I find myself in a calm and happy frame of mind, and write accordingly.' He added a request for further reading matter. 'Will you please send me a copy of Brandes's *Aesthetic Studies* and debit it to my account? While I was in Rome I heard that he was writing an essay on comedy, a subject on the theory of which I must confess to having no very clear ideas, and about which I should greatly like to be informed, especially by Brandes.' Lacking introductions, and cut off by his shyness from striking up acquaintances in cafés as Bjørnson would have done, he added a sad little plea. 'Do you know of no Dane who might stop off in Dresden this winter? I long much for Scandinavians. There may be some here already, but I haven't met any, and the consul knows nothing.' However, he was finding Dresden 'very pleasant and very cheap', and concluded: 'I go much to the theatre. It is one of the best in Germany, but is far, far behind that of Copenhagen in taste and accomplishment. But that is so everywhere in Germany'—an opinion which Hans Andersen had expressed twenty years earlier. One would like to know which plays Ibsen saw but, unhelpful as so often, he names none.

Hegel sent him a copy of *Aesthetic Studies*, a solid book of 318 pages. It comprised a section on 'The Nature of Tragedy' (the introduction to a thesis which had won Brandes the Copenhagen University Gold Medal in 1862–1863); two essays on 'The Theory of Comedy'; five studies of modern Scandinavian writers (Christian Rickardt, Frederik Paludan-Muller, Emil Aarestrup, Henrik Hertz and Ibsen himself); and three short pieces on individual plays, Oehlenschläger's *The Little Herdsman*, Heiberg's *The Inseparables* and Molière's *L'École des femmes*. The sections on tragedy and comedy read rather dully today, and are the kind of abstract theorising which Ibsen was accustomed to find particularly indigestible; but the studies of the individual writers sparkle with good sense, perception and breadth of outlook. To read them side by side with the cloudy utterances of Clemens Petersen, that feared pundit, is like comparing the essays of Matthew Arnold (the first volume of which had appeared three years previously) with those of the executioners of the Edinburgh and Quarterly Reviews. Ibsen devoured the book with delight, even, apparently, the abstract sections. 'It has', he informed Hegel on 22 December, 'been a veritable gold mine for me . . . Brandes is a remarkable man for seeing clearly, deeply and cohesively.' He must have been gratified to find that the essay on himself, of fifty-five pages, was more than twice as long as any of the others about individual authors.

Hegel had expressed doubts about the propriety of Ibsen's suggested subtitle for his new play; he feared that some might think *Our Lord & Co.* blasphemous, and Ibsen agreed to alter it. 'I was myself half of the same opinion', he told Hegel in the same letter, 'though the expression would not have offended anyone *once they had read the play*. It contains no word on religious matters; but people can't know that in advance, and the sub-title might well cause offence; so, away with it! The play will be the most artistically finished work I have yet written . . . I hope to send you the fair copy in February.' He was less good than his word, for he did not complete even his first draft until 28 February. 'It is a blessed feeling', he wrote to Hegel that day, 'to be done with something which for a whole year now has never for a single day been out of my thoughts.'

The fair-copying of his manuscript took him a further nine weeks, a long time, one might think, even allowing for a certain amount of rewriting. A more cogent reason for this apparent dilatoriness, however, may have been his reluctance to return (as he would then have had to have done) to the heart-searching labour of *Emperor and Galilean*, that burden which had for so long been on his back. Replying on 23 March to Martin Schneekloth, the young Dane who had so sharply observed his marriage, and who had enquired about the progress of the Roman play, Ibsen wrote: 'I am not thinking about "Julian" for the moment, and don't want to bother about him in the near future; to be honest, I shrink from both the man and the theme . . . We visit the theatre regularly . . . Life is fabulously cheap here. In the New Year Sigurd became a pupil at Dr Holbe's famous school, which is principally attended by foreigners, Americans, English, Russians, Poles, etc. . . . We shall stay here at least a year.'

Sigurd later recalled to his wife Bergliot[1] how poor his parents were during those first months in Dresden. He himself was looked down on by his school-mates because he was so ill-dressed; Suzannah made his clothes out of his father's old ones, and cut them big enough to allow for growth. His trousers were too long, and the boys in the street used to run after him shouting: '*Du tretst in deine Hosen!*' *Du tretst in deine Hosen!*' ('You're treading on your trousers!') Once, when Ibsen suggested that Sigurd should bring some of his schoolfriends home, he told his father that he 'didn't want to', ashamed that they should see how humbly his parents lived; at which his father gave him 'a long, wounded and questioning look', which left such an impression on him that 'I would have given years of my life to have unsaid it'. The neighbours' children mocked him too, and he had to make up fantastic tales to impress them, such as that his mother (who had been ill for some weeks, and had left the shopping to him) was a negress who never went out of the house, and that he had a brother whom his parents kept in a box. Suzannah brought him up austerely, continually drumming into him the importance of duty; once when

---

[1] Bergliot Ibsen, pp. 37–39.

he had cut his head so that it bled and he was running a fever, Suzannah simply bandaged it and sent him to school as usual.

When there was some occasion for celebration, such as the anniversary of his wedding, or Suzannah's or Sigurd's birthday, Ibsen would design an imitation banknote for a certain sum, to be cashed when sufficient funds should be in hand. Several of these banknotes have survived, the earliest from 1867 when he was on Ischia writing *Peer Gynt*, and continuing as late as 1875, after the move to Munich. Most of them contain drawings of either a cat or an eagle —both nicknames that he had affectionately coined for Suzannah. (His own nickname in the family was 'The Tiger' or 'The Bear'.) He also on occasion awarded them medals, often copied from real medals, and sometimes amused himself by sketching these in the margins of his manuscripts.

Each week, Sigurd received a tiny amount of pocket money, which he never spent but kept in a money-box; this he opened three times a year, at Christmas and on his parents' birthdays, to buy presents for them. Every evening, after he had finished his homework, Ibsen would play cards with him, and always let him win. One evening Ibsen won, and Sigurd was so upset that he threw the cards on the floor; thereafter, they never played cards, but always chess, which they continued to do for many years. They had a small music-box which played the *Tyrolienne* from Offenbach's *La Vie Parisienne*, Gounod's *Faust-Walzer* and *Klosterglocken*; Suzannah still liked to play it forty years later as as old woman. Sigurd remembered what a great reader his mother was, ploughing through the year's books and recommending to Ibsen what he should read. From the age of four Sigurd was regularly sent to the library with a basket to change the books; the first thing they always did when they came to a new town was to find the library. And whenever Ibsen had finished a new play he would read it to Suzannah and Sigurd; he had done this at least as early as *Peer Gynt*, when Sigurd, on hearing the speech in Act One in which Aase scolds Peer, cried: 'Why, that's just like mother!' This habit, too, continued all their lives; when Sigurd married, Ibsen, on finishing a play, said to his daughter-in-law: 'Bergliot, you mustn't take it ill if I don't ask you to listen with us. I'm used just to reading to Sigurd and his mother.'

Sigurd remembered too how Suzannah used to force Ibsen to write, when the mood was not on him. Gradually he realised that she was right. 'When you are not in the mood to write', he told Sigurd many years later, 'you must nevertheless sit down calmly at your desk, and the inspiration will come of itself.' Bergliot (who recorded her husband's memories) adds an interesting note on Suzannah which needs to be measured against the detractions of casual observers. 'From the very beginning of their marriage she tried to keep away friends or acquaintances who might distract him . . . She let nothing and no one disturb him . . . Nor could anyone give him enthusiasm as she could. When he was depressed she knew how to ignite his courage. One needs to have personally heard her proclaim her fanatical faith to understand the strength she gave him through the years. When hostile criticism depressed him she did not lose courage. Her eyes blazed and she said: "With your genius, what should you care what this rabble writes?" And it always ended with his walking calmly into his study.'[1]

He still, even after he had come to Dresden, hankered after painting, and it cost Suzannah much effort to dissuade him from pursuing it seriously. 'I had to fight with him', she told Sigurd, who commented to Bergliot: 'The world can thank my mother that it has one bad painter the fewer and got a great writer instead.'[2]

About this time, Ibsen spotted an item of news in the Danish press which must surely have caused those tight lips to allow themselves the luxury of a small smile. To few authors is it granted to see a hostile critic of their work publicly humiliated; but in March Clemens Petersen, whose review of *Peer Gynt* had so enraged Ibsen, became involved in a homosexual scandal concerning some boys at a school where he had been lecturing, and had to leave hurriedly for the United States, where for the next thirty-five years he devoted himself to religious journalism among the Scandinavian-Americans, a fate which even Ibsen himself might have hesitated to wish on a leading literary critic. 'This is a dreadful business about Clemens Petersen', he wrote to Hegel on 7 April. 'I have always had strong suspicions about his character; but such a thing—!' Petersen's passionate admiration of Bjørnson, which may have had a sexual element in it (not that Bjørnson would have approved of or been likely to perceive that) was probably partly responsible for his denigration of Ibsen's work; Ibsen may well have appeared principally to him as a challenger to his idol. As soon as he left Denmark, Petersen's name became taboo and his influence ceased. His friends subscribed to bring him home in 1904, and he died ten years later at the age of eighty-four, almost forgotten.

During 1869 the rift between Ibsen and Bjørnson gradually widened. They had not corresponded since the end of 1867, and their letters to third parties show that a mutual distrust had developed. 'From Ibsen', wrote Bjørnson to Hegel on 25 February, 'I've heard nothing but a discourtesy which he sent me through someone else. Whether I have deserved it, I don't know, nor care; for now I'm tired; he must sail his own moody sea.'[3] And on 15 July Ibsen cynic-

---

[1] Bergliot Ibsen, pp. 41–42.
[2] *Ibid.*, p. 41.
[3] *Gro-tid*, II, p. 298.

ally observed to Brandes, with whom Bjørnson had likewise recently quarrelled: 'For him [Bjørnson] there exist only two kinds of men, those whom he
might use and those who embarrass him'—an ungrateful and untrue remark.
More accurately, he added: 'However good Bjørnson may be at analysing his
own characters, he is a poor psychologist when it comes to dealing with real
people.'

The exact cause of their alienation remains unknown; but that it should
have happened when the two were separated by half Europe is hardly surprising. Both were sharp-tongued, free in their condemnation of other human
beings, inordinately sensitive to any kind of criticism and, as such men are, more
than usually ready to believe gossip. Even if they did not say caustic things
about each other, and they pretty certainly did, we may be sure that rumours
of such remarks reached both pairs of ears. 'Have I not experienced', Bjørnson
had publicly declared at Bergen six years earlier, 'that my friend Ibsen has
been held up against me for the purpose of disparaging me, and I against him
to disparage him?' and, as we have seen, they had both had to write and reassure each other on this score within a few months of Ibsen's departure from
Norway. If they had been able to meet, the differences might have been
resolved, as they were when, many years later, they did at last meet. But
Ibsen's suspicions were intensified by something, whether true or false we do
not know, which his old Holland acquaintance Jakob Løkke told him in
Stockholm later that summer. Bjørnson tried to mend things by writing Ibsen
a friendly letter in September, ten days before the publication of *The League of
Youth*, saying that he was looking forward to reading the play; but the implied
insult to him contained in the character of Stensgaard, and the continued success
of the play on the stage, widened the gap impossibly; and although Ibsen told
Hegel in December that he would like a reconciliation, it was to be eight years
before they corresponded again and fifteen before they met.

Hegel held *The League of Youth* over until the autumn, when the publication
of the play and its stage premiere would conveniently coincide, and Ibsen spent
the summer relaxing. 'I lead a pleasant and carefree life', he wrote to Lorentz
Dietrichson on 28 May, 'and plan to get down to "Julian" in the autumn.'
Asking Dietrichson to write a brief biographical sketch of him to preface a
German translation of *Brand* which was to be published that autumn,[1] he
exhorted him to 'forget the starving poet stuff; tell rather how the government

---

[1] As things turned out, although the translator, P. F. Siebold, a travelling salesman from
Kassel, completed his translation that autumn, he did not succeed in getting it published
until 1872, when it marked the first appearance of any of Ibsen's plays in a non-Scandina-
vian language. John Grieg, the brother of Edvard Grieg, had translated *The Pretenders* into
German as early as 1866, but never managed to find a publisher.

and Storthing have granted me a pension, how I travel, am happy in *dem grossen Vaterlande*, etc.' Dietrichson has recorded how, on receiving this letter, he failed to recognise the neat, elegant handwriting, so unlike the scratchy script of Ibsen's earlier correspondence; and a photograph which followed three weeks later, with the words: 'I enclose the requested likeness of my phiz; I don't know whether you will recognise me from my bearded period', surprised him equally, with its trimly barbered head and mutton-chop whiskers, and assured expression in the eyes. Ibsen's letter included a defensive note on *The League of Youth*: 'The play is a pure comedy and nothing else. People in Norway may say that I have portrayed specific persons and circumstances, but this is untrue; though I have used models, which is as necessary for a writer of comedy as for a painter or sculptor.'

On 26 June Ibsen wrote to Georg Brandes to thank him for the essay on him in *Aesthetic Studies*. 'You have written illuminatingly of my work as no one else has done. Please accept my warmest thanks . . . I have read it sixteen times and sixteen times again . . . But now I am very excited to hear what you will say of my new work. It is written in prose and, consequently, with a strongly realistic emphasis. I have paid particular attention to the form, and *inter alia* have been artful enough to manage without a single monologue, or even an "aside".' He then, however, began to have doubts whether Brandes would approve of *The League of Youth*, and on 15 July he wrote: 'I begin to feel that perhaps I should not have asked you to read my new comedy. On reflection, I think that what really interests you in a work is the tragedies or comedies that are played out inside each individual, and that you care little or nothing about factual circumstances, whether they be political or not. In which case you may well ask, when faced with my play: "What's Hecuba to me?" But this once I didn't want to write anything but what this play is about, and it must be judged accordingly . . . As regards certain aspects of *Peer Gynt*, I cannot agree with you. I do, of course, accept the laws of beauty, but I don't bother about its conventions. You mention Michelangelo; to my mind, no one has contravened the laws of beauty more than he; yet everything he has created is beautiful because it is individual. Raphael's art I have never really warmed to; his figures are from before the Fall; and in general, the southerner has a different aesthetic attitude from us; he likes things to be formally beautiful; for us, that which is not formally beautiful can be beautiful by reason of the truth that lies in it. But it is no use arguing about this with pen and ink; we must meet.'

Brandes's 'illuminating' essay on Ibsen was an expansion of an article he had published in *Dansk Maanedsskrift* in November 1867, surveying Ibsen's career only as far as *Brand*, which he had disparaged at the expense of *The Pretenders*. *Peer Gynt* had not yet appeared when Brandes wrote this, so for the essay in

Aesthetic Studies he added the review of *Peer* which he had written for *Dagbladet* the following month, modifying, however, some of his fiercer objections to Ibsen's supposed offences against the 'laws of beauty'. At first sight, it is a little surprising that Ibsen should have shown such enthusiasm about this article, which is a curious mixture of penetration and insensitivity. The main body of it, which deals with the early plays up to and including *Brand* (but excluding *The Warrior's Barrow*, *St John's Night* and *Olaf Liljekrans*, none of which had been published), is a remarkable piece of writing for a young man of barely twenty-five. 'It is the destiny of truth and beauty', declared Brandes, 'only to shine forth for a moment, like meteors which are extinguished as soon as they touch the earth . . . There is . . . something combative, rebellious, violent and melancholy deep down in [Ibsen's] being that is reflected in his works, and darkens even his love of the light . . . He makes start after start, each, as it were, the run before the leap that is to carry him into the promised land. But for a long time it seemed as though this leap would never be taken. His genius cannot come to rest; it tosses about like a sick, restless child; now it searches within among its dreams and thoughts, but does not find them clear or strong enough to be able to step forth in vigorous nudity; now it searches without, finds a delicate, spotless drapery, wraps itself in it so as to become almost unrecognisable, seeks for a style, nay, more, a language; then it throws away what it has found, realises at length that all borrowing is pure loss, and labours until at last it finds its true self . . . Strength of will is, to him, the really sublime.'[1] The individual plays are finely analysed, especially *The Pretenders*, and Brandes makes the valid criticism that Ibsen 'has not infrequently marred his works by speeches which seem to come from a spectator rather than an actor . . . letting the characters utter sentences that are far too general, self-conscious and suitable to a thousand occasions, when one would expect them to be exclusively taken up with what is happening to themselves personally, to them alone, in this particular situation'. Brandes observes, too, that Ibsen is 'especially successful in his female figures . . . One is tempted to exclaim: "Have you been a woman in some other life, that you thus know a woman's heart?" '

The study of *Peer Gynt* which concludes Brandes's essay, however, was (with slight modifications) the indictment which he had published in *Dagbladet*, and remembering Ibsen's reaction to Clemens Petersen's scarcely more hostile review one can only suppose that Ibsen regarded these five pages of disapproval as a fair price to pay for the preceding fifty pages of brilliant sympathy. 'It is clear to me', Ibsen had written to Jonas Collin on 21 October 1867 after

---

[1] The Jesse Muir translation, revised by William Archer and doubtless owing much of its quality to him. Whatever Archer's limitations in the rendering of dialogue, he is incomparable as a translator of narrative or critical prose.

reading Brandes's attack on the philosopher Rasmus Neilsen in the name of free thought, 'that this man will play a big role in the cultural and spiritual life of the north.' A modern Danish critic has shrewdly observed that Ibsen's intuition probably told him that 'a man who was ideologically progressive could not long hold to an antiquated aesthetic standpoint', that Brandes 'felt attracted by Ibsen's poetic genius and powerful personality, but at the same time repelled by the works in which that genius and personality manifested themselves', and that after Petersen's review of *Peer Gynt* Brandes took over the position of friend and ally which had previously been occupied by Bjørnson.[1] Ibsen wrote to Hegel on 10 June asking where Brandes was proposing to travel that summer and saying that if he was going to be in Germany he, Ibsen, would gladly go out of his way to meet him.

Brandes was much excited by Ibsen's letter of 26 June. 'I prize it', he wrote to his old tutor, Hans Brøchner, on 25 July, 'because Ibsen is not, like Andersen, a man who praises everyone who praises him.'[2] He told Ibsen of his own recent quarrel with Bjørnson, which must have endeared him further, and Ibsen, in his letter to Brandes of 15 July, expressed great joy at this new-found friendship. 'It is a great blessing to have discovered an integrated personality', he declared, and expressed the hope that, since Brandes had no immediate plans to come to Germany, they might perhaps be able to meet in Copenhagen, to speak 'not merely about all the literary matters on which we disagree, but also about many human matters on which we stand closer together.' Later that year he told Hegel that he hoped Brandes would review *The League of Youth*, since 'nobody could do it as he could, and I feel he is a true friend to me',[3] and that 'there is something in both his praise and censure which indescribably pleases me: the fact of being understood'.[4]

During the spring of 1869 Ibsen had applied to the Norwegian government for a stipend of 300 specie-dollars (£75) to enable him to spend a year in Sweden studying the art, literature and other aspects of that country's cultural life. This was granted him; and meanwhile he received an invitation to take part in an orthographic conference in Stockholm, convened in order to agree on a unified spelling for the three Scandinavian countries (a purpose in which it failed signally). After changing his lodgings in Dresden to a first-floor apartment at Königsbrückerstrasse 33, he departed for Stockholm on 20 July.

Stockholm was then, apart from its impressive public buildings, still largely a

---

[1] Fenger, *Ibsen og Georg Brandes indtil 1872*, pp. 180–181.
[2] *Brandes Brevveksling*, I, p. 69.
[3] 22 September 1869.
[4] 14 December 1869.

town of small wooden houses; a piped water system had only just been introduced, and men and girls with buckets on yokes could still be seen selling water
from the wells. Citizens were awakened at night by the collectors of night-soil,
thumping on the door with their long poles. As the closets were usually in the
attic, the soil was commonly thrown out of the windows into, or at, the carts;
foreign travellers compared Stockholm to Constantinople for its combination
of beauty and filth. Ibsen took lodgings at Herkulesgatan 5, a narrow street just
across the bridge from the royal palace, and was regally entertained. 'I live
here', he wrote to his brother-in-law, J. H. Thoresen, on 2 August, 'in an
endless round of festivities. I have not had a single day when I have not been
invited to dinner or something.' The other delegates to the conference included
Knud Knudsen, his old enemy from the Norwegian Christiania Theatre, and
Jakob Løkke of the Learned Holland circle, who widened the rift between
Ibsen and Bjørnson by telling the former of some unkind things which the
latter had reputedly said of him. He saw a good deal of Lorentz Dietrichson,
and renewed his acquaintance with Count Snoilsky, to whom he apologised
for the halter incident in Rome. He had, he said, changed his mind about
Manderström, who was Snoilsky's uncle, and had come to the conclusion that
he was not really to blame. 'Then we are still as far apart as ever on this subject',
replied Snoilsky, 'for I have come to the conclusion that he was.' Ibsen spent
several days with a family named Limnell, who had a villa on Lake Mälaren.
Herr Limnell held a high position in the railways, and his wife, the widow of a
famous newspaper editor, was the centre of a literary circle; Ibsen was to thank
her for her hospitality in one of his best longer poems. He met writers, actors
and politicians, one of whom, a lively young liberal named Adolf Hedin,
rebuked him for his conservatism—an incident which was later to provoke
another interesting poetic declaration.

Ibsen's appearance and demeanour caused astonishment. 'People had expected the author of *Brand*', writes Dietrichson, 'to be an earnest, severe old
ascetic, and there appeared an elegant, youngish man in a velvet coat, refined,
lively and likeable. People could not reconcile *Brand* with its author,[1] and several people openly expressed their amazement, amounting in some cases to
downright disappointment; but soon he had taken them all by storm, especially

---

[1] August Strindberg, who in 1869 was twenty and had just failed his medical exams
and concluded his brief and calamitous career as a professional actor, did not meet Ibsen
(then or ever), but eight years later he recalled the impression which Ibsen made: 'Who
does not remember the famous poet's appearance when he visited Stockholm a few years
back? Dressed in a velvet jacket, a white waistcoat with black buttons, and a cape of the
latest fashion, with an elegant cane in his hand and a protective self-mocking curl to his
lip, he went his way, avoiding all deep subjects of conversation.' (August Strindberg,
Konstakademiens utställning, 1877, in *Kulturhistoriska studier*, Stockholm, 1881, p. 125.)

the ladies.'[1] On 22 September, two months after his arrival, he told Hegel: 'My stay in Sweden has been, and still is, one long festivity. From all sides I meet a courtesy and friendliness which cannot be described . . . I have plenty of plans for new works; but to get down to them I must find solitude again; I cannot write here.'

Thus Ibsen, for the first time since his visit to Bergen in 1863, found himself lionised; and the experience was not distasteful. King Carl XV, who, in his enjoyment of the company of writers, artists and pretty women, much resembled our own Charles II, invited him several times to the palace, where (he later told John Paulsen), he spent 'unforgettable' and highly informal evenings, continuing long after midnight, with champagne and merry stories, 'not always for dainty ears'.[2] Shortly before he left, the director and actors of the Royal Theatre held a farewell dinner for him and Dietrichson (who was leaving at the same time) at the Hotel du Nord in Carl XII's Torg. The actor Daniel Hwasser, proposing Ibsen's health, recited a poem in Swedish which Ibsen only gradually recognised as a very free translation of one of his own songs from *Love's Comedy*. 'It was very droll', recalled Dietrichson, 'to see Ibsen's expression as, towards the conclusion of the first verse, he recognised his own child.'[3] Dietrichson wrote an article about him in the leading Swedish illustrated weekly, *Ny Illustrerad Tidning*, describing him as 'one of the greatest poets of our time, if not absolutely the greatest'; and so considerable was the impact which Ibsen made on Stockholm that someone advised the King to recommend that he be chosen to represent his country that autumn at the official opening of the Suez Canal. Ibsen received the invitation with unmixed delight. 'I get everything free', he wrote happily to J. H. Thoresen on 24 September, 'the trip from Paris and back included.' And on his last evening in Stockholm, Carl XV invited him to the palace and personally invested him with the Order of Vasa, the first of those many medals which he was to receive and in which he took so curious and childlike a pride.

These weeks of lionising in Stockholm left Ibsen with an affection for Sweden which he was never to lose. He had received the homage, not merely of his fellow artists, but of society; and the latter, remembering his gnawing sense of social inferiority, may well have seemed at the time the more important. His previous feelings towards Sweden had been almost entirely hostile. Vilhelm Bergsøe records an occasion in Sorrento in 1867 when Suzannah had begun to praise that country. 'For some time Ibsen endured her talk in silence,

---

[1] Dietrichson, I, p. 350.

[2] Paulsen, *Samliv med Ibsen*, I (Copenhagen & Christiania, 1906), pp. 51–52.

[3] Dietrichson, I, p. 353.

but when she began to speak of the Swedish war heroes, Gustaf Adolf and Carl XII, he exclaimed violently: "Stuff and nonsense! What are these fellows now? Still tramping around in Carl XII's boots, but they haven't any shoes to run in when it comes to the point!" Fru Ibsen tried to qualify this unreasonable verdict of Ibsen's, but when she praised the Swedish warriors afresh, he shouted: "Keep quiet! I won't listen, you make me sick!" And he hit the table a thump so that the bottle trembled. Little Sigurd, who had sat and listened to our conversation with big eyes, suddenly said: "Father can't stand the Swedes."[1] Ibsen had caricatured the nation unkindly in Peer Gynt through the character of the pompous Herr Trumpeterstraale; but the charm and elegance (and perhaps the snobbery) of Stockholm society had won him over.[2]

On 26 September, two days before he left Stockholm, Ibsen wrote a letter which must have been on his conscience for a long time. On 3 June his mother had died in Skien, at the age of seventy-one, and his sister, Hedvig, now married to a ship's captain, Hans Jacob Stousland, had sent him the news. Only now, three and a half months later, did he reply. It was, as far as we know, the first contact between Ibsen and his immediate family since he had paid his brief visit to them on the way from Grimstad to Christiania nineteen and a half years before:

Dear Hedvig!

It is months since I received your letter, and I have not replied. But there is so much that stands between us, between me and home; understand this, and do not think that my silence during these long years and now this summer is the result of indifference. I cannot write letters; I must be near someone and give myself completely. You are different; you can write; do so often! I will answer—at the least with a loving greeting, or with news which I hope will not sadden you.

I look inwards into myself; there is my battleground, where I now conquer, now suffer defeat. But I cannot write about all this in a letter. Do not try to change me. I want to be true to myself. What will be, will be.

So our dear old mother is dead. Thank you for so lovingly carrying the burden for us all. You are indeed the best of mortals.

I wander around much in the world. Who knows if I may not come to Norway next

---

[1] Bergsøe, pp. 237–238. Cf. also Ibsen's letter to Anton Klubien of 20 October 1865, not in the Centenary Edition but printed in Ibsen-Årbok 1953, p. 98. 'Some wretched Swedes come and go, but I don't bother with them . . . I wanted to annoy the Swedish dogs who were present [at the Club.]'

[2] John Paulsen remarked (Samliv med Ibsen, II, p. 224) that Ibsen liked the formality and aristocratic elegance of Swedes in contrast to what he regarded as the boorishness and provincialism of Norwegian manners—just as so many Irish exiles (Goldsmith, Burke, Wilde, Shaw, Yeats) preferred London society to that of Dublin.

summer, in which case I should like to see our old home, to which I am still held fast by so many roots. Give Father all my love; explain to him about me; you understand so well, he perhaps does not . . .

I enclose my photograph; if you have one of your husband and children, please send it to me. I wish you knew my wife; she is exactly the right one for me, and sends her love. Our address in Dresden is: Königsbrücker-Strasse, no. 33.

This letter is short and I have passed over much that you must have wished that I should speak of. It cannot, for the present, be otherwise; but do not think I lack that warmth of heart which must, above all else, be present if a person is to enjoy a true and healthy spiritual life . . .

Hedvig had always been the only member of his family with whom he had been able to feel any real affinity, and she was the only one for whom he retained any affection. A non-conformist in religion like himself, she needed, unlike him, to belong to a religious movement, and had joined a sect roughly corresponding to the Quakers. Her Paus relatives, shocked at this, had tried to exert pressure on her by threatening to discharge her husband from their employ; she resisted, and he got the sack. Ibsen was to remember this episode when, twelve years later, he wrote *An Enemy of the People*, in which Captain Horster is likewise sacked for befriending Dr Stockmann.[1]

His mother's death was not the only bereavement that Ibsen suffered that summer. On 7 July his old friend Paul Botten Hansen, who had published so many of his poems and given him such wise encouragement, had died of pleurisy at the age of forty-four. 'A less self-seeking man would be hard to find', wrote Ludwig Daae of him in an obituary memoir, 'and if any man was free from vanity, he was.'[2] To give some support to his four children, the city of Bergen bought his fine book collection for three thousand crowns, and established it as a free public library.

On 29 September Ibsen left Stockholm for Dresden. The next day, while he was en route, *The League of Youth* was published in Copenhagen.

The importance of *The League of Youth* to a modern reader lies in the fact that it was Ibsen's first attempt to write a play entirely in modern colloquial dialogue. The plot must be briefly summarised, since the play is little known, though its complexity is such that any summary must seem bewildering. The scene is a market town in southern Norway, generally thought to have been modelled on Skien. Stensgaard, an ambitious young liberal politician, in a burst of enthusiasm at an Independence Day celebration, founds an anti-capitalist

---

[1] A. E. Zucker, *Ibsen, The Master Builder* (London, 1929), pp. 238–239. His informant was Hedvig's son, Captain John Ibsen Stousland.

[2] *Vidar* (Copenhagen, 1888), p. 354.

G

party which he christens the League of Youth. In the course of his speech he
delivers an eloquent attack on the local ironmaster, Brattsberg; he does not
name him, however, and Brattsberg thinks he is referring to a landowner
named Monsen, whose daughter, Ragna, Stensgaard has been courting. Fickle
in love as in all else, Stensgaard now takes a fancy to Brattsberg's daughter,
Thora, and to restore himself to favour makes a public apology to her father,
who shows him the door in a fury. Then Stensgaard learns that Brattsberg's
son, Erik, has forged a bill, realises that Brattsberg may be disgraced too, and
turns his attentions back to Ragna Monsen. But he hears that Monsen may
likewise be involved in the scandal, so proposes to a rich tradesman's widow
named Mrs Rundholmen. Then he finds that Monsen was involved but not
Brattsberg, and renews his interest in Thora. She no longer wants him; in
despair, he announces his engagement to Mrs Rundholmen; but she has
accepted someone else, and he is left with nobody. Yet his future is by no means
gloomy. 'Mark my words', says someone at the end of the play. 'In ten or
fifteen years Stensgaard will be in Parliament or the Privy Council'; and
another character adds a quotation from Napoleon: 'Double-dealing is the stuff
of which politicians are made.'

Ibsen had for some time sensed that the dialogue of drama must move
towards a greater colloquialism, as the novel had been doing, and Bjørnson
had shown him the way four years earlier in a two-act comedy called *The
Newly-wedded Couple*, a slight piece about a young wife bound to her parents
of which Ibsen, on reading it, is said to have remarked: 'This is how we must
write modern drama.' He tried, in *The League of Youth*, to escape as far as
possible from all the old conventions of artificial drama (as witness his proud
claim to Georg Brandes that he had completed it 'without a single monologue
or aside'). Having raised poetic drama to its finest peak since Shakespeare (for
Brand and *Peer Gynt* are greater *plays* than anything by Racine, Goethe or
Schiller, none of whose works are tolerable in the theatre if performed in any
language but their own), he had set himself to cultivate, as he was later to phrase
it, 'the much more difficult art of writing the genuine, plain language spoken
in life'.[1] As William Archer observed: 'Having now outgrown his youthful
romanticism, and laid down, in *Brand* and *Peer Gynt*, the fundamental positions
of his criticism of life, he felt that, to carry that criticism into detail, he must
come to closer quarters with reality; and to that end he required a suppler
instrument than verse.'[2]

Over the next thirty years *The League of Youth* was to prove the most

---

[1] Letter to Lucie Wolf, 25 May 1883.
[2] Introduction to *The League of Youth* (London, 1907), p. viii.

popular (if judged by the number of performances given) of all Ibsen's plays in Norway. Since 1900, however, it has been staged less often than any other of his established plays, there as elsewhere. Edmund Gosse dismissed it as 'the most provincial of all Ibsen's mature works', an adjective that was often later to be aimed at Ibsen by his denigrators. In fact, *The League of Youth* is no more provincial than *The Pillars of Society* or *An Enemy of the People*, which likewise have as their themes the petty-mindedness which prevails in small communities, and anyway the word 'provincial' has ceased to be pejorative when applied to drama. The real reason for posterity's lack of interest in the play lies, despite Ibsen's professed aim in writing it, in the out-datedness of its technique. The synopsis given above is much simplified; it omits (otherwise it would have been as unravellable as those verbal cats'-cradles which confront us in opera programmes) a mesh of sub-plots which depend for their working on the old-fashioned machinery of misdirected letters, overheard conversations and the like which Ibsen had inherited from Holberg and which commentators have so often mistakenly attributed to his supposed admiration for Scribe. Holberg's plays, Ibsen wrote to Lorentz Dietrichson on 28 May 1869, shortly after sending the last pages of *The League of Youth* to the printers, were 'almost the only book I never tire of reading'; but the conventions of mannered comedy, amusing in their proper context, are destructive to any play that sets out to impress by its realism. They did not bother nineteenth-century audiences, but they bother us. To keep a tightly-knit plot (as opposed to the looser, freer and more modern structures of *Brand* and *Peer Gynt*) ticking over was something that Ibsen was not yet able to manage without recourse to the rusty starting-handle of co-incidence.[1] The play is, moreover, full of topical references which were a source of delight and fury to Ibsen's contemporaries, but which would be lost on a modern audience. As Archer remarked, it was essentially an experimental, transitional work; and by the time Ibsen became known abroad, ten years later, its technique was already outdated.

With all its faults, however, it was an advance on the technique of the day. The plot never stops moving—something that can scarcely be said of any other comedy of the period, apart from the farces of Labiche—and, like every play Ibsen had written since *St John's Night*, it contains a galaxy of minutely observed characters. Unlike Strindberg, who was often perfunctory in his drawing of secondary personages, Ibsen never, in his maturity, created the smallest role that was not worth the playing. Stensgaard, the leading character, has well been summed up as 'Peer Gynt as a Politician'; an 'inescapably split personality', as

---

[1] ' "It is much easier", he said, "to write a piece like *Brand* or *Peer Gynt*, in which you can bring in a little of everything, than to carry through a severely logical scheme, like that of *John Gabriel Borkman*, for example." ' (William Archer, *Ibsen as I Knew Him*, p. 18).

Dr Fjeldbo describes him in the play, he is another in the long line of self-deceivers which began with Julian Poulsen in *St John's Night* (or even with Severus in *Norma*), and was to continue through Karsten Bernick, Torvald Helmer, Hjalmar Ekdal and Ulric Brendel to its culmination in John Gabriel Borkman and Arnold Rubek. Ibsen once admitted that Stensgaard contained a good deal of himself, a curious confession, one might think, from the writer who, above all others, has come to be associated with a hatred of self-deception. But Brand, we must remember, Ibsen had declared to be himself 'in his best moments', and Stensgaard, like Peer Gynt, presumably represented that side of himself of which he was ashamed and which he sought, not always success-fully, to subdue—cowardice, readiness to compromise when faced with un-pleasant realities, and facile eloquence. Bjørnson, while possessing many quali-ties which Ibsen envied, at the same time personified one of the subtlest snares that can destroy a writer, the temptation to give full rein to those gifts which bring the easiest and most immediate success; and in this sense Ibsen may have been speaking honestly when, later, he asserted that Stensgaard was not (as his contemporaries assumed) a portrayal of Bjørnson, Johan Sverdrup or any other specific individual. The real model for Stensgaard, as for Peer Gynt, was any Norwegian with charm and eloquence, which in practice meant, then as now, almost any Norwegian, including Ibsen himself.

Of the other characters, Daniel Hejre, a clever and malicious man who has lost his money but retained his wit, is generally accepted as being a portrait of the dramatist's father; and Aslaksen, a timid and bibulous printer who was to reappear, still timid but now a teetotaller, in *An Enemy of the People*, seems to have been based on N. F. Axelsen, the publisher of the student magazine *Andhrimner*, who, like Aslaksen, apparently disapproved of provocative young writers. The most important character for Ibsen's future and the future of drama, however, was the minor figure of Selma Brattsberg, the ironmaster's young daughter-in-law who, chafing against the bonds of marriage, complains to her husband: 'You dressed me up like a doll; you played with me as one plays with a child.' When Georg Brandes read the play he suggested in his review[1] that she, or a character like her, might make a good central figure for a later work, a suggestion which ten years later was to bring forth remarkable fruit.

The League of Youth received mixed notices in the Scandinavian press. Georg Brandes, as Ibsen had feared, disliked it. He complained that 'it lacks some-thing of what characterises Ibsen's work, the *"Dieu dans l'âme, le diable au corps"* ', and that Stensgaard 'grows ever smaller and smaller, becomes more and more

---

[1] *Illustreret Tidende*, 10 October 1869. 'She is a new figure, and a whole play might be written about her relationship with her family.'

a simple blackguard and gradually loses any suggestion of significance . . . Ultimately one wearies of being present at the downfall of so feeble a wretch . . . And what we have said of the main character is true of most of the minor ones; they are too mean for us not, in the long run, to grow sick of their company . . . In the absence of any genuinely mirthful comedy one sighs for some beauty; one hopes to find at any rate one or two of Ibsen's pretty female characters in this monkey-house; but alas, they are not to be found'—though Brandes made a grudging exception of Selma. He granted that the play showed an advance in character drawing—'the author's characterisation in previous plays has been somewhat unsure and loose [!]', but found that the absence of monologues and asides made the plot somewhat difficult to follow. 'While admitting the great technical facility to which Ibsen has attained, one must point out that the monologue is not in itself an incomprehensible dramatic device, and that it is far better to be wholly comprehensible with the aid of an observation confined to the audience than to be unclear because of over-economy.' Brandes, lacking any practical experience in the theatre, was never to become a good dramatic critic; all his life, he was to judge plays as literature, and for their moral and philosophical content; but his remarks are frighteningly revealing of the kind of mental conservatism with which Ibsen had to contend in his readers and audiences.

An anonymous critic in the newly-formed *Dagbladet*[1] (20 October) objected to the play on the usual aesthetic grounds. 'The main impression one gains from a reading of Ibsen's later work is neither calm nor harmonious . . . [but rather] of discord . . . coarse and brutal characters . . . Idealism does appear but has no active part in the unfolding of the play . . . regrettable that the ingenious and carefully finished dialogue should be wasted on such insignificant material.' But another anonymous critic, writing in *Morgenbladet* (17 October) saw what Ibsen was trying to do: 'This latest work marks a new and significant phase in the author's artistic development, a step forward . . . He places us slap in the midst of real life, where we meet people who are unquestionably of flesh and blood, people such as we unfortunately meet every day.' The re-viewer concluded: 'It is inevitable in our small community that when a writer presents the contemporary scene on the stage through typical characters he will meet the same criticism as was levelled at Ludvig Holberg in former days; even though the figures be types, people will point to this or that living person and say: "It is meant to be him, it is he to the life." So it was with Holberg . . . It would be no less ridiculous to demand of a modern writer that

---

[1] An independent left-wing daily established in Christiania that year. There had long been a Danish newspaper of the same name (cf. p. 51 etc.).

he should abstain from presenting contemporary life on the stage. But if this should happen, Henrik Ibsen need not be ashamed to share such a fate with Ludvig Holberg.'

Further support for Ibsen came from a somewhat unexpected quarter. Erik Bøgh, the fashionable and successful Danish playwright whose vaudevilles had so often figured in Ibsen's repertory at the Bergen and Christiania theatres, might, one would think, have resented the work of this disturbing newcomer. In fact he saw more clearly than most of his contemporaries what Ibsen was really getting at, and his reviews of Ibsen's plays as they appeared from the press were (except in the case of *Ghosts*) remarkably sympathetic and penetrating, much more so than Brandes's. He found *The League of Youth* 'like all Ibsen's plays, an outstandingly powerful and fertile work, so original that it must be in most respects be called unique in its genre'. The many Danish admirers of *Brand* and *Peer Gynt*, he continues, must wonder why such a master of dialogue has not written for the stage, and Bøgh tells them of Ibsen's earlier works which, we must remember, were still unknown to most Danes, none of his plays yet having been performed in that country. The only disadvantage of *The League of Youth* from a theatrical point of view (Bøgh concluded) was that the plethora of excellent minor characters would make the play 'almost as long as [Bjørnson's] *Mary Stuart in Scotland*, and will demand more skilful actors than most theatres will be able to provide'. Bøgh ended by exhorting the public, as they read the play, to imagine the lines being spoken with a Norwegian accent.[1]

Ibsen's old friend Aasmund Vinje probably summed up the general feeling when he wrote in *Dølen* (24 October): 'Those who think that they or their friends are portrayed in the play complain and find it bad; but those who enjoy seeing these people so caricatured are happy, and find it a good piece.' As one of the former, he compared Ibsen to Don Quixote, expressed indignation at Ibsen's mockery of his country, and hoped that he would soon get bored with 'acting Brand'.

Ibsen, however, saw none of these reviews until several weeks after they had appeared, for on his return to Dresden at the beginning of October he had departed almost immediately by train for Paris on the first stage of his journey to Suez. What impression did Paris make on him? We do not know, for of this, as of his first sighting of Venice and Florence in 1864, he has left no word. With the other delegates from northern Europe he entrained for Marseilles, and thence, on 9 October, he sailed in the s.s. *Moeris* for Alexandria.

---

[1] *Folkets Avis*, 29 October 1869. The review is reprinted in *Dit og Dat fra 1869* (Copenhagen, 1870), pp. 200–206.

FOUR

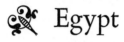 Egypt

(1869)

THERE WERE EIGHTY-SIX GUESTS of the Khedive aboard the *Moeris*:
Frenchmen, Germans, Dutchmen, Spaniards and Scandinavians, but no
Englishmen; they followed with the Russians and others in another ship the
next day. Surprisingly few of the names of Ibsen's fellow-travellers mean
anything today; one exception was Théophile Gautier, who fell down the
steps to the dining saloon on the first morning, dislocated a shoulder and spent
the rest of the voyage with his arm in a sling. Ibsen's ignorance of French
prevented him from holding any conversation with him. The only other
Norwegian delegate was an Egyptologist, Professor J. D. C. Lieblein, who had
condemned *Brand* as an insane work, but got on with its author well. Lorentz
Dietrichson should have accompanied them, but was prevented by illness.
Ibsen, as usual, kept mainly to his fellow-Scandinavians throughout his holiday.
These included a pleasant young Danish literary historian, Peter Hansen (later
to become director of the Royal Theatre in Copenhagen), and a Swedish army
captain, Oscar von Knorring, who had served as a volunteer in the first (1849)
Schleswig-Holstein war, was something of a composer, and later published a
naïve but readable account of his visit to Suez. He noted as his first impression
of Ibsen that he had 'elegant manners and an agreeable social tone'.[1]

The voyage across the Mediterranean was rough, and Lieblein, who sent
regular and lively despatches back to *Morgenbladet*, reported on the second day
that 'there has been some distress among the bulk of the passengers'.[2] They
sailed between Sardinia and Corsica, the high mountains of which reminded
Lieblein, and doubtless Ibsen too, of the Norwegian coast; then, the next day,
they passed close to Caprera, where Garibaldi was living in retirement, and
wondered which of the buildings there was 'the home of the great adventurer
and republican'. They skirted Sicily, and admired Stromboli; the Plough sank

[1] Oscar von Knorring, *Två månader i Egypten* (Stockholm, 1873), p. 14.

[2] *Morgenbladet*, 21 October 1869. Except where otherwise specified, all quoted references
to the Egyptian journey are from Lieblein's despatches to *Morgenbladet*, printed on 21
October, 6, 14 and 24 November, and 5, 17 and 23 December 1869.

towards the horizon and the moon rose higher towards her zenith as they proceeded south. The weather remained rough all the way, so that 'several of the party were unable to take full advantage of the Khedive's hospitality', which included four meals a day. At last, on 13 October, after four days at sea, they reached Alexandria.

Ferdinand de Lesseps, the creator of the canal, was there in person to greet them, and they were escorted to the Hôtel d'Europe, where 'the best rooms and carriages with dragomans' were placed at their disposal. Lieblein gives the menu of one of their dinners there:

> *1 potage varié*
> *1 relevé de poisson*
> *1 relevé de viande de boucherie*
> *1 entrée chaude*
> *1 entrée froide*
> *1 rôti de volaille, soit dinde, soit gibier*
> *1 salade verte*
> *1 entrée de legumes*
> *1 entremêts de patisserie*
> *4 desserts divers assortis*
> *fromage*
> *café noir et liqueurs assortis*
>
> —
>
> *vin ordinaire Médoc*
> *Madeira*
> *vin de Bourgogne*
> *Ch. Lafite*
> *Champagne*

This must have been by some way the best meal that Ibsen had ever eaten, even allowing for the hospitality he had received in Stockholm (unless something comparable had been provided in Paris and Marseilles); and, eating habits being what they were in those days, it was followed by 'a supper at midnight'.

They spent two days in Alexandria, visiting among other memorabilia Pompey's Pillar and Cleopatra's Needles (not yet removed to the Thames Embankment and New York's Central Park), and were banqueted in the Khedive's garden, where they were entertained with European military music and 'somewhat monotonous Arab melodies'. At eight in the morning of 17 October they left Alexandria and, five hours later, arrived in Cairo.

The guests stayed five days in the Egyptian capital, luxuriously accommodated at the Hôtel de l'Orient, where von Knorring notes that he and Ibsen 'spent many hours under palm trees on a terrace'. 'I take this opportunity', he added, 'publicly to record my gratitude for the many interesting and delightful moments which the amiable and truly cultivated Henrik Ibsen's company afforded me during both my journey to Egypt and our passage up the Nile.'[1] They walked through the bazaars, 'streets too narrow for any vehicle to enter', were shown the mosques and the citadel, from which they could distantly glimpse the Pyramids, and made expeditions to the museum at Bulak, old Cairo, where they saw the tombs of the Mamelukes, and Heliopolis, whence Ibsen sent Suzannah some flowers. The day after their arrival, the Khedive, 'a little, fat, powerfully built man in European dress', received them at his palace, Kasr-el-Nil; he was 'friendly, and talked with everyone . . . in fairly fluent French', which must have been lost on Ibsen. Von Knorring had an introduction to de Lesseps, who gave him a signed photograph; whether Ibsen accompanied him on his visit to the great man he does not say.

Not content with paying his guests' passages from Paris and back ('Who will finally foot the bill for all this hospitality may be questioned', reflected Lieblein. 'Probably the unfortunate Fellah, who is already poor enough without our coming and eating his last sheep'), the Khedive, Ismael Pasha, had arranged a three weeks' expedition for them up the Nile under the guidance of his conservator, the French Egyptologist Mariette Bey, who eighteen years earlier had discovered the subterranean catacombs of the Apis bulls. On the morning of 22 October they set off in three steamers, each towing a *dahaby*, or barge, covered by an awning for the greater comfort of the passengers. Ibsen and von Knorring shared a cabin on the s.s. *Ferus*, which also carried Lieblein, a Swiss, a Dutchman and seventeen Germans, whose behaviour was to earn them a derogatory simile in a poem which Ibsen later wrote about the trip, and which was to involve him in a controversy in the German press. They tried to insist that the German flag be hoisted on the ship, 'Scandinavians, Dutchmen and Swiss being of course pure Germans; but this was luckily prevented, and we still sail under the crescent of Turkey, whose guests we are. The Germans are frightened lest the French hear of their failure, but the secret is already abroad . . . The French and German guests are on very uneasy terms.' Lieblein found the Prussians 'more overbearing than ever after their military exploits of recent years'; only nine months were to elapse before the outbreak of the Franco-Prussian War.

Several of the places they had hoped to visit en route were unfortunately rendered inaccessible by heavy floods, including Gizeh, so that Ibsen, who had written about the Sphinx in *Peer Gynt*, glimpsed it only from afar; also

---

[1] von Knorring, p. 69.

Memphis, Sakkara, the tombs at Beni Hasan and the ruins of Abydos. On the second day von Knorring and Ibsen intervened to save an aged Arab from being flogged by the ship's dragoman for idleness, an action which earned them the good-will of the crew for the remainder of the expedition. One imagines that Captain von Knorring did most of the intervening. That same day they were surprised by a visit from Coptic monks from a monastery, who swam out to them, 'climbed up the stern and asked for *baksheesh* . . . Since they presented themselves to the passengers in a state of the utmost primitiveness, they had nothing to put the money in but stuffed it all, silver and copper alike, into their mouths.'

On the third day they stopped briefly at Roda, where they were shown round a sugar factory employing five thousand workers by the English manager, 'with great courtesy'. At Assiut they inspected the great tombs. As Ibsen and Lieblein were returning, they 'walked along the river bank and came to a great white brick house. Outside the entrance sat two distinguished-looking Arabs. They seemed glad to see us, offered us chairs and had us served with coffee.' One of the Arabs spoke fluent French and explained that this was a school and they the teachers; they invited Lieblein and Ibsen in, and the pupils demonstrated their skill in French and mathematics. Lieblein wrote a message of thanks on the blackboard. Upstairs they were shown a dormitory with a hundred and fifty beds; the pupils wore a kind of military uniform after the French pattern.

In the evening the travellers were entertained, on sofas, to a 'Fantasia by Torchlight', songs and dances performed by five expensively dressed and bejewelled girls. 'Since this was . . . enacted in the open air', comments Lieblein prudishly, 'the dance was reasonably decent, though certain wild Frenchmen did everything to persuade the performers into the licentiousness with which such dances customarily end.'

The heat grew intense as they approached the 26th parallel, reaching 28° Reaumur (95° Fahrenheit). The natives hereabouts wore nothing but figleaves, 'a fashion which the Europeans observed with envy, making a few, admittedly incomplete, attempts to imitate it'. They visited Kena, where there was more torchlight dancing, and the Hathor Temple at Dendera, and spent the last three days of October in Thebes. Here Ibsen and his companions walked round the twin cities, the Temple City on the east bank and the City of the Dead on the west; they saw the huge statue of Rameses the Great, eleven times lifesize, the Temple of Amon Ra with its one hundred and thirty-four pillars, the Temple of Rameses III at Medinet Habu, the Memnon statue of which Ibsen had written in *Peer Gynt*, and the great tombs. Arabs offered them pieces of mummy for sale, and Ibsen 'bought a little woman's hand with a scarab ring.

It must have come from a grand lady, perhaps from one of the ancient noble houses of Egypt, and now her hand was being sold for a shilling.'[1]

On the third day, 31 October, the Empress Eugénie arrived at Thebes amid spectacular ceremony. 'It was towards sunset', Ibsen recalled twenty-four years later. 'Far in the distance a pillar of smoke approached, rising from the polished river. A handsome great Nile ship glided towards us. This must be the Empress. But she was not there. Far, far away, a new pillar of smoke. An even larger ship, white, with silken banners. This *must* be she. No. A new Nile ship, bigger than the others, rose-pink. *Here* she sits, clothed in white, beautiful as Cleopatra, whilst the setting sun casts its gold over the banners and carpets and silken tents of the ship. Before a year had passed, she would be no mightier than the Kings we had just visited.'[2] She was greeted by a firework display and, at six o'clock, a banquet in a specially erected tent, which all the guests attended, while the crews and servants were given sheep to roast. They left Thebes the next day, and continued as far as the great cataract, pausing at Esna, Edfu, Gebel Silfilis, Kom Ombo and Assuan, whence they rode on donkeys a short way into Nubia, through the desert to the Isle of Philae, in a temperature of 31° Reaumur (102° Fahrenheit). At last, on 6 November, they turned back towards Cairo.

From Assuan to Cairo, with the following current, they travelled 'almost with the speed of a railway'. The floods had by now subsided sufficiently for them to be able to visit some of the places they had missed on the outward trip, including Luxor and Girgeh, where they had another donkey-ride, this time to inspect the ruins of Abydos. They stopped at Beni-Hasan and Gizeh, where they spent their last night aboard the *Ferus*; next morning, they visited the Great Pyramids and Sakkara, the necropolis of Memphis, to see the Step Pyramid, the oldest of them all. At last, on the evening of 13 November, after twenty-three days on the river, they returned to Cairo.

Ibsen kept a diary of his Egyptian experiences, which has not survived, but on his return to Dresden he began to write an account of his trip. He abandoned this after completing some four thousand words, apparently restless with the medium of direct narrative prose, and a year later summarised his impressions more succinctly in a long poem, *Balloon Letter to a Swedish Lady*—further evidence of the fact that he wrote most comfortably in verse or dialogue. The Egyptian prose fragment—which, apart from the prefaces to *Catiline* and *The Feast at Solhaug*, a few speeches and his unfinished childhood memoirs,

---

[1] Conversation with Ibsen recorded by Nordahl Rolfsen in the latter's *Læsebog for folkeskolen*, III (Christiania, 1894), and reprinted in *CE*, XIX, p. 191.

[2] *Ibid.*, p. 191.

was to be the last prose article that Ibsen was to write—is especially interesting for the rare evidence it provides of Ibsen's sharp eye as an observer of landscape:

'A kind of soundless peace rules over the landscape of the Nile valley. It possesses something of the Sphinx's dumbness. Today there was no breath of air to be felt save that caused by the ship's progress. The river flowed broad and swelling between its double banks of palm groves. Behind them the land rises on both sides towards distant lines of mountains, and everything that the Nile cannot touch, all the yellow limitless waste which glitters and throws its reflection into the air, is the desert; westwards the Libyan, eastwards the Arabian.

'On the mudbank, which the falling river reveals, stands here and there a solitary maribou on two stiff legs, drooping its beak and bald head on to its breast with a very human air of melancholy. Herons stalk and pelicans scrabble in the mud, and ibis birds rise from the *durrah* like a flock of white doves.

'Within an hour we have sighted the slender minarets of Girgeh before us; but it takes time for the ship to reach them, for the river is full of bends. At last, towards noon, we swing round and lay to. The three other steamers, which travelled more slowly, and had therefore been brought up from Quenneh the previous evening, lay with their *dahabies* or towed barges moored outside the town.

'It was a motley picture that now unfolded before us; Europe and the East in a picturesque composition. Directly in front of us stood a minaret, erect and sparkling in the sunlight. Beside it lay the ruin of a Coptic monastery, the whole front of which had collapsed into the river. For the rest, Arab huts, mounds of gravel, palms and sycamores. Inside the ruins of the monastery an Egyptian coffee-house proprietor had established himself; the coffee-room itself lay outside beneath a roof of withered palm-branches. Here we see a great concourse; long beards and long pipes are dominant; long Eastern silence and, too, long European chatter. And familiar faces. That handsome, brown-eyed man, who at a distance so strikingly resembles Abdul Kader, and who cannot be acquitted of playing the coquette a little in his elegant silk *koffie* and white-striped Beduin *burnous*, is the archaeologist Lenormant. Beside him, alert and friendly, with red fez and sky-blue flannel shirt, sits Dr Lambert, the Murray and Baedeker of Egypt in one person. That distinguished little white-haired man, with no parasol and his felt hat pulled down like Kilian in *Ulysses von Ithaca*, is the chemist Ballard. Out on the farthest slope of the shore stands Dr Bertholet, short, robust and jovial, with a thousand items of news to shout to us. A lady glitters, the sole representative of her sex in the party; her dress is European, her proportions oriental. She is of course Madame Collet, the Parisian *littératrice*. For the moment her attention is taken up with her diary, in which our arrival is noted, that the information may be transmitted to an important French magazine. A score of baying dogs send us the usual greeting from the housetops. In doors and corners stand Arab women, staring motionlessly from behind their long black veils, and up the high gravel mounds hasten the humbler members of the populace, the *fellahs*, amid laughter and cries, pursued by policemen who, with the aid of long palm staves, seek to persuade them to lend us a hand with the mooring of the ship.

'On the voyage up the Nile I felt for the first time that to belong to a small nation can have its advantages. Europeans bring bickering with them wherever they go, and so it is here. The Germans and French were, however, kind enough to take care of that, so that the rest of us had our time, and peace of mind, undisturbed. As things turned out, a few hours of intrigue and counter-intrigue ensured that our departure to Abydos should be postponed until the following morning. Only a rebellious minority of seven or eight broke away during the evening to spend the night among the ruins.

'As soon as lunch and its consequent siesta were over I went ashore to look round the town. Girgeh was in olden times the capital of Greater Egypt, and is still said to have about thirty thousand inhabitants. It takes its name from St Girgis, or George, to whose memory the aforementioned monastery is consecrated. In its time it is reputed to have been extremely wealthy, and at its peak housed over two thousand monks. By far the greater part of the population consists, naturally, of Arabs.

'If one can imagine the sites of many burned houses packed together, everything grey against grey, ramshackle, filthy, chaotic, buried in dirt and with narrow twisting lanes between, that is a fair picture of a south Egyptian town. Girgeh is no exception. I wandered among the bazaars, which were most humbly provided. A few tin and copper objects, a little pottery of the simplest kind, tobacco, millet, woollen goods, that was about all. Nor was there any detectable sign of family life; no friendliness between one human being and another. The oriental associates only with his superior or his inferior, never with his equal; his mind appears bewitched by the same silence and dumbness which paralyses the landscape. A torpid, dreaming apology for life seems to veil him. I doubt whether coffee, tobacco or opium transport him into any abnormal state of mind; they appear rather to extend his natural form of existence.

'If this is the case, one may easily appreciate what an immense task faces the government which is attempting to establish an overall civilisation in this country. The main problem here is not to introduce temporary improvements into the existing state of things so much as to recreate the whole spiritual *habitus* of the people, to break down the prejudices of millennia, even, to some degree, to violate the national character. Only an uninhibited autocracy could achieve such a transformation. A democratic parliament on the European model would merely get lost in gentle arguments over human rights; it would, like the river Nile, swell into an all-obliterating flood, though the resultant mud would scarcely fertilize any field save that of oratory . . .

'A couple of stark naked *fellah* children followed me faithfully on my saunter, never wearying of repeating: *"Baksheesh!"* A *"Rue!"* or a *"Mafish!"* sent them away for a moment; but at the next corner, there they were again. I walked on through the maize markets outside the town, and beyond them into the desert plain. The sun was sinking behind a cluster of palm trees, the long shadows of which it cast towards me on the yellow stretch of sand. Never have I felt the peace of sunset as here in Egypt. At home, I always found it oppressive; it made my spirit melancholy and impelled me to seek company. Here, where the philosophy of the hermit first found expression, one understands this philosophy, just as in Italy one learns to understand how a man can enter a monastery and be happy there.

'At a turning in the road I found a high sandbank between me and the western sky. On top of it perched several vultures, gnawing the carrion of a camel. They looked magnificent, sharply outlined against the background pregnant with light. Further off an Arab woman was driving her buffalo home; a calf capered behind; on the cow's back sat a naked brown Arab boy; his young brother was riding on the woman's shoulder.

'The road led back to the Nile. There, all was life and merriment. The Levantines in our crew were playing leapfrog, while the natives stood around in droves, watching; seriousness and decorum were cast aside as one salvo of laughter followed another. During all this, night fell, and long lines of pitch torches were lit in honour of us foreigners. On board, the signal was sounded to announce that our evening meal was ready.

'The night that followed was miraculous; its beauty grew and grew. The stars leaped forth, full and round on the transparent blue-black sky. A flat mist lay over the Nile valley, and redesigned the landscape into a gigantic bay, bounded to the south by mighty mountains. Now and then a barge glided past with the current. A paper lantern glowed large and

red on the prow; the monotonous rhythmical song of the crew was borne
to us and died away far down the river. We Scandinavians had gathered
in silence; I am sure our thoughts were in the north. In such an hour one
wishes to be reconciled with all mortals, and asks oneself: "How have
you deserved to witness all this beauty?" I felt that they stood before me,
all those many at home who annually perform their silent task—all those
who have a need and craving for what lies outside their sphere, but who
must renounce that craving and tread the millwheel of their days to the
end. Well, it was not long before I had to admit that we, too, had our
cross to bear; for it was after midnight, and time to grope our way down
into our torture chamber with its mosquitoes and its policemen snoring
against the threshold.

'At 4.30 the next morning the reveillé sounded. Two negroes, our
servants' servants, ran round the ship creating a fearful din with fire-tongs
and frying-pans. Swiftly we performed our toilet and ate our breakfast.
It was still dark, but with a faint shimmer of daylight in the east. On the
shore could be discerned a confused throng of asses, horses, camels and
Arabs, who had been organised to escort us to Abydos. Each of us selected
a beast and driver, and the company broke up singly, or into small groups.
I had acquired a well-saddled donkey with an Arab attendant who had
managed to learn some words of *lingua franca*, and to whom I could
therefore, with the occasional assistance of Italian, make myself understood.

'We rode southwards, with the Nile on our left, and within a few
minutes were outside the town. A dry stony plain lay before us; clumps
of palm trees could be indistinctly glimpsed in the morning mist, and the
stars grew ever fainter. After half an hour's ride we came to a canal, which
had been dug right across the plain, and across which, by means of a ferry
of the most primitive kind, expecting every moment to sink and in the
most perilous confusion, we were shipped to the further bank. Here we
continued our way along an endless dyke, beside another canal at a right
angle to the first. The landscape was very monotonous. Great plains of
maize stretched on the other side of the water as far as the eye could see;
a solitary sycamore or a clump of palm trees stood here and there upon
the plain, and at the field's edge a native family had erected its brown
woollen tent, with a pack of dogs baying at the entrance. On the slope
of the dyke clambered a flock of goats. Yellow-grey, with narrow faces
and shoulders, and long ears hanging down like corkscrews, they bore a
striking resemblance to English lady travellers. A native woman ferried
herself across the canal in a strange vessel, woven of branches and resembl-

ing a large inverted bottle-basket; it was filled with empty clay pots to give buoyancy, and was hauled to and fro by means of two fibre ropes.

'The dyke on which our road lay stretched in a straight line as far as the eye could see. The sun came up over the splendid mountains on the other side of the Nile. The innumerable birds of Egypt began to stir; suddenly they were flying in all directions; but quite soundlessly; no cries, no song, no twitter.

'Our caravan made an imposing procession. Warriors with drawn sabres mounted on Arab horses sped back and forth, as though some calamity were imminent. In the centre of our line rode the leader of our expedition, the famous Egyptologist Lepsius, with his Jovian head of youthful white curls, on a handsome ass with red velvet saddle hangings, surrounded by officials from Girgeh. "Leps, Leps!" whispered the natives as he rode past; everyone knew him from his three-year sojourn here, just as the scientific world knows him from his twelve-volume work on those travels and discoveries. His young and very tall Swiss colleague, Herr Naville, bore himself impressively on an almost unnaturally large thoroughbred, sent him by a rich Copt of these parts. The native herdsmen drove their buffalo away from the dyke and out into the canal; others stood motionless on the verge of the road, staring after us, leaning on their long palm staves.

'After an hour's ride we came on several hundred natives, mostly children, who had been driven in from the surrounding villages to improve the road and, especially, to render a collapsed bridge passable. It undeniably looked somewhat fragile as they built it before our eyes of branches and Nile mud, with of course no handrails; and I do not think I was the only person who felt a certain queasiness at the prospect of crossing it on ass-back. But all went well, and we emerged on to a richly fertile and well-tended plain with newly planted avenues and numberless groves of unusually luxuriant trees. A pleasant village lay on our right hand, surrounded by a ditch, where a crowd of natives slaked their thirst and washed their legs amid sociable chatter. Farther out in the plain lay the town of Bardies, the newly whitewashed houses of which, half-overgrown with a wonderful abundance of creepers, gave it the appearance of an immense floral display. A place I would happily have settled in! The inhabitants, evidently instructed, lined their houses and garden walls and greeted us civilly as we rode by. At every fork in the road guards were posted. Everything here suggested an unusually well-ordered communal life; many Copts live in the area.

'We came to another huge Nile dyke, and were soon riding as though

on a mole in the middle of a huge bay. Admittedly the floods were sub-
siding, but they were still considerable enough to give one an idea of how
they must be at their peak. Here, as elsewhere, one no longer wonders at
the information that the Nile annually emits into the sea a volume of
water five times that of the Danube.

'Suddenly we noticed that our outriders had halted, and as we came up
with them we stood there in a tight group, unable to proceed further. To
allow the flood waters free access to the plain the dyke had been breached
to a width of about a hundred yards, and there below us lay two Nile
barges making their humble preparations to ferry us over. It was an indescribable scene, all noise and confusion; everyone wanted to be first into
the boats; the horses reared and kicked as they were driven aboard with
sticks; the donkeys were literally thrown down into the vessels; the
Europeans swore and the natives shrieked at each other like madmen. The
water swirled through the gap in the dyke, and the boats swung across,
aided by a tattered rope. A similar scene ensued when we landed; first
one saw riderless donkeys and horses, then riders with nothing to ride;
for some of the attendants were still waiting to embark, and we had no
choice but to give chase to our long-eared mounts, which had straightway set forth along the dyke at a steady trot.

'Gradually the terrain began to rise, the arable soil ceased, and we rode
into the desert, which stretched for miles towards the western range of
mountains. A solitary Arab hut stood in the sea of sand; by its wall stood
a water trough; it was an old sarcophagus. On the roof stood a dog, and a
camel was tethered a short way from the house, standing there motionless
with its back to the sun. Its eyes squinted after us as we rode by; otherwise
it did not move.

'The desert is not completely flat. Here and there it rises in gentle waves,
and on these the sand is driven together in sharp crests, like the snow with
us. One cannot of course traverse these, but must find a way round. But
one seldom encounters this problem, as the drivers know instinctively
which route to follow.

'Thus we rode on, singly or in long lines; sun and sand trembled hotly
against each other, as one might imagine a sea of molten metal. Our
parasols gave scant protection, and gradually we gave one article of
clothing after another to our drivers' keeping. Far to the south several
dark mounds protruded into the air, and all our eyes were directed
towards these; for they were the burial mounds, which over several
millenia had gathered height so that they towered over ancient
Abydos.

H

'As is known, in olden times several places were named Abydos. The name arose here as the result of a Greek corruption of the Egyptian word *Ebot*; now the Arabs who live in the area call it *el matfun*, which means "the buried place". And burials there are, with a vengeance. A gathering of sand dunes sixty to eighty feet high adorn this immense city, which ancient authors described as the mightiest in Egypt after Thebes; when it is excavated, it will be that country's Pompeii.

'Abydos seems, like other Egyptian cities, to have been a necropolis, a place of burial as well as a city for the living. Here was discovered the grave of Osiris, and accordingly for thousands of years all rich Egyptians had themselves buried here that they might rest with their god and king in the earth he had sanctified. Many grave writings bear witness to this, and several of these date right back to the sixteenth dynasty, that is to say, 3,700 years ago.

'A stream had cut its course through the desert immediately below the town; here we rode along a poor strip of grass beneath sycamores and acacias. The mounds became more and more frequent, especially on our left. Here the *fellahs* were engaged in the famous excavations under the guidance of Mariette Bey, the Khedive's principal Egyptologist and the supervisor of all antiquities in the Nile valley. To the uninitiated, the work which this man is doing seems strange . . .'

There, as tantalisingly as with his unfinished childhood memoirs, the fragment ends. Ibsen was well able to write sharp and sensitive narrative prose; one can only surmise that it bored him, and that—which was his strength as a dramatist—he disliked writing in the first person, except under the mask of verse.

After returning to Cairo, the Khedive's guests rested for thirty-six hours before leaving by train for Alexandria, early on the morning of 15 November. There, trouble awaited them. A hundred guests needed transport to Port Said, where the Canal was to be ceremonially opened, and the steamer was found to have room for only fifty. No extra ship could be organised before the following day, so Lieblein and some others, including Ibsen, persuaded the authorities to lay on a special train to take them overland to Ismailia. It arrived there in oriental style six hours behind schedule, but by sailing up the still officially unopened Canal they managed to arrive at Port Said in time for the beginning of the festivities on 16 November. These were inaugurated with a double religious service, Catholic and Moslem, attended by the Empress Eugénie and the Emperor Franz Josef of Austria. The following day, Wednesday 17 November, the Suez Canal was declared open.

At nine in the morning the procession of ships began to enter the Canal, led by the Empress in *L'Aigle*. The Scandinavians travelled in the Danish corvette *Nordstjernen*; this should have gone with the second group of ships, but to their annoyance they had to wait while the third, fourth and fifth groups steamed past, 'doubtless', comments Lieblein, 'because the small nations have to stand aside for the big'. They did not get started until the next day, when further trouble awaited them, for the Egyptian ship in front of them went aground twice, so that the journey to Ismailia, which should have taken seven to eight hours, occupied three days. Determined not to miss the celebrations at Ismailia, the Scandinavians abandoned the Danish vessel and transferred to a barge towed by a small steamer, which, proceeding at 'the pace of a tortoise,'[1] got them there just in time.

Lieblein describes the scene at Ismailia as being 'like a story from the Thousand and One Nights', a phrase which Ibsen was later to borrow. 'The whole town and harbour glittered with light and colour. Ships, quays and the town were brilliantly illuminated, fireworks were exploded, and everything was decked with the flags of all the nations.' Tents had been erected everywhere; the huge crowds included people of 'every race and country'; there were carriages, camels, donkeys, European brass bands, orchestras playing dance music, and Asian flutes and pipes. In the evening a great ball was held in a palace especially built by the Khedive for the occasion; some of the furnishings had evidently arrived only just in time, for the huge wall mirrors from Europe were 'still uncleaned and bearing the makers' labels'. The dancing continued until three in the morning.

All this must have been heady stuff for Ibsen; and shortly before he had left Port Said to sail down the Canal, a letter had been handed to him on the quayside which, in that setting at that moment, must more than ever have underlined the narrowness and pettiness of life back home in Norway.

A month earlier, on 18 October, the day after Ibsen had first arrived in Cairo, *The League of Youth* had received its first performance at the Christiania Theatre. The political implications of the play, which by then had been in the bookshops for nearly three weeks, were already one of the chief talking points in the capital. Ibsen was later to protest that his characters were not meant to represent specific individuals ('There is a big difference between using someone as a model and directly portraying them'), but it had become a parlour game in Christiania to try to identify the models, and it was of little comfort to those selected that traits of other politicians were to be found in the same character. Stensgaard's facile eloquence, his readiness to make a patriotic

---

[1] Ibsen to Nordahl Rolfsen, *CE*, XIX, p. 192.

speech at the drop of a hat, and his repeated invocation of the Almighty, were irresistibly reminiscent of Bjørnson; and his penchant for proposing to rich ladies was a well-known characteristic of another of the liberal leaders, Ole Richter. Johan Sverdrup, who shared Bjørnson's love of speechifying, was declared by others to be the original of Stensgaard; and Lundestad, the rich farmer, was generally assumed to be a caricature of Ueland, the leader of the Peasants' faction in the liberal party.

The play, in short, as William Archer observed, offended the entire progressive front.[1] Ten days before its publication Bjørnson had broken his silence towards Ibsen by writing to him to tell him how much he was looking forward to reading it; but when he did, it struck him, not unnaturally, as a stab in the back for freedom. 'The League of Youth', he declared later, 'tried to paint our young freedom-loving party as a mob of speculating mountebanks.' 'Ibsen's play', he wrote to Rudolf Schmidt on 30 November, 'seems to assert that the young Norway is an intriguing and self-seeking society which abuses the name of freedom to satisfy its own ambition and covetousness'; and he expressed his resentment to Sverdrup in an eloquent verse:

> If poesy's sacred grove be made
> The assassin's hiding-place, if this
> The new poetic fashion is
> Then I for one renounce its shade.[2]

Twelve years later, in 1881, Bjørnson explained what he meant by this term. 'It was not the portrayal of contemporary life and known personages that I called assassination. It was the fact that The League of Youth sought to represent our young liberal party as a gang of ambitious speculators, whose patriotism was as empty as their phraseology; and particularly, that prominent men were at first rendered recognisable, and then had false hearts and shady characters foisted on them.'[3]

Ibsen later told Henrik Jæger that Stensgaard was not specifically based on Bjørnson, Richter or Sverdrup, but that 'in the Norwegian Society he had had the opportunity to study the liberal jargon of the time. There was then a group of not very talented people in Christiania who were Bjørnson's sworn admirers and who caricatured his mode of expression.'[4] And he protested to Hegel that

---

[1] Introduction to The League of Youth (London, 1907), p. x.
[2] Edmund Gosse's translation.
[3] Archer's translation (introduction to The League of Youth, p. x).
[4] Midbøe, p. 151.

the play was an attack, not upon true liberalism, but on demagogy: 'Bjørnson
. . . must surely realise that it isn't he but his damnable and lie-steeped clique
that have served me as models.'[1] But (to quote Archer again), 'it is difficult to
see how Ibsen can have expected Bjørnson to distinguish very clearly between
an attack on his "lie-steeped" clique and a lampoon on himself . . . The case,
in fact, seems to have been very like that of the portraiture of Leigh Hunt in
Harold Skimpole [in Bleak House]. Both Dickens and Ibsen had unconsciously
taken more from their respective models than they intended. They imagined,
perhaps, that the features which did not belong to the original would conceal
the likeness; whereas their actual effect was only to render the portraits
libellous.'[2]

Ibsen's apparent betrayal of the progressive cause seemed all the more
ungrateful when it was recalled that Bjørnson had organised the fund for
Ibsen five years earlier, and that both Richter and Sverdrup had been among
the subscribers, as well as signing the petition for him to be awarded a Civil
List pension. To quote Archer a third time, the cleavage between the right and
the left was now at its sharpest in Norway, not merely in politics but also in
religion, literature and even art; no one was regarded as an independent, and
so Ibsen, to his embarrassment, found himself hailed as a champion of conservatism, a charge which had also (as we have seen) been levelled against him
in Stockholm. As a consequence, the atmosphere on the opening night
resembled that of a political meeting. This is how Suzannah described it in
the letter which Ibsen received on the quayside at Port Said:

Dresden, 29 October 1869

Dear Ibsen,

I have received your letters, from which I see that you are having the
best possible time. Sigurd says it is that thought which comforts him, and
I say the same, take and enjoy everything which is offered you, one is not
a King's guest every day.

But while you are enjoying the splendour of the south, there is a terrible
storm in Christiania over The League of Youth. The first evening the first
three acts were greeted with loud applause, but in the fourth act when
Bastian says his line about what the nation is[3] the gallery started to whistle,
led by a few students who are fighting for the new language. What do
you think of that?

---

[1] Letter to Hegel, 14 December 1869.
[2] Archer, introduction to The League of Youth, pp. x–xi.
[3] 'The people who have nothing and are nothing, who lie in chains.'

According to *Morgenbladet* the evening went brilliantly, Krohn's and Isachsen's performances[1] were works of art, all the company were called, *Morgenbladet* printed several excellent reports. The evening ended with thunderous applause.

But then came the second evening, your benefit performance, they had already decided in advance that things were going to start now; the house was sold out, as soon as Lundestad finished his first speech the whistles began, time after time they were drowned by applause, but they would not stop. The curtain had to come down. The director had to come forward and ask for quiet so that the play could continue, and the commotion so grew that after the performance was over the lights had to be put out . . . But your play has not suffered . . .[2]

Indeed it had not. Within ten days of the premiere, the sales of the book had been such that Hegel had already brought out a second edition; and so heavy was the demand for tickets at the theatre that seats were even sold in the space normally reserved for the orchestra. The violent demonstrations continued, however; the atmosphere in the theatre was that of an angry debating-chamber. Ibsen's later plays were to arouse far more widespread debate than *The League of Youth*, but none was to provoke audiences to such immediate and noisy hostility. Ibsen carefully kept every hostile criticism. 'My enemies have helped me greatly', he is said to have remarked. 'They protested so much that in the end people wanted to know who this man was whom everyone was always abusing.'[3] On his return to Dresden, he recorded his reaction to these events in a poem, *At Port Said*:

> The eastern dawn
> Rose on the harbour.
> The flags of the nations
> Hung from the masts.
> The sound of music
> Preceded the hymn;
> A thousand cannon
> Baptised the Canal.

---

[1] Krohn played Lundestad, Isachsen Aslaksen. Johannes Brun was Daniel Hejre, Laura Gundersen Selma, Arnoldus Reimers Stensgaard and Lucie Wolf Mrs Rundholmen.

[2] Bergliot Ibsen, pp. 44–45.

[3] *Ibid.*, p. 42.

The steamers moved
Past the obelisk.
Whispers reached me
In my mother tongue.
The mirror I had polished
For male coquettes
Had been dirtied there
By a shower of saliva.

The gadfly bit me;
Memories stirred.
Bright star, I thank thee!
My home hasn't changed.
We hailed the frigate
From our small deck.
I waved my hand
And saluted the flag.

To the feasting, on!
Though the snake spit venom.
A chosen guest
Through the Bitter Lakes.
As the day dies, quenched,
Dreaming I slumber
Where Pharaoh drowned
And Moses passed over.

By the time he reached Ismailia, Ibsen had had enough of Egypt. Leaving
Lieblein and von Knorring to enjoy another month of the Khedive's hospitality, he returned to Cairo, took the train to Alexandria and embarked for
Marseilles. By the end of November he was back in Paris, where he stayed for
a fortnight at his own expense. These two weeks provide another infuriating
lacuna in our knowledge of Ibsen's life. No letters from him while he was
there have survived; we know only that he spent much time visiting art
galleries and exhibitions. What did he see? He was five years too early for the
first Impressionist exhibition, but he might possibly have noticed the odd
painting by Manet or Monet, who had begun to exhibit in 1861 and 1865
respectively; and one would like to think that he may have wandered in for
a drink at the Café Guerbois on the Avenue de Clichy, where the future
Impressionists (the name had not yet been coined) habitually gathered that
year. But art galleries and exhibitions close soon after dark; how did he spend

his later hours? Did he (we must remember his almost total ignorance of French) go to the theatre? Did he visit other, less decorous, places of entertainment? We do not know. He told no one; or if he did, they have not told us. In the middle of December he rejoined Suzannah and Sigurd in Dresden.

FIVE

 Doubts and Hesitations

(1870)

WHATEVER THE LIMITATIONS of Ibsen's physical courage may have been, he revelled in hostile criticism. 'The reception of *The League of Youth*', he wrote to Frederik Hegel on 14 December 1869, shortly after his return to Dresden, 'delights me. I was prepared for opposition to it, and would have been disappointed had there been none . . . I will write to him [Bjørnson] today or tomorrow, and hope the affair will, despite all our differences, end in a reconciliation.' But he does not seem to have written any such letter, and it is difficult to imagine that by this time it would have had any effect, except to add fuel to the flames. He was already meditating a successor to *The League of Youth*: 'I am planning a new, serious, contemporary drama in three acts; I expect to start work on it in the very near future.' Of his visit to Egypt he had little to say. 'I had a pleasant journey. I got right down into Nubia and the Red Sea, underwent many experiences and met many interesting people. But it is best to sit quietly at home and look back on it all.'

'I shall probably come up to Christiania in the summer', he informed his brother-in-law, Johan Thoresen, on 17 December. Year after year he toyed with the idea of revisiting Norway, without bringing himself to take the plunge. The reaction to *The League of Youth* must have confirmed his conviction that a writer did best to study his subject-matter from a distance. 'From the attacks that I read', he wrote to Jonas Collin on 4 January 1870, 'it seems that in Norway people regard empty phrase-making, hollowness and mean-mindedness as national characteristics which are therefore sacrosanct. But none of this bothers me in the least.'

Ibsen was not the only foreign writer who was studying his subject-matter from a distance in Dresden that year. One wonders whether he ever noticed a short, bearded Russian, even smaller than himself,[1] who haunted the art galleries and theatres (which he found poor), and consumed in the cafés great quantities of ice-cream, for which he had a passion. From August 1869 until

---

[1] Dostoevsky stood five feet six inches, Ibsen about five feet seven and a half.

July 1871 Fyodor Dostoevsky was living in Dresden, at Viktoria-Strasse in the
English quarter, not very far from Ibsen, writing *The Possessed*, and heartily
disliking both the city and its inhabitants, who were for ever short-changing
him in shops and restaurants and misdirecting him in the streets. 'Dresden is a
very dull place', he complained to a friend in December 1869, the month
Ibsen returned from Egypt. 'I can't bear these Germans.' His working routine
was very different to Ibsen's, though equally rigid. 'I get up at one o'clock in
the afternoon because I do my work at night. I work from 3 to 5 p.m., then
go for half an hour's walk to the post office and back through the Royal
Gardens—always the same route. We dine at home and then I go out for
another walk and back home through the Royal Gardens again. At home I
have tea and at half-past ten sit down to work and usually work till five o'clock
in the morning. Then I go to bed and punctually on the stroke of six fall asleep.
That is my life.'[1]

Since Ibsen, too, liked to walk in the Gardens, and both men frequented
the cafés on the Brühl Terrace, the two must surely have seen each other;
but Dostoevsky would not, any more than most other non-Scandinavians,
have heard of Ibsen, and although Ibsen must at least have heard of Dostoevsky,
who had already published *Crime and Punishment* and *The Idiot*, the latter's
presence in Dresden seems to have been known to very few. Nearly thirty
years later Ibsen was to name *Crime and Punishment* as the Russian novel which
attracted him most[2]—and he was a great admirer of the Russian novelists,
especially of Turgenev and even (despite Tolstoy's hatred of him) of *Anna
Karenina*. But we do not know whether he had yet read Dostoevsky when
they were neighbours in Dresden.

The 'contemporary drama' referred to in Ibsen's letter to Hegel of 14
December must have been *The Pillars of Society*, for his first notes for that play
date from this year. 'The main theme', he recorded, 'must be how women sit
modestly in the background while the men busily pursue their petty aims with
an assurance that at once infuriates and impresses.' But he found unusual
difficulty in (as he had written in another context) 'getting the beast under
him'. On 25 January he informed Hegel that he hoped to have it ready by the
following October, but two and a half months later he had to tell him that it
had not yet got beyond the draft 'and since I have to put my travel notes in
order it looks like being delayed for some time'. (He had promised articles on

---

[1] David Magarshack, *Dostoevsky* (London, 1962), p. 405. For other information on
Dostoevsky's life in Dresden, see *The Diary of Dostoevsky's Wife* (London, 1928), pp. 35–
172.

[2] Interview with Hans Tostrup in *Ørebladet*, 19 March 1898, reprinted in *CE*, Vol.
XIX, pp. 211–215.

Egypt to both *Morgenbladet* and *Dansk Tidsskrift*, but never completed them.) When October arrived, so far from having the play ready he could only tell Hegel that it had 'sufficiently developed in my mind for me to hope that any day now I may be able to start writing it'.

It was in fact to be a further seven years before he completed this next work, an extraordinary period of silence for one who had written three successful plays in five years and who was to be so prolific for the remainder of his life. Nor can this be explained away by the stumbling-block of *Emperor and Galilean*. This long gestation has been much debated by commentators; *The League of Youth*, it has been argued, shows that he had already and painlessly made the decision to abandon poetic drama for prose. Yet the reason is surely plain to see, and Georg Brandes, whose entry into Ibsen's life at this period was to be so important to both of them, stated it. Ibsen's artistic instincts, Brandes wrote in his autobiography, 'were unconsciously leading him in the direction of modern prose drama. He was to remain silent for several years while these new efforts were taking shape within him. Admittedly he had written the sharply modern satire, *The League of Youth*, in 1869, but without the intent of striking out a new path; which was why he straightway turned back to the distant past (in *Emperor and Galilean*).'[1]

The key word here is *unconsciously*. Commentators may argue whether *The League of Youth* is the first of Ibsen's 'new' dramas, or a bridge between the old and the new. The point is that Ibsen himself did not yet know in which direction he was moving. He had not yet taken the decision to abandon poetry for prose; he was to arrive at that standpoint slowly and agonizingly over the next few years, and the long gestation of *The Pillars of Society*, the gathering, revision and publication of his poems, and the unusually flawed quality of *Emperor and Galilean* are all evidence of the struggle within him, and of the hesitation with which he took that momentous step. Abandoning poetry, in which he felt so free, for prose, in which he felt so constricted, was for Ibsen like abandoning the Mediterranean to return to Norway. Georg Brandes was to remark that 'some time during the battle of life, a lyrical Pegasus must have been killed under him.'[2] It would be truer to say that he shot it himself, and that from this action, much as we may regret that *Brand* and *Peer Gynt* were to have no successors, the whole of modern prose drama was to stem.

Ibsen's shortage of acquaintances in Dresden, which had chafed him during his first months there, seemed now not to bother him. On 6 March 1870 he addressed a few words of fatherly advice on the subject to Georg Brandes,

---

[1] Georg Brandes, *Levned*, II (Copenhagen, 1907), p. 103.
[2] Georg Brandes, *Henrik Ibsen* (Copenhagen, 1898), p. 64. (Muir-Archer translation.)

now being reviled in Copenhagen for his open liaison with Caroline David, a lady who had left her husband (and whose daughter Marie, twenty-one years later, was to be accused by Strindberg, probably for once justifiably, of having a Lesbian affair with the latter's wife Siri). Brandes's letters to Ibsen have, like so many others which Ibsen received, disappeared, but he had evidently pictured himself as a kind of Ishmael.

'You say you have no friends at home', wrote Ibsen. 'I have often supposed this to be the case with you. When one stands, as you do, in so intensely personal a relationship to one's life-work, one cannot really expect to keep one's friends. But I think it is, in the long run, good for you that you are setting out[1] without leaving any friends behind. Friends are an expensive luxury; and when one invests one's capital in a calling or mission in this life, one cannot afford to have friends. The expensive thing about friends is not what one does for them but what, out of consideration for them, one leaves undone. Many spiritual ambitions have been crippled thus. I have been through this, and that is why I had to wait for several years before I succeeded in being myself.'

He returned to this theme in other letters that spring and summer, and the unusual emotion with which he, normally so uncommunicative a correspondent, expatiated on it seems further evidence of the split which was beginning to widen in his creative personality. On 29 May he warned Magdalene Thoresen (from whose clutches Brandes had only recently escaped, and who was now unsuccessfully refocussing her attentions on Bjørnson) against being over-sensitive to criticism. 'Most critical objections', he assured her, 'boil down to a reproach against the writer for being himself, thinking, feeling, seeing and writing as himself, instead of seeing and writing as the critic would have done, had he been able. The essential thing is to protect one's essential self, to keep it pure and free of all intrusive elements, and to draw a clear distinction between what one has merely experienced and what one has spiritually *lived through*; for only the latter is proper matter for creative writing.'

During the spring, a young Norwegian girl named Laura Petersen had published an emotional contribution to the debate on women's rights in the form of an imaginary sequel to *Brand* entitled *Brand's Daughters*. She sent Ibsen a copy, which one would have expected him to ignore or, at best, formally acknowledge; but young girls sometimes brought out the cavalier in him, or anyway the father-figure, and on 11 June he wrote her a long and kindly reply. 'Are you thinking of continuing to write?' he enquired. 'Much

---

[1] Brandes was about to embark on a long and fruitful European tour, which was to bring him the friendship of Taine, Renan and, especially, John Stuart Mill.

more is needed than mere talent. One must have something to create from, some genuine experience. If one lacks that, one doesn't write in the true sense, one just makes books . . . Intellectually, man is a long-sighted animal; we see most clearly from a distance; details distract; one must remove oneself from what one wishes to judge; one describes the summer best on a winter's day . . . The main thing is to be true and faithful to oneself. It is not a question of willing to go in this direction or that, but of willing what one absolutely must, because one is oneself and cannot do otherwise. The rest is only lies.'

To be true and faithful to oneself, to will what one must; this, more perhaps than anything, was to be the theme of all Ibsen's future work. Nora gave herself at any rate a chance of salvation by following her own convictions; Mrs Alving was destroyed because she did not follow hers, but stayed with the husband she despised. Yet Ibsen, even this early in his career, knew that to follow one's convictions may end in self-destruction; Julian the Apostate and Rebecca West destroyed themselves thus, and who knows whether Nora's life ended more happily than Mrs Alving's? To write in verse for the printed page, as in *Brand* and *Peer Gynt*, which had brought him fame with a comparative minimum of controversy, or to write in prose for performance, which had stirred up a hornet's nest about his head? To remain in exile or to return home? The easy course would have been to continue in the medium of verse drama for reading, but in artistic matters Ibsen was never to take the easy course, any more than he was ever to take the easy way out of a fifth act. He was never to write the same play twice, never to repeat a success; he was to remain for ever the most restless of experimentalists.

The problem of whether or not to return to Norway crops up as frequently in Ibsen's letters of this period as the importance of being oneself, a question of which, in Ibsen's case, it was of course part. He knew well that he could never deny the Norwegian in him, or turn his back, as other self-exiled writers had done, on the country that had at first rejected and now at last acclaimed him.[1] 'I long to come northwards', he wrote to Ole Schulerud's widow on 9 June (in the letter already partly quoted),[2] 'if only for a short while—I have grave doubts about settling permanently up there. I fear it would cramp my activity . . . Everything that is irrelevant or transitory acquires undeserved significance when one stands in the midst of the tumult; or so I have always

---

[1] He retained, like so many exiles, a nostalgic longing for the simple food of his homeland. Several times in his letters he begs friends to send him *gammelost*, the pungent Norwegian cheese, and on 22 January 1871, complaining of the lack of fresh fish in Dresden, he asked a chemist acquaintance in Trondhjem to send him a cask of a north Norwegian speciality: 'a very delicate fish called redfish, rosefish, rose-perch or some such name'.

[2] See *Henrik Ibsen, The Making of a Dramatist*, p. 196.

felt. I have wandered widely since we parted. I have lived and travelled in Italy for about five years; then two years in various places in Germany. I have, as you may perhaps know, also been in Egypt; have travelled all the way down into Nubia; have sat by the Red Sea and looked across to Sinai. Yet I feel more Norwegian in my soul than ever before; you must not believe, as so many do, that I feel hostile towards my native land. It is the excrescences of our social existence which I hate; but they are not organic to it.' And he concluded his letter to Laura Petersen: 'Sooner or later I shall come to Norway . . . You must not think me so ill-disposed towards my countrymen as many assert; and in any case I can assure you that I am no more tolerant towards myself than towards others . . .'

If Ibsen was getting nothing written that spring and summer of 1870, at least *The League of Youth* was being more widely performed than any of his previous plays. On 11 December it had been staged in Stockholm, at the Royal Theatre, and had been a success, for Sweden too had its Stensgaards in political life. In Copenhagen it at first seemed no more likely to get produced than anything else he had written. The censor of the Royal Theatre, old Carsten Hauch, an early befriender of Brandes but somewhat conservative in his literary judgments, reported to his board that the author had 'adopted an unfortunately fragmentary style which constantly, as it were, chops the dialogue into pieces', complained that 'one has to know about all the humbug which can be performed with false bills of hand, and the mysteries of fraud, to be able to follow the action and fully comprehend it', and concluded: 'The play is totally unsuited to the theatre.' But the board, doubtless mindful of the full houses which the play was attracting in Christiania, asked Hauch to think again, whereupon he grudgingly admitted that, despite the 'chaotic obscurity and formlessness from which the play, in my view, so sadly suffers', since the board felt that 'the play must possess some significance as a political satire which it lacks aesthetically', he would not oppose its production.[1] Johanne Luise Heiberg herself directed it, and it received its premiere in Copenhagen on 16 February 1870, the first Ibsen play to be performed in Denmark; and here, as in Christiania and Stockholm, despite some critical disapproval, it proved a success.

Ibsen spent the spring in a leisurely revision of *The Pretenders* for republication by Gyldendal, a task which principally involved amending the spelling so as to conform with the recommendations of the Stockholm orthographic conference. He also altered a few phrases to read more particularly and less

---

[1] Edvard Agerholm, *Henrik Ibsen og Det Kgl. Teater* in *Gads Danske Magasin*, 1910–1911, p. 278.

generally, in deference to an objection which Brandes had made on that score. When July came he packed Suzannah and Sigurd off for a holiday in Teplitz and, doubtless encouraged by his reception in Stockholm the previous summer and by the success of *The League of Youth* in Denmark, went off to get lionized in Copenhagen. He sailed from Lübeck on 19 July, a momentous day for Europe, for it marked the outbreak of the Franco-Prussian War. Brandes, unfortunately, was in England, being horrified by the poverty, disappointed with Oxford and with the theatres and ladies of London, enjoying the Zoo and Kew Gardens and talking French (since his English was poor) with John Stuart Mill at Blackheath. But Ibsen met his publisher, Frederik Hegel, for the first time, and renewed two acquaintances which he had fleetingly made on his study visit eighteen years before, with Johanne Luise Heiberg and Hans Christian Andersen.

Hegel had received a neurotic letter from Bjørnson warning him about his guest and concluding: 'Beware of Ibsen! He is ungrateful, and a man who is that is capable of anything!'[1] But he had by now doubtless learned to discount whatever the two writers said about each other, and he took excellent care of Ibsen throughout the latter's stay, though he never, throughout their long friendship, managed to penetrate Ibsen's reserve. 'Ibsen is an extremely courteous man and pleasant to do business with', he wrote eleven years later, 'but very cautious and withdrawn, and I have the feeling that I haven't got any closer to him now than in 1866 when I had the honour to publish *Brand* for the first time—and that saddens me.'[2]

Hans Andersen[3] was eager to meet the new dramatist, having apparently forgotten their brief encounter in 1852. On 11 August he noted in his diary: 'Fru Melchior told me that the poet Ibsen was dining today with Carl Bloch, and expressed surprise that I had not been invited. I was put in a bad humour

---

[1] *Gro-tid*, II, p. 356.

[2] Nielsen, I, p. 297.

[3] Edmund Gosse, who met Andersen at the Melchiors two years later, recorded a vivid impression of him: 'a very tall, elderly gentleman, dressed in a complete suit of brown, and in a curly wig of the same shade of snuff-colour. I was almost painfully struck, at the first moment, by the grotesque ugliness of his face and hands, and by his enormously long and swinging arms; but this impression passed away as soon as he began to speak . . . Gentleness and ingenuousness breathed from everything he said . . . He had but to speak, almost to smile, and the man of genius stood revealed.' Andersen read a story to Gosse but lost his voice during the conversation that ensued and had to be 'conducted to his bed with infinite precautions'. Gosse especially remembered his 'amazingly long and bony hand—a great brown hand, almost like that of a man of the wood—grasping my shoulder as he read to me'. (Edmund Gosse, *Two Visits to Denmark, 1872, 1874*, London, 1911, pp. 97–100).

by the thought of how little attention B. had paid to me.'[1] 'I wasn't there', he wrote the next day to Henriette Collin, 'but would have liked to have been invited to see at last this Norwegian poet who doesn't like the Norwegians.'[2] A week later he got his wish, when Moritz Gerson Melchior, a politician in whose eighteenth-century house overlooking the Sound Andersen had, by a generous arrangement, a permanent suite of three or four rooms, gave a party for the two writers. Andersen tried to prepare himself for the meeting with a little homework, and the result depressed him. 'Read *Peer Gynt*', he noted in his diary for 18 August, 'which is written by a mad poet. One goes crazy oneself reading this book. The poetry isn't good either, there is something sick and distraught about the whole thing. Am sorry I read it, as Ibsen is coming here this evening for the first time. I've never seen him; he's said to be taciturn and gloomy.'[3] But the occasion passed off unexpectedly well, for the diary continues: 'After dinner he arrived with Bloch, and made a good impression... He talked well and amiably. We all liked him.'

Andersen's diary conceals how close the evening came to being a disaster. According to John Paulsen, who had the story from Ibsen himself:

'Many of the city's most notable personages were among the guests. Everyone had arrived and was ready to sit down, but no Andersen descended from his rooms upstairs. A quarter of an hour passed, half an hour; a nervous restlessness settled on the company, and the hostess looked unhappy. Message after message was sent up, but he still did not appear. The hostess quietly went upstairs, but returned with a more worried expression than before. He would not come down. No one said anything to the guest of honour, but Ibsen sensed what was afoot. Andersen did not like to be with people of whose sympathy he was not sure. When people mentioned strange authors he would naïvely ask: "Does he admire me?" The atmosphere grew more embarrassed. It was now three-quarters of an hour past the appointed time for supper. The host and hostess were at a loss what to do. Were they to sit down without Andersen?

'Then Ibsen saved the situation. He took his host aside and asked to be allowed to go up to Andersen's room and speak with him. The host nodded and showed him the way. A minute later, to the joyful surprise of the company, the two great writers entered the room arm in arm, Andersen

---

[1] H. C. Andersens Brevveksling med Edvard og Henriette Collin, ed. C. Behrend and H. Topsøe-Jensen (Copenhagen, 1933–1937), IV, p. 163.

[2] Ibid., p. 163.

[3] H. C. Andersens Dagbøger og Breve, 1868–1875, ed. C. M. K. Petersen and Svend Larsen. (Copenhagen, 1906), p. 64.

evidently deeply moved, smiling through his tears. He was like a small child who has got his way.

' "But what happened between you and Andersen in his room?" I asked Ibsen. Ibsen smiled at the memory. "I embraced him and paid him a casual compliment. He was moved and, as he returned my embrace, asked: 'Then you really like me?' " Ibsen added: "It was one of the pleasantest evenings I have ever known. Andersen could be lovable and entertaining as few other men when he wanted to be." ' [1]

Andersen was delighted with his new acquaintance. He wrote to a friend that he had found Ibsen 'very amiable, unassuming and pleasant. I like him a lot, but *Peer Gynt* not at all.' [2]

Johanne Luise Heiberg, whose acting had been such a revelation to Ibsen on his previous visit, invited him to dine with her at her home, the beautiful seaside villa (not far from the Melchiors') where her husband's conversation had so disappointed Ibsen in 1852, and where he now, in turn, disappointed her by his taciturnity, a fault for which he was to make handsome amends in a poem the following year. Sadly for him, she had retired from the stage, and of the other actors whom he had admired then Michael Wiehe and N. P. Nielsen (whom he had seen as Lear) were both dead; but there was an exciting new talent to enjoy in Emil Poulsen. Fru Heiberg arranged a special performance of *The League of Youth* in Ibsen's honour. Stensgaard was played by Anton Wilhelm Wiehe, whom Ibsen had known and respected in Christiania —an unexpected but shrewd piece of casting, for Wiehe specialised in strong romantic roles, such as Oehlenschläger's heroes, and, as Edvard Brandes observed, 'all his faults as well as his virtues helped him in the part' [3] of Ibsen's narcissistic hypocrite.

The documentation of these weeks is scanty. The only letters of Ibsen which have survived, apart from a brief note thanking Wiehe for his interpretation, are two which one would be happy to do without, revealing as they do one of the quirkiest and least attractive aspects of Ibsen's character. Addressed (9 and 12 September) to a Danish lawyer named Anton Klubien whom he had known in Rome, they ask him to use his influence to obtain for the writer the Order of Dannebrog which, Ibsen reminds his correspondent, had been awarded to his fellow-countrymen Welhaven and Andreas Munch. 'I must

---

[1] Paulsen, *Samliv med Ibsen*, I (Copenhagen & Christiania, 1906), pp. 39–40.

[2] Letter to Henriette Collin, 26 August 1870. She replied agreeing that Ibsen was 'odd and likable, but why do you read *Peer Gynt*? Put it away and read *Brand* and *The Pretenders*.' (*H. C. Andersens Brevveksling med Edvard og Henriette Collin*, IV, pp. 164–165.

[3] Edvard Brandes, *Om Teater* (Copenhagen, 1947), pp. 146–147.

tell you', runs the first of these embarrassing documents, 'that I am greedy
for any recognition that I can receive from Denmark. You have no conception
of the effect this kind of thing has in Norway . . . A Danish decoration would
much strengthen my standing there . . . Seriously—the matter is important to
me.' One might have thought that the success of *The Pretenders, Brand, Peer
Gynt* and *The League of Youth*, his selection as delegate to Suez and the Swedish
Order of Vasa would have been enough. But medals were always to hold some
especial significance for Ibsen.

While he was in Copenhagen Ibsen received two letters from Suzannah in
Dresden. The first of these, undated, is worth recording if only to underline
the genuiness of the affection which bound this remarkable and difficult couple,
and which many casual acquaintances (such as Martin Schneekloth) and
envious gossips failed to appreciate:

Dear Ibsen!

We returned here on Thursday evening, and found your letter. I was
very happy, for I had been longing to hear from you.

I would have replied at once but I have had such bad pains that I have
not been able to hold a pen for four days. I am glad to learn that you are so
happy, but you must go to Norway too, my dear Ibsen! Do not put it off
for another year! It will look like indifference, and I am afraid may do you
harm. You can make it a short visit, but overcome your reluctance and
go there. Once you are there I am sure it will do you good.

We had a very nice time in Bohemia. Each day we received an excellent
Viennese newspaper which was filled with nothing but telegrams about
the war, as much about France as Germany. Here it is quite different, as
you can imagine, everything from one side, France, its Emperor, Empress
and Prince all mocked in the most common lampoons, caricatures of them
in the windows, that is what one sees here. In Bohemia everyone's sympathies were with the French. The people hate the Prussians, there was
great sorrow when the news came of France's defeat.

The woman we lived with was quite fanatical, she said she could not
sleep night or day; and she and Sigurd argued so, it was a delight to hear
them. He is all for the French, and champions his cause each day with his
fists at school, he is a real war-hero, there is no room for hesitation in this
matter, he says.

The boys told Herr Elbe that Sigurd was for the French. '*Das ist nicht gut,
mein lieber Sigurd.*' '*Aber Norwegen-Schweden hält auch mit den Franzosen,
und ich will keine Ausnahme machen*', the boy replied.

This is now your son's creed, I am myself horribly depressed by what is happening. The city is filled with wounded. Many Frenchmen. Otherwise, flags, cannon and victory celebrations. I have before me a special edition of a newspaper dealing with the victory at Metz; in a few days they will be in Paris, I cannot think of it, it hurts me so. The way is now open for the Prussians to take what they want.

Dear Ibsen, your long letter made me so happy, and I often long deeply for you, but of course it is much more important that you are where you are now.

Give my best greetings to Mother . . . After paying Herr Berger I still have 60 thalers left.

Be happy, my dear Ibsen. Warmest greetings from
Your affectionate
Suzannah Ibsen.[1]

Another letter from her tells how Sigurd had been beaten up daily for a fortnight 'because he would not declare himself pro-German'. She had complained to the headmaster, who had promised to see that the bullies were punished. 'It would look bad for his school, where over half the pupils are foreign, if such treatment were permitted; so now we have peace . . . Herr Elbe is quite mad; instead of religion he talks only politics and the wickedness of the French. The French teacher could not stick it, so they have had to engage an Italian . . . Last Saturday was a sad day for us. At eight in the morning we received telegrams announcing the fall of Napoleon. Huge crowds gathered, and there were horrible scenes, cheering and hooting. Marie and I were quite frightened to speak on the street, as all foreign tongues jar in their ears. All their flags made me quite sick. You cannot imagine what it is like to live here among such a coarse bawling mob.'[2] Dostoevsky was suffering similarly a few streets away. 'Even the German shopkeepers', he recalled a year later in his *Writer's Diary*, 'when talking to a Russian customer, invariably put in the remark: "Now that we've finished with the French, we're going to start on you." '[3]

Ibsen returned to Dresden towards the end of September. 'I had intended', he wrote to Johan Thoresen on 3 October, 'to visit Norway too, but the war made things so uncertain that I feared I might not be able to get back here, and when things were all right again the autumn was so far advanced that I decided to postpone my visit until next spring.' The excuse rings rather feebly; despite Suzannah's exhortations, he was still reluctant to see Norway again,

---

[1] Bergliot Ibsen, pp. 46–48.
[2] *Ibid.*, pp. 48–50.
[3] Magarshack, p. 419.

and four more years were to pass before he did. 'Life here just now', the letter continues, 'is anything but pleasant. The city is full of prisoners and wounded, and the atmosphere feverish and oppressive.' A week later (10 October) he informed Hegel: 'The city is filled with sick and wounded; at any hour of the day one can be sure of encountering a military funeral, or waggons filled with new patients for the hospitals. We have, besides, several thousand French prisoners; some of them walk around freely, enjoy good treatment and seem contented enough. There is no sign of enthusiasm for the war; what the papers say about this is completely untrue.[1] The country is suffering dreadfully; half-grown boys and middle-aged fathers are called to the colours and sent to France; almost every family wears mourning for someone; many have lost all their relatives; all this despite the fact that no casualty lists have been published for the past six weeks. As I say, it is horrible living here . . .'

On 28 October he wrote a long letter to Peter Hansen, his companion in Egypt, supplying information for a short biographical note which the latter was writing for a book entitled *Scandinavian Writers of the Present Century*, due to appear at Christmas. Most of the matter in this letter has already been quoted,[2] but two passages especially reflect the mood of this year of 1870. 'Everything I have written', runs the first paragraph of the autobiographical section, 'has had its origin in a mood and situation in which I found myself; I have never written anything because I had, as the saying goes, "found a good subject".' And the section concludes: 'The locality in which one writes has a great influence on the form through which the imagination works. May I not, like Christoff in [Holberg's] *Jacob von Thyboe*, point at *Brand* and *Peer Gynt* and say: "Such are the effects of wine"? And is there not in *The League of Youth* something which smacks of *knackwurst* and beer? I don't mean thereby to rate the play lower; I mean that my standpoint is different because I live here in a society well-ordered to the point of tedium. What will happen when I finally come home? I will have to seek peace in distance, and then I intend to get down to *Emperor Julian*.' The letter also contains those words on Suzannah which bear repeating: 'She is just the kind of character I need, illogical but with a strong poetical intuition, a bigness of outlook and an almost violent hatred of all things petty.'

The contemporary drama which he was planning still eluded him. On 6 November he wrote Hegel that he felt a 'strong inclination' to write an opera

---

[1] Ibsen's impression here is curiously at variance with that expressed by Suzannah in her letters to him; though, since Saxony had fought against Prussia in the Austro-Prussian War of 1866, any absence of enthusiasm would hardly have been surprising.

[2] See *Henrik Ibsen, The Making of a Dramatist*, pp. 137, 143, 192, 198, 225, 234.

libretto for the Danish composer Peter Heise, based on the saga of Sigurd
Jorsalfar. He got as far as completing a draft synopsis, from which it appears
that amongst other things it was to deal with the difference between the northern
and southern temperaments, the one dominated by a sense of duty, the other
by *livsglæde*, the joy of life. But he abandoned the idea (though coincidentally
Bjørnson wrote a play about the same character the following year).[1] In a
desultory way he began to think again about preparing a collection of his
shorter poems; the appearance in 1870 of such a collection by Bjørnson, plus
his lack of inspiration for any longer project, encouraged him to pursue the
idea to the extent of asking Jacob Løkke to get hold of and copy as many of
his poems as the latter could find in Norwegian newspapers and periodicals.
His own copies had disappeared during the auction of his goods in Christiania
and, surprisingly, he seems to have taken none to Italy.

The question of medals cropped up again that autumn of 1870, for on 23
November Ibsen addressed a supplicatory letter on the subject to a shadowy
character in Stockholm named Ohan Demirgian, an Armenian who had
brought some Berber horses as a gift from the Khedive of Egypt to Carl XV,
won that genial king's favour and landed the job of royal stable-master (but
evidently made enemies somewhere along the line, for he got sacked as soon
as the King died in 1872). The letter is couched in similar terms to the one
written to Klubien; after stating that he had learned while in Egypt that he was
to receive a decoration, Ibsen continues: 'This honour was in the highest
degree flattering to me, *as too it would be of the greatest help to my literary standing
in Norway*. It would likewise have been a consolation to me for the neglect I
have endured at home, where the Order of St Olaf has been given to several
artists, painters and musicians, while I have been passed over—and that despite
the fact that I faithfully support the government, with my pen and all my
talents . . . The [Egyptian[decoration would have been regarded in my country
as proof of the favour of my King and have been doubly precious to me.'

Of all the begging letters addressed to patrons from Grub Street (and a list
of signatories would include most of the great writers of the world up to that
date), this is one of the least appetising. A man may be forgiven for humbling
himself to obtain money, but not in order to get a medal, and a foreign one at
that. It is not easy to see how the award of an Egyptian or Turkish medal (in
the end it turned out to be Turkish, since Egypt was still part of the Ottoman

---

[1] Cf. Hans Andersen's glum letter to Edvard Brandes, 1 July 1871: 'Bjørnson is writing
a new work, *Sigurd Jorsalfar*. I hear Ibsen is writing one on exactly the same subject. I am
writing nothing, and wish I had never written anything!' (*H. C. Andersens Brevveksling
med Edvard og Henriette Collin*, p. 181.)

Empire, and the delay was due to the fact that the matter had to be referred
to Constantinople) could have been regarded in Norway as 'proof of the
favour of my King'. What is particularly nauseating is Ibsen's statement that
'I faithfully support the government', not because the supporting of governments is necessarily wrong but because it was untrue. Ibsen supported the
government no more than he did the opposition; his political position was one
of genuine independence, and one would have expected him to be proud of it.
This passion for medals and willingness to degrade himself in order to acquire
a further specimen is a trait in Ibsen's character with which it is difficult to feel
any sympathy. Still, a man's ethical shortcomings should not affect our judgment of his work. Milton's, Shelley's, Tolstoy's and Dostoevsky's treatment of
their wives was far more reprehensible than Ibsen's passion for medals. Most
of us are mean on one point of the compass.

Ibsen, however, felt no qualms about his position, and defended it eloquently
in another poem stemming from his Swedish visit, which he addressed to a
young liberal politician he had met there, Adolf Hedin. Hedin, a gifted and
imaginative statesman who should have become his country's Prime Minister,
but was kept out of office by the personal animosity of Carl XV's successor,
Oscar II, had accused Ibsen of becoming reactionary. Ibsen entitled his reply:
To My Friend Who Talks of Revolutions:

> You say I've become a conservative.
> I am what I have been all my life.
>
> I've never been one for shifting pawns.
> Blow the board to glory—*then* I'm your man!
>
> I can only recall one revolution
> That wasn't scamped half-heartedly.
>
> It makes all subsequent lettings of blood
> Seem small—I refer of course to the Flood.
>
> Though even then Satan was left the poorer;
> It was Noah who ended up as Führer.
>
> All right, let's do it again, my friends!
> But let's not scamp to achieve our ends.
>
> You unleash the waters to make your mark.
> I set a torpedo under the Ark.

The last verse summarises the attitude which Ibsen was to hold towards
reform for the rest of his life: that it was a writer's duty to aim at a bigger and

more basic explosion than politicians could dare to envisage. He believed that politicians, once they had achieved power, invariably compromised with their ideals, and that the only way to avoid doing the same was to keep oneself free from all party loyalties. Such compromise might be permissible in a politician if he were to achieve practical reforms, but for a writer it was not permissible; he must be totally independent and never sacrifice his integrity. It was an attitude which, seventy years later, George Orwell was to adopt, and which Ibsen himself was to epitomise in a phrase which is less un-Orwellian than might at first sight appear: 'The minority is always right.' At this early stage of its development he elaborated the theory in a letter dated 20 December 1870 (three months before the explosion of the Paris Commune) to Georg Brandes, then in hospital in Rome recovering from typhus: 'That glorious yearning for liberty—that is now past. I must confess that the only thing I love about liberty is the fight for it; for the possession of it, I care not . . . The old France of illusions is broken in pieces; and now, too, the new pragmatic Prussia is in pieces, so that suddenly we find ourselves at the start of a new era. How the ideas tumble about us now! And indeed it is time. All that we have been living on until now is but scraps from the table of the last century's revolution, and that gristle has been chewed and re-chewed for long enough. The ideas need to be scoured and re-interpreted. Liberty, equality and fraternity are no longer the same as they were in the days of the lamented guillotine. That is what the politicians refuse to understand, and that is why I hate them. These fellows only want individual revolutions, external revolutions, political, etc. But all that is just small change. What matters is the revolution of the spirit, and you must be one of those who march in the van.' The revolution of the spirit; the phrase epitomises what Ibsen was striving to achieve and, more perhaps than any man of his century except Karl Marx, was to achieve—and it is worth noting that Ibsen's distinction between freedoms and Freedom was one which Marx (whose first volume of *Das Kapital* had appeared in 1867, the year of *Peer Gynt*) was also to make.

Ibsen's restlessness with Bismarck's Prussia expresses itself in a letter he wrote the same day as the one to Brandes, to his old friend Consul Bravo. 'My wife and I both long deeply for our beloved Rome, and we shall probably be taking up residence there again. The only thing which makes me hesitate is whether there is any good Protestant school in Rome.' The answer was apparently no; once again, the question of Sigurd's education was to determine the residence of his parents.

That December the Christiania Theatre mooted the possibility of a stage production of *Peer Gynt*, and Ibsen wrote to Johan Thoresen, who was now managing his affairs in Norway, suggesting as terms the net takings of the first performance, with a minimum guarantee of 150 specie-dollars ($£42$).[1] But the project fell through, and *Peer Gynt* was not staged until 1876.

In 1870 Ibsen had begun to keep an account book, in which he meticulously noted (in careful copperplate) details of his income and investments. He continued to do this until his first stroke in 1900, and these two black books, now in the possession of his grandson, Mr Tancred Ibsen, provide fascinating statistics. For the year 1870 Ibsen's earnings were as follows:

	specie-dollars	$£$
Fee for *The League of Youth* at Christiania Theatre	301	84
Fee for *The League of Youth* at Royal Theatre, Copenhagen	600	168
Fee for 2nd edition of *The Pretenders*	200	56
	1,101	308

In addition to this, there was his Civil List pension of 400 specie-dollars ($£111$), and a balance of 100 specie-dollars ($£28$) which he had apparently managed to save from his Swedish travel grant. He had a balance of 282 specie-dollars ($£78$) to his credit with Hegel from previous years, and he notes that at the beginning of the year he had 74 specie-dollars ($£21$) in his *huskasse*, or domestic money-box. It is a measure of how cheaply he lived that he was able to ask his publisher to hold money for him; as he built up a small reserve, he was to invest all that he could possibly spare in the soberest and least speculative securities. He had no intention that he and his family should ever be faced with the spectre of bankruptcy as his father had been. Once, later, when Sigurd asked his father whether they could not occasionally eat a little less frugally, Ibsen replied: 'It is better to sleep well and not eat well, than to eat well and not sleep well.'[2]

---

[1] From 1870 until Ibsen's death in 1906, the exchange rate of the Norwegian crown varied between 18 and 18.80 to the $£$, i.e. a lower rate than earlier in the century. (At the time of Ibsen's birth it had stood at over 25 to the $£$.) For the purposes of conversion after 1870, I have calculated at 18 to the $£$.

[2] Information from Mr Tancred Ibsen.

SIX

❧ A Farewell to Poetry

(1871)

THE NEW YEAR brought a change of heart about the Danish medal, and on 8 January Ibsen wrote to Anton Klubien asking him to forget about it. The circumlocution of his language is evidence of his embarrassment at the importunity he had previously shown.

My dear Klubien,

There is nothing for it; I must write you while there is still time.

When I was in Copenhagen this summer, so close to my own country, it seemed to me so pre-eminently desirable to be able to return home under conditions which I regarded as essential that I expressed a wish which, could a calmer mood have prevailed, I would have left unsaid.

I now see clearly that I cannot explain this matter to you in any way which will acquit me of the charge of unpardonable vanity. Nor, consequently, will you have been able to evoke any other reaction in the people you would have had to approach.

This has troubled me since; I have felt as though I were walking unwashed on the street.

This I cannot bear; I must restore my self-respect. I therefore entreat you to forget the whole matter, and to strive your utmost to restore my standing in the eyes of those people whose respect I feel I cannot do without. All other considerations must, compared with this, be regarded as secondary.

Thank you for all the friendship and proofs thereof which you showed me in Copenhagen! And when The Pretenders *is staged, write me a long letter and tell me how it went. I have lately written a longish poem, entitled 'Balloon Letter' to a Swedish lady; it will probably be in today's* Morgenbladet. *Read it; it will tell you something about my attitude towards present-day problems.*

There! Now I feel better. Remember me once more as your old Roman carissimo *and devoted friend*

Henrik Ibsen.

Ibsen's change of heart came too late to affect the issue, however, for Klubien had talked to Fru Heiberg who had talked to the Minister of Justice who had talked to the Minister of Culture, and the machinery, as Ibsen was shortly to discover, had already been set in motion.

On 11 January the Royal Theatre in Copenhagen, encouraged by the success of *The League of Youth*, staged *The Pretenders*, and this, too, was well received. 'The audiences have not poured in to admire the brilliant acting of Mr A. or Miss B.', reported Johanne Luise Heiberg, who had directed it, to Ibsen on 25 April. 'It is the great play itself that has excited their wonder ... Not since 1807, when [Oehlenschläger's] *Earl Haakon* received its premiere, has any tragic drama gripped audiences as *The Pretenders* has done.'[1] Edvard Brandes thought she had cast it badly, with Wiehe too open and uncomplicated for Skule and Jens Nyrup a poor Haakon; but the young Emil Poulsen gave a memorable performance as Bishop Nicholas.[2] Hans Andersen went, and quite enjoyed himself, though he, like Brandes, had doubts about the production. 'There was too much music', he wrote in his diary that evening, 'so that it became almost melodramatic. It's a rambling piece, but with some splendid lines. It's the best thing I know of Ibsen's.'[3]

The *Balloon Letter to a Swedish Lady*[4] mentioned by Ibsen in his letter to Klubien was a belated expression of thanks to Fru Frederika Limnell for the hospitality she had shown him in Stockholm. Outside his plays, it is Ibsen's longest poem—four hundred and forty-four lines of rhymed octosyllabics, with an occasional septisyllabic—and one of his best. Apart from its technical accomplishment, it is of considerable psychological interest, for it crystallises (as he had found himself unable to do in prose) his impressions of the confused events of the past eighteen months—the accusations of conservatism, the Egyptian visit, the lionising in Stockholm, Egypt and Copenhagen, and the Franco-Prussian War.

The poem opens (like so many of his prose letters, but with a grace seldom apparent in them) with an apology for not having written sooner. He has entitled this a balloon letter, he explains, because

---

[1] In the same letter, she asked permission to cut the final line of the play ('Skule Baardsson was God's unwanted child on earth'), since she felt it blasphemous to suggest that God had any unwanted children. (She had made some cuts in Bjørnson's *Mary Stuart in Scotland* on similar grounds.) No reply by Ibsen has survived, but a sentence in Fru Heiberg's memoirs (*Et Liv gjenoplevet i Erindringer*, III, Copenhagen, 1892, p. 192) suggests that he acceded to her request. Cf. Herleiv Dahl, *Ibsen og Johanne Luise Heiberg*, *Ibsen-Årbok*, 1954, pp. 102–106.

[2] Edvard Brandes, *Om Teater*, p. 148.

[3] *H. C. Andersens Dagbøger og Breve, 1868–1875*, p. 79.

[4] Paris was being besieged by the Germans when Ibsen wrote this poem, in December 1870, and the Parisians were sending messages by balloon.

I have no doves. Doves are the birds of hope.
In this cramped grave but owls and ravens build,
No messengers for a lady.

He tells her of his Egyptian journey, comparing his fellow-travellers to various birds and animals:

Eleven cocks from France, four Spanish stallions . . .
A kind of ram from Switzerland . . . and, of course,
A herd of German wild pigs, almost tamed.

—which last remark was to cause great offence in Germany. After narrating how they voyaged up the Nile, Ibsen describes the still life of the desert:

Wading through endless streets where living nature
Is wedded to death, transformed by time
Into a mad architecture of stone.
Ribs, femurs, spines, poke up like shattered plinths,
And camels' skulls like fallen capitals.

What especially remained with him from his Egyptian visit, continues Ibsen—and it is typical that he should have referred so little to this in his letters, and have resorted to poetry to say what really mattered to him—was the total deadness of Egyptian religion. The gods of Greece, he writes, still live today; Zeus still moves in the Capitol. But

Where is Horus? Where is Hathor?
No trace exists, no memory.

The reason, he suggests, is easy to find, and in stating it he stated the essential difference between his plays and the nineteenth-century conception of drama against which he was rebelling—the greater urgency, as he saw it, of the individual as opposed to the idealised, that same contrast which he had remarked in Italy between Roman and Greek sculpture, between Michelangelo and Raphael:

Where personality is lacking,
Where there is neither hatred, indignation,
Nor joy, no beat of pulse nor flush of blood,
Glory is but a dry rattle of bones.
Who has not seen Juno in his mind's eye,
Pale in her wrath as she surprised her lord? . . .
But the Egyptian gods were otherwise.
Static, they never, like the gods of Greece

And men, sinned, groped, and raised themselves from sin.
And so this culture, four millenia old,
Lies like a bloodless mummy in a crypt.

A parallel, Ibsen suggests, is to be found today. Bismarck's Germany is as ossified as the Pharaohs' Egypt. Gustaf Adolf and Charles XII were poets of action, but Moltke has 'killed the poetry of war'. The poem concludes on a note of Apollonian detachment:

> Our age craves beauty.
> But that's a kingdom outside Bismarck's range.
> Shall we go to the feast, madame? Who knows when the dove
> Will descend with the invitation? We must wait.
> Meanwhile, I pace my room, kid-gloved. Till then
> I shall seek peace, tracing my words on vellum.
> This will anger the mob. They will doubtless
> Brand me a heathen. But I shrink from the mob.
> I have no wish to be clasped to their hot bosom.
> I shall await whatever time may bring
> In a well-pressed morning coat.

The *Balloon Letter* was (as Ibsen had told Klubien) printed in *Morgenbladet* on 8 January, and received praise from an unexpected quarter—Count Manderström, he of the halter, who, so Georg Sibbern, the Norwegian Minister in Stockholm, told Ibsen, was 'enchanted'. 'The old man', commented Ibsen to Hegel (16 February), 'is truly heaping coals of fire upon my head!'

Early that January Ibsen had received the copies of his lost poems which he had been awaiting from Jakob Løkke. 'They make a thick book', he informed Hegel on 8 January. 'But I am throwing out three-fourths of them and rewriting the rest.' Løkke had collected fifty-two poems—eight from the student magazine *Andhrimner*, five from *Aftenbladet*, three from *Morgenbladet* and no less than thirty-six from Botten Hansen's *Illustreret Nyhedsblad*. Ibsen set to work on them at once, as though happy to get away from the play that was tormenting him, and on 21 January he sent Hegel the first batch, promising to post 'a similar batch each week' (an undertaking which, for once, he kept). Further instalments followed on 31 January and 8 February, with requests concerning the typography. 'I earnestly beg [31 January] that the printer see carefully to it that the verses lie in the centre of the page, with no greater a margin on one side than the other; this is not always done, and the appearance suffers. And I greatly love the big French type-faces; I have never seen anything more beautiful for poetry; and, what is most important, they seem to me to match exactly the character of my poems. Printed thus they will be twice as good!' He seems to have kept no copies even of the poems (or some of them) which he had written in Rome, for he had to ask Hegel to get hold of the elegy on Abraham Lincoln 'which appeared in *Fædrelandet* in either March or April 1865', the drinking song from *Love's Comedy* 'since I don't have the book', and a dirge from *The Vikings in Helgeland* which he appears not to have had either. Has any other poet, major or minor, when preparing a collection of his own work for the press, been so dependent on friends to supply him with the material?

On 16 February he sent two more poems, which 'I supposed lost, and couldn't remember[!]; finally I found them among my travel papers.' Both were unusually personal statements (which some would say was a cause of his supposing them lost and being unable to remember them). One was a confession of the bond he still felt with Norway. He called it *Burned Ships*:

> He turned his ship's
> Prow from the north,
> Seeking the trail
> Of brighter gods.
>
> The snow-land's beacons
> Quenched in the sea.
> The fauns of the sea-shore
> Stilled his longing.
>
> He burned his ships.
> Blue smoke drifted
> Like a bridge's span
> Towards the north.
>
> To those snow-capped huts
> From the hills of the south
> There rides a rider
> Every night.

He placed this poem last in the book, as though to remind his compatriots that, whatever thunderbolts he might send from the south, his roots remained fast in the country which had rejected him. The other new poem, for Suzannah, he entitled simply *Thanks*:

> Her grief was the sorrows
> That cobbled my path.
> Her joy the spirits
> That lifted me o'er them.

Her home lies here
On Freedom's sea
Where the poet's ship
Finds its mirror.

Her children are
The shifting figures
Who glide, waving
Flags in my song.

Her goal is to fan
My vision's embers
So that none knows
Whence the fire cometh.

And because she asks
And expects no thanks,
I give her now
Thanks in a song.

The task of revising his earlier poems proved much more arduous than Ibsen had imagined. Never the man to skimp a job, he went through every poem he had decided to include, cutting away anything that now struck him as conventionally poetic or self-indulgent, making the language more natural and less redolent of Wergeland and Welhaven, his two earliest influences, and sometimes deleting whole sections of a poem which one is rather sorry to lose. The twenty-three sonnets which comprise *In the Picture Gallery*, for example, he omitted altogether, though he used five of them as the bases for new poems.[1] Among these was the Hardyesque *In the Gallery*, the mood and language of which were near-perfectly caught by a Victorian translator, F. E. Garrett:

With palette laden,
She sat, as I passed her,
A dainty maiden
Before an Old Master.

What mountain-top is
She bent upon? Ah,
She neatly copies
Murillo's *Madonna*.

---

[1] *The Ravine, A Swan, Fear of the Light, In the Gallery* and *My Young Vine* are, as Didrik Arup Seip has pointed out (*CE*, XIV, p. 491) based on sonnets 2, 3, 14, 17 and 21 of the earlier sequence.

But rapt and brimming
The eyes' full chalice says
The heart builds dreaming
Its fairy palaces.

The eighteenth year rolled
By, ere returning,
I greeted the dear old
Scenes with yearning.

With palette laden
She sat as I passed her,
A faded maiden
Before an Old Master.

But what is she doing?
The same thing still—lo,
Hotly pursuing
That very Murillo!

Her wrist never falters;
It keeps her, that poor wrist,
With panels for altars
And daubs for the tourist.

And so she has painted
Through years unbrightened,
Till hopes have fainted
And hair has whitened.

But rapt and brimming
The eyes' full chalice says
The heart builds dreaming
Its fairy palaces.

On 13 February Ibsen received 'an exceedingly beautiful document' announcing that he had been made a Knight of Dannebrog. The chain of action started by that word to Klubien in Copenhagen had had its effect, and his qualms seem to have vanished. 'Now', he assured Hegel on 16 February, 'my compatriots will think my poems twice as good as they would otherwise have done!'

'Since Christmas', he wrote the next day to Georg Brandes, who was still in his Roman hospital, 'I have been occupied practically day and night preparing this collection. It has been a damnable job to relive all those attitudes which I long since left behind. But together they form a kind of whole.' He returned to the obsessive question of freedom and its true meaning. 'I shall never agree to identify Freedom with political freedom. What you call Freedom I call freedoms, and what I call the battle for Freedom is nothing but the continuous pursuit of the idea of Freedom. He who possesses Freedom otherwise than as something to be striven for possesses something dead and meaningless, for by its very definition Freedom perpetually expands as one seeks to embrace it, so that if, during the quest, anyone stops and says: "Now I have it!" he shows thereby that he has lost it.' Ibsen found Brandes's suggestions for political reform inadequate, as he had found Adolf Hedin's, and was now (he, the most ordered of men!) suggesting that the only solution was anarchy. 'The state must be abolished!' he concluded in the same letter. '*There's* a revolution to which I will gladly lend my shoulder. Abolish the conception of the state, establish the principle of free will and all that is spiritually akin to it as the one pre-requisite for a universal brotherhood—*there* is the beginning of a Freedom that is worth something!'

This was a bit much even for Brandes. 'His radicalism really exceeds all conceivable bounds', he wrote to a friend on 22 February. 'My head grows dizzy with reading of all he wishes to revolutionise. I am afraid that had he power commensurate to his genius, or had he lived in another era, he would have been regarded as a greater radical than Marat in one field, Proudhon in another. Not only does he reject the established concepts of religion and morality, he even rejects the concept of the state.'[1] Ibsen's ideas as expressed in this letter are so close to those of Proudhon, who had died only six years earlier ('Government of man by man in every form is oppression', Proudhon had written. 'The highest perfection of society is found in the union of order and anarchy') that one wonders whether Ibsen may not have been reading him, or anyway had Suzannah read him and pass on the gist; but such ideas were, like those of Kierkegaard, so much a part of everyday conversation among thinking people then that he would have been a dull and out-of-touch fellow who had not absorbed something of them.

In that same letter of 14 February to Brandes, Ibsen cited the Jews as an example of the advantages of abolishing the State. 'How is it they have kept their place apart, their political halo, amid surroundings of coarse cruelty?' he asked. 'By having no State to burden them. Had they remained in Palestine, they would long ago have lost their individuality in the process of the State's construction, like other nations.'[2] He referred to the Jews as 'the aristocracy of

---

[1] Fenger, *Ibsen og Georg Brandes indtil 1872*, p. 189.

[2] I quote Archer's incomparable translation of this difficult passage, printed on p. 59 of the English edition of Brandes's *Henrik Ibsen* (London, 1899).

the human race'. This need for an aristocracy, not of birth but spiritual, was something that Ibsen was increasingly to stress, notably in *An Enemy of the People*, and it made him many enemies among Scandinavian liberals. Even today (as this writer knows from experience) Dr Stockmann's demand for this kind of aristocracy upsets many a liberally-inclined director and actor working on the play.

On 25 February Ibsen sent the (as he thought) last pages of his poems to Hegel, but as late as Easter week he composed a long and, again, technically intricate piece, *Rhymed Letter to Fru Heiberg*, which Georg Brandes, a quarter of a century later[1] was to describe as Ibsen's most artistically accomplished poem. In this exquisite work, two hundred and eighty-two lines of astonishing variety, Ibsen stated his attitude towards the rival media of verse and prose in a sentence that anticipated his imminent abandonment of the former for the latter. 'Prose is for ideas, verse for visions. The joys and sorrows of the soul, grief that snows upon my head, indignation's lightning-bolt—these I endow most fully with life, and express most freely, in the bonds of verse.' The renunciation of this medium, in which he moved so easily, was to be a continuation of the austere process which he had begun with the astringent revision of his poems.

The *Letter to Fru Heiberg* ends with an expression of faith, unfashionable for the period, that things created in the theatre may perhaps last longer than works which never leave the printed page. Ibsen intended this as a compliment to the great actress now living in retirement, but it plainly expresses a conviction which he himself possessed, and which is a little surprising when we remember that his two triumphs, *Brand* and *Peer Gynt*, were still both commonly regarded as unstageable. 'Some say', runs the poem, 'that the art of the theatre, born for and bound to the moment, must, like a soap-bubble or nocturnal meteor, dazzle, then burst to leave no trace. Free yourself from this dark thought! The very fact that your art is a child of fragrance, of the spirit, of a mood, of personality and imagination, and not something of wood or stone, or even a thought fixed fast in black on white, but a sprite for ever swinging free on beauty's vine, the fact that it lacks tangible form, renders it immune to the gnawing of time's worm. And [he concludes] that is what life truly means: to live in memory, to rest in people's mind free of the mildew and rust of age ... and this lot has been granted you.'

Ibsen's *Poems* were published on 3 May 1871. The edition was a large one, 4,000 copies (the equivalent, counting Norway and Denmark as one, of something approaching 50,000 in modern Britain). The reviews were generally

---

[1] *Henrik Ibsen: festskrift i anledning af hans 70de Fødselsdag*, p. 25.

K

most favourable. An anonymous critic in *Bergens Tidende* complained that 'he seems to look down at everything from a poetic iceberg', but found in the *Balloon Letter* 'hope that Ibsen, in addition to his latest brilliant but ugly works, will also give us something brilliant and beautiful'. The Danish poet Otto Borchsenius, writing in *Bergens-posten*, praised Ibsen for omitting his early poems, wished he had omitted some others (including, surprisingly, the *Elegy to J. L. Heiberg*), regretted the absence of the Priest's sermon in *Peer Gynt*, and feared that the lines about the 'well-pressed morning coat' (in the *Balloon Letter*) might imply an intent to withdraw from the battle. He hoped Ibsen might 'gradually mellow this half-ironical, half-melancholy view of life, people and their actions', but admitted that 'the age needs a disciplinarian, and we should be sorry to see Herr Ibsen withdraw from the battle as long as he can still wield his sword'.

Rudolf Schmidt, in *Fædrelandet*, compared the volume with Bjørnson's recent collection; he found Bjørnson's poems 'certainly the richer and weightier', and complained that 'Behind all doubt there must lie a conviction which must be equally strong, so that doubt strikes out in scorn and indignation. But sometimes with Henrik Ibsen this expresses itself rather as hesitation, as though doubt had struck inwards and quenched the spark of inner wisdom.' Bjørnson himself, predictably, disliked the book. 'I have now read Ibsen's poems', he wrote to his wife Karoline on 14 May. 'Except for the old ones and one to his wife and a few others, and apart from an almost too virtuoso style in some, such as the one to Fru Heiberg, I find nothing noteworthy about the collection. As with almost everything by Ibsen I am left so empty afterwards. His standing *vis-à-vis* his country is becoming almost comic, and his poem to the King, praising him for not daring to do anything in 1864, seems to me criminal.'[1]

The man about whose opinion Ibsen was most anxious had mixed reactions. 'I was so uncontrollably delighted with Ibsen's book when it arrived', wrote Georg Brandes to Frederik Hegel, 'that the reading of the poems put me in a most violent state of nervous emotion. It went through me like a storm through an Aeolian harp . . . But later my critical sense asserted itself, and my judgment on these poems is that only a few of them are good, and those the ones already known. Most of them are *obscure* to the point of incomprehensibility, many are clumsy, and the humour is nearly always unsuccessful. It's nearly all doggerel. But there are things in the book which carry me away, and despite everything I *was* greatly carried away.'[2] Writing to his family a

---

[1] *Breve til Karoline, 1858–1907*, p. 174.
[2] Fenger, *Ibsen og Georg Brandes indtil 1872*, p. 190.

month later, he declared: 'I was tremendously moved by *Terje Vigen*. It is a true masterpiece, a real classic . . . The only pity is that there is so much rubbish in the book'[1]—a not altogether unfair comment, for a number of the poems fall far below Ibsen's best standard. He was much more uneven as a poet than as a dramatist. Brandes did not review the book until the autumn, by which time he had met Ibsen, and his review was to reflect that meeting.

That first fortnight in May was a good one for Ibsen, for on 9 May, six days after the publication of his *Poems*, he at last received his longed-for Medjidje Order, 'a handsome object', he informed Hegel the same day, 'together with a large and unintelligible diploma from the Grand Turk himself'. With unusual (on this subject) candour he admitted that the main reason for his getting the decoration was that 'we brought a lot of Swedish and Norwegian decorations for Egyptian bigwigs, and this courtesy was merely being reciprocated'.

Down in Rome, Georg Brandes had at last left hospital after five months, his attack of typhus having been followed by a clot of blood in the leg. Brandes's sense of kinship[2] with Ibsen had been deepened by their correspondence; from his sickbed earlier in the year he had written a poem entitled *To Henrik Ibsen*, describing his lonely struggle and his longing for a comrade in arms:

> Brother! I found thee. What care I
> That thou art a matchless chieftain, I
> But an armourer? Our souls are kin.
> We shall sound a spiritual call to arms.[3]

Ibsen reciprocated the younger man's feeling; and so, as Brandes's biographer has put it, 'these two lonely men joined hands'.[4] None, alas, of Brandes's letters to Ibsen has survived, but Ibsen's side of the correspondence is proof of the warmth which already existed between them:

Dresden, 18 May 1871

My dear Brandes!

. . . Well, I never really believed you were in danger; one doesn't die in the first

---

[1] *Ibid.*, p. 190.

[2] The previous autumn Brandes had told a friend that he felt 'spiritually akin' to Ibsen, though he regarded himself as 'incomparably less gifted'. Ibsen, he declared, 'has quite overwhelmed me with his sympathy. Does not this arise from a kind of kinship?' (Letter to Emil Petersen, 15 October 1870, quoted by Fenger, *Ibsen og Georg Brandes indtil 1872*, p. 187.)

[3] Brandes wrote the poem on the night of 9–10 January 1871, but felt diffident about sending it to Ibsen and did not post it until 11 February.

[4] Henning Fenger, *Georg Brandes Laereår* (Copenhagen, 1955), p. 341.

act;[1] *the great world* dramaturge *needs you for a leading role in his* Haupt- und Staatsaction,[2] *which He is now doubtless preparing for our respected public.*

Warmest thanks for your portrait! . . . I always like to have a physical likeness to hang my conception on. I shan't rest till I have met you, when I think we shall prove to have more in common than a liking for velvet jackets.

During this somewhat long interval I have managed to persuade myself not to write to you. I sensed from your last letter that you were a little angry with me, and since my poems were about to be published I didn't want to do anything which might look like an attempt to conciliate you before you should read them. I know you would not let this affect your judgment, but a kind of diffidence bade me avoid even the appearance of having supposed any such thing. My dear friend, you will understand what I mean.

I trust you will long since have received the book from Hegel. It contains both old and new material, and much that I no longer set much store by; but it all belongs to the story of my development. So tell me what you think of it; I attach the greatest importance to your judgment.

And what are you up to now, down there in beautiful, warm Italy? Your illness will perhaps have had one good result, I mean, that you may have to spend a summer there. I think of you daily; sometimes I see you in Frascati, sometimes Albano or Ariccia. Which is right? And what new work are you preparing down there for our spiritual enlightenment? I am sure something must have matured during your long sickness. One of the blessings of being ill is that it gives a kind of purity and stature to so much which otherwise would not blossom. I have only once been really ill; but that may be another way of saying that I have never, perhaps, been totally well. Chi lo sa!

Is it not wretched of the Paris Commune to have gone and spoiled my excellent theory of the State—or rather, of the No-State? Now the idea is ruined for ages; I cannot even decently write a poem about it. But the idea is sound, of that I am sure, and some time it will be achieved without caricature.

I have often thought about what you once wrote, that I had not taken up the standpoint of modern scientific knowledge. How could I overcome this failing? But is not each generation born with the prejudices of its time? Have you never noticed in a painting of a group from some previous century a curious kind of family likeness between people of the same period? So it is in the field of intellect too. What we profane creatures lack in knowledge I think we possess, to a certain degree, in intuition or

---

[1] A reference to the Strange Passenger's cold comfort to Peer Gynt: 'One doesn't die in the middle of the fifth act.'

[2] 'A type of entertainment popular in Germany in the seventeenth and eighteenth centuries, consisting of a chronicle play, improvised farce and spectacular effects. The chronicle play presented the extravagant and absurd adventures of an emperor or general over a period of many years.' (Evert Sprinchorn, *Ibsen's Letters and Speeches*, New York, 1964, p. 111.)

instinct. And a writer's task is essentially to see, not to mirror; I am conscious of a particular danger to myself in indulging the latter tendency.

Dear Brandes—it is always a relief for me to talk to you, and a great, great joy to hear you talk, if only on paper. So give me that pleasure again soon.

Your affectionate

Henrik Ibsen

Brandes was overwhelmed. 'I received an extremely charming and flattering letter from Henrik Ibsen', he informed his family on 26 May, 'almost too flattering for me to believe that he was being completely honest.'[1] Visiting Walter Runeberg's studio in Rome he was interested to see the latter's 'remarkable bust of Ibsen, fiery yet overcast'.[2]

Meanwhile, Ibsen had at last broken the creative block that had been tormenting him. 'I have now begun my big play, *Emperor Julian*', he wrote to Johan Thoresen on 26 June, 'and hope to have it ready by Christmas ... I work blazingly fast, but only for a few hours[!] each day.' On 12 July he told Frederik Hegel: 'I am well into *Emperor Julian*. This book will be my masterpiece, and occupies all my thoughts and all my time. That positive view of things which the critics have so long demanded of me they will find here.'

At last, on 14 July 1871, Ibsen and Brandes met. Brandes had arranged his homeward journey to Copenhagen so as to pass through Dresden, and had arrived there the previous night. His autobiography contains a vivid account of his first sight of Ibsen: 'As I approached the house, which lay in an avenue, Dippoldiswaldaer-strasse, I saw him, easily recognisable from his portrait, leaning out of the window in his shirtsleeves. But when I entered he had put on a velvet jacket. He hugged me to his breast, almost suffocating me. I found him handsome (*smuk*), with an incomparable forehead, clear eyes, long curled hair. I was surprised how handsome I found him.'

They talked for two or three hours, 'partly of his work, partly of conditions at home, much of me'. Ibsen was wearing an order ribbon in his buttonhole, which slightly disturbed Brandes.[3] Later that day Brandes returned, and Ibsen took him to the Waldschlösslein 'where we ate and drank beer ... Ibsen told me how Bjørnson had tried to persuade him to avoid all contact with me, and promised to show me letters the following day. He told me how they had

---

[1] Fenger, *Ibsen og Georg Brandes indtil 1872*, p. 190.

[2] *Brandes Brevveksling*, IV, p. xxxi.

[3] 'I often regret that I so thoughtlessly repeated to you the impression I got last year from that trifle in his buttonhole. Ibsen no longer wears his decoration at home. But I have only now, for the first time, really got to know him.' (Letter from Brandes to Hans Brøchner, 29 September 1872, *Brandes Brevveksling*, I, p. 172.)

demanded, in the most shameless manner, that he should become co-editor of [the literary magazine] *Idea and Reality*, demanded it of him as his *duty* . . . He had replied that he felt no inclination to occupy a seat that was still warm from Clemens Petersen.' They discussed Danish writers. Brandes asked Ibsen if there was anyone he cared about. 'After letting me guess for some while in vain, he answered: "Once upon a time, somewhere in Zealand, there walked behind his plough an old man in a smock-frock, who had looked upon men and things until he was wroth at heart. That is a man I like." ' They agreed in their admiration of Heiberg and shared a feeling that Scandinavia was sadly backwards in its cultural development. 'Ibsen was full of plans and hopes, and overflowing with the spirit of battle. "You needle the Danes, I'll needle the Norwegians!" were the last words he smilingly addressed to me.'[1]

Brandes, no doubt, told Ibsen of the exciting actors and actresses he had seen in Paris the previous summer—Ristori as Lady Macbeth, Mounet-Sully as Hernani, Coquelin in Ponsard's *Gringoire*, the young Sarah Bernhardt in Georges Sand's *L'Autre*; no doubt, too, they argued about John Stuart Mill, whom Brandes so revered and whom Ibsen found tedious. Ibsen left no record of their meeting, but a vivid impression of how Brandes looked and behaved at around this time survives from a young Englishman who made his acquaintance three years later, Edmund Gosse. Gosse found Brandes 'a tall, thin young man . . . gentle and even mild in appearance, pale, with a great thatch of hair arched over a wide forehead . . . I never met anyone more impatient than Brandes, and this probably had something to do with the atmosphere of anger and suspicion which he had created around him in Copenhagen. He not merely did not hear fools gladly, but he was easily driven to distraction, and to the visible stamping of feet, by those who were not, even in his own measure, fools, but merely less arrowy in their mental movements than himself. Thus I immediately fell under his ban because I spoke Danish so slowly . . . Brandes went pacing, infuriated, between the sofa and the door, and snapped his long tapering fingers.'[2]

Gosse's account of the distrust with which Brandes was regarded by his fellow-countrymen helps us to understand why he and Ibsen, two difficult men whose views on literature and other matters often differed so widely, were drawn to each other. Brandes was, writes Gosse, 'the only man in Denmark

---

[1] For the information contained in this and the preceding paragraph, cf. Brandes's *Levned*, II, pp. 55 ff.; Henning Fenger's *Ibsen og Georg Brandes indtil 1872*, pp. 191–193; and Brandes's *Henrik Ibsen* (Copenhagen, 1898), p. 90 (Muir-Archer translation). The poet-ploughman was Christian Hviid Bredahl (1784–1860).

[2] Edmund Gosse, *Two Visits to Denmark*, 1872, 1874, pp. 167–168.

who represented the spirit of modern Europe in *belles-lettres*', and the Danes were angered by his cultivation of friendships with German authors such as Paul Heyse—hostility towards Germany still being fierce in Denmark—and his attempts to impose their writings on Danish readers.

'It was difficult to account for the repulsion and even terror of Georg Brandes which I heard expressed around me whenever his name came up in the course of general conversation . . . Brandes was a Jew,[1] an illuminated specimen of a race little known at that time in Scandinavia, and much dreaded and suspected. That a scion of this hated people, so long excluded from citizenship, should come forward with a loud message of defiance to the exquisite and effete civilisation of Denmark, this was in itself an outrage. . . The tone of Copenhagen was graceful, romantic, orthodox; there was a wide appreciation of literary speculation of a certain kind, kept within the bounds of good taste, reverently attached to the tradition of their elders. This, too, was markedly national. It was part of the political isolation of Denmark, of the pride which her two European wars had fostered, to be intellectually self-sufficient. It was orthodox to believe that the poetry and philosophy and science of the national writers was all that Danes needed to know of a modern kind. Here, then, was an angry Jew, with something of the swashbuckler about him, shouting that mental salvation was impossible without a knowledge of "foreign devils" like Taine and John Stuart Mill and Schopenhauer . . . There was something exasperating, too, in the lofty tone which Brandes adopted. He did not spare the susceptibilities of his countrymen . . . "How these Christians hate me!" he could not help saying. He belonged to the race of iconoclasts, like Heine before him, like Nietzsche after him, and he was expected to disturb all the convictions of his contemporaries. In religion a deist, in politics a republican, in ethics an extreme individualist, Brandes seemed at that time prepared to upset every part of the settled and convenient order of things.'[2]

In other words, Brandes was, as a critic, doing for Denmark what Ibsen, as a creative writer, was doing for Norway, and what August Strindberg, now a twenty-two year old student at Upsala, was shortly to do for Sweden: in Ibsen's own phrase, to 'wake the people and make them think big'.

The meeting with Ibsen had given Brandes the stimulation he had been hoping for, and the next months were for him a time of violent fermentation, as his diaries for August and September show. On 20 September he noted: 'Towards 2 a.m. I wrote a long, violent and ardent letter to Ibsen. Surely this

---

[1] His father had been born Cohen, but the family name was changed to Brandes when Georg's grandmother re-married with a man of that name.

[2] Gosse, *Two Visits to Denmark, 1872, 1874*, pp. 156–157, 164–166, 288.

will inflame him? Thought him worth more.' Doubtless he compared Ibsen
with John Stuart Mill, whom he was to describe in his autobiography as 'the
incarnation of the ideal I had drawn for myself of the great man . . . His boldness was not of the merely theoretic kind; he wished to interfere and re-
model.'[1] Ibsen was in fact to interfere and re-model contemporary thought at
least as much as Mill; what must have disappointed Brandes was Ibsen's lack of
inflexibility, and his willingness (like Schopenhauer) to compromise in his
private life. Brandes's letter to Ibsen of 20 September has disappeared, but we
have Ibsen's answer, from which it is evident that Brandes had tried to persuade
him to play a less detached and more active and committed role:

Dear Brandes!   *Dresden, 24 September 1871*

   *It is always with curiously mixed emotions that I read your letters. They are more
poems than letters; they come to me like a cry for help from a solitary survivor in some
immense and lifeless desert. I cannot but rejoice and thank you for addressing this cry
to me. Yet it worries me, for I ask myself: 'To what will such a mood lead?' I can only
comfort myself with the hope that it is merely transitional. It seems to me that you now
find yourself in the same crisis that I was in when I wrote* Brand, *and I am sure you
too will find the medicine to drive the sickness from your body. Energetic creation is an
excellent remedy. Above all, I would wish you a full-blooded egotism, to persuade you
for a while to rate yourself and your thoughts as the only things that have any value
or significance, and everything else as non-existent. Do not regard this as a sign of
brutality in me! You cannot serve your community better than by minting this metal
which lies within you. I have never really had any strong liking for solidarity; I have
always regarded it as just another traditional dogma—and if one had the courage completely to disregard it one might perhaps be rid of the ballast which weighs heaviest on a
man's individuality. There are times when the whole history of the world seems to me
but a mighty shipwreck, and the only sane course to save oneself. I hope for nothing
from isolated reforms. The whole human race is on the wrong track; that is the situation. Is there really any hope in the present state of affairs, with these unattainable ideals,
etc.? Human history seems to me like a young man who has left his work-bench and
gone to the theatre. We have made a fiasco of everything, both as lovers and as heroes;
the only role for which we have shown a faint talent has been that of the fool; and with
our increasing sophistication we shall no longer be able to play that. Nor do I think
things are better arranged in other countries; the masses, whether at home or abroad,
have no understanding of higher things.*

   And so I am to try to raise a banner? Alas, my dear friend, that would be like Louis

---

[1] *Recollections of My Childhood and Youth* (London, 1906), pp. 270–271. The excellent
and vigorous translation is anonymous.

Napoleon's arrival at Boulogne with an eagle on his head. When his hour of destiny eventually struck, he needed no eagle. Working on Julian has made me something of a fatalist; but this play will be a kind of banner. Don't fear, however, that this will be a tendentious work; I explore the characters, their conflicting plans, their story, and do not try to seek a moral—always remembering that one must not confuse the moral of a story with its philosophy; for it is inevitable that a philosophy must emerge as the final judgment on the conflict and the victory. But all this can be illustrated only in practice . . .

I have received your book [Criticisms and Portraits]. *I can only say that it is something to which I return again and again. Yes, my dear, splendid Brandes, I cannot understand how* you *can be despondent. You have received a spiritual summons as clearly and unmistakably as is granted to few people. So why this gloom? Have you a right to feel thus? Though don't imagine that I don't fully understand you . . .*

Finally, hearty thanks for the visit you paid me in Dresden; those were festive hours for me. Good luck, courage, good health and good everything!

Your affectionate

Henrik Ibsen

We have no record of Brandes's reaction to this letter, but his diaries of the period show how continuously Ibsen was in his thoughts. On 21 September, presumably just after he had sent his letter, Brandes noted: 'If only Ibsen would write me a powerfully *poetic* reply! Were he a ready and fertile writer he could hardly not do so.' And the next day: 'Is it I who am to raise the battle cry, is it really I who am the sole chieftain of the young? I feel like Moses and Jonah when the Lord chose them and they prayed for strength . . . Ought I to hold a lecture in the Students' Union to sound a trumpet call for the young? I think I *must*, I think it my duty.' On 30 September: 'Still no letter from H. Ibsen. I am hurt and indignant.' The same day he began to write a review of Ibsen's volume of poems, and a day or two later he received Ibsen's reply of 24 September which must have struck him as disappointingly evasive, and which inspired him to the deeply personal statement which that review, published in *Illustreret Tidende* on 22 October, represents—a wonderfully mature assessment which repays quoting *in extenso*. After apologising for writing about the volume so long after its appearance, Brandes continues:

'The book is in no way very rich, and does not contain many poems that broaden the soul . . . but . . . it brings us a message from a spirit who has the rare characteristic of being a warrior, in the fields of both artistic and human endeavour . . . Despite its faults, it is so passionate that it contains passion, and one likes to write about something by which one has been powerfully moved.' Ibsen's poetry is 'the poetry of loneliness, portraying the lonely need, the lonely strife and the lonely protest'; as examples, Brandes names *The Miner*, *The*

Murder of Lincoln and *On the Heights*. 'It is out of isolation that Ibsen writes. It is
irrelevant that he isolated himself partly out of discontent at not being able to
carry the public with him. It was loneliness that first drove Ibsen to become a
poet, and this collection of poems mirrors in microcosm the whole development of Ibsen's life, beginning as it does with a series of works of no marked
individuality.' There are those who attain to self-knowledge and originality
almost at their first contact with the world, with its society and personalities
so different to their own. 'But others, the lonely ones, achieve this only by the
gradual rejection of bonds and scruples, as being ever more weighty and useless
ballast. I remember I once heard a man of this ilk say: "It is good to be without
friends. Friends are an expensive luxury, and when one invests one's capital in
a mission, a calling in this life, one cannot afford to keep friends" . . . Ibsen is
like this man; he became himself by becoming a solitary.'

One of the tasks of poets, continues Brandes, is to give the lead in ideas to the
young—not that the young do not know what their password must be,
'but they wish to hear it uttered, for the first time, by inspired lips. If the poet
does not, at the right moment, give the answer that is awaited from him, it
forms itself without his help in the mouths of the young, and then it is the poet
himself who is challenged and asked if he knows the password; if he does not,
the young will strike him down and proceed. But where scatttered yearnings
do not work towards a single goal and seek a central point, no rallying-cry can
be expected, and then the poet withdraws into himself. Ibsen's character fits
such a situation and draws strength from it. His strength depends on the night-
stillness around him, on the calm darkness in which alone he can freely breathe.
Not the twelve fair hours of the day but the dark hours of the night stand god-
parents to his poetry. Alone, he divides more than he unites. He shows each
man the way back to the powers which he may discover within himself when,
without fear or scruple, he follows his own nature and his own star. But a
star shines only in the night. It is useless to ask Ibsen to raise a banner. He
writes only for himself and for those who are created like him; to them he
offers not a banner but an example . . . He, the enemy of apathy and sloth, is
alarmed and indignant at seeing his people sit out the sword-dance, retreat, like
Peer Gynt, turn their backs on the opportunity to be tested, and his mood has
called forth a string of his most notable works.' As examples, Brandes cites
Brand and *Peer Gynt*, *The Murder of Lincoln* and *A Brother in Need*, even the poem
to Carl XV which Bjørnson had mocked, *To One Unnamed*. 'In such protests
the poet's genius stands forth in its full strength, the axe glints, the torch
glitters in his hand. The axe and the torch! These are his emblems. One recalls
those words of Hippocrates which Schiller set on the title page of *The Robbers*:
"What medicine cannot cure, the iron will heal; what the iron cannot heal,

will be cured by fire." Can this lonely and passionate spirit seriously be regarded as one who delights in annihilation and renunciation?'

Wise readers, explains Brandes, find this kind of destroyer easy to understand, and such an instinct, Ibsen's character being what it is, natural. He quotes the anecdote from Lamartine's *Jocelyn* about the travellers who, desiring to cross a river in flood, laid their axes to the trees under which they had just rested, to the amazement and consternation of the birds and beasts of the forest; but by destroying these trees they were able to build a bridge, cross the river and continue their journey. 'Thus the human spirit fells what had once sheltered it, and thus it progresses over the corpses of what it has destroyed.'

As regards Ibsen's supposed lack of faith, Brandes asserts that: 'Faith consists in believing in truth though untruth reign and lies triumph and drug men's minds. In believing in justice though injustice inflict one defeat after another, in believing in the future despite the present.' There are, he concludes, two kinds of unbelievers. On the one hand, there are those who regard themselves as believers, but whose ideals lie 'not before them, but behind them, like some physical, tangible object of the past . . . While mankind strives forward, these men, calling themselves philanthropists, liberals, men of the future, cling on with all their might to protect what has fallen, shore up what is crumbling, curse the presumption of those who demolish and deny, lend all their strength to reaction. In contrast to these, those whose highest ideals lie not behind them but ahead of them, in the future which they are preparing, build bridges over the abyss from the trees which they have felled and, in the darkest night, believe, with all the passion with which they have demolished and denied, in the dawn and the sunrise.'

The poet of loneliness, of iron and fire, the divider not the uniter, the believer in truth and justice who 'shows each man the way back to the powers he may discover within himself'—has any critic in the century since Brandes penned these words more penetratingly epitomised what Ibsen stood for, even though the judgment was delivered before Ibsen had written most of the work on which his fame rests? No wonder that, however fallible Brandes's judgment may have been concerning individual plays, not only Ibsen, but Strindberg also, regarded him as the one contemporary critic whose opinion they could respect.

That autumn, Ibsen got involved in a public row with H. J. Jensen, formerly the publisher of *Illustreret Nyhedsblad*, who claimed the right, since *Lady Inger of Østraat* and *The Vikings at Helgeland* had first appeared in his periodical, to reprint the two plays in book form. Ibsen protested; Jensen defended his claim in the newspapers; Ibsen's friends, Ludvig Daae and O. A. Bachke, entered the controversy on Ibsen's side, and Ibsen himself published two open letters on the subject in the Danish newspaper *Dagbladet*. Jensen, undeterred, brought out his pirate edition of *The Vikings*, whereupon Ibsen sued him. When the case finally reached the courts, four years later after Dickensian delays, Jensen was fined and ordered to pay compensation, and the edition was confiscated. Ibsen's letters of September and October 1871 are scattered with neurotic references to the matter. On 28 October, writing to Michael Birkeland, he hysterically blamed Norway in general for the publisher's action, declaring: 'This business will leave its scar on me if I should live to be a hundred . . . From now on I must regard myself as completely homeless. I know that certain of my friends would not mind this—I know some people think I can do my bulldog act in their interests better abroad than at home, and that therefore they do not want me home. Now they have achieved their wishes.' The same day he wrote to Bachke: 'The law protects the salmon in our rivers and the deer on the mountains, but authors seem to be classed with birds of prey: they do their best to smoke us out.'

Simultaneously, he had become embroiled in an equally tedious controversy in the German press as a result of his uncomplimentary references to Germans in his Balloon poem. 'The newspaper *Im neuen Reich*', he informed Hegel on 27 December, 'which is published in Leipzig under the editorship of Alfred Dove and Gustav Freytag, has attacked me for some of the things I have said in verse about the Germans. The battle has also been taken up in the *Constitutionelle Zeitung*, and several other papers of less import. I have of course been compelled to reply.' Fortunately, these petty distractions did not hinder his work on *Emperor and Galilean*. 'My new play', he told Hegel in the same letter, 'goes forward unceasingly. Part One, "Julian and the Friends of Wisdom", comprising three acts, is already finished and *fair-copied* . . . I am now busily engaged on Part Two, and this will go more quickly and be much shorter. Part Three will, though, be somewhat longer; the whole thing will probably run to between 280–300 pages, all in prose, in a style mainly approximating to that of *The Pretenders*.' Camilla Collett, the novelist champion of women's rights, was now in Dresden.[1] 'She is thinking of proceeding to Rome', Ibsen

---

[1] Edmund Gosse, who met her in Copenhagen three years later, got on less well with her than Ibsen did. 'This lady, whom I found singularly unpleasing, had an air of affectation based, apparently, on her familiarity with Hamburg and Rome, but still more with Paris, where she seemed to have made a lengthy residence. She detested England and the English, and she stirred up Andreas Munch to satirical outbursts against us . . . "You belong, sir, to a nation of shopkeepers", Camilla Collett remarked to me across the dinner table. The hackneyed impertinence was applauded by the host.' (*Two Visits to Denmark*, p. 315.) But Gosse was always less happy with women than with men.

told Hegel, 'but I doubt if she will get any further, for she has no idea how to arrange a journey.' She was hopelessly unpractical, and kept her gold coins in a matchbox. They met much and indulged in many lively debates; she was scandalised at what she regarded as the old-fashionedness of his ideas about woman's place in society. Her forthrightly expressed views on the subject were to have a considerable influence on him.

1871 had been another thin year financially, even worse than 1870. *Poems* had earned him 562 specie-dollars (£156); a sixth edition of *Brand* had brought a welcome 212 specie-dollars (£59); and *Morgenbladet* had paid him 25 specie-dollars (£7) for the *Balloon Letter*—a total of 799 specie-dollars, or £222. His only other source of income had been his pension of 400 specie-dollars (£111). But this was enough for his very modest requirements. 'Everything has become dreadfully expensive here in Germany since the recent war', he wrote to Consul Bravo on 16 February 1872. 'Luckily my income has risen proportionally, so that we can live without worry; new editions of my books are appearing regularly[!] and I am always busy with something new.' He was miserly with his money, but not for selfish reasons. 'The little capital which I have succeeded in amassing during these years', he told Johan Thoresen on 22 February, 'must be further increased, if Suzannah and Sigurd are to be reasonably secured against all eventualities. This consideration precedes all others, as far as I am concerned. Nor can I be certain that my literary talents may not decline with time; I cannot rely on new editions of my books being printed every year.' He badly needed to complete *Emperor and Galilean* during the next twelve months; in the event, he didn't, and 1872 was to prove, financially, a lean year indeed.

SEVEN

⚜ An English Admirer: and a New Friendship

(1872–1873)

On 24 February 1872 Ibsen made a fresh monetary application to the Ecclesiastical Department in Christiania, this time for a stipend of 450 specie-dollars (£125) to enable him 'by comprehensive research in the Berlin Museum of Egyptology to complete my knowledge of Egyptian architecture and sculpture, and their connection with corresponding ancient forms of art in Europe. Next year family considerations will compel me to return home. I had planned to do so this year, but a big new work on which I am engaged makes this impossible. The mental disturbance inseparable from a change of residence and a re-entry into an environment which, after an absence of more than eight years, has in many respects become foreign to me, could not but leave an unfortunate mark on an uncompleted work.' What these 'family considerations' were is not clear, unless Sigurd's independence of outlook had been running him into further trouble at school. In any case, Ibsen's application was refused.

That month P. F. Siebold's German translation of *Brand* was at last published, the first foreign version of any of Ibsen's plays to be thus honoured. It was rapidly followed by German translations of *The Pretenders* and *The League of Youth*; and before they appeared, on 3 March, his name was printed for the first time in English.[1] The periodical was the *Spectator*, the article a review of

---

[1] At any rate in England. But some time in 1872 (I have not been able to ascertain the month) a native of Bergen named Johan A. Dahl published there his own English translations of *Norwegian and Swedish Poems*, including (together with items by Wergeland, Welhaven, Andreas Munch, J. L. Runeberg, Esaias Tegnér, the National Anthem and a prose story by Bjørnson) *Terje Vigen*. This brave effort is not always successful; e.g.:

> The sea rushed in thro' the opening broad,
> In two feet of water it sunk.
> And gone was the precious barley-load
> But not so our hero's spunk.

This volume is sometimes stated to have been published in 1874, but the title-page and preface are both dated 1872.

158

Ibsen's *Poems*, and the author a twenty-three year old member of the cataloguing department at the British Museum. While on a visit to Norway two years previously, Edmund Gosse, who then knew no Norwegian, had gone into a bookshop at Trondhjem to buy an English novel, entered into conversation with the manager, H. L. Brækstad, and asked him whether Norway had any poets. Brækstad (who later became Norwegian vice-consul in London and translated Hans Andersen into English) showed Gosse a copy of Ibsen's *Poems* newly arrived that day from Copenhagen. 'I put the small green volume in my pocket and left the shop. Of course I could not understand one word, but I could see that the versification was singular and good, and altogether felt much attracted to the unknown poet.'[1] That winter, at the suggestion of a colleague in the British Museum, W. R. S. Ralston, Gosse began a systematic study of the Dano-Norwegian language. Ralston probably thought it would be useful to have someone on the staff who could deal with Scandinavian literature; and Gosse had been told by the editor of the *Spectator*, R. H. Hutton: 'The reason why you get articles refused is because you write about the great familiar classics. Choose something out of the way, Scandinavian literature for instance, and you will get a hearing.'[2] That was probably one reason why Gosse had gone to Norway, and indeed a travel article about the Lofoten Islands which he wrote on his return was the first thing he ever got published (in *Fraser's Magazine* in November 1871).

There was no Danish or Norwegian grammar or reader available in English then, and Gosse taught himself by going through a Danish novel with an English crib. He then managed to work his way through the book of poems he had bought in Trondhjem, and wrote a review which Hutton accepted. As well as dealing with the poems, the article naturally referred to Ibsen's dramatic achievements; and Gosse, always an assiduous cultivator of the great, sent a copy, with an accompanying letter, to Ibsen in Dresden, and received a gratifying reply:

Dresden 2 April 1872

Most honoured sir!

Some days ago I had the great pleasure to receive your very flattering letter, accompanied by your kind review in 'The spectator' [sic].

---

[1] From an autobiographical sketch written by Gosse in 1875 for a 'profile' of him by K. A. Winter-Hjelm which appeared in *Ny Illustreret Tidende* on 14 February 1875. The sketch is quoted in full from the manuscript on pp. 82–85 of Elias Bredsdorff's *Sir Edmund Gosse's Correspondence with Scandinavian Writers* (Copenhagen, 1960), which gives (pp. 24–55 *et passim*) an excellent account of the development of Gosse's acquaintance with Ibsen, to which this chapter is much indebted.

[2] *Ibid.*, p. 2.

My knowledge of the English language is unfortunately not such that I dare attempt to write it, so I hope you will forgive me if I use my native tongue to express my deepest and most heartfelt thanks for the generous way in which you have written of my work.

I could not wish to be introduced to a foreign public better or more sympathetically than in your excellent article; nor is there any public by whom I should be prouder to be read than the English. Should this, thanks to your kind and perceptive assistance, come about, I shall feel boundlessly and permanently indebted to you . . .

The English people are so close to us Scandinavians spiritually, intellectually and emotionally—for which reason it has been especially painful to me that language should set a barrier between my writing and the whole of this great related world. So you will appreciate the pleasure you have given me by the prospect of removing this barrier.

Here in Germany several editions of my books are in preparation. A translation of Brand *has been published in Cassel, but I am not satisfied with it. Another translation of the same play is announced in Berlin. Also in Berlin there have appeared German versions of* The Pretenders *and* The League of Youth, *both excellently rendered by Dr Adolf Strodtmann, the admirable translater of Byron and Tennyson. Dr Strodtmann is currently engaged in translating my shorter poems.*

To be introduced to the English reading public is, though, my chief concern, and the sooner this could happen the happier I should be . . .

Your most respectful and obliged
Henrik Ibsen

Gosse's reply is not extant, but he must have explained that his contribution to the campaign would mainly be in the form of articles and reviews, for on 11 April Ibsen informed Michael Birkeland: 'The translations are to be executed by various hands, and Mr Gosse, though in charge of the enterprise, is not likely to be most active in this side of the work, but will do his utmost to advance the cause by placing articles in the English newspapers.' Gosse kept one half of his promise,[1] for he published a review of *Peer Gynt* in the *Spectator*

---

[1] Not without difficulty. 'I had an introduction to the *Saturday Review*, so I submitted a longish article on *Peer Gynt*. Mr Harwood, who was then the editor, said that I had used terms of so warm an eulogy that he could not publish the article unless I could find some other witness to the merit of this strange piece by an unknown foreign writer. But no sponsor for Ibsen's poetic respectability was forthcoming, and the review did not appear. A little later on I tried the same editor with an article on *The Young Men's League*, which was tartly rejected . . . I wrote more articles, which were rejected . . . Mr Archer is the host, and his the guests and dances; but it was I who swept the floor and lighted the candles.' (An article by Gosse congratulating Ibsen on his seventieth birthday, printed in *The Sketch*, 23 March 1898, and quoted by Bredsdorff, p. 184.)

An Italian *osteria* in the mid-nineteenth century: painting by Luigi Fioroni.

'*With the aid of our fogliette we built our dream-castles.*'

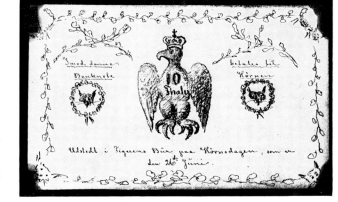

Ibsen's home-made banknotes. 'Cat' and 'eagle' were Ibsen's nicknames for Suzannah.

'*To be cashed when sufficient funds should be in the bank.*'

The jury at the Vienna International Exhibition, 1873. Ibsen is on the extreme right.

'. . . *seated noticeably apart, trimly barbered, in frock-coat and spats.*'

SUZANNAH, 1876

'*She is exactly the right one for me.*'

SIGURD, 1879. Portrait by H. Olrick

'*Very strange, withdrawn and brooding.*'

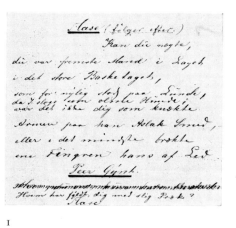

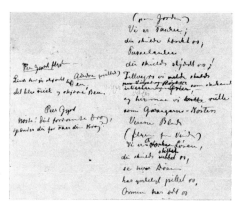

1

2

3

4

5

6

Extracts from Ibsen's manuscripts, with their curiously varying handwriting.

1. Act I of *Peer Gynt*. 2. Act 5 of *Peer Gynt* (the threadballs scene). 3. *Brand* as an epic poem. 4. Preliminary notes for *Ghosts*. 5. The opening of *The League of Youth*. 6. Act I of *Emperor and Galilean*.

Lower right: IBSEN in 1877. The portrait by Julius Kronborg of which Strindberg wrote: '*The face is Brand's: the high, broad brow of the fanatic . . . so repellent, so attractive!*'

Top right: CLEMENS PETERSEN. '*I would have struck him senseless!*'

Top left: CARL SNOILSKY, 1864. The Swedish poet on whom Ibsen based John Rosmer in *Rosmersholm.* Drawing by Severin Falkman.

HANS CHRISTIAN ANDERSEN, *c.* 1870

'*I like Ibsen a lot, but Peer Gynt not at all.*'

GEORG BRANDES, *c.* 1867

'*How these Christians hate me!*'

EDMUND GOSSE, 1874

'*It was I who swept the floor and lighted the candles.*'

LAURA KIELER in middle age

'*He called her his "skylark".*'

A Doll's House, Christiania, 1880. Sketch of the tarantella scene in Act 2, by the designer of the first Norwegian production, Olaf Jørgenssen.

Ghosts, Hälsingborg, 1883. August Lindberg and Hedvig Charlotte Winter-Hjelm in the first European production.

An Enemy of the People, Christiania, 1883. Arnoldus Reimers as Dr Stockmann and Henrik Klausen as Morten Kiil in the first Norwegian production.

JOHN PAULSEN

'*Scoundrel!*'

EDVARD GRIEG

'*. . . had a particular talent for getting Ibsen going.*'

BJØRNSTJERNE BJØRNSON

'*A poor psychologist when it comes to dealing with real people.*'

FREDERIK HEGEL. Ibsen's publisher and counsellor

'*The illegitimate son of a servant-girl.*'

'Henrik Ibsen as Disciplinarian'. A caricature in *Vikingen*, 9 December, 1882. Ibsen belabours the left in *The League of Youth*, and is applauded by the right; belabours the right in *The Pillars of Society* and is cheered by the left; and finally indicts all political parties in *An Enemy of the People*, and antagonises everyone.

'Henrik Ibsen receiving Mr William Archer in Audience'. Caricature by Max Beerbohm. (Note the wallpaper.)

on 7 July, another of *The Pretenders* in the *Academy* on 1 August, an article on *Norwegian Poetry since 1814* in the October issue of *Fraser's Magazine*, and, in January 1873, a long article in the *Fortnightly Review* entitled 'Ibsen, the Norwegian Satirist'. But in his attempts to arrange translations, he was less successful. He completed a blank-verse version of *Love's Comedy* in the spring of 1873, but failed to find a publisher, and (not surprisingly, considering how few English people knew Norwegian, and the indifference shown to his own single effort) does not seem to have found any willing collaborators.[1] No English version of an Ibsen play was to appear before Catherine Ray's translation of *Emperor and Galilean* in 1876.

While Gosse was learning Norwegian in London and introducing Ibsen's name to a tiny section of the English public, Ibsen's Danish champion had been running into trouble in Copenhagen. On his return there the previous summer after the meeting in Dresden, Georg Brandes had applied for a position at Copenhagen University, where it was obvious that a successor would soon be needed to the octogenarian Carsten Hauch as Professor of Aesthetics. Hauch himself had been an early champion of Brandes, and the latter was asked to give a series of lectures to show his qualifications. He chose as his subject 'Main Currents in Nineteenth-Century Literature', and delivered his first lecture on 3 November 1871.

The hall was filled, one-third of the audience consisting of women; not only was Brandes the translator of Mill's *The Subjection of Women*, he was also known to have been the lover of a married woman with six children.[2] The lectures were a tremendous turning-point in Scandinavian culture. Brandes declared that Danish thinking was half a century behind the times, that it was reactionary and divorced from reality instead of, like French literature (which Brandes, fresh from his meetings with Taine and Renan, took as his model) dealing with contemporary social problems. Danish literature, he asserted, lived in the past; it was the duty of writers to live in the present and the future. Harmless as these sentiments appear today, they infuriated the powerful conservative element in Danish society and its press organs. In November Brandes wrote a satirical piece about a modern Red Riding Hood, a free-thinking girl who is gobbled up by the *opposition* press (he despised the official

---

[1] Gosse also translated 'The Poet's Song' from *Love's Comedy* and 'Agnes' from *Brand*, and included them in his own collection of poems, *On Viol and Flute*, published in London in 1873.

[2] On these lectures, cf. Evert Sprinchorn's excellent note in his edition of *Ibsen's Letters and Speeches* (New York, 1964), pp. 120–121. I do not like Mr Sprinchorn's translation of the letters, except where it follows the Maurvik-Morison version of 1905, but his notes are informed and illuminating.

L

opposition party in Denmark as much as Ibsen did its counterpart in Norway). For this he was violently attacked in *Fædrelandet*; it and the other newspapers of the capital closed their columns to him, and to reply to the attack he had to insert a paid advertisement. When the first volume of Brandes's lectures was published in February 1872 it, too, was violently abused in every Danish newspaper; and when Carsten Hauch died in March, his recommendation that Brandes should be his successor was ignored, and Brandes was not given a position at the University until thirty years later—the penalty of following Ibsen's advice about 'needling the Danes'. He wrote to Ibsen, pouring out his troubles; the letter has perished, but we have Ibsen's reply, the rough comfort of a battle-scarred veteran to a subaltern enduring his first experience of shellfire:

Dresden, 4 April 1872

Dear Brandes!

I have this moment received your letter, and am replying immediately.

But what unbelievable news you tell me! And I imagined you revelling in success and triumph. Surely, though, you must have an army behind you. Remember that these are but recruits whom you are leading into battle. The first time, they will retreat; the second time, stand their ground; and after that they will follow you to victory.

So the liberal press has closed its doors to you. But of course! I once expressed to you my contempt for political freedom. You thought me wrong on that occasion. From your story of The Red Hat *I see you have gained some experience. My dear friend, the liberals are the worst enemies of Freedom. Spiritual and intellectual freedom flourish best under absolutism; that was proved in France, then in Germany and it is now being proved in Russia.*

But I must turn to what for these past weeks has continually filled my thoughts and disturbed my nightly rest. I have read your lectures.

A more dangerous book could never fall into the hands of a pregnant writer. It is one of those books which set a yawning gulf between yesterday and today. When I was in Italy I could not understand how I managed to exist before I went there. In twenty years people will not understand how anyone managed to live spiritually in Scandinavia before these lectures . . . Your book is not literary history in the accepted meaning, neither is it cultural history; what it is, I shall not attempt to describe. It is to me as the goldfields of California were to those who discovered them; they either made men millionaires or ruined them. Now, is our spiritual constitution in the North strong enough to survive this shock? I don't know; but it doesn't matter. Whatever cannot sustain these new ideas must fall.

You say everyone in the faculty of philosophy is against you. My dear Brandes, would you have it otherwise? Are you not fighting to destroy the philosophy of that faculty? A war such as yours cannot be waged by a crown servant. If they did not bar the door against you, it would show that you had failed to frighten them.

As regards this agitation which is being worked up against you, all these lies and calumnies and so forth, let me give you a word of advice which I know from experience to be sovereign. Be an aristocrat! Aristocracy of the spirit is the only weapon against this kind of thing. Appear indifferent; never write a word of reply in the newspapers; if you polemise in your writings, never direct your polemic against this or that specific attack; never write a single word which could make it seem as though your enemies had found their mark; in short, act as though you had no idea that anyone was opposed to you. What power of survival do you suppose that your enemies' attacks will have? In the old days when I read an attack on me in the morning, I used to think: 'Now I am finished, I shall never be able to hold up my head again!' But I did; no one any longer remembers what was written, and even I myself have long forgotten it. So, don't cheapen yourself by getting involved in mud-slinging. Start a new series of lectures, unperturbed, unmoved, maddeningly indifferent, cheerfully contemptuous of everything that is crumbling around you. Do you think that what is rotten to the core has any powers of resistance?

How this mortal combat between two epochs will end, I do not know; but anything is preferable to the status quo—of that I am certain. I do not promise myself that victory will result in any permanent improvement; every historical development has been but a lurch from one delusion to another. But the battle itself is good, healthy and invigorating; your revolt is a mighty and emancipating declaration of genius. When these old men complain that you mock God, they should reflect that they themselves are the mockers. The Great Aforesaid created you for a purpose.

I hear you have founded a society. Do not rely implicitly on everyone who joins you; what matters is whether they do so for the right reason. Nor am I sure that this will strengthen your position; my own conviction is that the strongest man is he who stands most alone. But I sit here outside it all while you stand there in the midst of the storm; that makes a big difference.

Au revoir, my dear Brandes! Keep a friendly place in your heart for me and mine, next to what must henceforth be the only important thing to you, because it is your own child in spirit and in truth.

Forgive the haste and incoherence of this letter!

Your affectionate
Henrik Ibsen.[1]

No wonder that Ibsen was so excited by *Main Currents*, which still reads wonderfully well today. The theme, as stated in Brandes's introduction, is

---

[1] Ibsen misdated the letter 1871 (cf. Halvdan Koht's note in *CE*, XIX, p. 497).

'the revolution waged by the first decades of the nineteenth century against the literature of the eighteenth, and the victory of that revolution', as reflected in French, English and German literature up to 1848; in other words, the gradual conquest of liberal ideas through such writers as Byron, Hugo, Lamartine and Heine. It is easy to realise what a revelation this brilliant survey of Ibsen's spiritual ancestors must have been to one ever conscious of his imperfect education and inability to read French and English.

Meanwhile, *Emperor and Galilean* was grinding slowly on, for ever falling further behind schedule. On 19 January he had told Hegel that he hoped to have the whole play finished by June; on 24 April he was still optimistic enough to write: 'I shall soon be ready with Part 2 of *Julian*. The third and final section will go easily. The spring has now arrived here, and I always work best in warm weather.' He was not in fact to complete even Part 2 until August, nor the whole play until the following February. 'We have had the pleasure of seeing several Danish travellers', continued this last letter to Hegel. 'H. C. Andersen is now here.' Andersen and Ibsen met on 22 April, and evidently got on well again, for Andersen (though he continued to spell his new friend Ipsen)[1] sent him a copy of the final volume of his *New Tales and Stories*, which had appeared that year. An undated letter from Ibsen thanking him, or rather a fragment of it, has survived: 'Thank you for your visit to Dresden; thank you for the book; thank you for everything else . . .' The rest of the letter has been cut away.[2]

On 7 July Edmund Gosse's review of *Peer Gynt* appeared in the *Spectator*. Not unnaturally, the play had considerably bewildered him, but much of the article still reads respectably. 'The dramatic power displayed in this poem', Gosse declared, 'quite raises it out of any mere local interest, and gives it a claim to be judged at a European tribunal.' Like so many Scandinavian critics, however, he was disturbed by the jagged and discordant quality of the work; indeed, his criticisms almost suspiciously resemble Brandes's. 'The book is not without marks of haste, and there is a general sense of incongruity and disjointedness . . . mixture of brilliant and crude elements; one is alternately delighted and scandalized. It is to be hoped that Ibsen will not be so led away in future by the perilous sweetness of the Lynean god as to neglect to give his work its due elaboration and polish.' English critics were saying very much the same kind of thing about Robert Browning.

Some time early in July Ibsen moved from Dippoldiswaldaer-Strasse to a

---

[1] Cf. Andersen's letter to Martin Henriques, 20 April 1872 (*H. C. Andersens Dagbøger og Breve, 1868–1875*, p. 118).

[2] *CE*, XVII, p. 46.

new apartment at Grosse Plauensche Strasse 9, and on the fifteenth he took Suzannah and Sigurd for a holiday to Berchtesgaden, where they had enjoyed themselves four years previously. There he received a request from Brandes to help him and his brother Edvard in a new magazine which they were planning, to be named *The Nineteenth Century* and to be published by Gyldendal. Ibsen replied (23 July) that he was thinking of writing some more rhymed epistles on the lines of the *Balloon Letter* and the *Letter to Fru Heiberg*, 'concerning our position, and that of our age in general, *vis-à-vis* politics, literature, etc. They would be a kind of declaration of faith.' But he refused to associate himself more actively with Brandes's project. 'They would be of no direct help to you and your cause; but, my dear Brandes, this is all I can do for you. I must confine myself within my own chosen sphere; here, all my thoughts are concentrated. Its range is not wide, but I exploit it as best I can. Please don't regard this as evidence of egotism! How soon I can begin these epistles for you, I don't know; the monster Julian still has so firm a hold on me that I cannot get away from him. But we can discuss this in more detail later, preferably when we meet. I do not in the least fear being regarded as holding partisan sympathies', he concluded suprisingly, 'I cannot understand why people now regard me as having no party allegiances.' Presumably he meant by this last sentence that his criticisms of the faults of the left did not imply that his sympathies lay elsewhere, and that one could owe allegiance to a party without toeing the line, just as a man can regard himself as a good Catholic while retaining the right to independent criticism.

On 18 July Norway celebrated her thousand years as a kingdom, and Ibsen wrote a special poem for the occasion which the University Library in Christiania printed on the day. It contained one of the most disturbing messages of thanks that any country or individual can ever have received. Edmund Gosse was not always the most accurate of translators, but his rendering of the first two verses of this poem will hardly be bettered:

> My countrymen, who filled for me deep bowls
> Of wholesome bitter medicine, such as gave
> The poet, on the margin of his grave,
> Fresh strength to fight where broken twilight rolls—
> My countrymen, who sped me o'er the wave—
> An exile, with my griefs for pilgrim-soles,
> My fears for burdens, doubts for staffs, to roam—
> From the wide world I send you greeting home.
>
> I send you thanks for gifts that help and harden,
> Thanks for each hour of purifying pain;

Each plant that prospers in my poet's garden
Is rooted where your harshness poured its rain;
Each shoot in which it blooms and burgeons forth
It owes to that grey weather from the north;
The sun's fire loosens, but the fog secures!
My country, thanks! My life's best gifts were yours.[1]

Ibsen worked hard on *Julian* in Berchtesgaden, and on 8 August he was able to write joyfully to Hegel that he had completed Part Two and assure him that the third and final part 'is so clear in my mind that it will go very much quicker than the others'. On 30 August he left for Dresden where, a fortnight later, he was joined by Georg Brandes. This time, Brandes stayed a month, during which period he saw Ibsen almost daily, and his autobiography contains some vivid reminiscences of their meetings:[2]

'Each day I walked from the small, very bad hotel which he had recommended me nearby, and collected him for a walk, often broken by a visit to an inn, where the waiters were impressed by the barbaric splendour of his buttonhole, but invariably ending with tea at his apartment. I received a new impression after the year that had passed since I had last seen him. Not very tall, but handsome, athletically built, with a mighty head, big neck, powerful shoulders—he looked as though one would need a club to overpower him. He spoke, in general, little, though he was communicative to me; but the curious thing about his speech was its calm and slowness, and the fact that he never smiled except when the person to whom he was talking smiled first. This sometimes had an effect that was almost of scaredness. If one had to choose a single adjective to describe him, it would be menacing (*truende*). He could look terrifying, as he sat with his watchful eyes. Then he resembled a judge. He looked a man who was accustomed, in intercourse with other men, to occupy the standpoint of a schoolmaster confronting his pupils, and to instil fear. For all his hostility towards the Norwegians he was, in essence, very Norwegian.

'There lay stored within him twenty-four years of bitterness and hatred; his contempt for humanity knew no limits. He was an aristocrat to his fingertips, with all that that implied. It was an article of faith with him that

---

[1] The Christiania magazine *Vikingen* printed a cartoon showing Ibsen standing in front of a magic mirror flanked by a beer-mug and a money-bag marked 'Poet's Pension 400 [specie-dollars]', the objects being reflected in the mirror as a pilgrim's staff and a glass marked 'wholesome bitter medicine'.

[2] *Levned*, II, pp. 99 ff. Cf. also Brandes's letter to Hans Brøchner, 29 September 1872 (*Brandes Brevveksling*, I, pp. 171–173).

all politicians—parliamentary politicians, that is, not men such as Bismarck
—were hypocrites, liars, drivellers, dogs . . . His hatred for false freedom
movements was supplanting his interest in genuine ones . . . The true
freedom was social freedom, spiritual freedom, freedom of thought,
freedom of conscience . . . He hated the liberals of Norway,[1] and regarded
most Norwegian peasants as sordid and self-seeking . . . He laughed at
Bjørnson's rustic tales, he chortled over the space that love occupied in
them, saying that nothing bothered the Norwegian peasant less, unless one
used the word "love" in its crudest sense. A youth of twenty would gladly
marry a woman of sixty if she were well-to-do. Let Bjørnson but continue
till his hero Arne got into Parliament, and we should see that fellow in his
true colours. Many years later I learned from Ibsen's letters that he at times
felt friendly towards Bjørnson, even infatuated. But on this occasion, and
others, I heard him name Bjørnson only with the most vehement distaste
and contempt. The violence of his fanaticism struck me one day when in
an angry outburst he decried Magdalene Thoresen's writings, damned
their language, called them artificial and false, and then broke off to
remark: "Mind you, she has more talent than that Bjørnson." One must,
however, add that, as Christian Rickardt once rightly observed, Ibsen
never spoke as disparagingly of Bjørnson as the latter did of him.

'Walking out towards Plauenscher Grund he said: "Scandinavia lies
outside the cultural mainstream. The unhappy consequence is that we
never get anywhere until the rest of Europe has moved on . . . It is as
though one were to introduce astronomy into Madagascar and begin with
the Ptolemaic system" . . . He spoke of the importance of written work
having "an intense connection with the author's spiritual life", and
thought the major advance of the age was that poetry was becoming more
and more psychological, and not merely poetry but all literature. "What
will ensure your latest book a future life is that it reveals how *you* have
regarded things. If you want objectivity, then go to the objects. Read
me so as to get to know *me*!" He thought that this was the great literary
revolution that he was attempting.'[2]

---

[1] 'In political matters he is very conservative, or rather absolutist . . . The political liberals
are almost illiberal in intellectual matters, and he says it is better to be under the rule of one
big tyrant than several little ones.' (Letter from Brandes to Hans Brøchner, 29 September
1872, *Brandes Brevveksling*, I, p. 172.)

[2] Another example of Ibsen's imperfect acquaintance with literary history. 'Read me so
as to know *me*' had been one of the principles of the Romantic movement throughout
Europe at the beginning of the century, as one would have expected him to know from his
acquaintance with Byron's work.

Of *Emperor and Galilean*, Brandes recalled: 'At first he could not be persuaded to read a line of it to me. When he wanted to rewrite a scene to refine
the dialogue, he would not let me see its first, inferior form. He said: "I never
write a line without asking myself: 'What will G.B. think of this?' So how
could I let you see it in the rough?" However, he shortly afterwards read me
long extracts, including the scene between Julian and the mystic Maximos.
His quiet voice lent itself well to the expression of what was powerful and
disturbing.' He took Brandes to more than one meeting of the Dresden
literary society (where, says Brandes, Ibsen regularly attended lectures);
amongst other subjects, they heard a talk on Tieck's essay on the monologues
in *Hamlet*, 'of which, strangely enough', comments Brandes, 'I was the only
person present who had foreknowledge.'

Another Danish visitor to Dresden that month was Meïr Aron Goldschmidt,
founder of *The Corsair*, that magazine on which, twenty years earlier, Botten
Hansen and Vinje had modelled *The Man*, to give Ibsen his first opening in
journalism. Goldschmidt invited Ibsen and Brandes to dinner at the Hotel
Berlin. The conversation turned to religion. Goldschmidt denied that Voltaire
was an atheist, and suddenly asked Ibsen if he believed in God. Ibsen 'replied
in astonishment at this inquisition: "Certainly." "Then I don't see how you
can associate with someone like Brandes who doesn't believe in any God" . . .
Ibsen replied in rising displeasure: "I have no idea what Brandes believes in or
doesn't believe in. I have never discussed it with him, and feel no cause to." '[1]

They talked of Brandes's plans for a new magazine, and Ibsen wrote to
Hegel to try to persuade him to back it. 'If *you* will publish it', he wrote on
15 September, 'I think, nay, I feel sure, that it will succeed and be able to
survive with profit for some considerable time. In my experience an enterprise of this kind depends almost totally on its publisher. I need hardly add
that, once assured of this, I shall gladly associate myself with the project as
closely or distantly as you may think fit. I long for a regular secondary
occupation, and had indeed thought of contacting one or another of our
public media when Dr Brandes and subsequently yourself mentioned this
project, which attracts me more than any other.' Hegel agreed, and the result
was *Det Nittende Aarhundrede* (*The Nineteenth Century*), edited by Georg
Brandes and his brother Edvard, which set a new standard for critical journalism in Scandinavia.

Ibsen does not record what Brandes said to him during these meetings in
Dresden; but some things, at least, we can guess at, and if we are correct, they
were to bear importantly on Ibsen's future work. As Dr Henning Fenger, the

---

[1] Georg Brandes, *Levned*, II, p. 107.

distinguished Brandes scholar, points out, Brandes had that spring followed up his lectures of the preceding winter with a series of six on the development of French drama from Beaumarchais to Dumas *fils*. In these lectures, Brandes had shown special interest in the connection between money and morality— the way French dramatists regarded money as playing a vital role in determining human destinies, the way false share dealings are brought to light, and so forth. This interlocking of money with morality was something that was to feature strongly in *The Pillars of Society* and *A Doll's House*. Moreover, from these unpublished lectures Dr Fenger quotes Brandes's description of the new type of woman who was threatening to replace the traditional romantic heroines: 'This young girl is no longer ignorant of life and the world. She walks forth into it self-possessed and sceptical. She does not throw herself at the first man who asks her. Even in extreme youth, she has a character of her own. She has a man's seriousness, power of decision, and will.' These words exactly describe the 'heroines' (did anyone then in conversation if not in print, ever refer to them then as anti-heroines?) whom Ibsen was henceforth to create, beginning with Dina Dorf, Nora and Petra Stockmann, and of whom Selma in *The League of Youth* was, as we have seen, in a small way (for she has very few lines) the forerunner.

Brandes also, in his lectures, praised Dumas *fils* for his realism and 'physiological, clinical view of human nature . . . a directness, a brutality, but at the same time a truthfulness of expression hitherto unparallelled'.[1] One must assume that Brandes expatiated on this to Ibsen during their Dresden walks; and any writer knows how immensely stimulating and strengthening it is when, apparently ploughing a lonely furrow, he meets someone who can crystallise in clear language his own unstated intuitions.

Most importantly, perhaps, Brandes had demanded in his lectures that the Scandinavian dramatists should employ 'careful and truthful study of human character' in the service of liberal thought—in other words, not stand objectively and ironically aloof, as Ibsen had done in *The League of Youth*, but use the drama as a pulpit for preaching the ideals of the new age. Dr Fenger rightly comments that to Ibsen this uncompromising demand that he should commit himself must have come as manna from heaven. 'Here was the answer to the problems he had wrestled with in 1869–70 . . . A wholehearted commitment to the ideals of the new age was something that would lift and animate the most realistic portrait of actuality.'[2] Remembering that these lectures of

---

[1] It is interesting that, according to the French scholar P. G. la Chesnais (*Œuvres Complètes d'Henrik Ibsen*, XI, p. 409). Dumas *fils* was probably partly responsible for the first (private) staging in France of *A Doll's House* in 1891.

[2] *Ibsen og Georg Brandes indtil 1872*, pp. 207–208.

Brandes were (and were to remain) unpublished, the conversations that Ibsen had with him in Dresden that September may well have been vital in stimulating Ibsen to make the leap from the uncommittedness of *The League of Youth* to the committed progressiveness of *The Pillars of Society* and its great successors.

In England, Edmund Gosse's review of *Peer Gynt* had been followed by another of *The Pretenders* published in the *Academy* of 1 August. Gosse sent copies of both articles to Ibsen as they appeared, from Denmark where he was holidaying, but Ibsen does not seem to have replied, or even to have acknowledged them. Undeterred, Gosse sent Ibsen another article early in October, on the subject of *Norwegian Poetry since 1814*, which had appeared in *Fraser's Magazine* of that month; and this, at last, elicited a response from Ibsen, the warmth of which must have consoled Gosse for the months of silence. 'A better, clearer or kinder interpretation of my poem I could not wish for', wrote Ibsen (14 October) of the review of *Peer Gynt*. 'I only wish that the praise you extend to my work were fully justified; the objections you make are reasonable enough; I can partly see the faults myself, now that time has set me at a sufficient distance to be able to consider it as though it were by another hand.' After praising the other two articles, Ibsen continued: 'I am working daily on *Julian the Apostate* and hope to have the whole play ready by the end of the year. As soon as the book is printed I will send you a copy, and can only hope it will win your approval. I have put a good deal of my own spiritual life into this book; I have myself lived through what I portray, in other forms; and the historical theme I have chosen has a closer connection with our own time than people might suppose before reading it. This I regard as an indispensable prerequisite to any modern treatment of material so remote in time, if it is to arouse interest as an original work.'

That autumn a new artistic director, Hartvig Lassen, had been appointed at the Christiania Theatre, and on 24 October Ibsen wrote to him suggesting that he consider staging *Love's Comedy*. 'The fears I once had regarding the presentation of this play', he explained, 'have long since disappeared. I have for various reasons become convinced that the public now realises that this is, in essence, a deeply moral work; and artistically, I am more than ever sure that it is irreproachable, and at any event not bettered by anything else I have written. All in all, I rate *Love's Comedy* among my best efforts. I think my standing in Scandinavian literature gives me a certain right to make this friendly request, which would be superfluous for an author similarly placed in any other country.' He enclosed a suggested cast list, adding: 'If Johannes Brun could, without damage to things generally, be kept out of it, it would in some ways ease my mind . . . As a fee I should require the gross receipts from the premiere against a guaranteed minimum of 300 specie-dollars (£83).' Lassen replied promptly, on 2 November, saying that he had only hesitated about staging *Love's Comedy* because he had feared his company was inadequate to the demands of the play; Ibsen's letter had, however, dispelled his fears, and he would present it as worthily as his resources would allow. Ibsen wrote again on 14 November with further casting suggestions, and explaining his doubts about Brun. 'Is Herr Brun capable nowadays of learning a part properly? Can he be persuaded to subject himself to the inconvenience? . . . If he plays it for comedy, Svanhild's decision, the trickiest thing in the play, may easily seem too crude; and if he plays it seriously, without comedy, he will be in a field foreign to him. Might it not be approachable to approach Herr Reimers? Herr R. is an intelligent man and if he can play the part I think he will act it in such a way that Svanhild's abandonment of Falk for the tradesman may not seem impossible, which would be a great gain.'[1]

Ibsen evidently assumed from Lassen's letter that the play would be put on that season, for the next week he told Hegel that it would be staged 'in the very near future'; but changes were made at the theatre whereby Lassen was reduced to the position of artistic consultant (the post which Ibsen himself had held briefly a decade earlier). The direction of the theatre was entrusted to a Swede, Ludvig Josephson—much to Ibsen's subsequent advantage—and *Love's Comedy* had to be postponed until the following autumn.

Some time during November Ibsen moved for the second time that year, from Grosse Plauensche Strasse to a first-floor apartment at Wettiner-Strasse 22. Thence on 20 November he assured Hegel that 'I definitely hope to have my new play finished by the end of the year . . . During the summer I plan to give *Lady Inger* a thorough going-over with the Royal Danish Theatre in mind, after which, if all goes well, I am thinking of writing a longish comedy, the plan of which is already pretty well matured.' This last project may have been *The Pillars of Society*, or (which is very possible) it may have been some other plan which never came to fruition.

Ibsen had a welcome visitor that month in Lorentz Dietrichson, whom he had not seen since his visit to Stockholm three years earlier. Dietrichson, like Brandes, enjoyed the unusual pleasure of hearing Ibsen read Part 1 of *Julian*, and remembered the disappointment of the thirteen-year-old Sigurd at being ordered into another room to do his divinity homework instead of being allowed to listen. 'I think there's as much divinity in Father's play as in my

---

[1] These two letters to Lassen were not discovered until 1960, and are not in the Centenary Edition. Øyvind Anker published them in his article *Kjærlighedens Komedie på Christiania theater* in *Edda*, 1961, pp. 59–81.

homework', he pleaded, but in vain. 'Although Ibsen has no outstanding talent for reading [tells Dietrichson], it was a rare and exquisite delight to hear him read his drama in his pleasant voice and noble, totally unaffected diction.' It was nearly midnight before Ibsen read the final line: 'For Thine is the Kingdom, the Power and the Glory'; and Dietrichson walked home 'quite shaken, and convinced that I had heard one of the most remarkable tragedies written since the time of Shakespeare. Its mighty figures haunted me even in my dreams.'[1]

Dietrichson (again like Brandes) was amazed that Ibsen had not made the acquaintance of Hermann Hettner, whose *Das moderne Drama* had so excited the dramatist twenty years earlier, and who was now living in Dresden. 'I tried to bring them together, but did not succeed in the few days I could spend in Dresden. Hettner knew Ibsen's name well, indeed, almost everyone I met in Dresden was aware that a great Norwegian writer was dwelling in their midst; but very few then knew his work, and those who had read his *Brand* in Siebold's translation . . . could not really get a grip on the work; they could of course sense the grandeur of its scope, but found its full meaning, to put it mildly, obscure.'[2] Ibsen's avoidance of Hettner may have been conscious; as we have seen, he had a neurotic fear of admitting that he owed a debt to anyone, a feeling which is perhaps tied up with his obsession about bankruptcy. He may, too, have felt that he had outgrown Hettner's teaching and would gain little from a meeting, for Hettner had written nothing very interesting since (though Brandes had met him several times and found him rewarding). The other fact which Dietrichson mentions, that Ibsen's German literary acquaintances had to take his reputation on trust—in the next five years, only *The Vikings at Helgeland* and *Lady Inger of Østraat* were to be translated, in addition to the three plays published earlier that year, and of his best work, *Brand* was most inadequately translated, and *Peer Gynt* not at all—no doubt helped to increase his already formidable reserve.

Ibsen spent the last months of 1872 combining Parts 1 and 2 of his *Julian* trilogy into a single part of five acts, and beginning the draft of his final section (the ultimate Part Two).[3] The great work was at last approaching its end; indeed, it was urgent that it should, as Ibsen must have realised when making up his balance-sheet for the year. His total earnings for 1872 were the 200 specie-dollars (£56) which he had received for the third edition of *The Pretenders*; and this was five years after the publication of *Peer Gynt*.

---

[1] Dietrichson, I, pp. 354–355.

[2] *Ibid.*, p. 354.

[3] Cf. J. W. McFarlane's note in *The Oxford Ibsen*, IV (London, 1963), p. 560.

EIGHT

🗝 The End of Several Phases

(1873–1875)

1873 OPENED PROPITIOUSLY for Ibsen, in several respects. On New
Year's Day the *Fortnightly Review* in London published a long article by
Edmund Gosse entitled *Ibsen, the Norwegian Satirist*, the first full assessment of
Ibsen in English. 'Where shall we look for a young great poet among the
continental nations?' asked Gosse. 'It is my firm belief that in the Norwegian,
Henrik Ibsen, the representative of a land unknown in the literary annals of
Europe, such a poet is found . . . Ibsen has many golden arrows in his quiver,
and he stands, cold and serene, between the dawn and the darkness, shooting
them one by one into the valley below, each truly aimed at some folly, some
affectation, of the everyday life we lead.' After surveying Ibsen's life and
development, Gosse passed on to a discussion of 'his three great satires', *Love's
Comedy*, *Brand* and *Peer Gynt*, quoting long extracts of the first and third plays
in his own translation. The article concluded: '*Love's Comedy*, *Brand* and *Peer
Gynt*, despite their varied plots, form a great satiric trilogy—perhaps for
sustained vigour of expression, for affluence of execution, and for brilliance of
dialogue, the greatest of modern times. They form, at present, Ibsen's principal
and foremost claim to immortality; their influence over thought in the North
has been boundless, and, sooner or later, they will win for their author the
homage of Europe. It was a white day with me when I first took *Brand* into my
hands in the languor of a summer's day at Trondhjem, and I may trust that
some competent translator will one day set these books before my countrymen in an English dress.'

News also arrived from Hegel that reprints were in hand of both *Brand* and
Love's Comedy; and Ibsen himself had good tidings to send in reply. 'I have the
great joy', he wrote on 6 February, 'to be able to inform you that my great
work is finished, and more happily so than anything I have previously written.
The book is entitled "*Emperor and Galilean*, a World Drama in two parts". It
contains: Part 1: Caesar's Apostasy, a play in five acts (170 pages). Part 2:
Emperor Julian, a play in five acts (252 pages). Do not let the description
"World Drama" frighten you! I shall begin fair-copying the play in a week and

shall send you a weekly batch of 48 pages . . . This has been a Herculean labour for me; not the work itself, that has gone easily, but the pain it has cost me to live myself freshly and vividly into so distant and alien an age.' The letter ended with a request for money. 'I have in my credit account with you and in the savings bank about 49 riks-dollars [£5 8s. od.]. Will you advance me as much as, added to this sum, will make 150 Prussian thaler, and send it to me? The Christiania Theatre's procrastination concerning *Love's Comedy* leaves me financially embarrassed, and I need money.' He explained his plans for the summer: 'I shall completely rewrite *Lady Inger of Østraat*, and it will be one of my best books'.

Ibsen at first kept pretty well to his timetable for the fair-copying; he posted batches of forty-eight pages to Hegel on 22 February, 1 March, and 9 March. Then there was a gap until 22 April, but further instalments followed on 30 April, 9 May and, finally, 24 May. 'There is much self-anatomy in this book', he told Edmund Gosse, who used the information to publish a brief note about its imminent appearance in the *Academy* on 1 April; and to Ludvig Daae, who was helping him with the spelling of the Greek names, he wrote: 'The play deals with a conflict between two irreconcilable powers in human life which will always be repeated, and that is why I call it "A World-Historical Drama".' It would, he assured Daae, 'be my masterpiece'.

Even the Dresden Literary Society began to take notice of him. Strodtmann's translations of *The Pretenders* and *The League of Youth*, and his praise of Ibsen in a series of articles in the *Hamburg Correspondent*, were the cause. The articles especially, he told Strodtmann (20 March) 'have added immeasurably to my standing here. They have been the subject of three separate lectures in the Literary Society, together with the two plays you translated. This has put me back into a good humour with my surroundings, so that I now feel happy again in Dresden—the only home I can imagine for myself north of the Alps.' Yet he concluded his letter: 'I stand unspeakably alone, today—which happens to be my birthday—more than ever.'

He tried to read Georg Brandes's translation of Mill's *Utilitarianism*, but found it, like most theoretical writing (apart from Brandes's own) unsatisfying. 'I don't know', he wrote to Brandes on 30 April, 'whether I dare express an opinion on a subject on which I have no professional expertise. When, however, I reflect that there are writers who lay down the law about philosophy without any knowledge of Hegel or German thought in general, it seems to me that anything is allowed. So I must honestly tell you that I cannot see any hope of progress, or any future at all, in the way Stuart Mill prescribes. I don't see why you have bothered to translate this book, the philistine sophistry of which harks back to Cicero or Seneca. I am convinced you could have written a ten times better book yourself in half the time it must have taken you to translate it . . . Come here soon! I long to see you, despite our many differences of opinion.' Brandes, he must have felt, was the only person who could relieve his loneliness.

While he was awaiting the publication of *Emperor and Galilean*, a pleasant diversion offered itself. He was invited to attend the International Exhibition in Vienna as representative for Denmark and Norway on the jury which was to award the prizes in the painting and sculpture sections. The Exhibition opened on 1 May, but Ibsen's services were not required until the following month. He left Dresden by train on the evening of 12 June, and the day after his arrival in Vienna he wrote to Suzannah. It is the earliest of his letters to her that has survived:

Vienna, 14 June 1873

Dear Suzannah!

A few hasty words, just to put you in the picture. I arrived here yesterday morning at nine o'clock, and was met at the station by Thomas,[1] *who brought me word from Tobias Møller that I could have a room next to his, which he strongly recommended. I could not have done better! The house, which is near the Exhibition, only fifteen minutes walk or five minutes ride for five* kreutzer, *is an excellent and respectable hotel in the most elegant part of the city. The first floor, which I have rented, overlooking the street, or avenue, belongs to a Baroness, who has left town and instructed her* Wirthschafterin, *or housekeeper, to rent out the room for the summer. She is an absolute pearl of amiability, honesty and helpfulness. Hildur*[2] *is enthusiastic about her, and rightly. For my room, with service, cleaning and valeting, errands within the city, etc., I pay 80* gulden *a month, i.e. about 2½* gulden *a day. She brings me coffee when I require it, with rolls and butter for breakfast, all for 30* kreutzer *or 6* groschen. *I ate breakfast here this morning, beautifully served on a silver tray with a cloth and napkin, a whole small pot of coffee, lots of milk, bread, butter and sugar, all of the best quality, and delicious.*

I visited the Exhibition yesterday, but cannot of course yet venture any opinion on it. I live next to the Møllers. Our admirable landlady lives quite alone in the house and sees to everything herself.

Møller and I have to go out now to pay our official respects. It is said to be expensive here, but I have found that I can manage economically for lunch, etc.

This must be all for today. Be patient in my absence and write soon to

Your affectionate

Henrik Ibsen.

---

[1] The elder of Magdalene's two sons by Dean Thoresen. They both died at the age of thirty, Thomas (who was a successful writer of vaudevilles) in 1876, Axel in 1881.

[2] The daughter of Randolph Nilsen, with whom he had stayed at Bergen in 1863.

When you write you can until further notice use the address I gave you. My lodging is: Augarten Alleé-Strasse no. 23, first floor.

Suzannah's birthday fell on 26 June, and Ibsen dutifully remembered it:

Dear Suzannah!   *Vienna, 25 June 1873*

Now that the good time approaches when there will be roasting and frying for three days on end, and the coffee-pot will simmer unceasingly from early morning, I write you a few words to wish you many happy returns of the day. The only handsome present that I can offer you for the moment is the enclosed banknote, which I beg you will not disdain, and which you will be able to change immediately into Prussian currency. Had Thomas not been inaccessible these past days, I would have sent some small thing with him. But he remained invisible, and left without saying goodbye. So you must be patient, dear cattttt!

The jury work has now started in earnest, so you must not expect long letters from me for a while. I have become a juror for both painting and sculpture, and have therefore double duties. My timetable is as follows: in the morning I rise at 6, and by 8 have completed my toilet, eaten breakfast, read the newspaper and smoked my morning pipe. Then I go out to the Exhibition, where the painting jury meets from 9 to 12. As soon as this is finished, I go to a restaurant nearby, where I eat a good meat dish, with admirable beer. At 2 the sculpture jury's meeting begins, and this lasts till 4.30 or 5. These meetings are, however, not always confined to the table; for example, these last days we have been walking round the huge Exhibition buildings studying the works of art. There has of course been no question of my midday siesta since I arrived in Vienna. When the jury meetings are finished I am, as you can imagine, tired. Then I sit down in one of the many open-air restaurants in the Prater and look at the thousands of people driving along the avenue while I eat my evening meal, comprising bread and cheese, with excellent beer. At 9 I go home and, immediately, to bed. I greatly enjoy this life here. They have not yet begun to offer hospitality to the jurymen, though I hear this is to come later.

Thank you for your letter and the strilen's [*Marie's*]. *Yes, I have received* Lady Inger. *Dietrichson is expected here. Each day I find myself in the company of many notabilities, and all the officials at the Exhibition have instructions to show us the greatest respect.*

Write again soon. I shall only be able to send our dear young student[1] my visiting-card today. I shall celebrate tomorrow by indulging in some luxury.

Happy birthday!   *Your affectionate*
                                           Henrik Ibsen.

---

[1] Koht (CE, XIX, p. 554) takes this to refer to Thomas Thoresen's younger brother Axel, but Bergliot Ibsen (p. 52) states that the phrase was one which Ibsen used affectionately of his fourteen-year-old son; presumably he enclosed a short note on a visiting-card to Sigurd as an apology for not writing him a letter.

Ibsen stayed in Vienna until the end of July. One of his fellow-jurors was a Swede, Fritz von Dardel, a gifted caricaturist (and much besides) whose diaries are an endless source of fascination to anyone interested in the Scandinavia of those years. In addition to a lively drawing of Ibsen, Dardel (to whom, almost alone among his fellow-jurors, Ibsen's name was known) noted in his diary: 'The black clothes and white cravat which he always wore, and the searching, penetrating glance which issued from behind his spectacles, gave him the appearance of a French notary rather than an artist. Throughout all our meetings he remained completely silent, spoke to no one and avoided all opportunity of making the acquaintance of his fellows, who were mostly eminent persons. When the rest of us went to take lunch together in the restaurant, Ibsen retired to the beer-hall, where he sat quite alone emptying his tankards. I joined him there a couple of times, and found much interest in his conversation. My fellow-jurors were amazed when I told them that their supposed notary was a famous dramatist.'[1]

On 8 July the jurors were presented to the Emperor Franz Josef, whom Ibsen had seen from a distance at the Suez opening; and four days later, they were taken by train to Murz to be dined by Baron Schwarz-Senborn, the director of the Exhibition. 'At every station where the train halted', the *Illustrated London News* of 19 July 1873 reported, 'troops of little children came running up with baskets of wild strawberries, bouquets of Alpine flowers and jugs full of fresh, cool water from the mountain springs . . . At the repast which followed the greatest conviviality prevailed.' Six days later he was awarded another medal to add to his collection. On 18 May the new King of Sweden and Norway, Oscar II (the younger brother of Carl XV, who had died of syphilis without male issue), having already been crowned in Stockholm in May, was crowned again before his Norwegian subjects in Trondhjem, and in the ensuing welter of decorating Ibsen received the coveted Order of St Olaf. On 26 July the jurors were invited on a trip to Budapest along the Danube, but Ibsen, surprisingly, seems not to have taken part in this; at any rate there is no mention of it in his letters, which there surely would have been if he had. It is possible that he had, by then, already left; the date of his departure from Vienna is not known.

He wrote a short report on the Exhibition for *Morgenbladet*, which that newspaper published on 30 August. What impressed Ibsen most were the entries from Eastern Europe. The Exhibition, he writes, 'will dispel certain prejudices which have hitherto existed; I refer especially to the outdated superstition that the Slav peoples have little or nothing to contribute to the

---

[1] Fritz von Dardel, *Dagboksanteckningar, 1873–1876* (Stockholm, 1916), pp. 28–29.

M

great common task of civilisation. The acquaintance which Europe has made in recent years with Russian writing should have ended such an attitude; but I have no doubt that the Vienna Exhibition will lead to a quite different and juster appraisal. It teaches us that in every sphere of graphic art Russia stands among the leaders of our age.' Ibsen concluded by asserting that Russia possessed 'a school of painters fully comparable with those of France, Germany or any other country'—a judgment hardly confirmed by posterity—and suggested that young Norwegian artists should be given grants to enable them to visit Vienna.

Ibsen's taste in painting was less discriminating than his taste in literature; for, explaining that 'medals could only be awarded to living artists and then only for works completed since 1867, a condition to which several countries, notably England, paid scant attention', he adds: 'Thus the English exhibits, though almost exclusively comprising masterpieces, gained comparatively few medals.' What were these 'masterpieces' provided by England? Ibsen does not name them, but a list is given in the *Official Catalogue of the British Section at the Vienna Universal Exhibition, 1873* (London, 1873). Turner, who had been dead for over twenty years, was represented by *Walton Bridges*, Whistler by six etchings and Cruikshank by five. Otherwise, there was W. P. Frith's *Ramsgate Sands* and *Lord Foppington relating his Adventures* (from Vanbrugh's play, *The Relapse*); Millais's *Portrait of Miss Nina Lehmann* and *The Sisters*; G. F. Watts's *Portrait of Robert Browning* and *The Angel of Death*; Landseer's *The Sanctuary* (lent by Queen Victoria) and *The Arab Tent* and *Self-Portrait* (both lent by the Prince of Wales); and Thomas Woolner's bust of Charles Darwin, lent by the subject. Also in the oils section were Mrs E. M. Ward's *The Tower, Aye, the Tower* and *The Last Sleep of Argyll*; W. B. Richmond's *The Lament of Ariadne*; George A. Storey's *The Shy Pupil*; C. V. Cope's *Othello relating his Adventures to Desdemona*; John Pettie's *Touchstone and Audrey*; and Sir G. Harvey's *School Dismissing*. It is a melancholy comment on Ibsen's taste in painting, which was always to remain curiously conservative (to the end of his life there is no record of his taking any interest in Impressionism),[1] that he should have described this collection as 'almost exclusively comprising

---

[1] Ibsen's apparent indifference to Impressionism is the odder when one recalls that Naturalism, as Mr Walter Allen has observed: 'was the literary equivalent of Impressionism in painting; just as the Impressionists painted objects seen in certain conditions of light and atmosphere, so the Naturalists depicted human beings in terms of their environment . . . It is part of Zola's strength, for instance, that in his novels he often sets out to describe a scene as nearly as possible as Manet might have painted it.' (Walter Allen, *The English Novel*, London, 1954, pp. 282–283.) One would have supposed that the author of *The Lady from the Sea* and *The Wild Duck* must have admired the Impressionists, especially as he himself was painted by Edvard Munch.

masterpieces'; nor could they even be defended on the ground of realism; they were the visual equivalent of exactly the kind of sentimental melodrama that he was trying to lead the theatre away from. A seventeen-year-old Scot, also in Vienna that August, making his journalistic debut as a roving correspondent for the *Alloa Advertiser*, condemned the whole of the English art section as 'glaringly inferior'. But the two men did not meet; William Archer had not yet heard of Ibsen.

Nor, one supposes, had a young Jew who had left school in Vienna that summer, and was likewise to become a passionate admirer. Sigmund Freud was then just seventeen, and in certain respects their lives and personalities were curiously similar. 'I could tell you about my long years of honourable, but painful, loneliness that began for me as soon as I got the first glimpse into the new world; of the lack of interest and understanding on the part of my nearest friends; of the anxious moments when I myself believed I was in error and wondered how it was going to be possible to follow such unconventional paths and yet support my family . . . and of the calm certainty which bade me wait until a voice from beyond my ken would respond.' That is Freud writing to Jung in 1910, but the words could have been Ibsen's; and in a few years Ibsen might well have echoed: 'I understood that from now onward I belonged to those who have "troubled the sleep of the world", as Hebbel says, and that I could not reckon upon objectivity and tolerance.' To Freud too, as to Ibsen, Rome 'became the symbol for a number of warmly cherished wishes', and a source of 'great happiness and even exaltation . . . experienced on every visit'. And one suspects that Ibsen, like Freud, had a 'confessed need for periodic experiences of intense love and hate'.[1]

One interesting relic of Ibsen's stay in Vienna has survived in the form of a photograph of the art and sculpture jury, twenty-five formidably bearded and whiskered figures. Ibsen, looking much the youngest (as, at forty-five, he probably was) is seated noticeably apart from the others, neatly barbered, in frock coat and spats, an order in his buttonhole, a top hat on his knee and a rolled umbrella between his legs.[2]

There was an outbreak of cholera in Dresden that July, so on leaving Vienna Ibsen spent a few weeks at Pillnitz, an hour from Dresden by steamer. Suzannah and Sigurd joined him there; and he had two other visitors. Lorentz Dietrich-son, who had missed him in Vienna, dropped in on his way north, and found him more grandly dressed than when they had last met in Stockholm. 'His outward appearance had undergone a change; instead of his smart short velvet

[1] Ernest Jones, *The Life and Work of Sigmund Freud* (Pelican edn., London, 1964, pp. 226, 238, 318, 384).
[2] See illustration no. 3.

jacket he was now wearing a long black coat that reached beneath his knees, of a very severe character.'[1] Dietrichson was not surprised when Ibsen told him that during their summer in the Tyrol the local children had kissed his hand and asked for his blessing, taking him for a Catholic priest.

Ibsen's other caller at Pillnitz was Ludvig Josephson, the young Swede who had succeeded Hartvig Lassen as artistic director of the Christiania Theatre. In Stockholm, Josephson had enjoyed considerable success as a dramatist, and had been director of both the Royal Theatre and the Opera, but had had to leave because the Swedish actors disliked being ordered about by a Jew.[2] In Christiania he had an equally rough baptism; as he tells in his memoirs, 'one director after another had been forced to resign because of the savage press criticisms, and public hostility',[3] and there was additional feeling against Josephson because he was (in addition to being a Jew) a Swede. The premiere of his first production that February had been repeatedly interrupted with boos, hisses and cries of 'Out with the foreigner!' and the police had to be called to restore order. One of the ringleaders was the son of Johan Sverdrup, the President of the Storthing. Bjørnson was rumoured to be behind the demonstrations; Josephson, who had directed several of Bjørnson's plays in Sweden and whose relations with him had hitherto been cordial, disbelieved this and went to Bjørnson to ask his help, but found him so hostile that he feared the rumour might be true.[4] He stuck to his post, however, and during his four years there raised the artistic standard of the theatre to a height it had never previously attained, as the list of plays that he presented bears witness.[5] Ibsen was to owe him a considerable debt, both now and later, when he ran the New Theatre in Stockholm; Josephson may be ranked as the earliest of those imaginative young directors, after Duke Georg of Saxe-Meiningen and his

---

[1] Dietrichson, I, p. 357.

[2] Per Lindberg, *August Lindberg* (Stockholm, 1943), p. 26.

[3] Ludvig Josephson, *Ett och annat om Henrik Ibsen och Kristiania teater* (Stockholm, 1898), p. 12.

[4] *Ibid.*, pp. 16 ff.

[5] They included: 1873, the first production in Norway of *The Merry Wives of Windsor* (with Johannes Brun as Falstaff), Molière's *Le malade imaginaire*, Schiller's *Joan of Arc*, Bjørnson's *The Newly-Married Couple*, *Between the Battles* and *Mary Stuart in Scotland*, Holberg's *Jeppe of the Hill*, and Ibsen's *The Pretenders* and *Love's Comedy*. 1874: *Coriolanus*, *A Winter's Tale*, *The Merchant of Venice*, Molière's *Tartuffe*, Sheridan's *The School for Scandal*, Musset's *Il faut qu'une porte soit ouverte ou fermée*, and Holberg's *The Scatterbrain* and *The Lying-In Room*. 1875: *Hamlet*, Goethe's *Egmont*, Molière's *L'Avare*, Marivaux's *Le jeu d'amour et du hasard*, Holberg's *The Political Potter*, Bjørnson's *A Bankrupt*, Ibsen's *Lady Inger of Østraat*. 1876: Calderon's *Life is a Dream*, *Peer Gynt* (then, on 15 January 1877, the theatre was badly damaged by fire, which curtailed the season). 1877: *Richard III*, *The Vikings at Helgeland*, Musset's *On ne badine pas avec l'amour*.

lieutenant Chronegk, who saw in Ibsen's plays the dawn of a new era in the theatre. He was the forerunner of August Lindberg, André Antoine, Otto Brahm, Aurelien Lugné-Poe, Konstantin Stanislavsky and J. T. Grein.

Josephson was anxious to make the acquaintance of the author of *Love's Comedy*, which was on the theatre's schedule for the coming season, and wrote diffidently to ask if he might visit him. Ibsen assented; and 'as the steamer approached the humble jetty, I saw a solitary figure walking to and fro on the shore, dressed in black with medal ribbons in his lapel, kid gloves and a tall black hat—a costume which suited neither the season nor the shabby surroundings . . . I recognised him immediately from the portraits I had seen. My astonishment at his dress and the formality of his manner (a weakness which never left him once he had gone abroad) vanished as soon as we had exchanged preliminary courtesies. Soon the total unpretentiousness of the man became clear to me beneath the formal surface, and I found him the most friendly, kind and unpretentious [Josephson repeats the word, *anspråkslös*] great man that I had ever met among famous authors. I have often since wondered at this curious passion of Ibsen's for appearing, if I may say so, dressed up. The appearance he chose for himself was more suited to a rich merchant or banker than to a philosopher and a poet.'[1]

Josephson accompanied Ibsen back to Dresden at the beginning of September, and they spent a good deal of time together, both in the cafés and at Ibsen's home. Josephson noted with curiosity the relationship between father and son. He found Sigurd 'handsome and elegant' but 'very strange, withdrawn and brooding' . . . I observed with surprise that the young Ibsen would at mealtimes make his entry at the last moment, bow deeply like a stranger to his parents and seat himself silently at table. In that house, where everything happened silently, scarcely a word was ever exchanged between father and son in a stranger's presence, and when the father or mother did speak the son always replied in a very few words, very slowly and formally . . . After eating the young man retired immediately with the same stiff ceremonious bow . . . We were happiest when we sat over our coffee and in the evening, when he had a great glass jug of ale brought in, which stood beside him on the floor and from which he himself filled our glasses . . . But I never saw his study . . . and I don't think many of his visitors were more favoured than I in this respect.' His favourite cafés, Josephson remembered, were those on the Brühl Terrace, the restaurants near the Wildsrufferplatz, and the Café Français in the Old Town, where there were Scandinavian newspapers available.[2]

---

[1] Josephson, pp. 38 *ff*.
[2] *Ibid.*, pp. 92–93 and 96–98

Ibsen liked the young Swede. On the whole, dare one say, he got on better
with Swedes than with his own countrymen; the Swedish formality suited him,
and he felt free of the reproach, unspoken or expressed, of being a 'bad
Norwegian'.

He restlessly awaited the publication of *Emperor and Galilean*. 'I hear from
Norway', he wrote to Georg Brandes on 8 September, 'that Bjørnson, although
he can know nothing of the book, declares it to be "Atheism", and says it
was inevitable that I should come to that.' Bjørnson's hostility towards Ibsen
had doubtless been sharpened by the latter's acceptance of the Order of St Olaf,
and although he was in Dresden that autumn he did not contact Ibsen.

On 2 October Hegel wrote that 'the orders for your new book have been so
large that I have had to have no less than eight hundred copies bound', and that
as an honorarium he had credited Ibsen's account with 3,200 riksdollars (£356).[1]
Ibsen replied on 6 October asking Hegel to invest the whole sum in gilt-edged
securities 'giving an interest of at least 4 per cent'. His letter ended with a
reference to 'new literary plans which have begun to stir in me'. These, again,
probably (though not certainly) refer to *The Pillars of Society*, though it was
to be four painful years before he completed it; its gestation was to be almost
as difficult as that of *Emperor and Galilean*. A few days later he learned from
Hegel that, despite the first printing of four thousand copies (twice that of
The League of Youth), a second edition was already being prepared; he greeted
this good news soberly by asking Hegel to use the new advance to buy Swedish
railway shares, adding: 'More profitable shares are nothing to have if one is
disinclined to speculate.'

Emperor and Galilean was published on 16 October 1873. 'The booksellers
were so interested in this work', Hegel informed Bjørnson, who cannot have
been overjoyed at the news, 'that the large edition . . . was almost entirely
subscribed, and the rest were taken by the Copenhagen booksellers on the day
of publication.'[2]

Of all Ibsen's plays, including even *When We Dead Awaken*, *Emperor and
Galilean* is the one most underrated by posterity; indeed, it is unique among
his major works in having been admired less by posterity than by his contemporaries. Ibsen himself several times referred to it as his masterpiece;[3] most
subsequent commentators have rejected it as a worthy failure. But few Ibsen
commentators can have seen it, and fewer still seem able to read a play as a

---

[1] Nielsen, II, pp. 313–314.

[2] *Ibid.*, pp. 51–52.

[3] Witness, e.g., William Archer's introduction to the English translation of the play
(London, 1907), p. xvi, and the report by Arnt Delhi in *Aftenposten*, 14 March 1928.

play, mentally excising (as a director of Shakespeare must) what on the stage would be tedious and superfluous—for we must remember that *Emperor and Galilean*, like *Brand* and *Peer Gynt*, was written not for the spectator but for the reader. *Brand* was regarded as unactable in England until 1959, *When We Dead Awaken* until 1968; in some countries they are still regarded as such, awaiting the director who can reveal their profound and exciting theatricality. The same is true of *Emperor and Galilean*. It has longueurs, especially in the first half of Part Two, but so have *Brand* and *Peer Gynt*; once one has stripped away the superfluous detail, a play is revealed which is a worthy successor to those two great dramas.

The action of *Emperor and Galilean* covers twelve years, from A.D. 351 to 363. Julian, who is nineteen when the play opens, and his brother Gallus live in terror of the mad Emperor Constantius, their cousin, who has already had their parents and nine others of their kinsmen murdered. Julian, like the Emperor, is a Christian, but is restless in his faith; under the influence of the philosopher Libanius ('There is a whole glorious world to which you Christians are blind') he goes to Athens to study the pagan religion. But in Athens he becomes equally disillusioned with paganism, and longs for a vision to show him his way. He hears of a mystic, Maximus, who claims to have power over ghosts and spirits, and visits him in Ephesus. There, Maximus expounds his philosophy to Julian: 'First, there is the kingdom founded on the Tree of Knowledge. Then the kingdom founded on the Tree of the Cross. The third kingdom is the kingdom of the great mystery, which shall be founded on both the Tree of Knowledge and the Tree of the Cross . . . Its life-spring has its source beneath Adam's grove and Golgotha.' In other words, Julian must combine the wisdom of Christianity and the wisdom of paganism.

Now Maximus summons up the spirits of three men who, as unconscious instruments of the world-will, most altered the course of history: Cain, Judas Iscariot, and—but the third does not appear. Then Maximus realises that this third is either Julian or himself; which, he does not know. Julian believes that he could alter the course of history, granted the companionship of a 'pure woman'. Then he hears that the Emperor has offered him his sister Helena as wife. This seems to him a further sign that he has been chosen by destiny.

The Emperor sends Julian to Gaul to quell a rebellion. His brother Gallus has been executed at the Emperor's orders, so that now Julian is the last of his line. He knows he is being spied on, and that the Emperor has sent him to Gaul so that if he fails at least the Emperor will be rid of him. When he defeats the rebels, a tribune comes from the Emperor to arrest him, lest he should march on Rome. Helena is pregnant; the tribune brings her a gift of peaches from the Emperor; she eats them and is poisoned—the Emperor's precaution lest she should bear Julian an heir. In her delirium before she dies she reveals that the child she is carrying is not Julian's. This extra disillusionment dispels Julian's last scruples; he decides to lead his army against Rome; but before doing so, he denies Christ and, under the guidance of Maximus, embraces paganism and appears before his soldiers smeared with the blood of the sacrifice. Here Part One ends.

In Part Two, Julian is Emperor, Constantius having died before Julian reached Rome. He proclaims a regime of tolerance; although he himself is a pagan, the Christians will be granted freedom to worship. But the Christians will not permit a return to paganism; they destroy the temples, and Julian is forced to take repressive measures against them. He becomes a worse tyrant than Constantius, because on a wider scale. He leads an army against the Persians, and is killed in the desert by a Christian who had been his friend but who now sees him as anti-Christ. As he dies he realizes that by his tyranny he has roused the Christians from their apathy and advanced their cause. Like Cain and Judas he has unwittingly, and in the opposite direction to that which he intended, altered the course of history.

Emperor and Galilean is full of extraordinary scenes: the opening in Constantinople, with Julian and his brother waiting for the mad Emperor's hand to fall on them as on their eleven murdered kinsmen; Julian's confrontation with the philosopher Libanius, who tempts him to forsake the church for the debating-halls; Maximus's evocation of the ghosts of the 'corner-stones' of history, and Julian's sudden realisation that he himself is to be the third of these; Helena's revelation that she is pregnant by another man, and Julian's order to the doctor not to save her; and the great climax to Part One, when Helena's body lies in the church, the army outside grows mutinous while Julian hesitates to lead them against Rome until he has taken the final step of renouncing Christianity, he learns that Helena's body is working miracles because she was 'the pure woman' and, maddened by the falsity of this, he makes the sacrifice and appears with the blood of the beast on his forehead. The first three acts of Part Two mark a certain slackening of tension, and are overweighted with grubbed-up knowledge which Ibsen does not carry very lightly; in any production, they would profit most by cutting. But the last two acts are of the quality of the whole of Part One; Julian's gradual submission to the force on which he has turned his back but which he cannot evade is as powerful and moving in its inevitability as the final acts of *Brand*, *Peer Gynt* or any of the great prose plays.

Emperor and Galilean marks a vital turning-point in Ibsen's development as a dramatist in that, although it is on an epic scale like *Brand* and *Peer Gynt*, he wrote it in prose; it is both the last play of one period, and the first of another.

The conviction which had been growing in him for several years that he must abandon the poetic medium in which he had gained his greatest triumphs found expression in a letter he wrote on 15 January 1874 to Edmund Gosse. Gosse, in a review of the play published in the *Spectator* on 27 December 1873, had regretted Ibsen's abandonment of verse; and we must be grateful to Gosse that he wrote as he did, for his remarks stimulated Ibsen to a clear statement of his new policy in play-writing. 'The illusion I wanted to produce', he informed Gosse, 'is that of reality. I wished to produce the impression on the reader that what he was reading was something that had really happened. If I had employed verse, I would have counteracted my own intention, and prevented the accomplishment of the task I had set myself. The many ordinary and insignificant characters whom I have introduced into the play would have become indistinct, and indistinguishable from one another, if I had allowed all of them to speak in one and the same rhythmical measure. We are no longer living in the age of Shakespeare. Among sculptors, there is already talk of painting statues in the natural colours. Much can be said both for and against this. I have no desire to see the Venus de Milo painted, but I would rather see the head of a negro executed in black rather than white marble. Speaking generally, the style must conform to the degree of ideality which pervades the representation. My new drama is no tragedy in the ancient acceptation; what I desired to depict were human beings, and therefore I would not let them talk in "the language of the gods".'[1]

In other words, *Emperor and Galilean* is at the same time Ibsen's farewell to the epic drama (at any rate until the final act of *John Gabriel Borkman* and *When We Dead Awaken*), and the forerunner of those naturalistic prose plays which were shortly to explode upon the nineteenth century like a series of bombs.

Despite the seeming remoteness of its theme, *Emperor and Galilean* is one of Ibsen's most personal statements, as self-analytical as *The Pretenders, Brand, The Master Builder* or *When We Dead Awaken*. Somewhat unexpectedly, he took pains to establish this fact. 'I have put a good deal of my own inner life into the play', he had written to Gosse on 14 October 1872, and again to Gosse on 20 February 1873: 'There is much self-anatomy in this book.' Three days later he told Ludvig Daae that it contained 'more of my own personal experience than I would publicly admit'. The problem that baffled and finally destroyed Julian was one that was always at the back of Ibsen's mind, though he seldom if ever mentioned it; where to find a faith to replace the Christianity of his upbringing. The third quarter of the nineteenth century was, more than

[1] Edmund Gosse's translation.

preceding ages, a time of revolt against conventional religious thinking, with bible criticism and natural science marching hand in hand, and *Emperor and Galilean*, in its search for a 'third kingdom' (a phrase which had not yet acquired a sinister significance) was as much a book of its era as *The Origin of Species*, Renan's *Life of Jesus* and *Das Kapital*. 'He who has once been under Him [Christ] can never be free', says Julian, and they are words that Ibsen himself, and many of his contemporaries, might have spoken.

It is a cliché that man is attracted by the qualities he lacks, and Ibsen's plays are permeated by a longing for what, in *Ghosts*, he was to term *livsglæde*, the joy of life. He deplored its absence in contemporary Christian teaching, which he probably (and with reason) blamed for his own inability to experience that joy; Brand and Pastor Manders, and those daunting lay preachers Rörlund, Gregers Werle and Kroll, denounce it as a sin; Bishop Nicholas and John Rosmer would like to enjoy it but cannot, as though castrated by their own church upbringing. To find a religion which would combine Christian ethics with the joy of life is a problem that has troubled many a piously educated man and woman; it was a problem which Ibsen personally was never to solve, and it is the central theme of *Emperor and Galilean* as it was to be the theme (or part-theme) of so many of his plays, whether explicitly as in *Ghosts* and *Rosmersholm*, or implicitly, as in *The Master Builder*, *John Gabriel Borkman* and *When We Dead Awaken*.

When Ibsen said that *Emperor and Galilean* contained 'more of my own personal experience than I would care to admit', I do not think there is much doubt that he was referring to the emotional strait-jacket in which he found himself confined, and from which, like his childhood Christianity, he could never escape. It is relevant to add here a remark that Professor Francis Bull once made to this writer: that his father, Edvard Bull, who was Ibsen's doctor during the latter's last years, once told his son that Ibsen was preternaturally shy about exposing his sexual organs even during medical examination. There was, indeed, much of Hedda Gabler in her creator.

Critical reaction to *Emperor and Galilean* was generally favourable, though somewhat bewildered. *Dagbladet* (25 October 1873) and *Morgenbladet* (13–16 November) both sat on the fence and contented themselves with discussing the theological and ethical implications of the play. Kristian Elster in *Aftenbladet* (19 November) praised it highly; Part Two, he thought, lacked the dramatic tension of Part One, but 'if this latter half makes a lesser impression . . . there is no doubt that its subject-matter demands even greater skill than the earlier play . . . It contains such a wealth of reflection, is written with such imaginative power and worked out with so rare an art that it nowhere essentially falls below the level of "Caesar's Apostasy" . . . Both plays comprised a masterpiece of high rank.'

Arne Garborg published a long pamphlet on the play before the year was out, and it is an interesting example of the kind of grudging admiration with which so many of Ibsen's contemporaries regarded him. 'He is read with interest, even greedily', Garborg admitted. 'His books are gutted with an eagerness otherwise unknown in our literary circles. As soon as the rumour spreads that a new work is expected from his pen, the public gets worked up into an anticipation which sometimes reaches fever pitch, and once it has been published and read it is discussed to the exclusion of all else for a long time afterwards in the circles where such interests hold sway.'[1] Yet with all this, continues Garborg, Ibsen is not the usual idea of a 'popular' author. He only asks, he gives no answer, he is but a seeker, and so people call him negative. 'Ibsen has somewhere said that the "gift of doubt", too, can make a man a poet. But this is unhappily where Ibsen is wrong. Doubt is not a gift, it is a standpoint—nay, more, it is only a temporary standpoint. As long as a soul doubts it is not yet fully developed, not free, and however mighty its talent it will stand impotent before its calling. Ibsen is an example of this. He has received the gift of creativeness in the richest measure, but doubt destroys his song. His poetry . . . cannot achieve full beauty because it is bounded by obscurity and darkness, and lacks reconciliation and harmony. This is the main reason why people are reluctant to acknowledge him. They are conscious of the sickness which lies at the heart of his work.'[2] Similar objections were to be raised against Ibsen's plays as they gradually came to be translated and staged in other countries.

Yet Garborg, though not realising that Ibsen's strength lay precisely in this power of arousing unease in people's consciences and forcing them to self-analysis, admitted his creative power ('Brand, Peer Gynt, Stensgaard, with what splendid strength do these figures not live in everyone's mind!'[3]), and granted that his lack of inner peace and harmony made him a true spokesman of his time—'for a lack of peace and harmony is the essential characteristic of our age'.[4] At the same time: 'It is with *Emperor and Galilean* as with all of Ibsen's works. One lays them down with a disagreeable feeling of dissatisfaction . . . With each book Ibsen merely throws a new *problem* at the

---

[1] Arne Garborg, *Henrik Ibsens* Keiser og Galilæer: *en kritisk studie* (Christiania, 1873), pp. 3–4.

[2] *Ibid.* p. 5.

[3] *Ibid.*, p. 8.

[4] *Ibid.*, pp. 16–17.

world—a new problem which always turns out to be the same old one. Ibsen's misfortune is that he cannot, like so many others, rest content with a half answer, and from the standpoint he occupies he will never find the whole answer.'¹ However, the pamphlet concluded generously: 'Viewed as a whole, it must be admitted that *Emperor and Galilean* is in many ways a truly monumental work, possibly without equal in any literature. It has its weaknesses, of course. But these weaknesses are mainly non-aesthetic, and the virtues of the book are so numerous and so important that one is inclined to excuse its philosophical shortcomings. All in all, our literature has good ground to be proud of it.'²

Erik Bøgh no doubt summed up many people's reaction when he stated in the Danish newspaper *Folkets Avis* (4 November) that, while *Emperor and Galilean* was 'an interesting work' with 'certain scenes of great power', it was so unlike what one had expected that 'many of his friends and the friends of his muse will surely lay it down sighing: "Thank God Henrik Ibsen has finished *that*!"' Ibsen's fellow-authors were less respectful than the critics. J. P. Jacobsen, the Danish novelist whom Rilke so revered, disliked it: 'There's no pace in the play, it's cold, the characters are without character.'³ So did Bjørnson. 'I've read Ibsen's *Emperor and Galilean*', he wrote to H. E. Schirmer from Florence on 19 November. 'It was a great disappointment.' But he added a perceptive prophecy: 'I think he's finished with *Brand*-style writing . . . and that we shall henceforth have what he will be a master at—plays of plot. We need them!'⁴

Georg Brandes did not at first like it. 'I am sitting in agony over Ibsen's *Julian*', he wrote to his mother soon after the book's publication. 'I can't really bear the play, though of course there's a good deal in it.'⁵ He did not review it until the following year, when he and his brother had founded *The Nineteenth Century*, and although his matured verdict was kinder he still, as usual where Ibsen's work was concerned, found himself divided. He found the dialogue 'full of dramatic strength and fire', and felt that in the best scenes 'Ibsen has never written with greater effect, perhaps never as greatly'. But he, like Garborg, questioned Ibsen's metaphysics: 'His strength and originality lie in psychological insight, and not in the solution of metaphysical problems . . . The sum impression of Ibsen's great new work seems to me then to be

---

¹ *Ibid.*, pp. 55–56.

² *Ibid.*, p. 69.

³ Letter to Edvard Brandes, 7 August 1884, *Brandes Brevveksling*, II, p. 261.

⁴ Bjørnstjerne Bjørnson, *Brytnings-aar* (*brev fra aarene 1871–1878*), ed. Halvdan Koht (Christiania, 1921), I, p. 168.

⁵ *Brandes Brevveksling*, IV, p. xxxv.

approximately the same as that of *Peer Gynt*. It is full of splendid things, in the highest sense profound and poetic . . . Had Part One been published first as a separate volume one would have praised it to the skies. A weaker section in Part Two has in some wise damaged the powerful effect of the earlier play.' But he ended by declaring that the work confirmed one's hopes for Ibsen's future, and that 'never previously has he understood and portrayed history as he has here'. With few of these judgments would one disagree.

Ibsen was delighted with the reception of *Emperor and Galilean*. 'I was especially pleased to hear that the first edition of the book has sold out so quickly" he wrote to Hegel on 13 November. 'And I am happy that the second edition can be expected so soon; for should the bookshops be without it any longer, every day would have reduced the advantage which we both might have had from its publication. I know my countrymen; they will save their money by borrowing it, and then not buy it. But this can't be helped; for who would have supposed that the whole large first edition would so soon disappear? From many letters from Norway I gather that none of my previous books has aroused such a stir up there. It has established itself in circles not normally concerned with literature.' Yet despite its (one would have thought) obvious dramatic possibilities, *Emperor and Galilean* was not to be performed even in part until 1896, when an adaptation was staged at the Leipzig Stadttheater. The first attempt to stage any of it in Norway was in 1903, when Part One was produced at the National Theatre in Christiania.

Ibsen had a row that November with Andreas Isachsen, the actor who had been the first *student* to join the Bergen company, and who had witnessed Ibsen's rolling in the snow during their walk to Hardanger. Without asking Ibsen's, or indeed anyone's permission, Isachsen gave a public reading of *Emperor and Galilean* in Christiania, in two parts, on 1 and 8 November. Ibsen read an advertisement of this event in a newspaper, and on 4 November he penned Isachsen a furious letter. 'You will doubtless recall', he reminded him, 'that I have repeatedly impressed on you the need of foreign travel. Being abroad does not merely develop one's artistic outlook; it also teaches one the requirements needful to behave like a gentleman . . . I have made it indubitably plain to you that I am wholly opposed to your interposing yourself between me and my public. I wish my books to come direct from me to my readers, and I cannot see what right you have to obstruct my wishes. Nor can I understand how you can find it in your conscience to make money from a work of art which you have had no share in creating. For you can scarcely deny that every penny you get from publicly reading my book you take from my pocket; and I cannot spare one of these; for I need money to live decently. Moreover, the fact of your choosing a new work for your performance shows that you have no idea what the purpose of a reading is. A work that is to be read publicly should be one with which everyone is familiar; otherwise what people will come to hear will be the work itself, and not the manner of its reading. And what is one to say to your presuming after so few days to seek to interpret by a public reading a work such as my latest? I can assure you that you need longer to get to the bottom of that.'

Morgenbladet devoted a leader to the matter on 18 November; Isachsen replied four days later that he had asked Ibsen a year or two back if he could give a public reading of some new work of his, and that Ibsen had, by implication, given him permission: 'His time was exclusively occupied with a big work, a trilogy, but once this was published I would find sufficient material there, which I took to be sufficient permission.' The author of the leader retorted with justice on 30 November that there was a difference between reading bits of a play and the whole of it. The incident, trivial in itself, underlines a problem which Ibsen was to face for the whole of his career: lack of copyright protection. Ibsen's letter to Isachsen is scarcely pricklier than what a modern playwright would write under similar circumstances to someone who had given an unauthorised performance of his work, and modern playwrights are not, as Ibsen then was, dependent on book sales for the bulk of their income.

That same month, on 24 November, *Love's Comedy* received its first performance, eleven years after publication. This, again, was thanks to Ludvig Josephson, the new director of the Christiania Theatre, who had just opened his second season that September with a revival of *The Pretenders*. There was much curiosity to see how *Love's Comedy* would act, the general opinion being (not unreasonably) that it was 'scarcely suited to the stage';[1] but the result exceeded all expectations, even though Sigvard and Laura Gundersen, as Falk and Svanhild, 'lacked the youth that these two roles demand'.[2] Johannes Brun, however, was excellent as Pastor Strawman, and so, despite his strained relations with Ibsen, was Isachsen as Guldstad. The play at once became a regular item in the theatre's repertory, and in the next twenty-five years was performed there seventy-seven times.

As the year drew to its close, Ibsen heard from Johan Thoresen that his debts in Norway had finally been paid off. 'I am particularly happy', he wrote to Thoresen on 12 December, 'that the business with Nandrup[3] has at last been settled. I am clear of debt and have several thousand crowns invested in the public funds, which Hegel has arranged for me over the years, and which

---

[1] T. Blanc, *Christiania theaters historie, 1827–1877* (Christiania, 1899), p. 281.

[2] Josephson, p. 36.

[3] See p. 59 above.

steadily increase in value, so that I look forward to the not too distant time when we shall be able to live exclusively on my interest and my pension.' When he came to make up his accounts for the year, he found it had been by a long way his best yet:

	crowns	£
3rd edition of *Love's Comedy*	645	36
1st edition of *Emperor and Galilean*	6,400	355
1st edition (supplementary fee)	640	35
2nd edition of *Emperor and Galilean*	3,200	178
2nd edition of *The Vikings at Helgeland*	609	34
3rd edition of *The Vikings at Helgeland*	609	34
Fee for performances of *Love's Comedy* in Christiania	1,200	67
	13,303	739

With his pension of 400 specie-dollars (£111), a grant of 100 specie-dollars (£28) which he had received from his trip to Vienna, and interest on his Danish and Swedish shares of 107 specie-dollars (£30), Ibsen's total income for the year amounted to £908. This was excellent by the average standard of Norwegian salaries. In 1870, a Professor ordinarius in Christiania received a basic salary of 4,500 crowns (£250), rising to a ceiling of 6,000 crowns (£333). An *adjunkt*, or qualified schoolteacher, got 2,800 crowns (£156), an *overlærer* or senior teacher 4,600 crowns (£256) and a headmaster 5,400 crowns (£300).[1] At the same time, it was pathetically little compared with what leading authors of a stature comparable to Ibsen's were receiving in the larger European countries. Anthony Trollope, for example, earned at his peak £4,500. John Ruskin averaged £4,000 from his book royalties during his later years. George Eliot had refused £10,000 for the copyright of *Romola* in 1862, and *Middlemarch* brought her £9,000 in seven years. Ibsen only started to earn one thousand pounds a year regularly when he was well into his sixties, long after he had become world famous; and, as we shall see, he often, thanks partly to his refusal ever to repeat the pattern of a success, made barely half that amount, sometimes less. Although he lived most parsimoniously until his death, and sold his copyrights outright, he left only a fractional sum compared with his peers abroad. Yet so humble was the rate of earning in Norway that the myth that he was a rich man has survived there to this day.

Still, 'This has been a good year for me', he was able to tell Hegel on 30

---

[1] Information from Mr Øyvind Anker.

December, adding: 'I have something new in my head and it grows clearer all the time, so that I think it cannot be long before I begin to write.'

The success of *Love's Comedy* on the stage stimulated Ibsen to think afresh about the possibility of a production of *Peer Gynt*, and on 23 January 1874 he wrote to Edvard Grieg asking him if he would consider providing a musical accompaniment and suggesting cuts, some of them surprising:

'Act One will be retained in its entirety apart from some thinning out of the dialogue . . . The wedding scene on p. 28 can be made much more of, with the help of ballet, than appears in the text . . . In Act Two the incident with the three peasant girls on pp. 57–60 should receive whatever musical treatment you feel appropriate; but there must be devilry in it! . . . There will have to be some kind of musical accompaniment to the scene in the troll palace, though here too the dialogue will be considerably thinned out. The scene with the Boyg, also, which will remain uncut, must have music; the Bird Voices to be sung; the church bells and psalm singing to be heard in the distance . . . Pretty well the whole of Act Four will be omitted in performance. In its place I thought we might have a great musical tone-picture to suggest Peer Gynt's wanderings in the wide world, with American, English and French melodies interwoven as changing and dis-appearing *motifs* . . . Act Five must be shortened considerably . . . The scenes on the upturned boat and in the churchyard will have to go . . . The scenes with the Button Moulder and the Old Man of the Mountains will be trimmed down. On p. 254 the churchgoers sing on the forest path; church bells and distant psalm singing should be indicated in the music during the dialogue which follows until Solveig's song concludes the play, at which point the curtain will descend while the psalm singing is heard again clearer and louder. That is roughly how I have imagined it . . . If you agree to come in with me on this, I shall immediately approach the man-agement of the Christiania Theatre, send them an acting script and ensure that the play is guaranteed a production. As a fee I propose to ask 400 specie-dollars (£111), to be shared equally between the two of us. I think it certain that we can also reckon on the play being performed in Copenhagen and Stockholm.'

Grieg accepted the invitation, though not with unmixed delight. 'It's a dreadfully intractable subject', he wrote to his friend Frantz Beyer that August, 'except for certain passages—e.g., the part where Solveig sings—I've done that all right. And I've made something of the Old Man's palace in the mountains, which I literally can't bear to listen to, it stinks so of cow-dung and Norwegian insularity and self-sufficiency! But I think people will sense the irony behind it.' On 12 September Greig complained to Bjørnson, who had told him that he was wasting his time: 'I can't but admire the way from start to finish it [*Peer Gynt*] splutters with wit and venom; but it will never win my sympathy. Though I think it the best thing Ibsen has written. Am I not right? But you don't imagine I had a free choice in the matter! I got the offer from Ibsen last year [*sic*], and naturally baulked at the prospect of putting music to this most unmusical of subjects. But I thought of the 200 [specie-dollars] and of the voyage, and made the sacrifice. The whole thing sits on me like a nightmare.' Grieg continued to grouse privately about the task, and it was not until eighteen months after he had accepted the commission, in August 1875, that he finished the music. Ludvig Josephson, on the other hand, to whom Ibsen broached the project in a letter on 6 February after having received an affirmative answer from Grieg, reacted enthusiastically to the proposal, begging him only not to omit the whole of Act Four, and suggesting instead several extra cuts, to which Ibsen agreed.

It was in fact only by the chance of a lost manuscript that Grieg was invited to compose the music for *Peer Gynt*. Ludvig Josephson tells in his memoirs how a gifted Swedish composer, August Söderman, 'had so fallen in love with *Peer Gynt* that, soon after its publication, he began to compose music for the play; and I still happily remember the many occasions when, sitting at the piano beside him, I went through scene after scene to the accompaniment of Söderman's personal performance of all the accompaniments he had provided to Ibsen's masterpiece. Unfortunately this composition could not be found at Söderman's death. It is known that in his lifetime he lent this work to various people, but when, later, *Peer Gynt* came to be staged, Söderman was dead and no one knew where his music was. So it fell to Edvard Grieg to set his great compatriot's ideas to music.'[1] Admittedly Ibsen offered the idea of a stage production to Josephson on the basis of Grieg's promise to write the music; but the idea of a performance was already on the Christiania files when Josephson took over, and I think there is little doubt that had Söderman's score been available Josephson, being familiar with and enthusiastic for it, would have suggested a production before Ibsen did. And even after getting Ibsen's letter, he would probably have succeeded in persuading the un-enthusiastic Grieg to withdraw from the project had a good score already been available.

Meanwhile, another continent was beginning to show a flicker of interest in the new dramatist. 'I am especially glad', Ibsen wrote to Hegel on 10

---

[1] Josephson, p. 9.

February, 'that a new market has been opened up for us in America. I think that *Brand*, *Peer Gynt* and *The League of Youth* will all, for different reasons, appeal to the taste of American Scandinavians. The only pity is that the sending of books there will involve so much extra expense.' The interest seems, however, to have been limited to those Americans who were able to read Ibsen in his own language (of whom there were already several thousand, after the large-scale immigrations of the past two decades). There was to be no American translation or performance of Ibsen for several years to come.[1]

That spring and summer of 1874 Ibsen worked on the rewriting of *Lady Inger of Østraat*. He asked Ludvig Daae if the latter had any comments on it as history, but Daae's reply, to the effect that it was historically very false and erred on the side of chauvinism, convinced Ibsen that to bring the play into line with the facts would involve too sweeping changes. So he limited himself to cutting asides, breaking up the longer monologues and sharpening the characterisation and dialogue.[2]

Georg Brandes visited Ibsen for a couple of days that June, and was disturbed at what seemed to him Ibsen's eccentric and conservative opinions. The gap between the two men had begun to widen. 'Kind though Ibsen was to me, as always', Brandes wrote to his mother on 18 June, 'I am too superior to him in education to get any use from long conversations from him'[3]—an astonishingly vain and foolish judgment which Brandes was later to retract. Three days later he described their meeting to a biologist friend in Copenhagen, Professor C. J. Salomonsen, as 'a visit on which I look back with a certain sense of despondency, though he received me most warmly. The man sits there producing very little, unable to draw intellectual nourishment from the world around him because he lacks the organs to do so, and is rigidly set in all kinds of prejudices and eccentricities. He has a sure eye for only one thing, namely, the prejudices of his homeland, everything that is obsolete in Norway and Denmark; but the lack of any kind of systematic education makes him desperately limited. Fancy—he seriously believes in a time when "the intelligent minority" in these countries "will be forced to enlist the aid of chemistry

---

[1] This same year, according to Koht (II, p. 74), there appeared the first French article on Ibsen, by a Mlle Leo Quesnel; but Koht gives no further details.

[2] P. F. D. Tennant (*Ibsen's Dramatic Technique*, Cambridge, 1948, p. 104) points out that of the fifty-nine asides in the original version of *Lady Inger*, Ibsen cut twenty-three in revision. Another thirty-one he replaced by stage whispers and thinking aloud; though what the difference is between them and an aside is not easy to see. Evidently it had some significance, for when revising *The Feast at Solhaug* in 1883 he replaced nineteen asides by stage whispers and thinking aloud. It is not until *Ghosts* that Ibsen dispenses with them and monologues.

[3] *Brandes Brevveksling*, IV, p. xxxv.

and medicine in poisoning the proletariat" to save themselves from being politically overwhelmed by the majority. And this universal poisoning is what he wants. The Germans, too, amongst whom he has lived for so long (without getting to know a single intelligent one and without reading more than one or two books a year—literally), the Germans too he knows very incompletely, and his acquaintance with one or two crazy Catholics has led him to throw in his sympathy with the Catholic faction, the while he calls himself a Freethinker. In short, he is lost in an endless chaos of characterlessness.'[1]

As a further example of Ibsen's eccentricity, Brandes recalled (eight years later, but referring to this same visit) that he was 'loud in his praise of Russia. "A splendid country", he said with a smile. "Think of all the grand oppression they have." "How do you mean?" "Only think of the glorious love of liberty it engenders. Russia is one of the few countries in the world where men still love liberty and make sacrifices for it. That is why she holds so high a place in poetry and art. Remember that they possess a writer such as Turgenev; and they have Turgenevs too among their painters, only we don't know them; but I have seen their pictures in Vienna." '[2]

Brandes thought that one reason for Ibsen's partiality for Russia lay in the fact that the country had no Parliament. 'Ibsen's whole character presupposes a distrust of and ill-will towards parliamentarianism. He believes in the individual, in the single great personality; the individual, and he alone, can accomplish everything. Such a body as a parliament is, in Ibsen's eyes, a mere assembly of orators and dilettanti.'[3] Like so many liberals who were working actively against conservatism in literature and politics, Brandes felt that Ibsen, by his contempt for practical politics, was not helping their cause; and it explains that growing coolness towards Ibsen which has already been noted. A couple of months after their meeting he was to describe Ibsen to a friend as 'remarkably receptive to every kind of reactionary influence'.[4] One can sympathise with Brandes's distress; ironical paradoxes of the kind with which Ibsen had loved to taunt his companions in Rome are infuriating to the earnestly committed. But that summer Ibsen was to undergo a series of experiences which were to alter his course sharply from the conservatism to which, as Brandes had observed, he was beginning to lean.

He had at last, under the influence of Suzannah's constant urging, taken the decision to do what he had been planning, and putting off, for so many years:

---

[1] *Ibid.*, I, p. 313.

[2] From Brandes's 'Second Impression' of Ibsen, written in 1882 and reprinted in his book, *Henrik Ibsen* (Copenhagen, 1898), pp. 79–80. Muir-Archer translation.

[3] *Ibid.*, p. 81.

[4] Letter to Hans Brøchner, 10 August 1874 (*Brandes Brevveksling*, I, p. 203).

to revisit Norway. He made the journey with the utmost trepidation; as he sailed up the fjord, he was to recall ten years later, 'I literally felt my chest tighten with a feeling of sickness and unease.'[1] It was ten years and one hundred and five days since he had last set foot on native soil when, at six o'clock in the evening of Sunday, 19 July 1874, he disembarked with Suzannah and Sigurd in Christiania from the s.s. *Aarhus*.

They lodged modestly at a pension in Pilestrædet, in the centre of town, and stayed two and a half months, apparently spending the whole time in Christiania apart from a week in Stockholm during August to attend an archaeological congress. The experience left him with, if possible, even more confused feelings towards his country than before. The people of whose friendship he had felt surest had, he found, become remote; and those about whose feelings towards him he had least evidence, and perhaps cared most, acclaimed him as a champion.

The first to seek him out were, naturally, his old friends from the Learned Holland circle, Michael Birkeland, Olof Rygh, Jacob Løkke (who had helped him with the poems) and Jonas Lie. But the decade that had elapsed since he had last seen them had separated their viewpoints, and he found himself much less in sympathy with them than before. Their cynicism, which he had previously found stimulating, now seemed to him to have stiffened into an extreme conservatism which he found distasteful. Moreover, he found that, thanks to *The League of Youth*, he was now hailed as a champion of the established order by those right-wing elements which ten years earlier had scorned and excommunicated him. The medals which he had sought so assiduously in the hope that they would give him a position in Norwegian eyes had had their effect, and he found the result not altogether to his liking. Ibsen had no desire to be regarded as a pillar of society. The experience must surely have reminded him that, although he had mocked the pretensions of the left in *The League of Youth*, and stood aloof from the liberal party, his political sympathies still lay to the left of centre, and with the young rather than with the old; and when he read in the right-wing newspaper *Morgenbladet* an editorial demand that a candidate for a professorship at the University should be rejected on the grounds that he was a free-thinker, he seized the opportunity to advertise his independence. He withdrew his subscription to *Morgenbladet* and changed to the left-wing newspaper *Dagbladet*. The uneasiness of the conservatives on hearing this would have been considerably increased if they had known what he was preparing for them.

This distant attitude towards his old friends was, by some at least of them,

---

[1] Letter to Bjørnson, 29 September 1884.

reciprocated. 'Ibsen is in town', wrote Jonas Lie to Bjørnson on 4 September. '. . . [He] has become a somewhat elderly gentleman with fixed opinions and personality', and he went on to describe Ibsen as 'Bismarckian'.[1]

But if Ibsen's old friends in Norway greeted him with reserve, the general public did not. The Christiania Theatre put on special performances of *Love's Comedy*, which Ibsen had not seen before, and *The League of Youth*. He attended both occasions, and was loudly cheered in the theatre which had so repeatedly humiliated him as a young man. After (appropriately) the performance of *The League of Youth* on 10 September, the Students' Union and Choral Society honoured him with a torchlight procession. They sang a song for him and thrice cried: 'Welcome home!' words which ten years earlier he can hardly have expected ever to hear in Christiania. In reply he delivered a cryptic yet, if one reads between the lines, revealing speech of thanks, in which he squarely identified himself with the young against the old:

'Gentlemen!

'When, during the latter years of my residence abroad, it became more and more clear to me that the time had now come when I must revisit my homeland, I will not conceal that it was with a certain unease and doubt that I prepared to return. My stay here was indeed to be but brief, but I felt that, however brief it might be, it might yet be long enough to shatter an illusion with which I wished to go on living.

'I asked myself: in what kind of spirit will my countrymen receive me? The sympathetic reception accorded to the books I had sent home could not wholly reassure me; for the question always remained—what is my *personal* relationship with my countrymen?

'It would be idle to deny that at several points a suspicion has prevailed. As far as I have been able to make out, the complaints against me have been twofold. People have felt that I regarded my personal and private relationship with my country with undue bitterness, and have accused me of attacking certain things in our national life which in the view of many demanded other treatment than that of scorn.

'I do not think I can use this, to me, so flattering and joyous a day better than by making a statement and a confession.

'I have never made my private relationships the direct subject of any work. These relationships were of much less consequence to me in those hard and early days than I have ever been able to explain to myself afterwards. When the eider bird's nest was plundered once, twice and thrice, it was of illusions and hopes that it was plundered. When, on festive occasions,

---

[1] Carl Nærup, *Jonas Lie og hans samtidige* (Christiania, 1915), p. 94.

I have reacted to reminders like a bear in the hands of its trainer, it has been chiefly because I shared the guilt of an age which drowned a beautiful ideal in songs and rhetoric.

'Well, what does it mean—to write? I realised late that to write is essentially to *see*, but—mark well—to see in such a way that the object seen becomes the possession of the reader in precisely the form in which the writer saw it. But only what one has *lived through* can be seen and possessed thus. And this business of living through what one writes about is precisely the secret of modern literature. Everything that I have written in the past ten years I have spiritually lived through. But no writer lives through anything in isolation. What he lives through, his contemporary fellow-countrymen also live through, together with him. If it were not so, what would become of the bridge of understanding between the writer and his audience?

'And what is it, then, that I have lived through and written of? The range has been wide. On the one hand, I have written of those visions of greatness and beauty which have stirred me in rare glimpses, in my best hours. I have written of what, so to speak, rose above my ordinary daily self, and I wrote of it in order to set it permanently before me and in my heart.

'But I have also written of the opposite—of what, when one looks inwards, one sees as the slag and sediment of one's personality. In this context writing has to me been like a bath, from which I felt myself to emerge cleaner, healthier and freer. Yes, gentlemen, no man can portray in his writing anything for which he does not, to some degree and at least on occasion, find the model in himself. And where is the man among us who has not now and then sensed and admitted in himself a contradiction between word and deed, between will and duty, above all between life and doctrine? Or who is there among us who has not at any rate now and then been self-sufficient in a selfish and egotistical sense and, half-unconsciously, half in good faith, attempted to extenuate this state of mind both to others and to himself?

'I believe that in saying this to you, who are students, I am addressing these words to their rightful audience. You will understand them as they are meant to be understood; for the student has essentially the same task as the poet, to clarify for himself, and thereby for others, those topical and timeless questions which are being asked in the age and the society to which he belongs.

'In this respect I dare claim for myself that during my exile I have striven to be a good student. A writer is by nature long-sighted. I have never seen my country, and the living heart of my country, so clearly or so closely as when absent and afar.

And now, my dear countrymen, a few words in conclusion which also relate to an experience which I have lived through. When Emperor Julian stands at the end of his road and everything is crashing about him, there is nothing which saddens him so much as the thought that all that he has achieved has been to be remembered with respectful homage by clear, cold minds, while his adversaries remained deeply loved in warm and living human hearts. This conclusion I have reached through deep personal experience; it has its origin in a question which I have sometimes asked myself down there in my solitude. Now the youth of Norway has come to me here this evening and given me my answer in words and song, an answer so warm and full as I had never expected to hear. I shall take this answer back with me as the richest fruits of my visit to my countrymen and my home; and it is my hope and my belief that what I am experiencing here this evening is an experience which will some day be mirrored in some future work. And if this should be, if I should some day send such a book home, then I beg that you students will accept it as a handshake and an expression of thanks for this meeting; I beg you to receive it as fellow-authors.'

Ibsen made one friendship during this visit to Christiania which, two decades later, was to have much meaning for him. Annette Sontum, the daughter of his old landlady at Bergen, had married an engineer named O. M. Andersen; he struck up an acquaintance with them and he enjoyed their company, and, too, that of their ten year old daughter Hildur, who already showed signs of becoming a talented musician. When he returned to Norway for good seventeen years later, Hildur was to become an important factor in his life.

'I have', he wrote to Hegel on 16 September, shortly before he left, 'been received with extraordinary friendliness by everyone. All earlier unpleasantness is now past. I am thinking of exploiting these good times by indulging in a little property speculation. Several of my friends have become well-to-do by this means, and I think things might turn out well for me too.'[1] But this did not mean that he was thinking of settling there himself. Ludvig Josephson, who saw Ibsen several times during his stay, recalls that he 'sensed that Ibsen did not yet really feel at home or at ease in his native capital, nor, to speak plainly, that he was happy. I and his wife had unceasingly sought to persuade

---

[1] In the end he decided against it, and instead bought 1,000 specie-dollars' worth of shares in the new Christiania railway company.

him to return to Norway for good, but he disliked having the matter raised, and was disinclined to consider it, the more so since this visit had failed to convince him that the move would bring him pleasure, fertilise his imagination or help him to reflect and meditate as he loved to do.'[1] Josephson adds that he thought Ibsen would have missed the art galleries and ancient buildings of Germany and Italy. Ten years later, Ibsen confirmed Josephson's impression. In the letter to Bjørnson already quoted in which he told how, on his journey up the fjord, he felt his chest tighten with sickness and unease. Ibsen continued: 'I had the same sensation during the whole of my stay there; I was no longer myself with all those cold and uncomprehending Norwegian eyes staring at me from the windows and pavements.' While his country had to some degree atoned for the neglect and contempt with which it had treated him during the first half of his life, he had not felt totally accepted there, in the way he had been in Stockholm and Copenhagen. He was to continue his voluntary exile for a further seventeen years. Some hard truths remained to be uttered, and Ibsen preferred to ponder and utter them from a distance.

On his return to Dresden at the end of September, Ibsen settled down to his rewriting of *Lady Inger*, interrupting it briefly to compose an epithalamium for the wedding of Hegel's son Jakob on 9 October. On 22 October he posted the final instalment of *Lady Inger* to Gyldendals, and Hegel published the play in November in an edition of 4,000 copies, together with a new edition of *The League of Youth*. Both were virtually fully subscribed before publication; and Hegel had the further good news for him that both *Catiline* and *Poems* were to be reprinted early in the New Year.

But the happiness of the Ibsen household was tempered by sad tidings. Suzannah's sister Marie, who had been spending a good deal of time with them in Dresden, and to whom they were both much devoted, fell seriously ill in Copenhagen, where she was living with her stepmother Magdalene. Suzannah went to visit her, and found her dying. Ibsen, who now found himself looking after not only Sigurd but also his nephew Thomas, with the aid of only a single servant, wrote a characteristic letter to Suzannah on 13 November:

Dear Suzannah!

I received your last letter the day before yesterday, but have not replied before because Sigurd has not had time to write. Don't worry, I am looking after him. We walk home together from our dining-rooms. Towards 5 we go out for a walk and

---

[1] Josephson, pp. 54–55.

return at 6.30. He gets up to far too many pranks when he is alone for me to dare to leave him by himself. So of course I never manage to get to the Literary Society. But he works hard and does his homework without my having to remind him.

I seem unable to do anything for Thomas just now. The humble food that I have to offer him does not seem to attract him, and he seldom comes here. He is working on a translation for the Christiania Theatre, and that may perhaps be another reason why he doesn't come here more often. He does not find the food good enough at the place where we eat dinner, so now he goes elsewhere. I don't think anyone would know he was ill; but when he has attacks he stays at home, and I have no time to visit him.

There is a lot of cleaning going on, as the winter windows have to be put in. But the cold weather has eased and it is very fine. The people of the house do everything for me excellently, and Lina [the maid] *is very helpful.*

I had intended to write some new poems for the second edition of my collection; but I cannot think about that while I have all the household affairs to bother about. We don't spend much; we have not had any extra expenses; in the evening we eat only bread and butter; we have not bought cheese, sausage or anything like that. Sigurd has got a very nice winter coat from my Roman woman, for only 2 thalers 15 groschen.

I must strongly insist that you fortify yourself with wine and nourishing food of the best quality; to stint on this could easily be a false economy.

Greet poor Marie from me, of course. You and she will know that I think of her with heartfelt sympathy.

I must stand by what I said in my previous letter about Herr and Fru Ludvigsen [Marie's sister and brother-in-law]. *You say that Sara has been good to Marie. Yes, the kind of goodness one shows to a sick servant. If Marie had been in Bergen the Baars* [her other in-laws] *would not have sent her to hospital but would have kept her at home with them. Likewise in Christiania; and so of course would we have done. Don't let yourself be fooled by such hysterical nonsense. But enough of that for today.*

I received the enclosed letter a moment ago. It must be from either Frøken Holck or the French Frøken Pradez; for it is postmarked Kallundborg and Count Lerche lives there. If it is anything that concerns me, keep it. If it is from Frøken Holck, tell her that I have written to her in Copenhagen and that it may not yet have reached her. She is one of our true friends, and a true sympathiser unlike certain others, despite all their forced empty phrases and protestations. Thomas very seldom remembers to ask after Marie. When he was in Copenhagen he did not visit her, although he knew he would never see her again. He says Sara told him it would disturb Marie to see her. Ask her if this is true; I should like to know.

Now it is getting towards dinner-time and I must meet Sigurd at the dining-rooms.

Write soon and let me know in detail how you are; for I don't really know at all. If anything critical happens you must telegraph.

Your affectionate

Henrik Ibsen

Two days later he had occasion to write again:

Dresden, 15 November 1874

Dear Suzannah,

   Yesterday afternoon we received your letter with the sad news of our dear Marie's death. So she is no longer with us; but we will cherish her in fond memory.

   Sigurd has told her closest friends here in Dresden of the event; Thomas came to see us last night and learned then.

   Now it is your task to make the last arrangements with composure and serenity. You do not say in your letter when you expect to be finished in Copenhagen. The Titania leaves on Wednesday. If you travel in her, drop me a line ahead. But if you feel too tired you must not leave so soon.

   I hope you will have received my previous letter today, Sunday. I am addressing this, likewise, to the hospital, though I don't know if you are still living there; but anyway you will have left your new address with them.

   You will of course see that the letters, etc. that Marie has left do not come into strange hands; in which category I include her Danish relatives.

   Make sure you have enough money and clothes for the homeward journey. It will be bitterly cold on the way south. Travel in a second-class ladies' compartment, and take amongst other things a bottle of good port wine with you. I have described your best route in an earlier letter.

   I am writing this on Sunday morning. Sigurd is at Thomas's. If possible, let me know the time of your departure from Copenhagen. Whether we shall be able to meet you at the station I do not know, since we cannot be sure which train you will be taking.

   Who will send the news to Marie's family and friends in Norway? I strongly urge that this should not be left to your mother, as I am sure you will agree.

Your affectionate

Henrik Ibsen

Suzzannah, with typical single-mindedness, had, on discovering that her sister had been taken to die in a public hospital, installed herself there so as to be with her day and night. 'Suzannah Ibsen came here from Dresden', wrote Magdalene to Lorentz Dietrichson on 1 December, 'and tended her and watched over her with a splendid devotion. You know Fru Ibsen. What she does she does with all her soul—nothing by halves.'[1]

---

[1] Dietrichson, *En Ibsen-myte*, in *Samtiden*, 1907, p. 97.

Suzannah's enforced trip to Copenhagen placed an additional burden on Ibsen's already strained finances. Already on 22 October, after their return from Norway, he had written to Hegel: 'This has been an expensive year for me. I am almost frightened to look at my account books.' For the financial promise of the previous year had not been fulfilled. This year, he had earned less than half as much:

	specie-dollars	£
7th edition of *Brand*	255	71
3rd edition of *Peer Gynt*	247½	69
3rd edition of *The League of Youth*	215½	60
2nd edition of *Lady Inger of Østraat*	568	158
Extra royalties from Christiania Theatre	200	55
	1,486	413

With his state pension of £111, dividends from his gilt-edged and railway shares of 170 specie-dollars (£47) and a win of £5 in the Danish state lottery, Ibsen's total income for 1874 had been £576; not much for a man approaching his forty-seventh birthday who was the most talked-of writer in Scandinavia and one of its best-sellers.

On 27 January 1875 Ibsen posted Hegel his foreword to the forthcoming reprint of *Catiline*. 'On reading through it [the play]', he explained, 'I clearly recalled my original conception, and realised that the form hardly anywhere achieved a full expression of what I had intended. I therefore decided to rewrite this youthful poem as I think I could have done even then, had I had the time and had circumstances been more favourable. But the ideas, conception and general development of the play I have not tampered with. The book remains as it was, save that it now appears in a fulfilled and completed form. These things remembered I beg that it may be accepted by my friends in Scandinavia and elsewhere, I beg that they will accept it as a greeting from me at the end of an era which has been, for me, rich in change and contrasts. Much of what I dreamed of twenty-five years ago has come true, if not always in the way I then hoped, or as quickly as I had hoped. But I think it was best for me thus; I would not wish that anything that has happened should not have happened, and when I look back on my experience as a whole, I do so with a sense of gratitude for everything that happened and to everyone who was involved.'

That winter Ibsen made up his mind to leave Dresden, for several reasons. One was, again, Sigurd's education. 'The school which Sigurd has been attending here', he wrote to Ludvig Daae on 4 February, 'has done away with its two senior *gymnasialklasser*, and the state schools of the city seem to me, in their general method and organisation, unsuitable for foreign pupils. Besides, I have again begun to feel the wanderlust, and during this past year more and more foreigners have been leaving Dresden. My move will, I fear, take me somewhat further from home; but as compensation for that I shall be a little nearer Italy, and shall moreover have the pleasure of living among Catholics, who in Germany are unquestionably preferable to the Protestants.'[1] A further reason was that of economy. 'Dresden, when I first went to live there in 1868', he told Jonas Lie (25 May 1879) 'was a cheap place to live in; but after the war rents and all other necessities so rose that in the last years we were there, up to the spring of 1875, we spent twice as much as when we first came'; and to Johan Thoresen, on 20 February, he complained: 'Dresden has now become the most expensive place to live in in all Germany.' He added: 'I have recently drafted the plan for a new five-act modern drama, which I hope to complete during the summer. I much look forward to getting down to this work, which has long been fermenting in my mind and has at last matured.'

The day before he wrote to Thoresen, on 19 February, *The Vikings at Helgeland* received its first performance in Denmark, at the Royal Theatre in Copenhagen, and proved such a success that the theatre, on their own initiative, doubled Ibsen's original honorarium of 1,000 crowns (£50).[2] On 20 March, Ibsen's forty-seventh birthday, the new edition of *Catiline* was published, to celebrate his twenty-five years of authorship, and, as a further act of homage, *Lady Inger of Østraat* was performed in its revised form at the Christiania Theatre, where the play had never been acted before.[3]

For some reason, a few weeks earlier, Ibsen had felt impelled to write to his father, for the first time in a quarter of a century. It may have been that, as he implied in his preface to *Catiline*, he now wished to forgive all that had happened and reconcile himself with the past. His letter has not survived, for Knud

---

[1] 'I think spiritual and intellectual life find fuller and more agreeable expression down there [in Munich] than here in North Germany, where the state has dragooned every power into its service and sequestered every interest', he wrote to Edmund Gosse on 10 March 1875. This letter is not in the Centenary Edition, but is printed in Bredsdorff, p. 36.

[2] Encouraged by its acceptance, Ibsen had, on 1 December, submitted another play which had been rejected when first offered, *Lady Inger of Østraat*; but the theatre's censor, Christian Molbech, reported that 'the picture this play presents is from first to last so gloomy and despairing that a stage performance would not elevate the audience but would have a saddening and depressive effect ... Poetry should not merely show death and defeat, it should also thereby proclaim life and resurrection' (Agerholm, pp. 276–280). The board agreed, and *Lady Inger* was never performed at the Royal Theatre.

[3] But it was not a great success, 'This youthful and sombre work did not succeed in arousing any very great excitement, partly because none of the main roles, except Lady Inger ... was quite adequately performed' (Blanc, p. 289).

Ibsen was so overjoyed at receiving it that he always thereafter carried it around on his person, showing it to all and sundry, until it fell to pieces. But the old man's reply (in Gothic script) has survived; it was one of the few personal letters that Ibsen kept:

Skien, 1875

My dear Son,

It gave me great joy to receive your welcome letter of 25 February, it was in truth unexpected, as I have neither heard nor seen anything of you, as you yourself say in your letter, for 25 years, none the less I have heard from you in your writings, *Brand, Peer Gynt, Love's Comedy, The League of Youth,* have all been given me. *Emperor and Galilean* I have received from Brøndlund, but I don't know if I may keep it.

It is a trial for me to write a letter, I wrote pretty well in my youth, but now age bothers me, for think I am 80 years old all but a couple of years, so writing tires me, so I have lived my best years and I only await my end. You will come to Norway this summer and then I hope we in Skien will hear from you, it will make me very happy. I expect Hedvig will have told you in her last letter about the family, so I will not repeat it as nothing has changed.

But I have one piece of news for you, and that is this, that Peder Lund Pedersen, who was confirmed with you, married a few weeks ago. He was previously engaged to a forester's daughter, but she would not marry him and he wanted to marry, so he had to make do with something terrible, one of his servants. Well now I must stop my prattling for I am boring my learned son with this nonsense. I wanted to read over this letter but couldn't decipher it, which made me very ashamed, so I must just end with a friendly greeting to you, your wife and son from

Your old and affectionate father
Knud Ibsen.[1]

It was the last contact between father and son; they neither met nor corresponded again before Knud Ibsen died two years later.

On 13 April Henrik, Suzannah and Sigurd Ibsen left Dresden. The seven years he had spent there had not, on the surface, been particularly fruitful, compared with his four years in Italy: two plays (one of them, admittedly, of double length), and a handful of poems. *The League of Youth* and *Emperor and Galilean* had both been successes, and his earlier plays were being steadily reprinted; but his reputation still rested principally on *Brand* and *Peer Gynt,*

---

[1] Bergliot Ibsen, pp. 73–74.

and many of his admirers must have felt, like Edmund Gosse, that the brilliant achievement of those two plays had not quite been followed up. At forty-seven his prospects must have appeared, possibly even to himself, not quite so glittering as they had been at forty, and if it had been known that he would never again write a poetic drama he might well have been written off as having passed his seemingly brief peak. But the apparently barren years of a writer's life are often, when viewed in retrospect, the most fruitful. *Brand* and *Peer Gynt* may, in themselves, be Ibsen's greatest plays, but his main contribution to the future of drama still lay ahead of him. Neither *Brand* nor *Peer Gynt* was to inspire many notable successors; whereas the 'contemporary' drama which he had been brooding on for nearly five years and was now, at last, about to write was, though it is seldom performed today, to be the foundation-stone of most of the plays that anyone has written since.

On 1 May 1875, after a fortnight's house-hunting in Munich, the Ibsens moved into a ground-floor apartment at Schönfeldt-Strasse 17, yet another corner-house, gloomy and barrack-like to judge from a contemporary photograph. The same day, in Christiania, the Storthing rejected by 54 votes to 42 a motion to increase his state pension.

PART THREE
THE CRITIC OF SOCIETY

NINE

⚰ Munich and Gossensass

(1875–1876)

IBSEN FOUND MUNICH much to his liking. 'Many Norwegians live here', he reported to Johan Thoresen on 21 May (how that recommendation would have surprised his countrymen!), 'and I find the air much fresher and more invigorating than in Dresden, a natural result of the proximity of the Alps.' Ibsen had an almost English passion for fresh air, as visitors to his apartment occasionally discovered to their discomfiture. 'He needs good air in quantity', an acquaintance was to note twelve years later. 'Lofty, airy rooms are an absolute necessity to him.'[1] He was a great one for leaving windows open.

Soon after his arrival, two unexpected windfalls came his way. *The League of Youth* in Stockholm and *The Vikings at Helgeland* in Copenhagen had both proved so successful that both theatres sent him an extra honorarium, and he found himself with an extra 500 specie-dollars (£139) to his credit. Thanks to this he was able to contribute to a wedding present for Edmund Gosse, for which a whip-round was being organised among Scandinavian writers. He also learned (through reading about it in *Morgenbladet*) that as an additional commemoration of his twenty-five years of authorship he had been awarded a special gold medal by King Oscar, from whom, on his last day in Dresden, Ibsen had received 'a very friendly letter in his own hand'. Moreover, Sigurd, he was able proudly to inform Thoresen, had, 'after an exhaustive examination', been accepted into the top form but one of the Royal Maximilian Gymnasium, 'although all acceptances should have been closed by last October'. Altogether, it had been a good month.

Ibsen's fondness for versification was dying hard, and he wrote three poems that spring. He had been invited to attend a meeting of students from the various Scandinavian countries at Upsala, and although he refused he sent them, to excuse his absence, an *Ode to Sweden*—a conventional piece stressing the importance of looking forwards and not backwards, and declaring his

---

[1] Henrik Jæger's notes of conversations with Ibsen in September 1887, first printed in Hans Midbøe's *Streiflys over Ibsen* (Oslo, 1960), p. 160.

209

O

belief that a new age was dawning. This was not much better than the hack celebratory poems he had turned out during his lean years in Christiania; on reflection, the sentiments he had expressed struck him as hollow, and he considered the subject more cynically in the first of an intended series of 'rhymed letters' which he had proposed to Brandes for the *Nineteenth Century*: thirty couplets of iambics and anapaests entitled *A Distant View* (*Langt Borte*). Hopes similar to those at Upsala, he recalls, had recently been voiced in Italy and Germany, but 'the ghosts of old grey men' had appeared to quench them. Nevertheless, the young men of these countries had eventually triumphed; 'they *willed* their dream', and so Europe grew up. We in the North, Ibsen concluded, must learn these hard lessons.

He posted this poem to Brandes on 8 June, promising to send a further poem each month 'unless unforeseen obstacles prevent me' (which they did). The following month, however, he kept to his promise, developing the same theme in a longer poem simply entitled *A Letter in Rhyme*, which, he told Brandes, had occupied him 'exclusively for four weeks'. Why, the poem begins, does modern man seem oppressed by restlessness and apathy, so that he is incapable of either true joy or true grief? As so often in his work, Ibsen chose as his central symbol a voyaging ship, but a ship with a difference. Sometimes, he says, a vessel will set forth, and all seems well. Then, suddenly, in mid-ocean, a blackness settles on her and on all aboard her; the sail falls slack, even the sea-birds' cry seems to bode ill. When this happens, sailors have a saying that 'there is a corpse in the cargo'. So, suggests Ibsen, it is with us today. A voice has whispered in his ear: 'I think we're sailing with a corpse in the cargo.'

What this corpse is, Ibsen does not say. 'I only ask. My task is not to answer', runs a line in the poem—a line that his enemies were often to use against him, apparently unaware that great writers very rarely answer the questions they ask, unless it be to preach resignation. In fact, though, Ibsen was to state clearly and repeatedly what he believed this corpse to be: a willingness to let oneself be dominated by one's past. The idea that we can only become ourselves, true individuals, if we slough off the past was a theme which he was to develop throughout his final twelve plays from *The Pillars of Society* to *When We Dead Awaken*, finding its fullest and most vivid expression in *Ghosts* and *Rosmersholm*.

This *Letter in Rhyme* was not merely to be the last of Ibsen's promised contributions to the *Nineteenth Century*. It was to be the last poem of any length which he was ever to write.

Another event that summer of 1875 strengthened Ibsen's conviction that prose was the path which he must now follow. The previous year Bjørnson, in Rome, had completed two new plays, *A Bankrupt* and *The Editor*, both written in prose on contemporary themes (he had begun *A Bankrupt* first, but finished it after *The Editor*). Both had been printed in the summer of 1874, but their publication had been held back to coincide with their production, an event which turned out to be considerably delayed. The Christiania Theatre refused to stage *The Editor* on the ground that the main character, a ruthless journalist who comes to a bad end, too obviously represented the then editor of *Morgenbladet*, Christian Friele, and indeed it was not performed in Norway until 1917, seven years after Bjørnson's death. Indignant at this censorship, Bjørnson offered the two plays to Nya Teatern in Stockholm, which accepted them, performing *A Bankrupt* in January 1875 and *The Editor* in February. Georg Brandes was greatly excited, and wrote: 'At last it seems as though we of the north, too, are to have plays in which those two great forces, the present and reality, demand respect and enter into their right.' He noted, correctly, that Ibsen had sketched both an editor and a bankrupt in *The League of Youth*, but thought that Bjørnson's were the first genuinely modern realistic dramas; and Strindberg (then twenty-six) later described them as 'signal-rockets'.

Neither *The Editor* nor *A Bankrupt* reads very well today. *The Editor* is impossibly melodramatic and is hardly ever performed even in Norway; *A Bankrupt* works reasonably well until the last act, when it declines into one of those facile endings to which Bjørnson was so fatally prone. (He defended it on the ground that 'it is good for people to know that a man can raise himself up again', and that 'it shows a true family life, good, happy people',[1] confusing, as he so often did, art with morality). Ibsen had treated contemporary problems far more profoundly in *Love's Comedy* and *Brand*, but these had been in verse; and although *The League of Youth* nowadays strikes one as both more serious and more penetrating than *A Bankrupt*, it was, ostensibly at any rate, a comedy, and comedies were expected to be in prose. But *A Bankrupt* and *The Editor* dealt with contemporary problems seriously and in everyday prose, and as such represented, at the time of their writing, an important break-through not merely in Scandinavian but in European drama.

Brandes's claim on behalf of the plays needs some qualification. Gogol and Ostrovsky had both written plays at least as modern and realistic as Bjørnson's; but these were as unknown in western Europe as *Woyzeck* and *Danton's Death*. And in 1873, the year before *The Editor* and *A Bankrupt*, Emile Zola had written *Thérèse Raquin*, so often named by historians as the first proletarian stage tragedy. Zola was indeed fully conscious of the need to do away with the artificially 'well-made' play. 'I have no taste for watchmaking, and a great taste for truth', he had written as early as 1865, two years after the Goncourt brothers

---

[1] Letter to Edvard Stjernström, 25 May 1874; *Bjørnstjerne Bjørnsons brevveksling med svenske, 1888–1909*, ed. Øyvind Anker, Francis Bull and Örjan Lindberger, (Oslo and Stockholm, 1960–1961), I, pp. 150–151.

had written *Henriette Maréchal*, which Zola himself regarded as the first naturalistic play. But although *Thérèse Raquin* represented a considerable step forward from the old Scribean dramas of intrigue, its language was highly melodramatic, running directly counter to Zola's demand that actors should not act but *live* before the audience (a theory which André Antoine was to put into practice at his Théâtre Libre a decade later). Zola wanted the drama to do what the naturalistic novel had done, as in Flaubert's *Madame Bovary* and his own works. But, unlike Bjørnson, Zola did not know much about writing plays; his own dramas, *Thérèse Raquin* included, are much less interesting than his prefaces and programme notes.[1]

The success of *A Bankrupt* in Scandinavia quickly spread to Germany, where before the end of the year it was performed in practically every town that boasted a theatre. Bjørnson was never to have another success to equal it in that country. Ibsen asked Hegel to send him a copy when it at last got published in 1875, and in June he saw it acted in Munich. Its success gave him the stimulus he had been needing to get his own new play off the ground. On 22 August he was able at last to write to Hegel from Kitzbühel in the Alps, where he had gone to escape the city heat: 'I have now completed my plan for the new five-act play about contemporary life which I have long been thinking of writing, and which, if nothing unforeseen happens, I shall finish during the winter.' The block that had obstructed him for so long seemed to have been broken. 'My new work is progressing swiftly', he wrote to Hegel on 23 October from Munich. 'In a few days I shall have completed the first act, which I always find the most difficult part. The title will be *The Pillars of Society*, a play in five acts. In a way it can be regarded as a counterblast to *The League of Youth*, and will touch on several of the more important questions of our time.' On 25 November he wrote: 'Act 1 of my new play is finished and fair-copied; I am now working on Act 2', and by 10 December he was 'working at it daily and am now doubly anxious to get the manuscript to you as quickly as possible'.

So 1875 ended on a hopeful note. He was busy with, and excited about, his new play; a new production of *The Vikings at Helgeland* had opened in Stockholm on 3 November, and in Christiania preparations were under way for the first stage production of *Peer Gynt*, Edvard Grieg having finished the music that July. Moreover, the first complete book about him had appeared: *Henryk Ibsen, poeta norwegski*, published in Warsaw, and written by Count Lars von Engeström, a Pole of Swedish descent. And the first days of 1876 were to see

---

[1] Of the other early realistic prose dramas which have survived, Henri Becque's masterpiece, *Les Corbeaux*, was to be completed in 1876 but remained unperformed until 1882. Tolstoy's *The Power of Darkness* was written in 1886, and Strindberg's first effective modern play, *The Robbers* (later rewritten as *The Comrades*) in 1886–1887.

the first publication of an Ibsen play in English—Catherine Ray's translation of *Emperor and Galilean*. It created little stir; of the only three reviews which appeared, one was by Edmund Gosse and the other two probably by him;[1] still, it was a beginning.

When he totted up his earnings for 1875, they were as follows:

	spd.	£
Fee for *The Vikings at Helgeland* at Royal Theatre, Copenhagen	250	69
2nd edition of *Catiline*	328½	91
Fee for *Lady Inger of Østraat* at Christiania Theatre	300	83
Fee for *The League of Youth* at Royal Theatre, Stockholm	250	69
Fee from *Nineteenth Century* for *A Distant View*	25	7
Extra fee from Royal Theatre, Copenhagen, for *The Vikings at Helgeland*	125½	35
Fee from *Nineteenth Century* for *A Letter in Rhyme*	25	7
4th edition of *The Pretenders*	281¼	78
4th edition of *The Vikings at Helgeland*	150	42
2nd edition of *Poems*	243¼	67
	1,978½	548

This, though better than the previous year, was nothing like as good as 1873. His stocks and shares at the end of this year amounted to over £1,300, but this was the result of considerable parsimony; his *huskassebeholdning*, or money in hand, was only 25 specie-dollars, a little under £7.

Posterity must be grateful that Ibsen was never able, like his more fortunate fellow-dramatists in countries where there was copyright protection, to rest on the laurels of his past successes. He could not afford either to slow down his production or to let his quality decline. It was plainly necessary that he should complete his new play with all possible speed. Asking Hegel to advance him the 400 crowns (£22) due to him as interest on his investments, he explained (10 December): 'You will think that I have become a spendthrift or that life is very dear in Munich, since I am spending so much money here. But neither is the case; the fact is that we have been compelled to part-furnish our present apartment, which we have now done, so that in future we shall live more cheaply. But this has been an expensive year for me.' He ended the letter on a nostalgic note. 'This time ten years ago I was uneasily awaiting the publication of *Brand*. Thank you for all that has happened since! No one has contributed

---

[1] Cf. Bredsdorff, p. 37. The signed review was in the *Academy* on 10 June, the anonymous ones in the *Examiner* on 29 January and the *Athenaeum* on 12 February.

as much as you to the difference between my situation as it was then and as it is now. Be sure that I shall never forget this.' Nor did he.

By now Ibsen was making friends among the local Germans, something he seems never to have done in Dresden. 'I have begun to mix in a large literary group', he informed Johan Thoresen on 6 February 1876, 'where I have been greeted with exceptional kindness and courtesy.' This group was known as the Crocodile, and its members included several well-known German literary figures: the poets Hermann Lingg and Karl Streler, the comic writer Ferdinand Bom, Franz Grandaur, dramaturge and director of opera at the Munich Hoftheater, and, the most talented among them, the novelist and short story writer Paul Heyse, who had recently published two acclaimed novels, *Kinder der Welt* and *Im Paradiese*, the latter being a *roman à clef* about writers and artists in Munich. (It is a pity Ibsen did not come to Munich a year earlier, or he might well have appeared in it.) Heyse was also a prolific dramatist (though he was less successful in this field), a fluent linguist (he even ultimately learned Norwegian), and a distinguished translator of, amongst other authors, Shakespeare and Leopardi. 'Visit him often', Ibsen was to advise a young fellow-Norwegian. 'You will always learn something from this excellent and artistic writer.'[1] Two years younger than Ibsen almost to the day, Heyse was (though he disapproved violently of *Ghosts*) to maintain a long friendship with him—and he was to achieve one literary feat which Ibsen never did, for in 1914 he received the Nobel Prize for literature, although, as with so many recipients of that prize, posterity has not confirmed the verdict of the Swedish Academy.

Among the younger members of the Crocodile was a writer named Paul Lindau, who forty years later recalled their meetings.[2] He remembered that Ibsen looked much older than his years, and that he combed his hair frequently and never tired of looking at himself in mirrors. In the street he would stop before every mirror and comb his hair back from his forehead. Although Ibsen enjoyed jokes, he disapproved (surprisingly, for so ostentatious a free-thinker) of any jests concerning religion. Once when Lindau made such a jest Ibsen became very tight-lipped, snapped: 'There are some things one doesn't make fun of', and left the table. Lindau also recalled that Ibsen once told him that every time he finished a play he felt it was the last he would write, because he had said in it everything that he had to say.

The Crocodile used to meet daily at noon, first at the Café Probst, subsequently at their favourite rendezvous, the café of the Hotel Achatz in the Maximilianplatz. Another member was a young Norwegian painter named

---

[1] Paulsen, *Samliv med Ibsen*, II, p. 43.

[2] Paul Lindau, *Nur Erinnerungen* (Stuttgart & Berlin, 1917), pp. 369, 374–376, 383.

Marcus Grønvold, whom Ibsen liked and who has left an interesting account of him at this period. According to Grønvold, Ibsen at first attended these gatherings regularly, and even stood a couple of parties himself at a restaurant —'but since he was afraid that his work might suffer and social life gain the upper hand, he later began to attend less regularly'.[1]

Grønvold describes Ibsen's routine. He would breakfast simply on a small cup of black coffee and a roll, and would then work till one. After lunch he would rest, and then walk in the streets 'his sharp eyes perceiving everything, however buried in his own thoughts he might seem. People, shop windows, even dogs, were the objects of his attention. Sometimes he pondered what he would put on paper the following morning. On winter evenings his figure would appear like a phantom in the dark arcades of the Hofgarten. On these walks Ibsen did not like to be disturbed; he was as scant of speech then as, at other times, he could be communicative. When he returned home he again usually remained silent, and after his evening meal would walk up and down the room, smoking his pipe and listening to the conversation. But he listened carefully, taking pleasure in it, and sometimes partaking greedily, especially when eccentric characters whom he had known in his youth, gifted wrecks, were mentioned—characters such as he was to create in the persons of Ulric Brendel and Ejlert Løvborg. He once referred to such a man as "an ex-human being."'

As in the old days, in Rome, he loved to start an argument, but when he got bored with it he would break it off curtly, saying, 'Well, there are two sides to every question.' He loved to question people about their jobs, 'but if he saw that they had come to study him or were expecting witty or Sphinx-like utterances, he withdrew into his shell.' He enjoyed stories and anecdotes, especially risqué ones; 'He regretted that one could not use such stories and events in one's writing, since they were usually the best' (a pleasant corrective to the customary picture of Ibsen as a puritan). He also once remarked to Grønvold how difficult it was to finish a play when the spiritual process was already completed and other ideas were beginning to crop up. 'It demands so much self-discipline *properly* to complete a work', he said, 'for interest ceases at a comparatively early stage.' He added: 'At the moment of conception one must be on fire, but at the time of writing, cold.'

Like so many of those who knew Ibsen well, as opposed to his casual acquaintances, Grønvold speaks very highly of Suzannah. He calls her 'understanding, warm-hearted and moreover . . . free from all pettiness and narrow-

---

[1] For this and the following quotations from Grønvold, cf. his *Fra Ulrikken til Alperne* (Oslo, 1925), pp. 137 ff.

mindedness, intellectually independent . . . a woman of aristocratic intelligence'.[1]

On 24 February *Peer Gynt* was at last staged, at the Christiania Theatre. It was the most expensive production hitherto attempted in Norway, and proved a tremendous success. The reception at the premiere, recorded Ludvig Josephson, who directed it, was 'such as I have rarely experienced'.[2] The play seems to have been produced with the accent on the lyrical rather than the satirical aspects (as it was to be for many years to come and, sadly, still often is). Few musical scores can have so softened an author's intentions as Grieg's *Peer Gynt* suite, which turns the play into a jolly Hans Andersen fairy tale; but Ibsen was too unmusical to perceive this, and was delighted with the result, though he might have been less so had he seen it. 'Thank you for *Peer Gynt*!' he wrote to Josephson on 5 March. 'The outcome of this bold enterprise by your theatre has exceeded all my expectations.'[3] The play was performed thirty-seven times during the next ten and a half months, an unprecedented number for so serious a work, when one remembers that *The Pretenders* was reckoned to have done creditably with eight. It would have continued longer had not a fire destroyed the expensive scenery and costumes the following January.

Munich theatrical circles had, meanwhile, begun to take note of the foreign dramatist in their midst, and on 10 April the Hoftheater (thanks perhaps to its dramaturge's acquaintance with Ibsen in the Crocodile) staged *The Vikings at Helgeland*, the first performance of an Ibsen play outside Scandinavia. 'The house was virtually full', Ibsen reported to Hegel the following day, 'and the play was received with a storm of applause. I watched the performance from the wings, and was called on to the stage five times. After the performance the writers of Munich [presumably his colleagues in the Crocodile] improvised a party for me, which continued long into the night.' He even received a congratulatory letter from that passionate theatre lover Ludwig II, the mad King of Bavaria, Richard Wagner's friend, who was to kill himself (and his doctor) ten years later.

The success of *The Vikings* was good enough, but better was to follow. 'I have this moment', Ibsen informed Hegel on 30 May, 'received an invitation from the Duke of Meiningen to go to Berlin, where on Saturday his company is to act *The Pretenders* for the first time . . . The story that a Danish paper printed about the play being acted in Meiningen and receiving no applause is

[1] *Ibid.*, p. 145.
[2] Josephson, p. 62.
[3] But Ibsen seems to have had second thoughts about Grieg's score later (see vol. 3).

untrue. It was only a trial performance without the new decor and without any cuts.' To appear suitably dressed at so important an occasion required more money than Ibsen had to hand, and he begged Hegel to send him 450 reich-marks (£22) to him in Berlin and a like sum to Suzannah in Munich. This was hardly a loan, for Hegel had 400 crowns (£22) to Ibsen's credit from the Stock-holm production of *The Vikings*, and the interest on his shares was due in June. Hegel obliged as always, and so Ibsen saw for the first time the greatest theatri-cal company of his age.

The influence of the 'Meiningers' on the technique of stage production was almost as great as that of Ibsen on the technique of dramatic writing, and we may pause for a moment to consider it. André Antoine, who saw them in Brussels in 1888, and Konstantin Stanislavsky, who spent a year with them, have both described how the Meininger productions opened their eyes to the possibility of a theatrical realism of which they had never dreamed. Stanislavsky, indeed, recalled that it was their appearance in St Petersburg which first fired him to enter the theatre. The company was the creation of the new ruler of Saxe-Meiningen, Duke Georg II. Meiningen itself was a tiny town of only seven thousand inhabitants, but Duke Georg was no dilettante; the great Viennese actor, Josef Levinsky, described him as 'the finest theatrical director Germany has ever known', adding significantly: 'His deep understanding of dramatists' intentions is far more important than any amount of splendid decor.'[1]

Many of the innovations which we today accept as a natural prerequisite of any good production, and which are commonly attributed to Antoine, Stanislavsky, Reinhardt and Granville Barker, were introduced by Duke Georg in the eighteen-seventies. Ensemble acting; the conception of decor as an integral and imaginative part of the production instead of a mere back-ground; intelligent and searching characterisation, instead of the kind of theatricality that used the text as a trampoline; and above all, the treatment of crowds as so many individuals and not as a dumb and uncomprehending col-lection of extras—these were the innovations (or rather, since nothing is wholly new in the theatre, the re-creations) of Duke Georg which astonished and ex-cited his contemporaries. What these methods meant to an imaginative man of the theatre may best be evoked by quoting the reactions of Antoine and William Archer on seeing them for the first time. Here is Antoine writing to the critic Francisque Sarcey after seeing the Meiningers in Brussels in 1888:

'They showed us things absolutely new and very instructive. Their crowds are not like ours, composed of elements picked haphazard,

---

[1] Bjørn Bjørnson, *Bare ungdom* (Oslo, 1934), p. 153.

working men hired for dress rehearsals, badly clothed, and unaccustomed
to wearing strange and uncomfortable costumes, especially when they are
exact. Immobility is almost always required of the crowds on our stage,
whereas the supernumeraries of the Meininger crowds must act and mime
their characters. Don't understand by that that they force the note and
that the attention is distracted from the protagonists. No, the tableau is
complete and, in whatever direction you may look, you fix your eyes on
a detail in the situation or character. At certain moments, its power is
incomparable.

'The troupe of the Meininger company contains about seventy actors
of both sexes. All those who do not take a part are expected to figure in the
play, and every evening too. If there are twenty actors occupied, the fifty
others, without a single exception, even in the case of the leading players,
appear on the stage in the tableaux, and each leading actor is the chief, the
corporal, of a group of real supernumeraries, whom he directs and watches
as long as the company is under the eye of the public. This obligation is
such that the wife of Hans von Bülow,[1] one of the stars of the Meininger,
having refused to perform this service, which she considered beneath her
talent, was dismissed, although her husband had the title and functions of
Kapellmeister to the Duke of Saxony. In this way they obtain ensembles that
are extraordinarily true to life ... Mlle Lindner, their star, playing in *A
Winter's Tale*, took a silent part in the tableau of the seat of Justice, and
mimed a woman of the people as conscientiously and as carefully as she
interpreted on the following evening the important role of Hermione in
the same piece.'[2]

William Archer covered the company's visit to London in June and July,
1881, as a young critic of twenty-five for the *London Figaro* (4 June and subsequent issues). Of their opening production, *Julius Caesar* (in which Bjørnson's
son, Bjørn, the only non-German member of the group, acted Casca), Archer
noted: 'In the first scene already, a peculiarity of stage management is noticeable. The crowd does not remain *au deuxième plan*, acting as a background to
the tribunes. On the contrary, Flavius and Marullus mix with it and elbow
with it, sometimes almost hidden in its midst. It has all the uncertain fluctua-
tions of an actual crowd. Its splendid drill produces the effect of absolute freedom from drill.' Of the scene when Antony addresses the crowd in the
Forum, Archer wrote that the actor, Ludwig Barnay, 'did not address himself

---

[1] Marie Schanzer. Bülow's first wife, Cosima, had left him to become the mistress, later
the wife, of Richard Wagner.

[2] S. M. Waxman, *Antoine and the Théâtre Libre* (Harvard, 1926), pp. 95–96.

to the imagination of the audience, but to the living and moving populace before him . . . It is rather by inference than by personal sensation or intuition that we recognise the power of Mark Antony's oratory. We see how it moves the crowd, and by an act of judgment we decide that it should and must be so moved . . . The scene is presented in a manner far surpassing anything of the kind as yet attempted in England. Indeed, I search my memory in vain for anything with which to compare it even for an instant.'

Of their decor, Archer wrote: 'They take the trouble to distinguish between tree and tree, whereas our scene-painters have one recipe for every species of foliage, varied only by a dash of red-brown when an autumn landscape has to be depicted. Their handling of tree-stems and bark struck me as particularly admirable.' In their production of *William Tell* ('a marvellously fine and thoughtful presentation'), he noted the effect of rain which they achieved by 'a peculiar arrangement of light, and some motion in the backcloth'; the use of steam to represent dust when the Swiss tear down the Austrian castle; the small boys with beards on scaffolding at the back of the stage to give the effect of perspective; their presentation of the figure of Time as a young girl; and the care and individuality of their make-up. And they were far in advance of other European companies in their treatment of comedy; Archer thought that their *Malade imaginaire* 'need not shrink from comparison with the Comédie-Française itself', though he had seen Coquelin in the part.[1] Henry Irving saw them during their visit, and admired, and was influenced by, their crowd work and lighting.

The Meininger production of *The Pretenders* in Berlin was a great success; how one would love to have seen what Duke Georg did with the crowd scenes in which the play abounds, and especially his treatment of the battle scenes. Writing to Ludvig Josephson on 14 June, Ibsen described the performance as 'brilliant and spectacular. The play was received with great applause, and I was repeatedly called. I don't think this much pleased the Berlin critics, most of whom are themselves playwrights. However, the play

---

[1] Irrelevantly but interestingly, one may mention that in his column of 4 June Archer quotes an American paper as reporting that 'the adoption of a revolving stage, such as is seen in Japanese playhouses, is contemplated by several European theatres', and that on 13 July, reviewing a production of *Romeo and Juliet* by the Oxford Agamemnon Company, he observed with pleasure that 'Shakespeare's original text was followed throughout, instead of the ordinary acting version.' Archer's criticisms during his six years with *London Figaro* and his twenty-one years with *The World* are a fascinating mine of theatrical history.

Bjørn Bjørnson records that when they acted in Meiningen itself the Duke used real soldiers from his own army for the crowd scenes, and that when they played in big theatres they would have five or six hundred people on the stage (*Bare ungdom*, p. 176).

has run for nine successive performances, and would have continued longer had the Meiningers not been scheduled to end their season on the 15th. After the opening performance I was invited by the Duke to visit him at his summer palace at Liebenstein in Meiningen, where I have been staying until I came back here [to Munich] the day before yesterday.' And as if that was not enough, 'On my departure he decorated me with the Knight Cross of the Saxon-Ernestine Order, First Class. *The Pretenders* is to be given in Schwerin too, and *The Vikings* has been accepted by the Burgtheater in Vienna, where Charlotte Wolter is to play Hjørdis.' Ibsen got on well with monarchs, and the Duke, who plainly liked Ibsen, as Carl XV and Oscar II had done, invited him to come back in the winter. Indeed, the time was to come when Ibsen had to give up visiting a certain resort because Duke Georg, who had a place in the vicinity, so pestered him with invitations as to make it impossible for him to work.

Did the Meininger methods influence Ibsen's future writing? It is possible; the realism of that production of *The Pretenders* may well have had its effect on *The Pillars of Society*, which he was at last to complete during the following year. Mr Peter Tennant suggests: 'The setting and detail of the stage directions, with their references to gesture and expression, could almost have been taken out of a Meiningen producer's manuscript, and the detailed realism of the play strikes one as a reminiscence of the Meiningers and an exploitation of Meininger methods in the interest of modern social drama. The influence of the Meininger Company on Ibsen's technique cannot be proved, but circumstantial evidence goes to show that it was a factor.'[1] In fact, Ibsen had already, by the time he saw the Meiningers, completed his first draft of Act One and Part of Act Two, with stage directions almost as detailed as in the final draft; but their methods must have given him the assurance that a technique of production and acting was developing which might eventually be equal to the demands he was planning to make.

On 5 August Ibsen took Suzannah and Sigurd for their usual holiday in the mountains, but this year, instead of Berchtesgaden, they tried somewhere new. 'We shall be staying', he informed Edvard Grieg, who was in Bayreuth for the opening of the Festspielhaus with the first complete performance of Wagner's *Ring*, 'at Gossensass, a country town near the Brenner railway, between Brenner and Sterzing. You must come via Munich, Rosenheim and Innsbruck, it being only 3–4 hours by rail from the last-named town to Gossensass. We shall probably be lodging at the "Brauhaus" Inn—in any case, you will find out where we are even if you don't warn us of your arrival. You

---

[1] Tennant, pp. 54–55.

will be most warmly welcome, and I hope you won't make too brief a stay. After the exhausting pleasures of Bayreuth you will need fresh mountain air, and you will find it up there.'

Grieg duly arrived in Gossensass, bringing with him a young writer from Bergen named John Paulsen, who had accompanied him to Bayreuth. Paulsen, then twenty-five, had published a few things, including some poems which Grieg had set to music, and he was to become a prolific, if not greatly talented, novelist and playwright. His poems and novels are scarcely read today, and his plays will never be performed again, but in a series of memoirs he was to leave one of the most vivid and intimate pictures of Ibsen that we possess. He was inclined to romance from hearsay when reporting, but his first-hand observation was perceptive and lively.

Paulsen had his first sight of Ibsen as he and Grieg walked from the station into the little town. They had not warned Ibsen of their arrival, and chanced on him as he was taking a walk.

'Ibsen . . . reminded me of a bridegroom going in his best clothes to meet his beloved. The black tail coat with order ribbons, the dazzlingly white linen, the elegantly knotted cravat, the black, correct silk hat, the precise movements, the reserved expression, all put me in mind of his poem:

I shrink from the mob.
I have no wish to be clasped to their hot bosom.
I shall await whatever time may bring
In a well-pressed morning coat.

'Grieg introduced me. The conventional courtesies were exchanged. Ibsen's face expressed neither joy nor displeasure at seeing us. Gradually I studied his remarkable physiognomy—the small, blue-grey eyes behind the gold spectacles, the high, unusually broad brow, seemingly gnarled with thought, the long grizzled whiskers, the fine, pursed mouth, thin as a knife-blade . . . I stood before a closed mountain-wall, an impenetrable riddle.'[1]

Paulsen could not help contrasting this figure with the poet in his Christiania days as described to him by an unnamed friend who had known Ibsen then: 'seated alone at one of the humbler cafés, his cheek resting on his hand and a careworn expression round his mouth, his beard allowed to grow unchecked, his hair an unkempt mane, on his head an old slouch hat'.[2]

Each evening they ate together in the Brauhaus, 'the cosy little room with

---

[1] Paulsen, *Mine Erindringer* (Copenhagen, 1900), pp. 10–11.
[2] *Ibid.*, p. 15.

the Madonna painting on the wall, the friendly young Tyrolean landlord who knew Latin and Italian . . . the meal, which usually consisted of ham and fried eggs, with home-brewed beer or *vin ordinaire*, and a bunch of grapes for dessert, the itinerant zither-player who occasionally appeared to my delight and Grieg's distress . . . All day Ibsen would be silent and unapproachable. He often invited me to accompany him on his walks, but never uttered a word . . . Yet when we parted he never failed to thank me for my "pleasant company" . . . In the evenings he usually thawed and became communicative and cheerful.' Grieg, adds Paulsen, had 'a particular talent for getting him going'.[1]

Lorentz Dietrichson joined them at Gossensass, with his wife and daughters; he too (noted Paulsen) was good at 'getting Ibsen going'. One morning the four men left the ladies and went for a walk; but a flurry of snow caused them to seek shelter in a small wooden pavilion. Paulsen slipped back to the hotel to fetch some brandy, hot water, sugar and glasses, and they sat in the pavilion drinking toddy and telling stories. Paulsen was surprised to discover (as Marcus Grønvold had done) that Ibsen enjoyed slightly *risqué* anecdotes, which he would acknowledge with 'silent, chuckling laughter'.[2] Ibsen himself told one about an unnamed author, then much admired, 'one of those hyper-aesthetic characters whom Germany possesses in such abundance, who would like to forget that we humans, for all our spiritual qualities, share certain needs with animals'. Once, while travelling by rail (related Ibsen) this gentleman was afflicted with a painful stomach-ache and, unhappily, the train possessed no W.C. In addition to the hat he was wearing he had in his trunk a *chapeau-bas* 'which, since he was fortunately alone in the compartment, was now pressed into service'. It having served its purpose, the man threw it out of the window; but he had unluckily forgotten that the hat carried his visiting-card in the inside band. It was a slow, stopping train, and when it reached the station of the tiny town where he lived, and of which he was the leading inhabitant, the station-master ran up as the great man emerged with dignity on to the platform and proffered the hat with a respectful bow, it having been found on the line and rushed to its famous owner. The author was furious, at first denied that the hat was his, and ended by throwing it in the station-master's face.[3]

Ibsen told another story about an old man from Skien whom, to his surprise, he once met in Christiania, dressed like an undertaker in a white cravat and old black gloves. When Ibsen asked what he was doing in the capital, the old man replied: 'Herr Ibsen, my only joy in life is following corpses and being present at burials, but I have little opportunity to do these things in Skien,

---

[1] *Ibid.*, pp. 16–17.

[2] Paulsen, *Samliv med Ibsen*, I, pp. 183–184.

[3] For this and the following anecdotes, *ibid.*, pp. 10 ff.

where people live to too great an age and refuse to die. So I have now sold my little house there and moved to Christiania, where people pass on like flies and, the Good Lord be praised, I can follow corpses almost every day of the year.'

Grieg talked of Wagner and Liszt, whom he had seen at Bayreuth, especially of Liszt, whose warm testimonial had been largely instrumental in Grieg's receiving a civil list pension from the Storthing. He also, surely (though Paulsen does not mention it) told Ibsen of Wagner's experiments in staging at Bayreuth, such as his plunging the auditorium into total darkness throughout the performance, something that had not been done in the theatre before (though the Meiningers were to follow suit), and his concealment of the orchestra, so that the audience was separated from the stage by a 'mystical abyss'. But even the shortest concert bored Ibsen, and he never visited Bayreuth.

From Liszt, the conversation moved on to Ole Bull. Grieg told how the young Queen Isabella of Spain, who was 'more interested in love than politics', conceived a passion for the handsome Norwegian violinist and commanded him to play privately for her at the palace. He obeyed; no other person was present at the recital. Afterwards he received a Spanish medal carrying the inscription: 'Pour le vertu.' When he came to Stockholm old Queen Desirée, who in her youth had been the fiancée of Napoleon Bonaparte, asked Bull what he had got this medal for, and he replied: 'Pour le vertu, votre majesté'.

They discussed German women, and Ibsen remarked that 'a German lady in grande toilette always reminds me of a prize cow with gilt trappings and paper flowers between its horns'. He added that he thought animals realised that such decorations were a token of praise, since they resisted when anyone tried to remove them. On the subject of Bjørnson he observed: 'Bjørnson and I are not enemies, as many people believe. It is our disciples who are enemies.' At this interesting stage in the conversation the ladies surprised them over their glasses, and the three famous husbands were led back to the hotel 'with their tails between their legs'.

Grieg said that he was looking for a new subject for an opera. Ibsen suggested Olaf Liljekrans, but this did not appeal to Grieg, who suggested that Ibsen should write something new for him; but Ibsen said he was too preoccupied with his new play.

In September Ibsen and his companions moved south from Gossensass to the little town of Kaltern on the Italian border, where the Ibsens lodged with the burgomaster. They several times went fishing in a boat. 'Ibsen', writes Paulsen, 'turned out to be a passionate fisherman, and had miraculous luck. Every time he casually, and as though absent-mindedly, cast his line, a big fish immediately bit at the hook. In the space of half an hour he had caught a dozen . . . This put him in an excellent humour. His success as a sportsman pleased him more than if he had achieved some great artistic triumph.'[1]

Meanwhile, the success of *The Vikings* in Munich and of *The Pretenders* in Berlin had led to a rapid and widening increase in performances of Ibsen's work in the theatres. On 15 September he reported to Hegel: 'The Vikings is to be staged at the Burgtheater in Vienna in October; I have received an official invitation to attend, as also in Schwerin, where *The Pretenders* is to be done in November. *The Vikings* is to be performed at the Dresden Hoftheater in a few weeks; the same play is also in rehearsal at the Stadttheater in Leipzig, and is now being acted again with great success in Munich. From all of these theatres I receive ten per cent of the gross takings from all performances during my lifetime, and my heirs for a further fifteen years. This is undeniably a great deal better than what Herr Berner thinks proper to offer me, and people will now understand why I regard it as pre-eminently important to make my work profitable here. A German translation of *Lady Inger* is already completed in manuscript, and will be performed, for a start, in Meiningen and Munich. My preoccupation with all these matters has necessitated my postponing the completion of my new play; but on my return to Munich at the beginning of next month I intend to get it finished, although it is not very tempting to write for the theatres at home . . . I have long been waiting to see the new edition of *Peer Gynt* advertised; I hope it will soon appear. And perhaps there might be a call for a new edition at Christmas of one of my other books? I should be very happy if this were possible; for I need money, and theatre royalties down here are only paid quarterly or half-yearly. May I, therefore, notwithstanding my debt to you, ask you to be so kind as to send me 450 reichsmarks [80 specie-dollars, £22] at the above address? You would be doing me a great service, and I sincerely hope it will not be long before my account with you is balanced.'

Ibsen's reference to the lack of temptation to 'write for the theatres at home', and to the importance of making his work 'profitable' for the German theatres, may partly explain the apathy he had been showing towards *The Pillars of Society*, on which he had been working with such enthusiasm the previous autumn and winter. His successes in Germany had been with sweeping historical plays in the grand manner (*The Vikings at Helgeland* and *The Pretenders*), and, despite the success of Bjørnson's *A Bankrupt*, *The Pillars of Society*, with its very parochial and Norwegian atmosphere, must have struck Ibsen as unlikely to appeal either to German theatrical taste or to that country's traditional style of acting. It was with reluctance and doubt that he was to finish *The Pillars of*

---

[1] Paulsen, *Mine Erindringer*, p. 35.

Society; but his fears were to prove totally unfounded, and it was to set the style for all his future work. Not only was he always thereafter to write in prose and on contemporary themes; he was never to set any more of his plays outside Norway, though he took good care to give his characters names that could easily be pronounced by foreigners.

Ibsen left Kaltern at the end of September; apart from other considerations, Sigurd had to be back at school in Munich by 1 October. Paulsen accompanied them back to Munich; as the train drew in, Paulsen exclaimed: 'What a big city!' and Ibsen surprised him by replying: 'One can't live anywhere smaller.'[1]

Ibsen's letters during the last three months of 1876 contain, significantly, no reference to *The Pillars of Society*. Even when writing to Hegel he avoided the subject. In October *The Vikings at Helgeland* was performed in Vienna and Dresden, and also in Bergen. The director of his old theatre there annoyed him by suggesting that he should public-spiritedly allow them to stage it without payment, to which he replied (30 September): 'It should be the task of rich men, not authors, to bear the cost of such experiments . . . It has long vexed me to see how at every possible opportunity people at home try to put the burden on to artists and writers. For the restoration of Haakon's Hall [in Bergen] artists were blackmailed into presenting paintings each of which is worth 600–800 specie-dollars. I should be interested to know what the merchants of Bergen have contributed.'[2] In November *The Vikings* was revived at the Royal Theatre, Copenhagen. A fourth edition of *Peer Gynt* appeared this autumn; German translations of *Lady Inger* and *Brand* (the third German version of that work, this time by Baron Alfred von Wolzogen) were promised for the winter, and he was able to report to Hegel that the German edition of *The Vikings* was almost sold out. The inexpensiveness of book production in Germany amazed him; the first thousand copies of *The Vikings*, printed on 'very handsome paper', cost only 325 reichsmark (£16). Unfortunately, such fees as he might expect from all this lay in the future, and he had to ask Hegel to advance him another 400 crowns (£22).

Paulsen stayed in Munich until December, and recorded some further perceptive notes about Ibsen's routine in that city. In some respects his habits had changed since the early days in Dresden. He never now went to the theatre, unless to see one of his own plays; such as *The Vikings*, to which he took Paul-

---

[1] *Ibid.*, p. 36.

[2] Eventually, by a contract signed on 28 October, it was agreed that he should receive 100 specie-dollars (£28) for the first performance of each new play staged at the Bergen Theatre, 10 specie-dollars (£2.80) for each of the next five performances, and 5 specie-dollars (about £1.40) for each subsequent performance—except for *Catiline* and *The Feast at Solhaug*, which it was reckoned would each occupy only half an evening, and for which he was to receive half the above fees.

P

sen, who found the production 'exciting and spectacular', especially 'a grand snowstorm'.[1] The picture galleries which had attracted him as a young man he no longer visited, nor the studios of the numerous Norwegian painters who were in Munich at that time (and who included such distinguished artists as Erik Werenskiold, Eilif Peterssen, Christian Skredsvig, and Gerhard Munthe).[2] He isolated himself more and more, and was now even reluctant to accept invitations to dinner in other people's houses.[3] 'Social life does not merely steal one's time', he told Paulsen. 'It stultifies. An author who wants to achieve anything must isolate himself. Live alone in his thoughts and for his work.' He remarked of a Norwegian novelist (unnamed) who always allowed himself to be entertained to dinner: 'When does that man write? I wonder he manages to accomplish anything.' But unwilling as he was to partake in social life, he was very curious to know what went on there. When Paulsen had attended any such dinner, Ibsen would question him minutely about everything that happened—what topics had been discussed, what the hostess had worn, even how much people had tipped the footman.[4]

Arriving punctually at his fixed hour at the Café Maximilian, he would (Paulsen noted) always seat himself opposite a large mirror which reflected the

---

[1] Paulsen, Samliv med Ibsen, II, p. 27.

[2] But he had already given up visiting picture galleries during his time in Dresden. John Paulsen (Samliv med Ibsen, I, p. 152) quotes Julius Lange: 'I had to promise Ibsen yesterday that I would go with him to the gallery one day, since he, who has lived here two years, is so ignorant of its contents that it's a disgrace. It is amazing how incapable he is of really appreciating a work of art, and how little inclination he has for looking at anything of that kind.'

[3] This had not always been so; Lorentz Dietrichson, who was in Munich for two years from Christmas 1875 to February 1877, records that 'Ibsen entertained an unusual amount at this time . . . How many travellers must there be who retain grateful memories of the Ibsens' apartment, and especially Fru Ibsen's untiring kindness towards young and lonely compatriots of either sex during their stay in the Bavarian capital' (I, pp. 356–357). Bergliot Ibsen (who presumably had it from her husband, Sigurd) confirms this, with an embarrassing rider which explains Ibsen's subsequent unwillingness to accept invitations. 'At first they offered much hospitality. Once a week they held open house for the Norwegians in the city. But after a time Ibsen heard that the Norwegian guests found the fare offered not good enough, with the result that the Ibsens closed their doors to them.' She adds: 'It is curious to reflect on the kind of criticism which the Ibsens have always encountered from Norwegian sources. Even now, more than forty years after his death, people write disparagingly of the food Fru Ibsen cooked . . . When after his parents' death Sigurd presented his father's furniture, etc., to the nation the newspapers expressed nothing but contempt for Ibsen's bad taste.' She sums up: 'Ibsen hated people's perpetual scrutiny of his private life and especially the incessant nagging about his modest circumstances. That was one extra reason why they kept themselves more and more withdrawn . . . The first time Sigurd encountered this meanness of spirit was probably with the Norwegian guests at Munich.' (De tre, pp. 62–64.)

[4] Paulsen, Samliv med Ibsen, II, p. 42.

door. 'Here, without needing to turn his head, he could observe everything in the mirror, and sat there behind his big newspaper like some fiction detective. Nothing escaped his sharp eyes. He noticed, not merely people's appearance and habits . . . but picked up bits of their private conversations,[1] and noted characteristics which were peculiar to them and which he had not perceived elsewhere . . . He also learned much from the newspapers. There he found the answers to so many of his unuttered questions about the people amongst whom he lived . . . From a small article or advertisement which other readers overlooked he could learn more than they from years of study . . . But Ibsen was no ordinary newspaper reader. He read the advertisements minutely, and remarked that they were not the least informative section of the paper. He began reading from the title at the top of page one and read right through to the names of the printer and publisher at the foot of the final page.'[2]

Paulsen was surprised to find that Ibsen liked to do as many domestic tasks as possible himself. If a button came loose on his trousers, he would 'go into his room, close the door firmly and, after various preparations as humorous as they were unnecessary, would sew on the button with the same care with which he would fair-copy a new play'.[3] One of Ibsen's convictions was that 'women never know how to sew on a button so that it stays, whereas when he sewed one on himself it remained fast for ever'. Suzannah, however, told Paulsen that after Ibsen had sewed on a button she would stitch it, 'which Ibsen always forgets, and which is the most important thing. But let him go on believing it, it makes him so happy.' On the other hand, Ibsen hated seeing his wife doing anything manual such as knitting, and Paulsen says he never saw Suzannah thus occupied because she knew her husband's aversion to such things.[4] This business of independence Ibsen carried to unexpected lengths. One morning he startled Paulsen by asking him 'with an earnest and worried expression' whether he polished his own boots. Paulsen confessed that he did not. Ibsen said: 'But you must . . . One should never let another person do for one what one can do for oneself.' He was even, unexpectedly, something of a cook, and 'especially liked making soups'.[5]

As Paulsen had discovered at Gossensass, Ibsen could, when the mood took

---

[1] 'Ibsen listened all his life, though he often seemed to be otherwise preoccupied' (Lugné-Poe, *Ibsen*, Paris, 1936, p. 74).

[2] Paulsen, *Samliv med Ibsen*, I, pp. 31–33.

[3] For the information contained in this paragraph, *ibid.*, pp. 33–35.

[4] Cf. Helmer's lines in *A Doll's House*: 'Knitting—that's an ugly business—can't help it. Look—arms all huddled up—great clumsy needles going up and down—makes you look like a damned Chinaman.'

[5] Paulsen, *Samliv med Ibsen*, II, p. 220.

him, be an excellent raconteur. But despite his enjoyment of risqué anecdotes, such as the gentleman in the railway carriage, 'Ibsen, with a bashfulness unusual among writers, avoided all sexual topics.'[1] On this subject he was evidently inhibited to a degree unusual even for the nineteenth century. Paulsen reflects: 'And yet this man, according to his fellow students, had been in his youth soft, emotional, almost sentimental, as ... letters and poems from that time confirm. But the same cold hand that closed his eloquent lips laid itself early, like a frost, over his emotional life too ... Lest the world should cause him further pain he built a shell of satire over everything in him that was tender and vulnerable ... His heart gradually died, and with it his dreams of personal happiness. The door to the world of love and friendship was slammed shut.'[2]

Ibsen once astonished Paulsen by declaring that there were three things that meant nothing to him: flowers, music and children.[3] The last part of this claim is contradicted by several witnesses, such as Johanne Lie[4] and Bolette Sontum, who have testified to the kindness and affection he showed them when they were small. His indifference to music has already been remarked; I do not know of any other evidence of his feeling for or against flowers. What is perhaps most interesting about Ibsen's claim, however, is not whether it is true, but that he should have made it. It is very much the statement of a man who has turned his back on all things of the heart.

Ibsen was almost theatrically fortunate in being permitted to witness the humiliation of former enemies. Clemens Petersen's fate has been related; and one day after dinner in Munich, Paulsen was standing at the window with Ibsen looking out into the street when they noticed a curious old man dressed like a priest in black with a white cravat slouch past. 'Did you ever meet him in Bergen?' Ibsen asked. He had identified him as Poul Stub, the pedant who had corrected Ibsen's Norwegian essays when he was studying in Grimstad, and had attacked the policy and inexperience of the Bergen company shortly after Ibsen's arrival there in 1851. 'I looked long at the old, bowed schoolmaster, once Ibsen's merciless critic, now pensioned and, for economical reasons, compelled to live in Munich because of its cheapness. I thought how differently their

---

[1] Paulsen, *Mine Erindringer*, p. 18.

[2] *Ibid.*, p. 19.

[3] Paulsen, *Samliv med Ibsen*, I, p. 36. When Ibsen died Strindberg gleefully quoted (in *A Blue Book*, I) the remark: 'He has written his epitaph himself in an interview, viz: "This man who rests here could not endure flowers, children and music." Known as the light-bearer, he was a black soul, for he came from the dark and was always out of his mind, since he did not know what he was saying or doing'—an instance, if ever there was one, of the pot calling the kettle black. Cf. Göran Lindström's *Strindberg contra Ibsen*, in *Ibsen-Årbok, 1955–6* (Skien, 1956), pp. 77–78.

[4] Cf. p. 278 below.

lives had shaped themselves since their clash in Bergen. Ibsen sat there, a famous man in an elegant home, while Poul Stub was—still Poul Stub.'[1]

Paulsen noted, as Vilhelm Bergsøe had on Ischia, Ibsen's physical timidity. 'In windy weather he was always apprehensive lest a tile might fall on his head, and it always amused me to see how he glanced up over his gold spectacles at the threatening rooftops. His fear of dogs was also marked; he moved quickly aside if a bulldog approached.'[2] Paulsen comments that in this respect, as in the contrast between the conventionality of his life and the unconventionality of his thought, Ibsen resembled Goethe. Another weakness was his unwillingness that strangers should know of his liking for a nap after lunch. 'When Fru Ibsen once mentioned his long afternoon sleep, he got angry and declared: "It isn't true. I merely lie on the sofa and reflect." "How can you say such a thing, my dear Ibsen?", said Suzannah. "You sleep so heavily that we can hear your snores in the living-room." At this Ibsen left the room without speaking, evidently insulted.'[3] Suzannah also confided in Paulsen that Ibsen 'likes us to have maids who look pretty; he can't stand old, ugly ones', adding: 'Though he never looks at them—that is, he looks at them, but only aesthetically, as one looks at a statue or a painting.'[4] One is reminded of Irene's accusation of Rubek in *When We Dead Awaken*.

Ibsen had an extraordinary dislike of using Christian names, even with his close friends; Suzannah told Paulsen that Ibsen had addressed her as 'De' (the Norwegian equivalent of *vous*) throughout their engagement, 'which caused much amazement in the circles in which the young couple moved'.[5] He used affectionately to address Suzannah as 'the cat' or 'the eagle', the latter name having been given her long ago by her brothers and sisters because of her bold character (hence his drawings of these creatures on the family's home-made banknotes). Sigurd he called 'the old one';[6] and he amused Paulsen by exhorting him not to disturb the boy at work, for Paulsen knew that 'Sigurd's "studies" just then consisted of smoking cigarettes and reading a novel by Zola, which on his father's approach he would hastily conceal behind a large dictionary.'[7]

As regards Ibsen's method of work, Paulsen tells that he would (like so many writers) break off at an appointed hour even if in the heat of composition or in

---

[1] Paulsen, *Samliv med Ibsen*, II, pp. 37–38.
[2] *Ibid.*, p. 41.
[3] *Ibid.*, p. 37.
[4] *Ibid.*, p. 39.
[5] *Ibid.*, p. 221n.
[6] *Ibid.*, p. 220.
[7] *Ibid.*, pp. 39–40.

the middle of a scene, since 'instead of the mood evaporating it would carry over to the following day, when he would find the inspiration still fresh and could continue immediately without having to search for the central thread'.[1] He once surprised Paulsen by declaring that 'the creative function operates exactly like the stomach. One receives certain material from without, digests it, and excretes it—*voilà tout*!'[2] Nevertheless, Suzannah told Paulsen that Ibsen 'always approached his desk like a sanctuary, *soigné*, in a "well-pressed morning coat" '.[3]

In December, Paulsen departed for Rome. 'Promise me you won't write a line the first year you are in Italy', was Ibsen's advice to him as they said farewell. 'Just take in impressions.'[4]

Considering that he had not completed any new work during the year, 1876 had, thanks mainly to the continued success of The Vikings at Helgeland, the Christiania production of Peer Gynt, and the reprints of Peer Gynt and Brand, been financially fair:

	crowns[5]	£
Fee for The Vikings at Helgeland at Royal Theatre, Stockholm	1,000	55
Fee for The Vikings at Helgeland in Bergen	100	5
Fee for Peer Gynt in Christiania	2,024	112
Royalties from The Vikings at Helgeland at Munich Hoftheater	344	19
Extra fee for The Vikings at Helgeland in Copenhagen	500	28
4th edition of Peer Gynt	1,650	92
Extra fee for The Vikings at Helgeland in Bergen	400	22
Extra fee for Peer Gynt in Christiania	843½	47
8th edition of Brand	1,700	94
	8,561½	474

---

[1] Paulsen, Nye Erindringer (Copenhagen, 1901), p. 137.
[2] Paulsen, Samliv med Ibsen, II, p. 217.
[3] Paulsen, Nye Erindringer, p. 135.
[4] Paulsen, Samliv med Ibsen, II, pp. 28–29.
[5] From 1876 Ibsen recorded his income in crowns instead of specie-dollars.

TEN

❧ The Pillars of Society

(1877–1878)

IBSEN OPENED THE NEW YEAR, 1877, with an eloquent appeal on 4
February to Johan Sverdrup, as President of the Storthing, for an increase in
his pension, and his letter again underlines the disadvantage he suffered through
Norway and Denmark not having copyright agreements with other European
countries:

'As a result, our books can be translated without let or hindrance anywhere and by anyone. And this is happening all the time. In England the
whole of *Emperor and Galilean* was translated and published last year; I had
not at that time the money available to arrange this at my own expense;
now the translator and publisher take the profits; I take nothing. In Berlin
A. Strodtmann has taken my poems from me, as well as my plays *The
Pretenders* and *The League of Youth*. Now these works are being widely read
and performed in Germany, which brings money to the translator but not
to me. The same has happened with *Brand*, of which three separate
German translations now exist without providing me with a penny. Even
in Sweden the situation is the same for us; we have no legal right to payment either from the theatres or from the publishers who have us translated. One Swedish translation of *The Vikings at Helgeland* has already
appeared and another is in the press. All I have managed to keep for myself
has been the editions I commissioned personally of *The Vikings at Helgeland*
and *Lady Inger of Østraat*, but these editions cost me a considerable outlay
which I can expect to regain only gradually over the years.
    'I appreciate that the Norwegian government cannot consider entering
into cultural agreements with the great countries of literature. The advantage to us of the present anarchic situation is so evident that none of us,
out of respect to our general reading public, would wish it altered. Should
free access to foreign literary works be denied us, the source of intellectual
progress and freedom in virtually every walk of life would be blocked, or
at any rate rendered less accessible to us. Of that there must be no thought.

But, Mr President, I appeal to your sense of justice whether it is fair that the financial loss resulting from such an arrangement should be borne by us four or five writers? Give each of us an extra 200 specie-dollars (£55) supplement to our pensions as compensation for what we lose on the majority's behalf. With this extra help we could at least save some of our works from falling into the hands of foreign translators; we could keep them for our own benefit, and thereby also ensure that our literature is presented to foreign readers in a more correct form than is now commonly the case.'

Eleven days later Sverdrup moved in the Storthing that all pensions of composers and authors should be raised by 800 crowns (£44). This modest proposal was rejected. Ibsen's finances were now so low that on 27 February he had to ask Hegel to advance him the honorarium due on the forthcoming reprint of *Love's Comedy*, and Hegel generously obliged with 1,000 specie-dollars (£278). With this, plus a windfall of 400 crowns (£22) from the Bergen Theatre for *The League of Youth*, which had opened there on 25 February, Ibsen was able to look round for new lodgings 'where I can work undisturbed, my present apartment leaving much to be desired in this respect'.[1] On 1 May he moved to a first-floor flat at Schellingstrasse 30.

Meanwhile he had at last begun to make progress with *The Pillars of Society*. 'I shall have it ready during the summer', he told Hegel, who must have received the news with scepticism. But by 20 April it was 'moving rapidly towards its conclusion', and at last, on 24 June, for once on schedule, he was able to report: 'Today I take advantage of a free moment to tell you that on the 15th inst. I completed my new play and am now going ahead with the fair-copying.' He posted the fair copy to Hegel in five instalments between 29 July and 20 August.

While he was engaged on the copying, Georg Brandes visited him for one evening, accompanied by his wife; for the previous summer he had married Gerda Strodtmann, the ex-wife of Ibsen's German translator. The hostility towards Brandes in his native country had reached such proportions that he had decided, as Ibsen had done, and as Strindberg was shortly to do, to go into exile—though in his case (unlike theirs) his departure was regretted, for forty-five eminent Danes published a joint letter thanking him for what he had done, and even Bjørnson, who had quarrelled so deeply with him, added his thanks in an article in a Danish newspaper. Brandes was struck by the impersonality of Ibsen's living conditions, an impression which other observers were to record of his various dwellings. 'Since 1864', Brandes was to write five

---

[1] Letter to Hegel, 27 February 1877.

years later, 'he has not had his feet under his own mahogany, nor slept in his own bed . . . He has lived as though in a tent, among pieces of hired furniture, which could be sent back on the day appointed for his departure . . . When I last visited him [on this occasion in 1877], on my asking whether nothing at all in the apartment belonged to him, he pointed to a row of paintings on the wall. They were the only things that were his own . . . He feels no longing to possess a house and a home, still less a farm and lands like Bjørnson.'[1]

This unhomeliness which was always so characteristic of Ibsen's apartments is especially curious in a writer whose plays are so often permeated by a deep sense of home. Fifty years ago Gunnar Heiberg (a distinguished director of Ibsen's plays) pointed out how important it is when staging *A Doll's House* that the audience should have the feeling that a *home* is being broken up,[2] and the same is true of *An Enemy of the People* and *The Wild Duck*. Unless Dr Stockmann's house is given the feeling of a home, the effect of the last act when we see it with the windows broken is greatly minimised. And one has seen productions of *The Wild Duck* ruined by a failure to present the four Ekdals as a closely-knit family. By contrast, there are other plays, such as *Ghosts*, *The Master Builder* and *When We Dead Awaken*, in which the characters sadly remark on the fact that the house they live in is not in the fullest sense a home (as is also implied in *Hedda Gabler*, *Little Eyolf* and *John Gabriel Borkman*). Neither Ibsen nor Suzannah, for all their strong sense of family, seems to have had the gift of making the place they lived in homely—which need cost very little, as anyone who has lived in a bed-sitter can testify. One remembers Ibsen's admission of his indifference to flowers.

Another visitor to Ibsen that summer was Ole Bull, making what proved to be his last concert tour. They spent an evening together reminiscing over old times, and Marcus Grønvold, who was present, noted Ibsen's amusement that Bull expressed such pleasure in *Peer Gynt*, for which he himself had been the part-model.[3]

A week after he had sent the final instalment of *The Pillars of Society* to Hegel, Ibsen left for Sweden, having borrowed 600 crowns (£33) from his ever-willing publisher to pay for the ticket. The cause of his visit was an agreeable one; Upsala University, the oldest in Scandinavia, was celebrating its

---

[1] An article written in 1882 and reprinted (as 'Second Impression') in Brandes's *Henrik Ibsen* (Copenhagen, 1898), p. 59. Muir-Archer translation. The young Danish novelist Herman Bang, visiting Ibsen around this time, received the same impression, of a man 'curiously homeless, amidst a mass of rented furniture' (Herman Bang, *Ti Aar*, Copenhagen, 1891, p. 185).

[2] Gunnar Heiberg, *Ibsen og Bjørnson på scenen* (Christiania, 1918), pp. 5–6.

[3] Marcus Grønvold, p. 138.

four hundredth anniversary, the occasion was to be marked by festivities, including the awarding of honorary degrees, and Ibsen was to be made a doctor of letters. (For this he had to thank Lorentz Dietrichson, who had been informed that he was to receive a doctorate and suggested that Ibsen should be similarly honoured). Suzannah took the opportunity to pay a visit to Norway, taking Sigurd with her and leaving Ibsen to fend for himself for ten days in Munich before leaving—which, in his way, he managed to do, as appears from the following letter:[1]

Munich, 21 August 1877

Dear Suzannah!

As soon as I received your letter and Sigurd's yesterday I telegraphed that everything was all right here, and I hope the telegram reached you safely. I am glad the sea trip went so well, and I hear from Sigurd that you praised your own dress at the dinner table![2]

The whole manuscript is now despatched, and I am making preparations for my departure, which will probably be on Monday. I don't expect to be away longer than strictly necessary, i.e. about a fortnight. Here everything is as usual. Helene is very good, makes good coffee and does all her work very punctually and exactly the way she has seen that I want it. I usually dine at Schleich's, which is better than the Museum and not wickedly dearer. For 1.75 [about 7½p.] I get an excellent soup, fish, two meat dishes with all kinds of vegetables, and a compote, followed by pastries, cheese, bread and butter. This is pretty well my only meal, for I always stay at home in the evenings and then eat only a sandwich. Vullum has also been eating at Schleich's till yesterday when he left. I have been with Grønvold once or twice and intend to invite him to dinner, since his brother has been so kind to you in Bergen.

I hope you are enjoying yourselves up there; but don't run any risks, and take good care of Sigurd and of your money and don't let the locals rob you.

I will write again from Sweden and hope to receive another letter from you there. No more for today. Enjoy yourselves.

Your

Henrik Ibsen

He enclosed a Polonius-like letter to Sigurd, exhorting him to 'be sure to be

---

[1] Suzannah had written him from Bergen that all the people 'were as though taken from *The Pillars of Society*, portrayed to the life, even Rørlund [the puritanical schoolmaster]. Sigurd said he couldn't understand how you could know how everything was.' Her old family home, she found, had become a coffee-shop. 'I think of you every day', she concluded. 'It seems so long since I left you, yet it is only five days.' (Bergliot Ibsen, pp. 64–65.)

[2] Forgetting that she was among Scandinavians, Suzannah had said at dinner the first day aboard the ship: 'I think my dress is much smarter than the other ladies.' (*Ibid.*, p. 65.)

careful both ashore and at sea; the least carelessness can bring consequences . . . Don't go out too much on the water, and not in a sailing boat!'

Ibsen spent a fortnight in Sweden. After a few days in Stockholm, he accompanied the other guests to Upsala, fifty miles north of the capital, on 4 September. 'The aquavit will begin to flow', he wrote to Grønvold, 'and I don't expect to get any peace for letter-writing during the next few days.' The festivities in Upsala began on the 5th with a dinner. On the 6th the honorary degrees were handed out, and Ibsen had a laurel wreath placed on his head by the Archbishop. That afternoon a banquet was given in the Botanical Gardens, attended by fifteen hundred people, the doctors still wearing their laurel wreaths; in the evening there was a firework display and a torchlight procession, and the Finance Minister, Hans Forssell, who was also a distinguished man of letters, gave a party attended by several of the leading Swedish writers of the day, including Snoilsky, Victor Rydberg and Zacharias Topelius. 'Within five minutes', says Dietrichson, who was there, 'it was Ibsen who led the conversation and made it interesting. How Ibsen has acquired the reputation of being so excessively silent I have never been able to understand.'[1] The following evening there was a ball in the Botanical Gardens in a specially created building, looking (to judge from an engraving in *Ny Illustrerad Tidning*) remarkably like Paddington Station. During these days at Upsala Ibsen had several meetings with King Oscar II, who had already shown him several marks of his favour, and got on with that prickly giant nearly as well as he had with his much more open and attractive brother, Carl XV.

When the Upsala celebrations had ended, the King gave a farewell banquet for the guests at his palace at Drottningholm, just outside Stockholm, with illuminations in the park; and the Royal Theatre honoured Ibsen with a special performance of *The Vikings at Helgeland* (how antiquated that play, now twenty years old, must have seemed to the man who had just written *The Pillars of Society*!). Such a week, one might think, would have moved even Ibsen to write a spirited description to his wife, but she received only the following:

Stockholm, 12 September 1877

Dear Suzannah!

You will have read in the papers of the tremendous festivities in Upsala, which are now over. On Monday The Vikings at Helgeland *was performed; full house; the author repeatedly called, amid the greatest enthusiasm. I will tell you all about this when we meet. Throughout my whole stay in Sweden I have received only one letter from you and Sigurd, i.e. that in which you tell me of your visit to Folgefonden; I hope to find a letter awaiting me in Copenhagen—I leave for there today. I am tired now*

---

[1] Dietrichson, I, p. 360.

and long to be back in Munich; here there have been invitations and receptions every day. In Upsala I spoke with the King every day and was at once received by him in the friendliest manner. This is just to let you know that all is well with me; let me soon hear the same from you . . .

Ibsen spent a couple of days in Copenhagen, where Hegel put him up in style at the Hotel d'Angleterre opposite the Royal Theatre, refused to let him pay for anything, and gave a party in his honour at his villa. Unwittingly, however, Ibsen offended Georg Brandes by not contacting him, having been wrongly informed that Brandes was out of town. Brandes, as touchy as any of the many touchy persons in this narrative, was mortally offended. 'Ibsen and I', he wrote to Bjørnson the following June, 'have been good friends for so many years that I am unwilling to say any hard or unfriendly words about him. He seems to me to be an enclosed, shy person who has difficulty in finding words, is reluctant to open himself, and is full of suspicion and distrust, even to those who have never done him anything but good' (another case of the pot calling the kettle black). Amazingly, Ibsen seems to have been unaware of Brandes's change of attitude towards him; a year and a half later, on 18 February 1879, thanking Hegel for Brandes's book on Disraeli, he was to praise it as an 'absolute masterpiece' and to ask Hegel to convey to Brandes his admiration and best wishes. But he did not write direct to Brandes for four years, from 1877 to 1881 (for which the blame must largely rest with Brandes; their correspondence had always in the main been a case of Ibsen replying to Brandes's letters); and this silence unwittingly fed Brandes's suspicions that Ibsen's feelings towards him had cooled.[1] So there was another friendship down the drain.

By 20 September Ibsen was back in Munich, whence three days later he again wrote characteristically to Suzannah:

. . . You must have read in the newspapers how hugely I was fêted in Upsala. The Danish papers say I was the most fêted of all the guests in Upsala, and this was indeed the case. But now I am content to be at peace again, although things are not very comfortable; it is tiresome to have to eat out every day, the food does not suit me, the evenings are long, cold and gloomy. I sit here alone since Grønvold is in the country . . . If you could find the time to buy me 6 pairs of gloves in Copenhagen, I should be grateful; they must be of fine, thin leather, preferably dark brown, size 8½; I bought a pair there for 1 kr. 70 øre (9 p.) in a shop on the corner of Østergade and Kongens Nytorv. Perhaps Sara [Suzannah's sister] could help you with this; but pack them deep in your trunk, for the customs inspection.

---

[1] Cf. *Brandes Brevveksling*, IV, p. xxxvi.

As he awaited the appearance of *The Pillars of Society*, Ibsen learned to his annoyance that John Paulsen had passed on to a Norwegian journalist a few facts about the play which Ibsen had confided to him, and that the journalist had printed these, getting many of the details wrong. Amongst other errors, the title of the play was given as *Samfundets Piller* (*piller* is an archaic word for 'pillars', but more commonly means 'pills'). Didrik Grønvold (the brother of Marcus) visited Ibsen at Schellingstrasse just after he had discovered this, and found him 'walking up and down his room like a lion in its cage, sparking with anger, not so much at the leak of information as at the mutilated title'.[1]

Ibsen had been painted that summer by Julius Kronborg, wearing his new doctor's cloak—a portrait which Ibsen kept until his death. Strindberg, a much better painter and judge of painting than Ibsen, saw this portrait at an exhibition in Stockholm, and wrote an eloquent description: 'The face is Brand's; the high, broad brow of the fanatic, the strong mouth of the witness whose lips have never uttered the truths that his hand has penned, the cold, determined look that never wavered when it stared "the spirit of compromise" in the face; that is Ibsen, the fanatical sceptic . . . so impressive and terrifying, so repellent, so attractive!'[2]

On 11 October 1877 *The Pillars of Society* was at last published, and achieved an immediate and widespread success. The first edition of 6,000 copies sold out within seven weeks, and a further 4,000 had to be printed. A German translation appeared before the end of November, and the play was, as we shall see, to make a considerable impact there, especially on the young.

Since *The Pillars of Society* is an indictment of a particular kind of right-wing figure, contemporary opinion naturally varied according to the political views of the reader; the liberals and radicals hailed it with the same delight with which the conservatives had greeted *The League of Youth*. Curiously, the Christiania papers scarcely noticed it at all; it was reviewed less in the capital than any play he had written since he had left Norway in 1864;[3] not only the right-wing *Morgenbladet* but (inexplicably) the liberal *Dagbladet* ignored it. Indeed, only three Christiania publications printed reviews, and two of these were disparaging. Ditmar Meidell in *Aftenbladet* (3 November), though granting the play certain virtues, dismissed it as 'one of Ibsen's weaker works', and Arne Garborg, in *Fedraheimen* (27 October), after complaining that Ibsen, having mocked the peasants in *Brand*, the language reformers in *Peer Gynt* and the liberals in *The League of Youth*, 'has no sympathy with those who believe

[1] Didrik Grønvold, *Diktere og musikere*, pp. 8 9.

[2] August Strindberg, *Konstakademiens utställning, 1877*, p. 124.

[3] J. B. Halvorsen, *Norsk forfatter-lexicon, 1814–1880*, III (Christiania, 1892), p. 58.

in a future for Norway', continued: '*The Pillars of Society* gives me the impression that Ibsen is on the downward path. It lacks the fire and bounce of his earlier works . . . Its structural virtues are but tame routine . . . He could never write really badly . . . but the blaze and spark of his best work seem here to have been quenched . . . Ibsen . . . seems burned out.'

The provincial newspapers were more perceptive. An anonymous critic in *Bergens Tidende* (27 October and 3 November) wrote: 'He has satisfied the demands of the stage to a degree which as far as we know has not been equalled in Germanic literature since the English Renaissance'; and, comparing the play favourably with Bjørnson's *A Bankrupt*, rightly remarked that the probable reason why Bjørnson had not brought his dramatic talent to full flower in the same measure as Ibsen was that Ibsen had concentrated on drama and not dissipated his efforts on novels and short stories (and, he might have added, journalism and political agitation). And Nordahl Rolfsen, in the first of four articles in *Bergens-posten* (24, 26 and 28 October and 4 November), which Ibsen praised as 'saying everything I should most like to be said about the play',[1] was shrewd enough to see (24 October) that *The Pillars of Society* was more than a mere political salvo. 'It will help', he wrote, 'to dispel the idea that Ibsen is primarily a polemical writer. The real targets of Ibsen's indignation are mean-mindedness and pettiness, wherever they may be found. He does not position the sheep and goats so that all the goats are to be found on one side and all the sheep on the other.' He also shrewdly observed that the 'lack of harmony' for which Ibsen was so continuously condemned was the source of the intensity of his satire.

In his final article (4 November), Rolfsen quoted a *Punch* cartoon of the siege of Sebastopol, showing a room with the door blown in by a bomb and a man in bed crying: 'I'm a little deaf. Did someone knock? Come in!' Rolfsen comments: 'Ibsen believes our society is like the man at Sebastopol. People will not say "Come in" until a bomb has blown open the door . . . In this his latest play [as compared with *Brand* and *Peer Gynt*] Ibsen's satire has changed its form. It is no longer a Homeric spread, a broad stream of mocking words to accompany each sword-thrust; it is a quiet duel to the death, with no rattle of harness nor clash of blades; one watches, in a deathly silence, the elegant fencer's sure and piercing passes. His satire has gained in objectivity without losing in strength . . . Many may prefer the lyrical beauty and kaleidoscopic display of epigrams [in his earlier work] to this dramatic astringency—the beauty of the youth to that of the man. To us it seems that scarcely one of Ibsen's earlier satires can be compared to *The Pillars of Society* in the way the action reveals

---

[1] Letter to B. E. Bendixen, 21 December 1877 (*CE*, XIX, pp. 252–253).

the characters and the dialogue naturally reflects the personality not of the author but of the speaker.'

The Danish reviews were all good, apart from an anonymous complaint in *Fædrelandet* (19 November) that 'one hears too seldom the beating of a great and warm heart'. The writer of light vaudevilles, Erik Bøgh, again generously acclaimed the new dramatist whose fame was so far exceeding his own: 'It is a mighty test of strength that Henrik Ibsen has essayed in trying a fall with one of "The Pillars of Society" . . . He has gone about it like a Samson, and even if his shaking has not brought about the upheaval which levelled the Temple of Dagon, several Philistine hearts must surely have trembled as it groaned to its foundations in his mighty grip . . . Ibsen does not suffer from the Danish malaise of never doing anything whole-heartedly [a disease which Ibsen had in fact condemned in *Brand* as being peculiarly Norwegian]. If falsehood is to be stripped bare, he will work at it till its fine feathers cling protectively to the wearer's skin like the shirt of Nessus. If necessary, he will remove the skin too, and should a little flesh be adhering to the skin, that will not deter him.'

Like Rolfsen, Bøgh compared the play favourably with Bjørnson's *A Bankrupt* ('Ibsen never perpetrates a fifth act showing his hero restored to prosperity and converted as Bjørnson did'), and concluded with a shrewd criticism: 'there are too many speeches which delay the fall of the curtain after the action is finished and the play is over'. It was an error which (except in *An Enemy of the People*) Ibsen was never to commit again; anyone who has tried to cut one of his plays (for television, for instance) knows that, while a good deal of the exposition can usually be thinned out from the first act, and a certain amount from the middle, there is scarcely a line in any other of his last acts from *A Doll's House* onwards that will bear removal.

Surprisingly, especially for men of their political leanings, neither of the Brandes brothers liked it (which may be the reason why neither reviewed it). 'Ibsen is so anxious to provoke', wrote Edvard to Georg on 30 November, 'that there is nothing *big* about his play. It's a big problem seen small and treated small.'[1] And Georg wrote to J. P. Jacobsen on 16 December: 'Ibsen's play is technically fine, but it taught me nothing.'[2]

The Pillars of Society is not often performed today on the professional stage, though in England, at least, it pops up frequently in the drama schools. The reason in both cases is the same: the size of the cast. There are nineteen characters, not including the crowd at the end, an advantage to students and amateurs

---

[1] *Brandes Brevveksling*, II, p. 6.
[2] *Ibid.*, III, p. 132.

but an expensive obstacle to any unsubsidised company. *Peer Gynt* needs as many actors, but *Peer Gynt*, like Shakespeare, can usually be sure of an audience. This neglect of *The Pillars of Society* is sad, for until the last five minutes it holds the stage splendidly, quick-moving, strongly plotted, sharply characterised and full of feline wit. Were it not for those last minutes—but since the play is generally little known, one must pause briefly to outline its plot (a procedure which will not be inflicted on the reader when more famous plays come to be discussed).

It is set in a small port. The chief character, Karsten Bernick, a wealthy ship-owner, has (like John Gabriel Borkman) married a woman he does not love, to further his career. His life has been a series of successes founded on double-dealing, sometimes above the law, sometimes not. Caught in an actress's bedroom while still engaged (fifteen years before the play opens) he allowed his fiancée's brother Johan to take the blame. Planning a railway to the town, he has secretly bought up all the land through which the line will pass. When Johan returns from America and threatens to expose him, Bernick lets him go to sea in a ship he knows is rotten and must sink—only to find, seemingly too late, that his own son has stowed aboard. In the unconvincing ending, the ship is discovered not to have sailed, and Bernick in his relief confesses his crimes and is left not only unpunished but rather better off than he was before.

Such a summary omits the various sub-plots and several of the play's best characters: Lona Hessel, Bernick's former love, returning robustly (with a knapsack on her back) from America to let fresh air into the closed society of the little town; the narrow-minded schoolmaster, Dr Rørlund; Dina Dorf, the young orphan daughter of Bernick's former mistress, and his ward; Aune, the shipyard foreman, fearful of the unemployment that new machines may bring; Hilmar Tønnessen, Mrs Bernick's cousin, an indolent aesthete; Martha, Bernick's sister, who has loved Johan and waited for his return only to find that he has no eyes for her, but only for Dina who is half her age; and Bernick's three shifty capitalist associates and their gossiping wives. The pettiness of provincial life, which was one of the things Ibsen hated most about Norway (in its capital no less than in its small towns) is mercilessly detailed; and in two important respects the play marks a notable advance on *The League of Youth*. One is the clarity with which the sub-plots are interwoven with the main plot, instead of the play being a Congrevian maze; the other is the sharpness with which individual modes of speech are differentiated, something which was to be one of Ibsen's supreme strengths, and one of his main contributions to the technique of prose drama. Lona Hessel, for example, fresh from America, has a breezy, slangy way of speaking which contrasts markedly with the prim speech of the local stay-at-homes; and Hilmar Tønnessen talks in an extraordinary, fanciful manner, overloaded with adjectives and ridiculous flights of imagination, like Hjalmar Ekdal in *The Wild Duck*. Ibsen was a wonderfully minute observer of the way people talked (as of the way they looked and dressed), even to noting that we speak differently at different times of the day, and that women phrase their sentences differently from men. Other playwrights, such as Bjørnson, had attempted to differentiate the speech of their characters, but their efforts are crude compared with Ibsen's. These different modes of speech are one of the most difficult problems that face a translator; if one fails, one deprives the actor of his subtlest weapon.

The Pillars of Society is full of memories of Grimstad, the little port where Ibsen had spent six years as a chemist's apprentice (just as *The League of Youth* is full of memories of Skien). *The Palm Tree* (a ship which appears importantly in the play) was the name of a Grimstad ship. An actress belonging to a touring theatrical company had returned there in Ibsen's time after being involved in a scandal, and had tried to keep herself by taking in washing and sewing like Dina Dorf's mother, but had been shooed out of town by local gossips. Foreign ships came in for repairs, and foreign visitors turned the place upside down, like the American crew of whom the citizens in the play complain. In the autumn of 1849, six months before Ibsen left for Christiania, the socialist Marcus Thrane had come to Grimstad and founded a Workers' Association, like the one Aune the foreman belongs to. And the Bernicks had their origin in a family named Smith Petersen. Morten Smith Petersen, the original of Karsten Bernick, returned to Grimstad from abroad in the eighteen-forties, and ran his aged mother's business for a while, but finally had to close it down. He then started his own shipyard and an insurance company; he had died in 1872, but his sister Margrethe Petersen survived. She was an elementary schoolteacher and the original of Martha Bernick.

The play dealt with two problems of especial topicality for the eighteen-seventies, and it is a measure of its emotional and dramatic content that it has retained its validity despite the fact that both issues have long been settled. One was the question of women's rights; the other, that of 'floating coffins'. Controversy over the former problem had reached its height in Norway (as elsewhere) during the seventies; in 1876 Asta Hansteen, a great champion of the cause, began a series of lectures on the subject, but was so furiously assailed that in 1880 she emigrated to America. She was the original of Lona Hessel (Ibsen at first gave the character the surname of Hassel, but changed it, presumably so as to avoid too direct an identification with Hansteen). Camilla Collett, the novelist, another doughty warrior, had probably exerted a good deal of influence on him when they had met in Dresden in 1871 and in Munich in 1877, when he was writing the play and they had many arguments about mar-

Q

riage and other female problems; and Suzannah, too, had long felt strongly about these things. Ibsen had already touched tentatively on the subject in *The League of Youth*, and he was to deal with it more minutely in his next play. His original intention in *The Pillars of Society* had been to be even more outspoken than he finally was, for in one of the preliminary drafts Dina announces her decision to go off with her lover, Johan, without marrying him; but he evidently doubted whether the theatres would stage a play which suggested anything quite so daring, and legalised their relationship.

The question of the 'floating coffins' was first forced upon Ibsen's attention by an English Member of Parliament. In 1868 Samuel Plimsoll had sought in the House of Commons to have the State interfere against the cold-blooded and unscrupulous sacrifice of human life by sending men to sea in rotten ships. In 1873 he succeeded in getting a law passed to enforce seaworthiness; but this proved too slack. On 22 July 1875 he created a tremendous commotion in Parliament by a boldly outspoken attack on the people responsible for such a policy; he called the owners of such ships murderers and the politicians who supported them scoundrels. This so roused the conscience of the nation that a temporary bill went through in a few days, and its principles were made permanent by the Merchant Shipping Act of the following year. Plimsoll's protest echoed throughout the world, and in a seafaring country such as Norway it rang especially loudly. A particularly scandalous case had occurred in Christiania during Ibsen's visit there in 1874. On 2 September of that year, at the annual general meeting of the shipping insurance company Norske Veritas, which had been founded by that same Morten Smith Petersen, questions were asked about a ship which, after having been declared seaworthy, sprang a leak while at sea and was shown to be completely rotten. At the annual general meeting a year later two similar cases were mentioned, and a storm of indignation was aroused. The matter was reported in detail in the newspapers, and Ibsen can hardly have failed to read about it.

The presentation in a dramatic form of problems that were urgent and topical rather than eternal was not unprecedented; it was the depth and subtlety of Ibsen's characterisation, his psychological insight and ability to strip respected people and institutions of their masks, that made *The Pillars of Society* a revelation to its contemporaries, especially the young, in a way in which *The Editor* and *A Bankrupt, La Dame aux Camélias*, and *Thérèse Raquin*, for all their theatrical effectiveness, had never been. Two of the rising stars of the German theatre, then both in their early twenties, have recorded the effect that the play had on them. 'Our young eyes', recalled Paul Schlenther, 'were opened to the false tinsel of the theatre that was being offered to us. We thrilled with joy. We returned incessantly to the theatre where it was being played; when it was full, we read the play in Wilhelm Lange's terrible translation. Until then, Ibsen had been but an empty name to us. It was this play that taught us to love him, a love that lasted for life. I can testify on behalf of many of my generation that under the influence of this example of modern realism there was implanted in us, at that formative age, an orientation of taste which was to be decisive for the whole of our lives.'[1] And Otto Brahm, at twenty-two a year younger than Schlenther, wrote: 'It was there that we gained the first inkling of a new world of creative art, first felt ourselves face to face with people of our time, in whom we could believe, and with a criticism which embraced the whole society of our time.'[2] In a few years Schlenther and Brahm were to be leading spirits in the founding of the Freie Bühne, which was to do for the German theatre what Antoine's Théâtre Libre was to do for the French.

So exciting and new were the qualities of *The Pillars of Society* that Ibsen's contemporaries as a whole (political opponents and the Brandes brothers excepted) forgave the weakness of the last act; but it is a weakness we find less easy to forgive. It has been suggested[3] that this ending possesses 'ironic potential'; that Ibsen, by showing how a double-dealer can survive exposure and remain at the helm, underlined the danger that such men are to the society they control. The idea may indeed have been at the back of his mind; and if it was, and if he betrayed his real belief by settling for a happy ending, this may explain why that ending is so unconvincing. Erik Bøgh, in the review quoted above, wrote: 'Ibsen never perpetrates a fifth act showing his hero restored to prosperity and converted, as Bjørnson did [in *A Bankrupt*]', but this in fact is exactly what Ibsen did in *The Pillars of Society*, and it is a fault that no amount of sophistry or skilful acting can conceal. Yet the rest of the play is so fine that with a good production we forgive this unlikely ending, as we forgive the equally unlikely ending of (for example) *A Winter's Tale*.

The Pillars of Society was not (as it is sometimes claimed to be) the first realistic prose play. Nor was it even the first that Ibsen had written in colloquial prose; he had done that in *The League of Youth* (and to some extent in *Emperor and Galilean*). But it can be fairly claimed to have been the first (always excepting Büchner and Gogol) to combine the three elements of colloquial dialogue, objectivity and tightness of plot which are the requirements and characteristics of modern prose drama. And it is the first in which we can iden-

---

[1] *Henrik Ibsens sämtliche Werke in deutscher Sprache*, ed. Georg Brandes, Julias Elias and Paul Schlenther (Berlin, 1898 ff.), VI, pp. xvii–xviii.

[2] Otto Brahm, *Kritische Schriften über Drama und Theatern* (Berlin, 1913), pp. 447 ff., reprinted in *Henrik Ibsens brev*, ed. H. Koht and J. Elias (Christiania, 1904), I, p. 48.

[3] J. W. McFarlane, *Meaning and Evidence in Ibsen's Drama*, in *Contemporary Approaches to Ibsen* (Oslo, 1966), pp. 38–39.

tify several of those elements which we nowadays instinctively associate with Ibsen's name—a marriage founded on a lie, passionate women stunted and inhibited by the conventions of their time, and an arrogant man of high intellectual and practical gifts who destroys, or nearly destroys, the happiness of those nearest to him. It also exhibits, unlike his earlier plays, what Henry James admiringly described as 'the operation of talent without glamour . . . the ugly interior on which his curtain inexorably rises and which, to be honest, I like for the queer associations it has taught us to respect: the hideous carpet and wallpaper (one may answer for them), the conspicuous stove, the lonely central table, the "lamps with green shades" . . . the pervasive air of small interests and standards, the sign of limited local life'.[1] Above all, *The Pillars of Society* has, despite its overtones of comedy, that peculiarly Ibsenish quality of austerity which contrasts so sharply with the exuberant cornucopia of his earlier work; what Henry James, on another occasion, described as 'the hard compulsion of his strangely inscrutable art'.[2] No wonder, when we remember the technical problems imposed by this new form, that *The Pillars of Society* took Ibsen longer to write than any of his other plays except the triple-length *Emperor and Galilean*. As *Peer Gynt* had been a farewell to the old drama, so *The Pillars of Society* was the harbinger of the new.

By the end of 1877, *The Pillars of Society* had received three separate productions, at the Royal Theatre in Copenhagen[3] on 18 November, at the Bergen Theatre on 30 November and at the Royal Theatre in Stockholm on 13 December. The Christiania Theatre, however, had incurred Ibsen's wrath by permitting a performance that June of Act Four of *Brand* without reference to him and, worse, forcing the resignation of Ludvig Josephson, who had done so much for him (and for the theatre) over the past four years. 'The board would have acted more in the interests of the theatre if . . . they had sacked them-

---

[1] Henry James, *On the Occasion of Hedda Gabler* (*New Review*, June, 1891), reprinted in *The Scenic Art; Notes on Acting and the Drama, 1872–1901* (London, 1949), p. 249.

[2] Henry James, *On the Occasion of The Master Builder* (*Pall Mall Gazette*, 17 February 1893), reprinted in *The Scenic Art*, p. 258.

[3] The Royal Theatre's new censor, Christian Molbech, had reported to his board that the play possessed considerable merit: 'although here, as in several of the author's works, the ideal is sadly outshadowed by the real, and the satire is sharper and more intense than the sympathy, the overall impression is a healthy and attractive view of life, leaving a satisfying impression'. The production achieved twenty-one performances that season. (Agerholm, pp. 276–280). Johanne Luise Heiberg (according to John Paulsen) remarked that Lona Hessel would have been a part for her ('I never got roles of that kind when I acted. The writers of that time hadn't enough sense of reality'). Paulsen was amazed that she, who had specialised in romantic queens and princesses, should have hankered after playing an emancipated woman who washed her hands at the town pump. (*Samliv med Ibsen*, I, p. 43.)

selves', Ibsen wrote to Hartvig Lassen on 2 November. '. . . And what kind of a successor have you appointed! This successor was here in Munich last summer, and talked about his job like a five year old child. How long do you suppose this miserable and totally useless fellow will survive? He won't last the season.' Ibsen added sadly that Josephson had had plans to stage a shortened version of *Brand*, and Part One of *Emperor and Galilean*. Not only did Ibsen allow the Bergen Theatre to give the first Norwegian production of *The Pillars of Society*; he rubbed in the lesson a year later by permitting a Swedish company to act it in Swedish at the old Møllergaden Theatre in Christiania (on 6 November 1878), and it was not performed in the capital in Norwegian until the following March, seventeen months after publication.[1]

Ibsen marked the appearance of *The Pillars of Society* by sending a copy of it to Bjørnson, with a brief but affectionate note, the first contact between the two for eight years. The chief reason for this olive branch was, ironically, Bjørnson's public declaration of thanks to Georg Brandes, whom Ibsen, though he did not realise it, had himself now mortally offended. 'This one step [of Bjørnson's]', Ibsen wrote to Hegel on 28 October, 'in my eyes greatly expiates much else; it was a noble action. I should now like to bring about a closing of the gap between him and me, and therefore beg you to send him the enclosed note with a copy of *The Pillars of Society*.' The note read:

Munich, 28 October 1877

To Bjørnstjerne Bjørnson!

Your utterance on the occasion of G. Brandes's departure has delighted and deeply moved me. This is the true you. Will you be so good as to accept the enclosed book from me and give it to your wife?

H.I.

The olive branch was rejected. 'He has sent me a warm message of thanks and his last book because of what I wrote about you in D.F.', Bjørnson informed Brandes on 10 June 1878. 'I didn't answer him, for I find his conduct towards me shabby. I think he's a pipsqueak with his titles and decorations and nauseating letters to every little person who praises him in the tiniest newspaper . . .

---

[1] And when Ibsen did at last grant the Christiania Theatre permission to stage *The Pillars of Society*, he stipulated that the 'miserable and totally useless fellow', Johan Vibe, should have nothing to do with the casting, that he himself should have a veto on the casting, and that he should receive a lump payment of either 2,000 crowns for twenty-five performances or 2,500 crowns for forty performances; thereafter, two and a half per cent of the gross takings. They agreed to the former alternative, the biggest fee they had yet paid to any author. (Cf. Ibsen's letter to Harald Holst, 2 November 1878, printed in Ø. Anker's *Henrik Ibsens brevveksling med Christiania theater, 1878–1899*—Oslo, 1965, pp. 11–18.) Ibsen was not far wrong in his assessment of Vibe, who lasted only two years in the job.

People excuse Ibsen because he comes from "simple folk" [*sic*]. He needs it for his self-esteem. Well, well!'[1]

That autumn, on 24 October, Ibsen's father died, and as though to reconcile himself with the past and blot out old quarrels he penned a letter to his uncle, Christian Paus, in Skien, the circumlocution and stiltedness of which mirrors the guilt and embarrassment underlying the awkward words:

Munich, 18 November 1877

Dear Uncle Christian!

Although one of your closest relatives, I fear you must almost, and with good ground, regard these lines from afar as coming from a stranger. To uncomprehending eyes I know it must look as though I had voluntarily and deliberately cut myself off from my family, or at any rate permanently set a distance between me and them; but I think I may say that impossible circumstances from a very early stage were the principal cause.

You will of course guess the reason why I am writing to you today. From foreign newspapers, and also through a letter from Hedvig, I learn that my old father has passed away, and I feel a need to express my most grateful thanks to all you members of the family who have so lovingly helped to ease so many years of his life, and have thereby taken upon yourselves on my behalf, or in my stead, a task which, until very recently, I felt in no position to fulfil.

From my fourteenth (sic) *year I was sent away to care for myself. I have for many long years been compelled to fight hard to make my way and achieve my present position. That I so seldom wrote home during all these years of struggle was chiefly because I was unable to be of assistance or to support my parents. I thought it vain to write when I could do nothing practical to help them; I stood in constant hope that my circumstances might improve, but that happened very late and not long ago.*

It was therefore a great consolation to me to know that my parents, especially in recent years my old father, were surrounded by loving relatives. And when I express my thanks to all those who have stretched out a loving hand to him who is now gone, these thanks also incorporate the help and relief that I have thereby found on my journey through life. Yes, my dear Uncle, I say to you, and please tell this to my other relatives, that the portion of my duty and my love that they have taken on their shoulders has to a considerable degree sustained me during my longings and strivings, and has contributed to the fulfilment of what I have accomplished in the world.

During my last visit to Norway I felt a strong inclination to visit Skien and, especially, my family; but I felt also a strong reluctance to come into close contact with certain spiritual truths, then prevalent, with which I could feel no sympathy and a collision with which could easily have provoked unpleasantness, or at any rate an atmosphere of discord, which I wished to avoid. I have, nevertheless, not abandoned the

---

[1] *Brandes Brevveksling*, IV, pp. 57–58.

thought that I may some day see again my old childhood home. In a year my son will matriculate here, and then we shall be able to live anywhere we choose. We shall probably first pay a short visit to Italy and then take an apartment in Christiania, although I fear I could not in the long run be happy or work in Norway. The context in which I live here is far more advantageous; I mean, the intellectual freedom and broad view of life which a cosmopolitan way of living inculcates. Though to live thus demands certain sacrifices of various kinds.

I enclose my photograph. It is now twenty-seven years since we saw each other, and you will of course not recognise me; but I hope we shall see the day when the family will have the opportunity personally to decide whether or not the portrait is a good likeness.

And with this, my dear Uncle, I shall close. Warmest regards to yourself and the family from

Your grateful and affectionate nephew
Henrik Ibsen

When, at the end of 1877, Ibsen reckoned up his accounts, he had reason to feel satisfied:

	crowns	£
Royalties from *The Vikings at Helgeland* at Munich Hoftheater	250	14
Royalties from *The Vikings at Helgeland* at Dresden Hoftheater	92	5
Royalties from *The Vikings at Helgeland* at Wien Burgtheater	960	53
Fee for *The League of Youth* at Bergen Theatre	400	22
4th edition of *Love's Comedy*	1,000	56
Extra fees from Bergen Theatre	360	20
Miscellaneous fees from German Society of Dramatists	67	4
1st edition of *The Pillars of Society*	4,637½	258
Advance for *The Pillars of Society* from Royal Theatre, Copenhagen	1,000	56
Extra fee for *The Vikings at Helgeland* from Royal Theatre, Stockholm	1,000	56
Advance on 2nd edition of *The Pillars of Society*	3,091	173
Fee for *The Pillars of Society* at Odense, Denmark	600	33
Fee for *The Pillars of Society* at Bergen Theatre	400	22
	13,857½	772

It is noteworthy that despite the number of theatrical productions, nearly two-thirds of this sum was from book sales in Scandinavia. For many years yet, performance rights were to remain a subsidiary source, and foreign translations, as he had complained to Sverdrup when appealing for an increase in his pension, were seldom to bring him anything at all.

This fact was particularly exemplified at the beginning of 1878. The success of *The Pillars of Society* in the three Scandinavian countries did not pass unnoticed in Germany where, in the absence of copyright protection, translators and theatre directors fastened upon the play like vultures. In addition to the translation authorised by Ibsen, two pirate versions appeared before the end of January. One was by a man named Emil Jonas, whom Ibsen described to Hegel (28 January) as 'a frightful literary bandit', and to whom, ten days earlier, he had addressed one of those formidable rebukes which he so well knew how to word:

Munich, 18 January 1878

Herr Emil Jonas,
Berlin.

    In reply to your communication I must remind you of a fact of which you cannot be unaware, namely, that I myself, at the beginning of November last, published with Messrs Theodor Ackerman a German version of my play, The Pillars of Society. *A translation from your hand is therefore utterly superfluous, and I must totally disassociate myself from any adaptation such as you envisage.*

    Your suggestions for cuts in Act One are quite senseless and show that you have totally failed to understand this work which you regard yourself as worthy to adapt. Even to the most ignorant literary hack I should have thought it obvious that in this play no roles can be omitted and not a single line deleted[!]. The play has already been accepted in an unabridged and unbowdlerised form by many German theatres . . .

    If, in spite of me, you permit the proposed monstrosity to be put before the public, you at least owe it to me to clear my name by seeing that the placards outside the theatre carry the caption: 'Travestied by Emil Jonas'.

Faithfully,

Henrik Ibsen.

The extent to which this pirating cut into Ibsen's earnings soon became clear. In February *The Pillars of Society* was performed at five separate theatres in Berlin alone within a fortnight. Before the end of the year, it had been staged at no less than twenty-seven theatres in Germany and Austria. But financially, these productions brought Ibsen little joy. The play was performed almost exclusively in pirated versions. In a letter to the Swedish newspaper *Göteborgs Handels-och Sjöfarts-Tidning* (nr. 60, 1887), Jonas, defending his adaptation by declaring that it 'suited German taste', pointed out that it had been accepted for performance by thirty-two German theatres, whereas Ibsen's authorised translation had been played only at the Nationaltheater in Berlin and the

Munich Hoftheater. (Even the other pirate version, by Wilhelm Lange, had been performed at four theatres.) Most of Ibsen's German royalties and fees (excluding those from the Munich Hoftheater and one or two other theatres which had honourably offered to deal with him direct) were henceforth collected for him by the German Society of Dramatists, and appear only as unitemised lump sums in his account books; but from these twenty-seven productions, excluding Munich, he earned that year only 626 Norwegian crowns (under £35), plus another 251 crowns (£14) which arrived early the next year. Most of the German theatres do not appear to have paid him anything at all. Georg Brandes reckoned that Ibsen was robbed thus of 15,000 marks (13,284 crowns, £738) which he should have earned from *The Pillars of Society* in this year alone—'and his [German] publisher has lost much, much money, for three (*sic*) other pirate publishers sold it for 2 groschen while his own publisher was asking 2 marks'.[1] How much Emil Jonas made from the play is not on record.

In England, however, he had a new admirer, and one who was to do far more for him than Edmund Gosse, whose interest in Scandinavian literature had rapidly faded.[2] William Archer, now twenty-two, had spent much of his childhood in Norway and had grown up bilingual in English and Norwegian (his grandparents had settled in Larvik in 1825 and spent the rest of their lives there, and one of his uncles, Colin Archer, was to build Nansen's famous ship, the *Fram*). Archer had first made the acquaintance of Ibsen in 1873 (the year in which he had, unknowingly, been in Vienna at the same time as Ibsen), and at once became an addict.

'A *chokolade-selskab* [chocolate party] was going on, and I, a boy of seventeen, sat listening to the chatter of a lot of ladies. One of them, whom I never saw before or since, but whose face I remember as though I had seen it yesterday, said: "*Jeg synes* Kjærlighedens Komedie *er saa glimrende vittig*" ["I think *Love's Comedy* is so brilliantly witty"]. "Hullo", I thought, "have they got anything *glimrende vittig* in Norwegian? I must look into this—and forthwith went and bought the book. Then I read *Kongsemnerne* [*The Pretenders*], *Hærmændene* [*The Vikings*] and all that he had written up to that time, with increasing

---

[1] Letter from Georg Brandes to V. Pingel, 14 April 1878 (*Brandes Brevveksling*, III, pp. 273–274).

[2] After contributing over twenty essays or reviews concerning Ibsen to English periodicals between March 1872 and March 1878, Gosse was to write nothing about Ibsen for five years. During these years the only two other articles, etc., published in English about Ibsen were an account by Edith Pradez of Ibsen's 1874 visit to Norway in the *Academy*, 10 October 1874, and Archer's review of *The Pillars of Society* in the *St James's Gazette* in 1878. Cf. Bredsdorff, pp. 38–39 and 175.)

delight." [1] When *Emperor and Galilean* appeared that autumn of 1873, 'I remember locking myself up in a little bare hutch of a bathing-house by the fjord in order to devour its ten acts in the luxury of unbroken solitude . . . I laid in provisions to enable me, if necessary, to stand a siege. Even in those days, you see, Ibsenite and Ishmaelite meant much the same thing.' [2]

Archer waited impatiently for the publication of Ibsen's next play, and when *The Pillars of Society* at last appeared it so excited him that he made a hurried translation (rather uninspiredly entitled *The Supports of Society*), and on 2 March 1878 published an analysis of the play, with extracts from his translation, in *The Mirror of Literature*. He tried to interest publishers in his translation, but 'no publisher would look at' [3] it, and people 'used to jeer at my rapture over this incomprehensible Hyperborean'. [4] With Scottish resolution, he settled down to prepare another, more careful version which, eighteen months later, was to meet with better luck.

A young Norwegian woman named Laura Kieler, whom Ibsen had met a few times over the past seven years, now re-entered his life, with results which were to prove significant for both of them. As Laura Petersen, a decade previously, she had written a sequel to *Brand* in the form of a novel entitled *Brand's Daughters*; then, in the summer of 1871, she had visited Dresden for a couple of months and had called on him. He must have liked her, for they saw a good deal of each other during her stay; he called her his 'skylark', and encouraged her to write more.

She married a Danish schoolmaster named Victor Kieler, and in 1876 visited Ibsen again, in Munich. She now had a sad story to tell him (or rather, she told Suzannah, and Suzannah told Ibsen). Her husband had contracted tuberculosis, and she had been advised that the only way to save his life was to take him for a while to a warmer climate. They lacked the means for this and, since Kieler became neurotically hysterical at any mention of money, she took it on herself secretly to obtain a loan, for which a friend stood security. The trip (to Italy) had been successful, for Kieler, unluckily for Laura, lived for another forty years; but the matter weighed on her mind, and Ibsen noticed sadly that his little skylark 'could no longer sing her happy songs'.

During the first months of 1878 Suzannah received a letter from Laura enclosing the manuscript of a novel she had written and begging her to ask Ibsen to recommend it to Hegel. Ibsen found himself embarrassingly placed, for the book struck him as really bad; any writer who has been asked by a friend

---

[1] Letter to Edmund Gosse, 23 March 1898 (Bredsdorff, pp. 184–185).
[2] Charles Archer, *William Archer* (London, 1931), p. 37.
[3] *Ibid.*, p. 72.
[4] Letter from Archer to Edmund Gosse, 23 March 1898 (Bredsdorff, p. 185).

to pass on a poor manuscript to a publisher will sympathise with his position. He replied in stern but kindly terms, telling her that he could not possibly recommend it. 'You speak', he wrote to her on 26 March, 'of circumstances which compelled you to write this book under pressure. I do not understand. In a family where the husband is alive it can never be necessary for the wife to sacrifice her heart's blood as you have done. I am amazed that he should permit you to do so. There must be something which you don't tell me and which colours the whole situation; that is my impression after several readings of your letter . . . It is unthinkable that your husband knows everything; so you must tell him; he must take on his shoulders the sorrows and problems which now torment you . . . Hegel would never have accepted your manuscript even if I had recommended it . . . Confide all your troubles to your husband. He is the one who should bear them.'

She had, indeed, not told him the full story; perhaps she feared he might take it as an attempt to touch him for a loan. Repayment had been demanded of the money she had borrowed to take her husband to Italy two years earlier. She did not have it, and dared not tell her husband because of his neurotic attitude towards such matters; worse, the friend who had stood security had himself fallen into straits, and told her he would be ruined if pressed for payment. Laura, who had published a book of sketches and a novel (*Everil*, about an unhappy marriage) had seen no way out but to write another book and hope for an unusually large advance; hence the hasty and unfortunate manuscript. Ibsen's reply (though he can scarcely be blamed) was to have disastrous consequences.[1]

The success of *The Pillars of Society*[2] not surprisingly stimulated Ibsen to think immediately about following it up with another play in the same genre, just as the success of *Brand* had stimulated him to follow that work with another drama-for-reading. On 5 May he informed Hegel: 'I have begun to busy myself with plans for a new play with a contemporary setting; it will, like the last, be in four acts. When it will be ready, however, I can as yet have no idea.' His other letters of that spring and summer deal exclusively with business matters. He was to ponder his theme for another twelve months before writing the first line of dialogue—a routine he was to adopt with every play he subsequently wrote, with but one exception.

---

[1] B. M. Kinck, *Henrik Ibsen og Laura Kieler*, in *Edda*, 1935, pp. 504–506.

[2] Not that the conservatives liked it any more in Germany than they had in Norway. Karl Frenzel, the influential critic of *Deutsche Rundschau*, who had written of *The Pretenders* that Ibsen was poor at dramatic construction and did not know how to work out a plot, found *The Pillars of Society* an effective criticism of social conditions but reiterated that Ibsen was 'no dramatist'. (W. H. Eller, *Ibsen in Germany, 1870–1900*, Boston, 1918, p. 32).

That summer Sigurd took his matriculation, and passed with high honours. He was a far better student and examinee than his father had been; but he had been better taught. Now that the boy's schooling was finished, Ibsen felt free to do what he had been longing to do for several years; to return to Italy. He had enjoyed his three years in Munich, but the Mediterranean beckoned to him, and on 2 August he wrote to Hegel:

'Towards the middle of this month we shall be leaving for the south; we plan to spend the winter in Rome, where I hope to find time and peace to complete my new work. The weather here has been beastly the whole time, so that we have had no real summer. I greatly long to get across the Alps . . .

'Mrs Laura Kieler has, as you probably know, suffered a sad calamity. Her husband informed us rather curtly that she had been admitted into a mental clinic. Do you know the exact circumstances of this, and whether she is still there? . . . As soon as I have settled in at Florence, where we expect to spend a couple of months, you will hear from me again. Sigurd . . . will probably continue his studies at the University here [in Munich] when we return next autumn.'

When the full news of the Kieler affair reached Ibsen, it must have shaken him. On receipt of his letter of 26 March she had burned the manuscript and forged a cheque. The forgery was discovered, and the bank refused payment; whereupon she told her husband the whole story. He, regardless of the fact that she had done it purely for his sake, treated her like a criminal, told her she was unworthy to have charge of their children and, when she in consequence suffered a nervous breakdown, had her committed to a public asylum (where she lived in a ward among lunatics) and demanded a separation so that the children could be removed from her care. After a month she was discharged from the asylum and, for the children's sake, begged her husband to take her back, which he very grudgingly agreed to do.[1]

The story must have seemed especially relevant to a writer whose last play had dwelt upon the unequal position of woman in contemporary society, and Georg Brandes's advice nearly a decade earlier that he should make such a woman the chief character in a play must have come to his mind, if it had not already done so (we do not know how far the news changed Ibsen's plans).

On their way south, the Ibsens visited Gossensass, and remained there for several weeks till the last days of September. Ibsen wrote to Nils Lund on 23 September cancelling the *gammelost* which he had asked the latter to send him as early as 25 March, and which seems to have been a long time coming (not that a few months one way or the other would have made much difference to

---

[1] Kinck, pp. 506 ff.

that particular delicacy). They forsook their original plan to stay in Florence 'since I greatly long for familiar surroundings, so as to find peace for work',[1] and by the end of September, for the first time in ten and a half years, Ibsen was back in Rome.

[1] Letter to Hegel, 8 October 1878. John Paulsen observed that Ibsen seemed to feel the same indifference towards Florence as Goethe, who likewise never stayed long there but always moved on quickly to Rome. (*Samliv med Ibsen*, I, p. 30).

ELEVEN

℘ A Doll's House

(1878–1880)

WITHIN THREE WEEKS of his arrival in Rome Ibsen, installed in an apartment in a pleasant, five-storied corner house next to a church on the Via Due Macelli, jotted down the following:

Rome, 19.10.78

'NOTES FOR A MODERN TRAGEDY

'There are two kinds of moral laws, two kinds of conscience, one for men and one, quite different, for women. They don't understand each other; but in practical life, woman is judged by masculine law, as though she weren't a woman but a man.

'The wife in the play ends by having no idea what is right and what is wrong; natural feelings on the one hand and belief in authority on the other lead her to utter distraction.

'A woman cannot be herself in modern society. It is an exclusively male society, with laws made by men and with prosecutors and judges who assess feminine conduct from a masculine standpoint.

'She has committed forgery, and is proud of it; for she has done it out of love for her husband, to save his life. But this husband of hers takes his standpoint, conventionally honourable, on the side of the law, and sees the situation with male eyes.

'Moral conflict. Weighed down and confused by her trust in authority, she loses faith in her own morality, and in her fitness to bring up her children. Bitterness. A mother in modern society, like certain insects, retires and dies once she has done her duty by propagating the race. Love of life, of home, of husband and children and family. Now and then, as women do, she shrugs off her thoughts. Suddenly anguish and fear return. Everything must be borne alone. The catastrophe approaches, mercilessly, inevitably. Despair, conflict and defeat.'

But although he told Hegel on 7 December that he was 'concerning myself only with the preparations for my new play', it was to be another six months before he wrote the first line. Meantime, as was his wont, he pondered the theme and characters until he knew them in depth. One day he surprised Suzannah by saying: 'Now I've seen Nora. She came right up to me and put her hand on my shoulder.' 'What was she wearing?' asked Suzannah, as a woman should; to which Ibsen 'with great earnestness' replied: 'A blue woollen dress.'[1]

'A lot of Scandinavians have arrived here, but we have got to know few of them at all well', he wrote to Marcus Grønvold on 30 December. 'On the other hand, we have made several acquaintances among German and Italian scholars, artists and writers, whom I meet frequently. Sigurd attends lectures at the University here, and has already pretty well brushed up his old forgotten Italian; he follows the lectures completely and without trouble. We shall stay in Rome until the University holidays begin in June or July; we have made no plans beyond that, but intend to return to Munich in early October.'

Lady Inger of Østraat had just received its first German production in Berlin. But when he made up his accounts for 1878, a year in which his most recent play had been performed at over thirty theatres in Scandinavia and Germany, they offered no scope for extravagance. With only one new reprint, and that a small one, the improvement of the last three years had not been maintained:

	crowns	£
Fee for *The Pillars of Society* at Nya Teatern, Gothenburg	1,000	56
Royalties for *The Vikings at Helgeland* at Munich Hoftheater, 2nd half-year of 1877	122	7
Extra fee for *The Pillars of Society* at Royal Theatre, Copenhagen	500	28
Extra royalties for *The Pillars of Society* from Royal Theatre, Stockholm	2,425	135
Actor Brock's reading of [unspecified] work in Nordhausen	18	1
Further extra fee for *The Pillars of Society* from Royal Theatre, Copenhagen	500	28
5th edition of *The Vikings at Helgeland*	720	40
Fee for *The Vikings at Helgeland* at Trondhjem	100	6
Fee for *The Pillars of Society* at Trondhjem	400	22
Fees from Bergen Theatre for 8 performances of *The Pillars of Society* and 3 performances of *The League of Youth*	320	18

[1] Paulsen, *Samliv med Ibsen*, II, p. 60.

Royalties from Munich Hoftheater for *The*
Pillars of Society and *The Vikings at Helgeland*
for first half of 1878   818   45
Royalties and fees from German Society of
Dramatists   626   35
                                                        ————   ————
                                                        7,549   421

Ibsen was touchy and nervous that winter in Rome. 'We live in general pretty quietly', he wrote on 22 January to Marcus Grønvold. 'Lunch is brought in to us, and our landlady prepares our breakfast and supper. Everything is much cheaper here than in Munich, and wine especially is to be had for practically nothing this winter, so that in the Sabine villages one can buy excellent wine for 3 soldi [a penny-halfpenny] a litre!' Despite his poor earnings for the past year and his habitual economy, he now indulged himself in an unexpected direction. 'I am taking the opportunity', he informed Grønvold in the same letter, 'to buy old paintings, and have already purchased eleven, all good and valuable and at a comparatively modest price. I intend to buy more, so that I shall be able to furnish my next apartment in Munich solely with works of art. If only I can find somewhere suitable!' These paintings, or most of them, came from the collection of a recently deceased Cardinal, and included a supposed Titian. Lorentz Dietrichson, who, as a Professor of Art History, ought to have known, refers to them as 'important pictures, especially by the older Italian masters'.[1] One would like to know more about them.

He visited the Scandinavian Club regularly, but mainly to read the newspapers; although he occasionally entered into a conversation he was evidently in one of those long combative moods which periodically settled on him for weeks on end. Once he got into a violent argument about religion with two Danish theologians after drinking Swedish punch. He attacked the teachings of the orthodox church as being slanted to prop up an antiquated society, got angrier and angrier, and had to be supported home in the small hours by the Danish novelist and botanist J. P. Jacobsen and a young Norwegian named Gunnar Heiberg, later to become a fine theatrical director and playwright. On the way he grew more and more abusive of the human race and its aims and ambitions; and when Heiberg tried to mollify him by suggesting that at any rate Ibsen himself had written some great truths, and started to quote from his *Balloon Letter*, Ibsen roared contemptuously: 'Verse, verse! Just verse!'[2]

---

[1] Dietrichson, I, p. 361.

[2] Heiberg, *Salt og sukker* (Christiania, 1924), pp. 51–52.

It was in this prickly mood that, on 28 January, he put two proposals before the Club: that the post of paid librarian (which he had coveted himself fifteen years earlier) should be thrown open to women, and that women should have the right to vote on all Club matters. When these proposals came to be debated on 27 February, he delivered a lengthy and impassioned speech; Sigurd, who was present, tells[1] that he got so worked up that he occasionally abandoned his prepared text and improvised with that eloquence which, when the mood was on him, he knew how to command. Even his written text (which has survived) was fiery enough, if ill-calculated to gain support from the older members who formed the majority:

'Is there anyone in this gathering who dares assert that our ladies are inferior to us in culture, or intelligence, or knowledge, or artistic talent? I don't think many men would dare suggest that. Then what is it men fear? I hear there is a tradition here that women are cunning intriguers, and that therefore we don't want them. Well, I have encountered a good deal of male intrigue in my time, not least recently . . . Is it perhaps the supposed unpracticality of women in matters of business? Even if women were as unpractical as many an unpractical gentleman would like to suppose, are artists so especially practical in business matters? No, gentlemen, I think not. I hold it to be good and profitable that we should have ladies present at our annual general meeting just as I hold it good and advantageous that we should have young people there, those young people whose presence is now threatened by a proposal that the vote should only be allowed to those who have been resident for a year in Rome. I repeat that I am not afraid of these so-called unpractical women; women have something in common with the true artist, just as young people in general have—something that is a good substitute for worldly understanding. Look at our student societies in Norway! Matters are decided there which are ten times more complicated than ours; yet do not they manage well, although youth, untried, unpractised and unpractical youth, there enjoys an overwhelming majority? And why? Because youth has this instinctive genius which unconsciously hits upon the right answer. And it is precisely this instinct which women share with youth, and with the true artist. And that is why I want us to allow women to vote at our annual general meeting. I fear women, youth and inexperience as little as I fear the true artist. What I do fear is the worldly wisdom of the old; what I fear is men with little ambitions and little thoughts, little scruples and little fears, those men who direct all their thoughts and

---

[1] *CE*, XV, p. 469.

R

actions towards achieving certain little advantages for their own little and subservient selves. Should the affairs of this Club fall into such hands, I should greatly fear for its survival, at any rate as a society of artists. And that is why I wish to have ladies included at our annual general meeting, so that they, together with the young, may see to it that power is placed into true, and truly artistic, hands.'[1]

The first of Ibsen's motions, that concerning the librarianship, was accepted; but the second failed by a single vote to get the necessary two-thirds' majority. Ibsen was furious.[2] He left the Club immediately and sat alone in a café, refusing to speak to anyone who had voted against him. Some days later, however, to the general amazement, he attended a gala evening at the Club, and Gunnar Heiberg, who was present, has left a picturesque account of what happened:

'No one would have guessed it—but Ibsen came. He looked magnificent, in full panoply, with medals to boot. He ran his hand ceaselessly through his rich, grizzled hair, greeting no one in particular, but everyone in general. There was a deep peace in his face, but his eyes were watchful, so watchful. He sat alone. We all thought he had forgiven his fellow mortals, and some even supposed him penitent. This helped the atmosphere to be unusually gay and euphoric. Then, suddenly, he rose and stepped forward to a big table, so that he was facing the whole ballroom with its dancing couples.

"Ladies and gentlemen!" It was a tense and dramatic moment. What was going to happen? Was he about to admit the error of his ways? Surely he was not going to propose a toast? . . . He stroked his hair calmly. Then he began, softly, but with a terrifying earnestness. He had recently wished to do the Club a service, he might almost say a great favour, by bringing its members abreast with contemporary ideas. No one could escape these mighty developments. Not even here—in this community— in this duckpond! He did not actually use the word duckpond, but the contempt around his mouth proclaimed it loudly. And how had his offer been received? As a criminal attempt! Rejected by a paltry couple of votes. And how had the women reacted—the women for whom his gift had been intended? They had intrigued and agitated against him. They had thrown

---

[1] *CE*, XV, pp. 402–403.

[2] Feelings evidently ran high on both sides, for J. P. Jacobsen, who supported Ibsen's motion (as did the Swedish painter Ernst Josephson) tells that a Captain of Marines all but challenged Ibsen to a duel on the matter (*Brandes Brevveksling*, II, p. 344.)

his gift into the mud. What kind of women are these? They are worse—worse than the dregs, worse than scum—

'Now he was no longer speaking calmly, no longer thoughtfully stroking his hair. He shook his head with its grey mane. He folded his arms across his breast. His eyes shone. His voice shook, his mouth trembled, and he thrust out his underlip. He resembled a lion, nay, more—he resembled that future enemy of the people, Dr Stockmann, He repeated and repeated: what kind of women are these, what kind of ladies, what kind of a sex, ignorant, in the truest sense ill-bred, immoral, dregs, contemptible—

'Thump! A lady, Countess B., fell to the floor. She, like the rest of us, flinched from the unspeakable. So she took time by the forelock and swooned. She was carried out. Ibsen continued. Perhaps slightly more calmly. But eloquently and lucidly, never searching for a word. He intoxicated himself with his rhetoric against the ignorant, contemptible and rigid resistance that mankind, and especially women, was attempting to offer to these new ideas, whose purpose was to make people bigger, richer and better. He looked remote, ecstatic. As his voice thundered it was as though he were clarifying his own secret thoughts, as his tongue chastised it was as though his spirit were scouring the darkness in search of his immediate spiritual goal, his play—as though he were personally living out his theories, incarnating his characters. And when he was done, he went out into the hall, took his overcoat and walked home. Calm and silent.'[1]

In February Hegel sent him the good news that fresh editions of both *The Pretenders* and *Poems* were in preparation; the fifth of the former and the third of the latter. Spring arrived. 'The almond trees have already blossomed', he wrote to Marcus Grønvold on 9 March. 'The cherry trees are in full bloom, and all the fields are covered in fresh green grass and violets.' Yet something was missing in Rome. He no longer found the same excitement there which had so stimulated him fifteen years earlier. 'I have often thought of sending Sigurd back [to Munich] to continue his studies alone', he wrote in the same letter. 'But in various respects it is desirable that I should get back into German literary life. Down here one is in most respects too much outside the movements of the times.' Was it, he may have wondered, that he was no longer as young as he had been? Edvard Brandes, meeting him this spring, was surprised by the venerability of his appearance. 'I spoke a few words with Henrik Ibsen in the street', he wrote to his brother Georg on 1 May. 'How old he is! I'd imagined him different, alert.'[2]

---

[1] Heiberg, *Salt og sukker*, pp. 68–71.
[2] *Brandes Brevveksling*, II, p. 43.

Old he may have looked; but the following day, he began the first draft of his new play, and, as usual, once he had started the work went swiftly. He finished the first act in three weeks. The second act took him six weeks, but was interrupted by a holiday move. 'We had at first thought to go to one of the mountain villages around Rome', he told Hegel on 19 June, 'but the sanitary conditions there leave much to be desired [he had grown fastidious since the old days at Genzano and Ariccia] and so we have decided to retire to Amalfi, on the coast south of Naples, where there are facilities for sea-bathing.' He left for Amalfi on 5 July, armed with an inscribed copy of Edmund Gosse's *Studies in the Literature of Northern Europe*, published that February, and containing an essay on Ibsen (a revised reprint of Gosse's article in the *Fortnightly* in 1873, plus his reviews of *The Pretenders* and *Emperor and Galilean* and an account of *The League of Youth*). 'English causes me some difficulty', he had written to Gosse the previous day. 'But when we leave tomorrow . . . your book will be about the only one I shall take with me.' At Amalfi they took 'two small rooms with three plain iron bedsteads'[1] in the Albergo della Luna, an old monastery converted into a hotel, situated (still) on a cliff overlooking a sheer drop into the sea. Here he was well cossetted by the proprietress, Marietta Barbaro; he had an ante-room where he could write, and the desk at which one of the most influential of all plays came to be written may still be seen there. When not working he bathed in the sea and took long walks in the hills.

Shortly before he finished Act Two, he received a letter from Bjørnson, the first for nine years, seeking to enlist Ibsen's support in a campaign to remove the mark of union with Sweden from the Norwegian flag. A more unfortunate subject for the re-opening of correspondence between the two men could hardly have been chosen. The business of the flag lay very close to Bjørnson's heart, and was exactly the kind of concern that Ibsen regarded as chauvinistic and irrelevant.

I have not much sympathy for symbols [he replied on 12 July, a remark that many an Ibsen critic might ponder]. *Symbols no longer have any meaning except in Norway. Up there people bother so much about symbols and theories and ideas that no practical progress is ever made . . . I regard it as a sin against our people to make an issue burningly important when it is not. A people can never get seriously concerned about more than one burning issue at a time . . . We have only one thing which I think worth fighting for, and that is the introduction of an up-to-date education for our people. This embraces all other issues; if it cannot be brought about, what use are*

---

[1] Bergliot Ibsen, p. 78.

all the rest? It is quite immaterial whether our politicians bring about isolated reforms if they do not achieve liberty for the individual. They call Norway a free and independent kingdom; but I don't set much store by this freedom and independence as long as I know that individuals are neither free nor independent. There are in the whole of Norway no more than twenty-five free and independent individuals. They just don't exist . . . I have tried to acquaint myself with our educational system, school plans, timetables, teaching material and so forth. It is disturbing to see how much class time, especially in the primary schools, is taken up with old Judaic mythology and saga history and mediaeval distortions of a moral code of teaching which in its original form was undoubtedly the purest that has ever been preached. This is the field in which we should all, with one voice, demand a 'pure flag'. Let the mark of union remain, but take the mark of monkishness from people's minds; take away the mark of prejudice and narrow-mindedness and short-sightedness and subservience and unthinking trust in authority, so that every individual can sail under his own flag . . . I don't think it is our job to make ourselves responsible for the liberty and independence of the state, but rather to awake as many individuals as possible to liberty and independence.

Ibsen's dismissal as trivial of this question of the 'pure flag' deeply offended Bjørnson, to whom it was a matter of almost religious significance, and the gap between the two men, which had seemed about to close, now became so wide as to appear unbridgeable. Georg Brandes tells how he found himself next to Karoline Bjørnson at a dinner at Hegel's around this time, and asked her if she could not use her friendship with Suzannah to bring her husband and Ibsen together. The next day Bjørnson came to Brandes in a great rage and 'rode his hobby-horse, his contempt for decorations; Ibsen had his chest covered with orders, and a whole dog-collar around his neck. Bjørnson thought it disgusting; rather than offer him his hand he would plunge it into a toadstool.'[1]

Having got the matter of the Norwegian flag off his chest, Ibsen returned to

---

[1] Georg Brandes, *Levned*, II, pp. 350 ff. In fairness to Bjørnson, however, one must remember that the years 1875–1885 were a peculiarly frustrating time for him, especially coming as they did just after the success of *A Bankrupt*. Of the plays that he wrote during this decade only one, *Leonarda*, was immediately accepted for production in Christiania. *The New System* had to wait eight years, *A Glove* three, while *The King, Beyond Mortal Power, I* (his finest play) and *The Editor* never got played until the National Theatre opened its doors there, with his son as director, in 1899. His plays were similarly rejected in Copenhagen, including even *Leonarda*. He was attacked continuously by the press in Norway, Denmark and Sweden, suffered from a deep sense of persecution, and around 1880 was in such financial straits that he even tried to sell his beloved home at Aulestad. The success of *The Pillars of Society* and *A Doll's House* must have been galling to him, especially that of the latter, overshadowing as it did *The New System*, published only six weeks earlier.

the more important business of finishing his play. He started Act Three on 18
July and completed it in less than three weeks, on 3 August. 'I cannot recall any
work of mine', he informed Hegel on 15 September, enclosing the fair copy,
'that has given me more satisfaction in the solving of specific problems.' And
indeed, the technical advance on *The Pillars of Society* is enormous; no one
could complain of *A Doll's House* that it was let down by the final act.

He left Amalfi at the end of September, with the plan for a new play already
in his head, and stayed a week in Sorrento, at the Hotel Tramontano. Another
guest at the hotel was Ernest Renan, the great French orientalist whom Ibsen
had met briefly in 1856, when Renan had visited Bergen as a member of
Prince Napoleon's suite. Renan was now working on the final stages of his
Origins of Christianity, and in view of what Ibsen had just written to Bjørnson
about the Church's perversion of Christ's teaching they might have found
much common ground: but Ibsen's ignorance of French and shyness of
strangers inhibited him from introducing himself (though since Renan was
equally shy, conversation might anyway have been difficult). On leaving
Sorrento, Ibsen spent a week in Rome, and by 14 October was back in Munich,
where he moved with his Italian paintings into a new and larger apartment in
an elegant house at Amalienstrasse 50.

That autumn Magdalene Thoresen visited them; and Bjørnson, too, came
to Munich. He stayed a stone's throw from the Ibsens, at the Hotel Bamber-
gerhof, and John Paulsen, also back from Rome, tells how Ibsen and Suzannah
sat hoping that he would visit them, but in vain. Sigurd, who was Bjørnson's
godson and had not set eyes on him since childhood, went along to the Café
Probst to see what the great man looked like. When he returned, and Paulsen
asked him how Bjørnson looked, Sigurd replied: 'An Emperor! An Emperor!'[1]
Ibsen's friend Paul Heyse gave a dinner for Bjørnson during his visit, but
(according to Georg Brandes) disliked the 'missionary and world-improver'
in him.[2]

In November an old painter named Knud Både died in Munich, and Ibsen
attended the funeral. Paulsen, who was present, noted: 'I shall never forget the
manner in which he approached the open grave and cast a handful of earth on
the coffin. He did it with a solemnity and deep intensity which moved us all
and brought tears to my eyes . . . Ibsen must have been a deeply religious
person; no one who saw him at this moment could doubt that.'[3] His demeanour
put Paulsen in mind of Brand. Living painters seemed to concern Ibsen less;

---

[1] Paulsen, *Samliv med Ibsen*, I, pp. 195–196. Paulsen quotes Bjørnson as later saying: 'I
now think I was wrong; anyway, I regret that I didn't visit him.' (*Ibid.*, p. 198n.)

[2] Georg Brandes, *Levned*, II, p. 353.

[3] Paulsen, *Samliv med Ibsen*, II, pp. 40–41.

when Paulsen took him to the studio of one Nils Hansteen, Ibsen showed less interest in the paintings than in the model of a ship which hung from the ceiling. On the way home he told Paulsen that if he ever returned permanently to Norway he would live in a fjord town smelling of pitch and seaweed where he would be able to see many ships and shipyards, 'especially the latter'.[1]

On 4 December 1879 *A Doll's House* was published in Copenhagen, in an edition of eight thousand copies, the largest first printing yet of any of Ibsen's works. Its success was immediate and sensational. Despite its size, the first edition sold out within a month; a second edition of three thousand copies appeared on 4 January and a third of two and a half thousand copies on 8 March. Such sales (proportionately equivalent to something around 150,000 in the United Kingdom today) were without precedent for a play in Scandinavia; and certainly no play, in Norway or anywhere else, had had quite such an effect. '*A Doll's House*', recalled Halvdan Koht, who was a child when it appeared, 'exploded like a bomb into contemporary life. *The Pillars of Society* . . . though it attacked reigning social conventions, still retained the traditional theatrical happy ending, so that it bit less sharply. But *A Doll's House* knew no mercy; ending not in reconciliation, but in inexorable calamity, it pronounced a death sentence on accepted social ethics.'[2]

Several times during that famous last act Ibsen seems about to settle for a happy-ending—when Krogstad promises Mrs Linde to take back his letter, when he returns Helmer's I.O.U., and when, in the closing moments of the play, Helmer remembers and echoes Nora's words: 'The miracle of miracles —?' But the terrible offstage slamming of that front door which brings down the curtain resounded through more apartments than Torvald Helmer's. No play had ever before contributed so momentously to the social debate, or been so widely and furiously discussed among people who were not normally interested in theatrical or even artistic matters. Even Strindberg, who disapproved of it as being calculated to encourage just the kind of woman he dreaded most (and was infallibly drawn to), and attacked it in his volume of stories *Marriage* (1885), admitted in his preface that, thanks to *A Doll's House*, 'marriage was revealed as being a far from divine institution, people stopped regarding it as an automatic provider of absolute bliss, and divorce between incompatible parties came at last to be accepted as conceivably justifiable'. What other play has achieved as much?

Many voices were, naturally, raised against it. 'Those who were against revolution', wrote Koht, 'against social and moral upheaval, against female

---

[1] Paulsen, *Samliv med Ibsen*, I, pp. 152–153.
[2] Koht, II, p. 107.

emancipation, came to see in Ibsen their greatest and most dangerous enemy.'[1] There were aesthetic objections too. Frederik Petersen spoke for the tradition-alists when he complained in *Aftenbladet* (9 January 1880) that 'one does not leave this play in the mood of exaltation which, ever since the days of the Greeks, has been regarded as a *sine qua non* for every work of art and literature. We have seen something sorely unbeautiful, and retain only the sense of pain which is the inevitable outcome when no conciliation shows us the final victory of ideals.' But most critics accepted Ibsen's implied thesis that a play need not merely provide an aesthetic experience, but had a right to upset people and cause them to re-think. An anonymous reviewer in *Morgenbladet* (10 December) praised his 'most profound insight into the essentials of dramatic art and marvellous technical mastery', and Erik Vullum, in *Dagbladet* (6 and 13 December) perceptively noted the absence of imagery in the writing compared with Ibsen's earlier works. 'One can read the book from first to last page and find scarcely one image. Ibsen no longer needs them. He has so worked out what he wants to portray that he no longer needs to resort to any graphic aid to natural dialogue.'

So explosive was the message of *A Doll's House*—that a marriage was not sacrosanct, that a man's authority in his home should not go unchallenged, and that the prime duty of anyone was to find out who he or she really was and to become that person—that the technical originality of the play is often forgotten. It achieved the most powerful and moving effect by the highly untraditional methods of extreme simplicity and economy of language—a kind of literary Cubism. Erik Bøgh, perceptive as usual, spotted this when *A Doll's House* received its first performance, at the Royal Theatre in Copen-hagen on 21 December.[2] 'It is long', he wrote in *Folkets Avis* (24 December) 'since any new play was awaited with such excitement, and even longer since a new play brought so much that is original to the stage, but it is beyond memory since a play so simple in its action and so everyday in its dress made such an impression of artistic mastery . . . Not a single declamatory phrase, no high dramatics, no drop of blood, not even a tear; never for a moment was the dagger of tragedy raised. . . Every needless line is cut, every exchange carries the action a step forward, there is not a superfluous effect in the whole play. . . the mere fact that the author succeeded with the help only of these five characters to keep our interest sustained throughout a whole evening is sufficient

---

[1] *Ibid.*, pp. 107–108.
[2] Despite the fact that the Royal Theatre's censor, Christian Molbech, had only grudg-ingly recommended it, finding the break-up of the Helmers' marriage 'not merely painful and unsatisfying but psychologically somewhat inexplicable'. (Agerholm, p. 279.)

proof of Ibsen's technical mastery.'[1] *The Pillars of Society* had used nineteen characters. And there are other ways in which *A Doll's House* marks a considerable technical advance on *The Pillars of Society*. The characters do not (as occasionally happens in the earlier play) tell each other what the listener already knows for the benefit of the audience; points once made are not drummed home in the manner beloved of politicians; the final curtain is not tediously delayed after the climax has been reached (an elementary fault which every playwright learns reluctantly to avoid, the more reluctantly if he has ever written a novel in which such rapid wind-ups seem melodramatic). Only in the sub-plot of Krogstad does a trace of the old melodramatic machinery remain.

Edvard Brandes had mixed feelings about the play. Admitting that 'it made a powerful impression on the stage', he complained to his brother Georg on Christmas Day: 'I don't really believe in the psychology. Is the marriage of those two very credible?' Then he read it and liked it better. 'It is a fine work', he wrote to J. P. Jacobsen. 'I hadn't read it when I saw it.' But a month later, on 8 February, he wrote to Alexander Kielland: 'The play evades the issue. It ends where it ought to begin . . . If the first scene had shown the relationship between the two as Nora realises it to be in the last act, and the whole play had dealt with their separation instead of that coming as it does now, like a *Satan ex machina*, the audience wouldn't have clapped, but Ibsen's plot . . . would have been clearer and better.'[2] (It would in fact have been much more talkative and less explosive.) Yet the play's influence on Edvard Brandes was such that the next year Brandes wrote his first play, and followed it during the next quarter of a century with eleven more, all bearing the clearest signs of Ibsen's influence. Brandes's correspondents saw the play's merits more clearly than he did. '*A Doll's House* is really refreshing', Alexander Kielland wrote to him on 8 January. 'So simple, and spare as a statue—you can positively hear the superfluities clattering away from the slim figure after the merciless hacks with which the Master has for the past two or three years been chiselling away everything unnecessary. I know nothing so perfect.'[3] And J. P. Jacobsen on 14 March 1880, wrote: '*A Doll's House* seems to me decidedly the most important and successful thing Ibsen has ever done.'[4] Bjørnson hated the play.

---

[1] Reprinted in *Dit og Dat, 1879* (Copenhagen, 1880), pp. 252–263.

[2] *Brandes Brevveksling*, II, pp. 57 and 342, and V, p. 117. Brandes's doubts following the performance may have been partly due to the fact that (as he later recalled) it was not well acted or directed—he thought Emil Poulsen's Helmer the only really adequate performance —though 'this fault was scarcely noticed amidst the enormous sensation and controversy which the play aroused'. (Edvard Brandes, *Om Teater*, pp. 149–150.)

[3] *Brandes Brevveksling*, V, p. 112.

[4] *Ibid.*, II, p. 349.

'It is technically excellent', he wrote to Sophus Schandorph on 9 January, 'but written by a vulgar and evil mind.'[1]

It is the tragedy of books carrying a particular message for their times that they tend to be remembered by posterity for the wrong reasons. *A Doll's House* and its successor, *Ghosts*, are particular examples; critics still occasionally write about *A Doll's House* as though it was a play about the outdated problem of women's rights (an attitude largely conditioned by the habit, among British and American critics, of consulting Bernard Shaw's *Quintessence of Ibsenism*, that brilliantly misleading book, before writing about any Ibsen play). *A Doll's House* is no more about women's rights than Shakespeare's *Richard II* is about the divine rights of kings, or *Ghosts* about syphilis or *An Enemy of the People* about public hygiene. Its theme is the need of every individual to find out the kind of person he or she really is, and to strive to become that person. Ibsen knew what Freud and Jung were later to assert, that liberation can only come from within; which was why he had expressed to Georg Brandes his lack of interest in 'special revolutions, revolutions in externals', and had declared that 'What is really wanted is a revolution of the spirit of man.' The effect of *A Doll's House* in the theatre today is less explosive than when it was written, but scarcely less hypnotic, because there is hardly a married woman in the audience who does not sometimes want (or has not at some time wanted) to leave her husband. The unspoken thoughts in the cars and taxis returning from a modern performance of the play cannot vary much from those in the returning carriages of ninety years ago.

One woman to whom *A Doll's House* did not bring joy was Laura Kieler. Her tragedy was known to enough people in Copenhagen for them immediately to realise that Ibsen had based Nora's story very closely upon hers (except for the ending), especially as she had been proud to advertise her friendship with him; and the link soon became common knowledge. It must have made the situation between her and Kieler, which was already bad enough, even less tolerable; and she was also much hurt by the reference in Act Three to Nora's father's 'recklessness and instability'. Yet it is hard to blame Ibsen. The play is an admiring vindication of her conduct, and he may well have supposed that she would be happy to be recognised as the original of so sympathetic and courageous a character, as later Julius Hoffory was proudly (and with much less reason to be proud) to advertise that he was the original of Ejlert Løvborg in *Hedda Gabler*. It is ironical that the play which established Ibsen as the champion of women should have been so deeply resented by the woman who had inspired it.

---

[1] *Bjørnstjerne Bjørnsons brevveksling med danske, 1875–1910*, ed. Øyvind Anker, Francis Bull and Torben Nielsen (Copenhagen and Oslo, 1953), I, p. 175.

A Doll's House was to make Ibsen internationally famous. But this (contrary to popular supposition) did not happen at once, or even quickly. It was to be two years before the play was performed outside Scandinavia and Germany, and ten years before a recognisably faithful version was seen in England or America, although (as we shall see) perverted adaptations were to make brief and unsuccessful appearances.[1] France, even further behind the times, did not see the play until 1894. By the time it took its place in the general European repertoire, Ibsen was over sixty and had moved on to a very different kind of writing.

The success of *A Doll's House* in book form made 1879 a somewhat better year for Ibsen financially, though considering the impact of the play his earnings remained unremarkable:

	crowns	£
Royalties and fees from German Society of Dramatists for last quarter of 1878	251	14
Royalties from Munich Hoftheater for previous half-year	261	15
Fee for *The Pretenders* at Bergen	400	22
Fee for *The Pillars of Society* in Christiania	2,000	111
Fee for *The Pretenders* in Stockholm	1,000	56
5th edition of *The Pretenders*	1,125	62
Miscellaneous fees from Bergen Theatre	360	20
3rd edition of *Poems*	947	53
1st edition of *A Doll's House*	5,288	294
Fee for *Love's Comedy* at Bergen	400	22
2nd edition of *A Doll's House*	1,969	109
	14,001	778

1880 opened with what must by now, for Ibsen, have been the familiar mixture of public acclaim and stolen rights. On 8 January the Royal Theatre in Stockholm presented *A Doll's House*, and Christiania and Bergen followed suit within the month. In all three cities the play was a triumph (though Edvard Brandes, on a visit to the Christiania production, was shocked to hear how the two principals, Johanne Juell and Arnoldus Reimers, 'both rephrased in the most shameless manner practically every line').[2] The Germans, however, were,

---

[1] It is significant that even Bernard Shaw does not mention Ibsen in his letters before 1889.

[2] Edvard Brandes, *Fremmed Skuespilkunst* (Copenhagen, 1881), p. 27.

as usual, treating him badly. Wilhelm Lange's authorised translation was being freely sold in Copenhagen at a lower price than the original—a serious matter in a city where educated people read and spoke German as readily as educated Russians spoke French. 'I receive no payment from the publisher', Ibsen complained to Hegel on 22 January. 'The translator has to give me such copies as I need for the German theatres, and that is all.' Hegel estimated the Danish sales of this German version to be as high as 2,000 copies. However, he was able to comfort Ibsen with two good pieces of news: that a fourth edition of *The League of Youth* and a fifth of *Emperor and Galilean* were in preparation, and that 'the last five performances of *A Doll's House* [at the Royal Theatre, Copenhagen] have brought you an honorarium of 2,270.12 [crowns] [£126], i.e. 3,904.99 [£217] in all. The next five performances will bring you a third of the takings, excluding subscription seats; so far the play has been sold out for every performance.'[1]

But far worse than the undercutting of his book sales was what was about to happen to *A Doll's House* on the German stage. A well-known actress of the day, Hedwig Niemann-Raabe, had announced her intention to present the play with herself in the leading role, but she refused to act the final scene as written, on the grounds that 'I would never leave *my* children!' In the absence of copyright protection, Ibsen's hands were completely tied; and he decided that, as the lesser of two evils, a 'happy' ending written by himself would be preferable to one by another hand which could be published and performed at other German theatres. 'To forestall any such possibility', he explained in an open letter (17 February 1880) to the Danish newspaper *Nationaltidende*, 'I sent my translator and agent for use in an emergency a drafted emendation in which Nora does not leave the house but is forced by Helmer to the doorway of the children's bedroom; here a few lines are exchanged, Nora sinks down by the door and the curtain falls. This emendation I have myself described to my translator as a "barbaric outrage" on the play . . . But if any such outrage is threatened, I prefer, on the basis of previous experience, to commit it myself rather than submit my work to the treatment and "adaptation" of less tender and competent hands.'

Frau Niemann-Raabe accepted this distorted version, and acted it in February at Flensburg, and later in Hamburg, Dresden, Hanover and Berlin. In the last-named city there was a public protest at the perversion (though when, subsequently, the original ending was used, there were further protests on the ground that the play had obviously been shorn of its final act!). The 'happy ending' was never a success, and eventually Frau Niemann-Raabe

---

[1] Letter from Hegel to Ibsen, 5 February 1880 (Nielsen, II, pp. 343–344).

reverted to the original text. Meanwhile, on 3 March, an unbowdlerised production took place at the Munich Residenztheater, with Ibsen himself in the audience. John Paulsen accompanied him, and recorded his reactions. Ibsen had attended several rehearsals; the play was, to Paulsen's mind, well acted, and went down excellently with the public. After the premiere, Ibsen thanked everyone who had taken part in the production warmly. But afterwards, at home, he was full of criticisms, not merely of the interpretation of the play and the various roles, but of details such as that Nora had the wrong-sized hands (whether too big or too small Paulsen could not remember), and that the colour of the wallpaper in the Helmers' apartment was wrong and conveyed a false atmosphere. Paulsen wondered that Ibsen had not mentioned at any rate this last point during rehearsals; but the actors later told Paulsen that Ibsen had 'neither praised nor blamed, but just remained silent', and that when they asked him if they had fulfilled his intentions, he merely complimented them, which frustrated rather than pleased them 'since they knew they were far from perfect'.[1] Even now that he was famous, and anything he said would have been obeyed, Ibsen was as reluctant to offer advice as in the old days in Norway. Paulsen recalled that the Norwegian actress Lucie Wolf told him that, when a director in Christiania, Ibsen had 'always seemed happy with what we had done, though this was often moderate'.[2]

A Doll's House had a mixed reception in the German theatres, and was in general coolly received by the German critics. Karl Frenzel reiterated in *Deutsche Rundschau* (nr. 26, 1881) that Ibsen was poor at dramatic construction, and added that he seemed to love the repulsive; and Paul Lindau (later to become an admirer and friend of Ibsen) declared in *Die Gegenwart* (nr. 18, 1880) that the ending as originally written was both illogical and immoral. Georg Brandes sadly commented that Ibsen would never be understood in Germany.[3] But if he was not understood, he was immensely discussed. 'Down here', he wrote to Hegel on 14 April, '*A Doll's House* has excited as much controversy as at home. People have taken sides passionately either for or against the play, and it has hardly ever happened before in Munich that any play has aroused such lively debate.'

One extraordinary version of *A Doll's House* appeared this year in the form of an English translation by a Danish schoolteacher, T. Weber, published in Copenhagen, and surely one of the most sustained specimens of unconscious humour in all literature. The final scene contains the following examples:

---

[1] Paulsen, *Samliv med Ibsen*, I, pp. 60–61.
[2] *Ibid.*, p. 58.
[3] Eller, pp. 36–39.

NORA: Don't utter such stupid shuffles . . . Doff the shawl . . . From
          this moment it depends no longer on felicity; it depends only
          on saving the rest, remnants and the appearance.

HELMER: You are first of all a wife and mother.
NORA: . . . I believe that I am first of all a man, I as well as you—or
          at all events, that I am to try to become a man.

NORA: As I am now, I am no wife for you.
HELMER: I have power to grow another.

HELMER: Change yourself in such a manner that—
NORA: That cohabitation between you and me might become a matri-
          mony. Goodbye.

Of this last line, Harley Granville Barker wrote that he was 'not indisposed
to offer a prize at the Royal Academy of Dramatic Art to the student who
could manage to speak [it] without making the audience laugh'.[1]

During the early months of 1880 Ludwig Passarge asked leave to prepare
the first German (or, indeed, foreign) translation of *Peer Gynt*. Ibsen, as we
have seen, was dubious about the possibility of the play succeeding with any
but a Scandinavian public, but granted permission. In Finland, meanwhile, a
young scholar named Valfred Vasenius published the second book to be
devoted entirely to a study of Ibsen's work, a not unperceptive doctoral thesis
covering the plays up to and including *The Pretenders*. In Sweden, the Gothen-
burg Theatre acquired the rights to *A Doll's House* (for an outright payment of
500 crowns, £28); and in Stockholm Ludvig Josephson, now doing his best
on a shoestring at the little Nya Teatern, asked permission to present not
merely new productions of *The Vikings at Helgeland* and *The Pretenders*, but
also the first Swedish production of *Love's Comedy*, and the first production
anywhere of *Catiline*. Ibsen granted him the rights in return for outright
payments of 100 crowns (£5.50!) for each of the first two plays and 400
crowns (£22) for the other two.

Knowing that he would not start on a new play before the following year,
and anxious to have a new work in the shops by Christmas, Ibsen suggested
to Hegel on 31 May that he might prepare 'a small volume of 10–12 signatures
[160–192 pages], consisting of prefaces to his various plays on the lines of the
one he had written for *Catiline*. 'For *Lady Inger* and *The Vikings* I could describe

---

[1] Harley Granville Barker, *The Coming of Ibsen*, in *The Eighteeen-Eighties*, ed. Walter
de la Mare (Cambridge, 1930), p. 196.

my time in Bergen; for *The Pretenders* and *Love's Comedy*, the years that followed in Christiania; my life in Rome while I was writing *Brand* and *Peer Gynt*, etc., etc. . . . I plan to spend the summer doing this, for I don't intend to write another play this year and have nothing else with which to occupy my time.' Surprisingly, Hegel dissuaded him from this project:

Copenhagen, 6 June 1880

Dear Dr Ibsen!

Since you ask my opinion regarding the plan you propose in your kind letter, I must tell you why I very definitely entreat you not to go ahead with this. A foreword such as that which you wrote to *Catiline* can have, and has, value as relating to a youthful work later revised and re-issued by a then fully matured writer. Outside these special circumstances it is in my view a statement of a semi-private character which would scarcely interest the public did it not bear the signature of Henrik Ibsen. But even in this special instance a thing of this nature should appear only once. Repetitions would weaken the effect, and if stretched out to cover a succession of works they would assuredly strike the reading public as the kind of anecdotal writing which should at all costs be avoided.

Your works stand on their own as clear and characteristic entities, the significance of which does not need to be tied to such slight footnotes which would unconsciously work themselves into the consciousness of their readers and introduce a new and distracting element . . . It would be quite another matter, I feel, if you ever wanted to write an *aus meinem Leben*, in which these fragments would then appear in context and thereby cease to be fragments. But I think you would be wise to postpone writing such a work just yet . . .[1]

The last paragraph reads like good sense, and might tempt one to forgive Hegel. But when, eighteen months later, Ibsen suggested writing just such an autobiography, Hegel again dissuaded him. Ibsen meekly accepted his advice, and the details which he could have given us about the gestation and composition of his plays remained unwritten.

Ludvig Josephson visited Ibsen in Munich that summer, on the way home from seeing the passion play at Oberammergau, and enjoyed the interesting experience of accompanying him on a visit to his tailor, where Ibsen ordered a black velvet coat and amazed Josephson by the minuteness of his instructions to the man. Ibsen, he noted, now usually wore a white cravat and white gloves with his invariable black coat, and a tall, shiny felt hat with a very

---

[1] Nielsen, II, p. 347.

broad brim, which, with his 'long dark hair not yet grizzled or white' gave him rather the appearance of a sectarian minister.[1] As a companion to Oberammergau Josephson had taken a young Swedish actor-director named August Lindberg, who had just acted a remarkable Hamlet for him at Nya Teatern, and who was to become one of the foremost interpreters of Ibsen's plays, both as actor and as director. He advised Lindberg, who was returning later than him, to visit Ibsen, warning him that Ibsen was 'an odd person, difficult to make conversation with'. 'Don't talk to him about the theatre', advised Josephson 'nor about plays, his or anyone else's'. 'As I had just come from Oberammergau', records Lindberg, 'I began to talk of Jesus, Mary and all the apostles in the moving drama I had seen amidst the mountains, but it was heavy going, and in the end I sat silent on a rock and when I left retained only the memory of a pair of spectacles.'[2] In three years time Ibsen was to have cause to be profoundly grateful to Lindberg.

In the beginning of August Suzannah and Sigurd went to Norway, partly so that Sigurd could investigate the chances of his being able to study law at Christiania without going through the preliminary examinations, and Ibsen, shortly before they left, addressed a letter to King Oscar pleading, unsuccessfully as it turned out, that his son should be granted exemption. While awaiting the royal reply, he made preparations to leave with John Paulsen for a holiday in Berchtesgaden.

The preparations for this excursion, which would have occupied most people for perhaps a couple of hours, caused Ibsen extraordinary distraction. A week before they were due to depart Paulsen chanced to visit him at Amalienstrasse and found him walking up and down in great agitation with an open trunk on the floor. 'When Ibsen was going away', Paulsen explains, 'he began to pack, not a day or two, but a whole week ahead, and, for fear of arriving late, would come to the station at least an hour before the train was due to leave.'[3] When the day came, 'although I reached the station in good time, Ibsen was of course waiting, dressed in a new, elegant travelling suit and a big broad-brimmed felt hat which rendered him half unrecognisable'. They took the train as far as Salzburg. There, while they awaited the diligence which was to convey them to Berchtesgaden, Ibsen showed Paulsen round the town, 'the white houses with their flat roofs and green awnings, the marble buildings, the numerous churches, fountains and palaces, and the archbishop's ancient palace', though not, which seems strange even when one remembers

---

[1] Josephson, pp. 40–41.

[2] Per Lindberg, *August Lindberg* (Stockholm, 1943), p. 36. Per Lindberg, like his father, was a fine actor and director, and his book is one of the best of theatrical biographies.

[3] Paulsen, *Samliv med Ibsen*, II, p. 75.

Ibsen's indifference to music, Mozart's house. When they reached Berchtesgaden, they had to share a bedroom for the first night at the Salzburger Hof;
but, to Paulsen's surprise and relief, Ibsen 'slept as silently as a child'.[1]

Living à deux with Ibsen was less difficult than Paulsen had feared. He took
an inordinate time to dress in the morning, often an hour or more—'and when
he was ready, there was nothing particularly special about his appearance;
he was attired like everyone else'. He was inclined to be prickly during the
morning, and did not much like being spoken to before noon. But 'later in
the day he would begin to talk a little; after lunch he became amenable and
friendly, and in the evening warm and lovable'. He bought a coloured feather
and stuck it in his hat, which caused the local children to stare after him. He
was brooding on his next play, and once, in bad weather, when Paulsen
tentatively asked him about it, he replied: 'It is a family story as sad and grey
as this rainy day.'[2]

Paulsen noted with interest the respect which Ibsen showed towards priests,
despite the contempt with which he portrayed them in his plays. Whenever
a priest passed them on their walks Ibsen would bow respectfully. At the hotel
he got annoyed because another guest kept taking the copy of Berliner Tage-
blatt which was reserved for him; but when he learned that the offender was
a priest, Ibsen offered him the newspaper next morning with a deep bow. In
contrast to this, he showed little respect for actors. A young German-American
actor who was staying at the hotel and was an admirer of Ibsen tried to strike
up an acquaintance, but Ibsen ostentatiously avoided him.[3] He enjoyed,
however, talking to artisans about their work. One day on their walk he saw
a cobbler working outside his house and engaged him in a lengthy conversation. 'He took the boot, examined the leather and stitching carefully, and
asked in surprise: "Does one do that now? In my day one did so-and-so." '
When they left, the cobbler bade farewell to Ibsen 'with the respect of a
fellow-craftsman'.[4]

He ate little, but extremely slowly, chewing each mouthful almost as many
times as Gladstone.[5] They spoke of literature. Paulsen, while in Paris, had met
Turgenev and his platonic mistress, Pauline Garcia-Viardot, and declared his
amazement that any woman could have so 'demonic an influence' on a man
that he could become her slave. This problem interested Ibsen. 'A man is easy

---

[1] Ibid., pp. 76–79.
[2] Ibid., pp. 79–80.
[3] Ibid., pp. 104–105.
[4] Ibid., pp. 134–135.
[5] Ibid., p. 108.

S

to study', he said, 'but one never fully understands a woman. They are a sea which none can fathom.' He expressed to Paulsen (as he later did to William Archer) his admiration for Turgenev and 'the Russian writers' in general;[1] we know from other sources that these included Dostoevsky and Tolstoy, but his opinion on Gogol (whom one would expect him especially to have enjoyed), Pushkin and Ostrovsky is not on record. Of French literature, on the other hand, Paulsen, found that Ibsen was largely ignorant. He had read nothing of Georges Sand, despite Suzannah's admiration of her (she re-read *Consuelo* almost annually) and the only thing he knew about Madame de Staël was her remark: '*Tout comprendre est tout pardonner*', on which he commented that anyone who had written that must be 'an unusual woman'.[2] He praised Paul Heyse's work, especially the elegy for his dead child and his stories, *The Last Centaur*, *Salamander* and *The Widow of Pisa*,[3] and exhorted Paulsen to read Kleist's *conte*, *Michael Kohlhaas*, 'which he averred to be a true masterpiece'.[4] But he spoke contemptuously of Heine as a poet for adolescents.[5] Goethe and Schiller he admired as poets but not as dramatists; and when anyone spoke, as Germans often did, of Goethe's *grosse, reine Liebe* (great, pure love), Ibsen would laconically comment: 'That d—d old goat!'[6] As regards Italian authors, Paulsen 'gained the impression that he had in his time studied Dante in translation', but 'the modern Italian writers, such as Verga, Edmondo De Amicis, Fogazzaro and Gabriele D'Annunzio were merely names that Ibsen had seen in the newspapers'.[7] English authors he does not seem to have been reading at all. One would have expected Suzannah to have admired George Eliot (who was to die this year), and Thomas Hardy, who at forty had already published several of his finest novels, including *Far from the Madding Crowd* and *The Return of the Native*; but there is no record of Ibsen ever mentioning either writer.

On the subject of other Scandinavian authors, Ibsen expressed little sympathy for Henrik Wergeland, whose early influence he had long since rejected, but considerable admiration for his old professor J. S. Welhaven, both as a poet and as a man. He told how once, after a particularly brilliant lecture by Welhaven in Christiania, he had been surprised, when standing outside the lecture hall, to hear the great man complain to his wife as he emerged that his trouser

---

[1] *Ibid.*, pp. 93–94.
[2] *Samliv med Ibsen*, I, p. 171.
[3] *Samliv med Ibsen*, II, p. 102.
[4] *Mine Erindringer*, p. 162.
[5] *Samliv med Ibsen*, II, p. 226.
[6] *Samliv med Ibsen*, I, pp. 72–73.
[7] *Ibid.*, pp. 29–30.

buttons were loose and he had spent the whole hour wondering if they would fall off. He also related with approval a story of how Welhaven (who, like Ibsen, could be rude to people who bored him) once attended a party at which the hostess was a very fat lady with an enormous double chin and, exhausted by her conversation, put his finger to the crease between her chins and said: 'Couldn't you manage one little smile?'[1] Of Alexander Kielland, whose proletarian novels Ibsen regarded as meretricious, he remarked: 'I have the impression that after a good dinner he suddenly remembers, over his coffee and Havana cigar, that there are poor people in the world, takes out a sheet of vellum and writes with a golden pen of their needs, thus, by the law of opposites, increasing his gourmet's pleasure in the moment.'[2] He praised Carl Snoilsky's poetry, and also mentioned approvingly Strindberg's novel about Bohemian life in Stockholm, *The Red Room*, which had appeared the previous year[3] (and which contains a scene in which the young hero is struck dumb with admiration on meeting a man who was permitted to call Ibsen 'Du'). This was the book which established Strindberg's reputation and probably provided Ibsen with his first introduction to an author whose work, despite Strindberg's oft-declared hostility to him (mainly because of his championship of women) he was to read with continued interest and respect.

On 17 August Ibsen's old mentor Ole Bull, who had given him his first job in the theatre, died at the age of seventy. He had lived a full life to the last (at the age of fifty-eight he had married an American girl of nineteen, and that was by no means the last of his conquests). Marcus Gronvøld tells that on hearing that Bull, on his death-bed, with a sprig of heather in his hand, had thanked God for everything, Ibsen remarked with a quiet smile: 'Ah, he thought he'd get away with it all?'[4]

Ibsen spoke much to Paulsen of Sigurd and, when Paulsen remarked on the young man's talent for languages, declared: 'He has inherited that from me.' 'But', ventured Paulsen, 'you are poor at languages, Herr Ibsen, you have said so yourself.' 'Yes', replied Ibsen, 'but I flatter myself that I know *our* language minutely—and this feeling which I have toiled to perfect I have passed on to my son.' Ibsen related with relish how Sigurd, as a small boy, on being spanked and ordered from the room, had turned on his father and shrieked: 'Poet! Poet! All you know is how to tell lies and rubbish!' Ibsen rubbed his hands as he told this story. It evidently amused him that the title which in the eyes

[1] *Samliv med Ibsen*, II, p. 211.
[2] *Ibid.*, p. 207.
[3] *Ibid.*, p. 224.
[4] Marcus Grønvold, p. 139.

of Europe was a term of honour was used by his small son as a term of abuse.'[1]

One day a letter arrived at Berchtesgaden from Sigurd telling his father that there seemed little chance of his being excused the preliminary examinations before being admitted to read law at Christiania University, and that he would probably be required to study there for eighteen months first. Paulsen was with Ibsen when he received this letter. 'He sat silent, angry and tight-lipped . . . I scarcely dared to look at him. He refused the food that was brought to him and limited himself, with a martyr's expression, to eating a little bread and salt. I can still hear the rasping sound of the salt crystals as he crushed them with his knife . . . After a long and indescribably oppressive silence he said: "But I shall raise a memorial to that black band of theologians who rule in Norway. They shall remember how they have treated me." '[2] A foolish priest was to be one of the central characters of the play he was meditating, and was to dominate it to the point of imbalance.

This decision of the Ecclesiastical Department, which controlled matters of education in Norway, affected Ibsen's own future as well as that of his son. Bergliot Ibsen says that had Sigurd been accepted at Christiania University Ibsen would have settled there himself so as to be near Sigurd.[3] As things were, he was to spend a further eleven years in exile.

'His mood', recalled Paulsen of this summer, 'could change like an April day. He could be uncommonly gentle and irrigate one with his calm smile, his good humour and his merry Peer Gynt-like fantasies, but he could also be dark and angry . . . There were times when the satirist in him awoke and his sharp tongue spared nothing . . . And he had other, huger moments when, filled with a holy indignation at the meanness and unjustness of humanity, he could thunder like Brand or an Old Testament prophet. By nature he was talkative, but if an unexpected reverse met him which awoke bitter memories of the old days, his mouth shut tight in bitterness as though padlocked, and there emanated from him an icy coldness which silenced everything about him. And once I caught a glimpse of the bird of prey in him, as later portrayed in Solness and Rubek, the falcon questing for a victim, some poor fellow-human whom he could dissect and then throw away.'[4] Sometimes he would indulge in a macabre humour. When, for instance, he related the story of a German painter who had tried repeatedly to commit suicide in different ways

---

[1] Samliv med Ibsen, II, pp. 98–99.
[2] Ibid., p. 115.
[3] Bergliot Ibsen, p. 84.
[4] Samliv med Ibsen, II, pp. 116–117.

and had succeeded only at the fourth attempt, 'Ibsen told these horrible details with a merry laughter, as though the story were funny rather than tragic . . . At such moments there emerged a demonic side to Ibsen's character which he normally concealed.'[1]

Rather than waste a year and a half on formal and useless studies, Sigurd suggested to his father that he should abandon all thought of trying for a legal degree in Norway and should instead continue his education in Italy. Ibsen telegraphed his approval, and followed his telegram with a letter. 'Since I received the Ecclesiastical Department's reply', he wrote on 18 September, 'I have naturally given much thought to the matter, and have come to the conclusion that you are probably best served by the turn which, thanks to our imbecile and superannuated regulations, events have taken. What would it have profited you to have studied law in Norway? It was not your intention to become a civil servant up there. The only positions which attract you are still within your reach: you can become a Professor or enter the diplomatic service without taking any civil service examination; for we have foreign professors at the University . . . But don't think further ahead than studying abroad; you should wait before deciding whether it would be advantageous to become an Italian citizen.'

Ibsen's old fellow-student from Christiania, Jonas Lie, by now a distinguished novelist, was spending the summer in Berchtesgaden with his wife Thomasine (who was also his cousin) and their children. Success had come late to Lie, as it had to Ibsen; but during the past decade such novels as *The Visionary*, *The Pilot and his wife* and *Adam Schrøder* had established him as an imaginative portrayer of human relationships. The Lies were living in a small white house in which Ibsen himself had stayed during his first visit to Berchtesgaden in 1868, and he visited them every Saturday evening, sometimes with Paulsen. Lie's son Erik, then a boy of twelve, recorded his father's memories twenty-eight years later, and added his own in another and equally rewarding book.

Jonas and Thomasine Lie were the kind of warm-hearted, sensitive people with whom Ibsen relaxed most easily. In their company 'he talked away about everything, told anecdotes, enjoyed himself to the full and never left before three in the morning.' 'I have never seen that closed face which people attribute to Ibsen', Lie once remarked (and he must have been almost the only acquaintance who never did). 'When we were together in Berchtesgaden I always had the impression, as we sat together of an evening, of two front teeth which appeared more and more often as time went on—two front teeth with a gap between. And the higher his humour rose, the more he laughed and glowed,

---

[1] *Ibid.*, pp. 182–183.

till at last he sat there like a good prattling midwife.'[1] The observation about the gap between the teeth, surprising at first sight, reminds us that there exists no photograph or portrait of Ibsen with his mouth open. Apart from those Saturday evenings Ibsen and Lie virtually never saw each other, by mutual agreement, since Lie was working on a new novel. But, the latter remembered, 'more than once Ibsen walked past the house where we were living, and it was observed that he often paused before the lighted windows on the ground floor and peered tentatively in at the family as we sat at our evening meal'.[2]

Ibsen's passion, already remarked, for sewing on his own buttons manifested itself during this holiday. 'One morning', recalled Jonas Lie, 'Ibsen suddenly appeared and asked to speak to my wife. She was not to disturb me; it was only a trifling matter, to wit, a button. He had brought needle and thread. "But may I not sew it on for you?" asked Thomasine. No, he wanted to do it himself. "But what's the matter, then?" "I wondered if you could help me to thread the needle. I have tried and tried, but I must confess it is a more difficult art than I had imagined." Fru Lie of course immediately helped him. A week later she asked him if there was nothing else she could help him with. To thread another needle, perhaps? "No, thank you", replied Ibsen. "Once I had the thread in, I took enough to last me the whole summer." '[3]

The Lies particularly remembered Ibsen on his country walks, 'following the same precise routes along the rustic roads as, later, he was to do down Carl Johan [in Christiania] to the Grand Café'. As soon as a cart appeared Ibsen would move off the road until it had passed and the dust had settled. 'He would then take out the silk handkerchief which he carried in his left breast-pocket, wipe his spectacles and carefully refold it . . . and walk on with his small, tripping steps, elegant and finical, despite the green Tyrolean hat which he had acquired soon after his arrival, and into which he had put a cock's feather which nodded at every step.' Erik Lie also remembered how Ibsen loved to sit among the village children watching Punch and Judy shows, continuously wiping his spectacles as the puppets killed each other; how he rebuked John Paulsen angrily for making jokes about a Dowager Duchess; how he once remarked that he would ideally like to live on an island guarded by two hungry bloodhounds; and how little Elizabeth Lie, Jonas's elder daughter, on hearing her parents refer admiringly to Ibsen's *Doll's House*, supposed him to be a toymaker and was bitterly disappointed that he never brought any present for her. The youngest daughter, Johanne, recalled that he was 'nice, and very kind to children', and

---

[1] Erik Lie, *Jonas Lie, oplevelser, fortalt af Erik Lie* (Christiania and Copenhagen, 1908), p. 256.

[2] *Ibid.*, p. 257.

[3] *Ibid.*, p. 257.

(confirming Paulsen's observation) that he loved to talk with the local cobbler, Jacob Hasenknopf.[1]

Ibsen, as far as we know, did no writing that summer at Berchtesgaden. It was to be the last time he visited the little town; they had recently extended the railway to it, and the seclusion he so prized was gone. At the end of September or the beginning of October he returned to Munich, whence, on 25 October, he informed Hegel that 'we are now returning to Rome, where he [Sigurd] will complete his legal studies, and then become naturalised'. Whether he had in fact taken this decision or whether it was still under discussion, we do not know. Ibsen went on to repeat, almost precisely, the words he had used to Paulsen on first hearing the news of the rejection of Sigurd's petition. 'To the black band of theologians who temporarily rule in the Ecclesiastical Department, I shall in due time raise a fitting memorial.'[2]

That October Ludwig Passarge's German translation of *Peer Gynt* appeared. On 2 November the Ibsens left Munich, arriving in Rome (the journey took thirty-one hours) on the 4th. They stayed the first week in a hotel, and on the 11th moved into 'a very handsome and spacious, but somewhat expensive apartment' at 75, Via Capo le Case, close to where they had lived twelve years earlier. The description occurs in a letter Ibsen wrote to Hegel the next day asking him to send 1,600 crowns (£89), adding, however, that 'luckily accommodation is practically the only thing which can be called dear down here'. He added that he was 'turning over new literary plans, which I hope will have sufficiently matured within the next few months for me to begin on the actual writing'. Edmund Gosse wrote to him asking permission to translate *A Doll's House* into English, to which Ibsen agreed; but Gosse never translated the play, nor even (as he had Ibsen's earlier works) reviewed it.

Ibsen received evidence that autumn of how his plays could be misinterpreted. A Scandinavian lady appeared in Rome with her lover. Having found her marriage unsatisfactory, she had left her husband and children. The Norwegians in Rome condemned her action as unnatural; and Ibsen, when asked his opinion, said: 'It is not unnatural, but it is unusual.' When the lady sought out Ibsen at a public function he treated her rather coolly; and when she complained that she had only behaved as his Nora had done, he replied: 'But my Nora went alone.'[3]

---

[1] *Ibid.*, pp. 254 ff.; *Erindringer fra et dikterhjem*, pp. 43 ff.; *Urd, Ibsen-nummer* (Oslo, 1928), p. 150.

[2] The similarity of the phrasing has led some critics to doubt the truth of Paulsen's reminiscence. But Ibsen often used in his letters (and plays) phrases which he is known previously to have used in conversation.

[3] Zucker, p. 182. The story was told to Zucker by Julius Elias's widow.

The English theatre at last paid brief and belated recognition to Ibsen's existence that winter. On the morning of 15 December 1880 William Archer's revised translation of *The Pillars of Society* was given a single performance at the Gaiety Theatre in the Strand, the first in England, amateur or professional, of any Ibsen play—though Ibsen might have had some difficulty in recognising it as his, for it was much abridged and adapted, and was entitled *Quicksands*. Charles Archer, in his biography of his brother William, describes how the play at last found its way on to the stage: 'Having failed to find a publisher for his translation of *The Pillars of Society*, Archer had set himself, as the only way of bringing Ibsen to the front, to adapt the play for the English stage; for in those days it was unthinkable that a faithful translation, even of a French piece, much more of a play by an unknown Hyperborean dramatist, should ever make its way on to the London boards. By the end of 1878 an "adaptation", which might better have been described as an abridgment, had been accepted by Mr W. H. Vernon, who was much struck by the part of Consul Bernick. But Mr Vernon had no theatre at his disposal, and negotiations for a London production dragged on for nearly two years. At last, since no better might be, the piece was produced experimentally at a Gaiety Theatre matinee on December 15, 1880—and fell perfectly flat. The production, as a whole, was inevitably scrambling and ineffective. But the best setting and acting could not have made the play a success with the English critics and audiences of that day. Ibsen's time was not yet come.'[1]

The *Athenaeum* (24 December) praised the play as 'a good and telling story which introduces some novel, if not very powerful, types of character . . . extremely fine comedy . . . we shall be glad to know more of its author's workmanship'. *The Theatre* (February 1881) described the performance as 'tentatively produced and fairly successful', but felt that 'Bernick's cold-blooded villainy appears somewhat inadequately punished'. The Danish correspondent of a Copenhagen newspaper reported that at the final curtain the audience called loudly for the author, 'a request which was readily met, without any trace of embarrassment or reserve, by Mr Archer, the English translator'.[2] Archer's translation was not published until 1888, and then in a much revised form.

At the end of 1880 Ibsen found that he had, for the first time, earned over a thousand pounds in a single year.

	crowns	£
Fee for *A Doll's House* in Christiania	2,500	139

[1] Charles Archer, p. 82.
[2] J. W. McFarlane, *The Oxford Ibsen*, V, p. 434. He does not name his source.

Fee for *A Doll's House* in Gothenburg	500	28
Fee for *A Doll's House* in Bergen	400	22
4th edition of *The League of Youth*	898	50
Miscellaneous fees for *A Doll's House* from Norwegian touring companies	800	44
3rd edition of *A Doll's House*	1,406	78
Extra fee from Royal Theatre, Copenhagen, for *A Doll's House*	6,103	336
Extra fee from Gyldendal for *The League of Youth* and *A Doll's House*	177	10
Fee for *A Doll's House* in Swedish provinces (Åbjörnsen)	200	11
Royalties from Munich Hoftheater, 1st quarter	253	17
Fee for *A Doll's House* in Swedish provinces (J. F. Smith)	200	11
3rd edition of *Emperor and Galilean*	1,600	89
Extra fee from Royal Theatre, Stockholm, for *A Doll's House* (after 30 performances)	2,451	137
Fee for *A Doll's House* from theatre-director Rylander	100	6
Royalties from Munich Hoftheater, 2nd quarter	83	5
Fee for *A Doll's House* at Flensburg and Schleswig	62	3
Extra fees from Bergen Theatre	620	34
Royalties from Munich Hoftheater, 3rd quarter	106	6
Extra fee for *A Doll's House* from Royal Theatre, Copenhagen (16–21 performances)	1,966	109
Extra fee for *A Doll's House* from Royal Theatre, Copenhagen (22–26 performances)	709	39
Extra fee for *A Doll's House* from Foght's travelling company in Norway	400	22
	21,534	1,187

Several features of this year's accounts are interesting. For once, book sales constituted a minority of his income 4,081 crowns, (£227). Performing rights represented approximately five-sixths of it, and these were almost entirely from a single play, *A Doll's House*. The fees from the Royal Theatre in Copenhagen alone for the year (8,778 crowns, £484) exceeded his total income for many a previous year, and underline how much he lost by not getting similar royalties from all theatres. The German theatres, be it noted, paid him a total of 504 crowns (£28).

But if Ibsen supposed that a period of financial affluence lay ahead of him, he was to be disillusioned. It was to be another ten years before his annual income again reached £1,000. The decade from 1881 to 1890, which was to see the composition of *Ghosts*, *An Enemy of the People*, *The Wild Duck*, *Rosmersholm*, *The Lady from the Sea* and *Hedda Gabler*, was to bring him a total income of under £6,500—less than playwrights of far inferior stature in larger countries, such as Scribe, W. S. Gilbert and Pinero, would expect to make in a single year.

TWELVE

 Ghosts

(1881–1882)

FURTHER EVIDENCE THAT IBSEN, as he approached his fifty-fourth
birthday, was becoming, if not an international figure, at any rate one of the
few Scandinavians whom other countries bothered to consider at all, appeared
in the form of foreign articles in the early months of 1881. The January issue
of *Unser Zeit* contained a long essay on him by Eugen Zabel, the first, other
than reviews of individual plays, to be devoted to him in a German paper.
It was by no means wholly favourable; drawing parallels between Ibsen's
philosophy and German pessimism, Zabel thought that both *Brand* and *Peer
Gynt* had much in common with Goethe's *Faust*, but declared that Ibsen's
imagination, although fertile, was enclosed in a frigid sheath of intellect, and
that much of *Peer Gynt* belonged to the realm, not of poetry, but of pathology
—an unconsciously penetrating observation.

At the same time, a far shrewder and more balanced assessment of Ibsen's
work was placed before the English reading public in the form of two articles
in the January and February issues of the *St James's Magazine* by William
Archer. Instead of condemning Ibsen, as so many of his critics were doing,
for pessimism, discord and 'lack of idealism', Archer, familiar with the novels
of George Eliot and Thomas Hardy, recognised that in these supposed defects
lay much of Ibsen's strength. 'His countrymen', wrote Archer, 'admire, fear
and hate him. The lash of the satirist has fallen heavy upon them as a nation
. . . While admitting his greatness, they maintain that the negativeness of his
aims detracts from, or almost nullifies it . . . [But] Ibsen depicts a real world,
not the ideal where satisfaction and reconciliation are possible . . . The old
theory that all great work comes from a positive age is rapidly dying away.
Ibsen is one of the great negative voices of a negative age which tries in vain,
by shrieking in falsetto and thundering in the deepest bass, to convince itself
that it is positive.'

This was remarkably mature criticism from someone aged barely twenty-
four; and before the year was out Archer was to introduce Ibsen's work to a
chance acquaintance who was to become, not merely his most influential

283

apologist, but also his most distinguished disciple as a dramatist. 'In the winter of 1881-2', Archer recalled, 'I used to go almost every day to the British Museum Reading Room in London. I frequently sat next to a man of about my own age who attracted my attention, partly by his peculiar colouring—his pallid skin and bright red hair and beard—partly by the odd combination of authors whom he used to study—for I saw him, day after day, poring over Karl Marx's *Das Kapital* and an orchestral score of Wagner's *Tristan und Isolde*. How we first made acquaintance I have forgotten; but one did not need to meet him twice to be sure that George Bernard Shaw was a personality to be noted and studied . . . We became fast friends.'[1] As Archer's brother and biographer, Charles Archer, comments: 'This friendship, founded on a common idealism in fundamentals, was to endure for more than forty years, standing the strains of radical difference of temperament and wide divergence of views, and was to be of . . . some consequence in literary history.'[2] Not only did Archer introduce Shaw to Ibsen; he also got Shaw his first critical work, first as a book reviewer, then as art critic and finally as music critic.[3] The debt of English and Irish literature to William Archer is inadequately realised; he was also one of the first people to encourage the young James Joyce.

In America, too, that February, Ibsen's name was praised, the first record of its mention in the New World. The writer was none other than Bjørnson who, having delivered an oration at Ole Bull's funeral in Bergen, had been invited by Bull's young widow to visit her in Boston, and had stayed in the States for seven months. In the course of a long article entitled *Norway's Constitutional Struggle* in *Scribner's Monthly*, Bjørnson declared: 'I do not hesitate to say that in my opinion Henrik Ibsen possesses the greatest dramatic power of the age. I am so much the more certain of my judgment from the fact that I do not always like his dramas. It is surprising to me that he is not translated in America. He is one whom his contemporaries should know.'[4] This was an extraordinarily generous tribute from a man whose own star was sliding into eclipse.

Several of Ibsen's old friends and acquaintances were in Rome that winter, including Lorentz Dietrichson, Camilla Collett and Kristofer Janson; and among the newcomers whom he met was a young Swedish poet, Werner von Heidenstam, later to become a Nobel prizewinner, but at this early stage in his career still regarded as a rich dilettante. John Paulsen, who was there too,

---

[1] Charles Archer, p. 119.
[2] *Ibid.*, p. 119.
[3] *Ibid.*, p. 135.
[4] *Scribner's Monthly Magazine*, 1881, vol. xxi, p. 606.

records that Ibsen used to go every day to the Café Artisti, where the Scandinavians gathered, to see if anyone new had arrived. He began, too, to hold soirées, 'cosmopolitan rather than homely, but very agreeable. One arrived between nine and ten, and an Italian servant offered tea. On the sideboard stood wine, fruit and cakes, to which one helped oneself during the course of the evening. Ibsen, dressed in a black frock coat without decorations, received the guests with a calm and impressive dignity.'[1]

Paulsen, who was there on a travelling scholarship from the Norwegian government, which he had received largely thanks to Ibsen's recommendation, achieved something of a record on his arrival by becoming, surely, the only man ever suspected of being Suzannah Ibsen's lover. Calling at the Ibsens' apartment, he found them out, and asked the Italian maid to tell Suzannah that her *amico* was in Rome and would return in the afternoon. The maid conspiratorially warned Suzannah on her return, knowing that then *il signor commendatore* (a title by which Ibsen was known among the Italians, because he was a Commander of the Medjiji Order) might be at home, and adding delightedly; 'How rash of the young man!' The incident became, whilst their friendship with Paulsen lasted, a standing joke in the Ibsen household.[2]

Among the other Scandinavians then in Rome was the Swedish painter Georg Pauli, who was amazed one day to see a figure walking towards him down the street wearing medals—'not ribbons but medals'. The two became acquainted, and it was not long before Pauli, like others before him, found himself assisting Ibsen back to his apartment, with the help of the Norwegian painter Christian Meyer Ross. 'We supported the great man on either side', Pauli noted in his diary, 'and he showed his gratitude by incessantly giving us his confidential opinion of our insignificance. I, he said, was a "frightful puppy" and Ross "a very repulsive character".' On another occasion Pauli asked Ibsen what books he was reading, and was surprised to receive the answer: 'I don't read books, I leave them to my wife and Sigurd.' But, Pauli confirms like other observers, he read the newspapers most minutely, from the top of page one to the printer's name at the foot of the final page, including the advertisements (sometimes, in the Scandinavian newspapers of those days, not the least interesting part). Pauli noted that Sigurd, now twenty-one, was very much his father's son, meticulous in dress and demeanour, reserved, buttoned-up and 'seldom ungloved, even on the most informal occasions'.[3]

Ibsen's dislike of reading books has disturbed many a man of letters, starting

---

[1] Paulsen, *Nye Erindringer*, pp. 103–104.
[2] *Ibid.*, pp. 87–89.
[3] Georg Pauli, *Mina romerska ar* (Stockholm, 1924), pp. 111–120.

with Edmund Gosse, but it is not surprising that he, whose principal interest was modern people and modern ideas, should have found the newspapers more rewarding. They kept him better abreast of his subject. 'He has often seemed to me', wrote Georg Brandes of him, in an essay published the following year, 'to stand in a sort of mysterious correspondence with the fermenting, germinating ideas of the day. Once or twice I have even had a distinct impression that new ideas, which were on the point of manifesting themselves publicly, but were not yet perceived by others, had been preoccupying and indeed tormenting him'; and he added in an eloquent phrase that Ibsen possessed the true poet's ear for 'the low rumble that tells of ideas undermining the ground . . . for the throb of their pinions in the air'.[1]

Not long after Ibsen's arrival in Rome the two Swedish princes Oscar and Carl visited the city. The Scandinavian Club gave a fancy-dress ball in their honour, which Ibsen attended, not, sadly, in fancy dress (what could he have gone as but himself?), but, as the saying was, in full gala, with his decorations on his chest and a *chapeau-bas* in his hand. King Oscar had given the princes a letter to Lindstrand, the Swedish Minister in Rome, commanding him to introduce them to Ibsen, 'from whom they might learn much'; but Lindstrand, instead of inviting Ibsen to the dinner he gave for them, merely asked him to join them for tea afterwards. Ibsen, well able to answer one snub with another, replied by sending his visiting card bearing the brief message: 'I do not drink tea.'[2]

In fact he liked tea, and often visited Christian Meyer Ross at the latter's studio to drink it of an afternoon, even though it involved listening to music, his unconcealed boredom with which offended a young New England girl married to a Danish diplomat. 'There is always a little music', she noted in her diary. 'Ibsen sits sullen, silent and indifferent. This is not, as you may imagine, inspiring to the performers. In fact, merely to look at him takes all the life out of you. He is a veritable wet blanket.'[3]

One day John Paulsen risked promulgating some theories about Ibsen's work, and received a warning against 'looking for obscurities in his work where none existed'. Ibsen complained that 'critics were eager to find a double meaning, a hidden symbol, in every word or action', a tendency that has not lapsed with

---

[1] Georg Brandes, *Henrik Ibsen*, pp. 83 and 94 (Muir-Archer translation).

[2] John Paulsen, *Nye Erindringer*, pp. 126–127. The story is confirmed by Fritz von Dardel, who had it from Ibsen himself, and adds that the Princes took the hint and invited Ibsen to dinner the following day. (Fritz von Dardel, *Dagboksanteckningar, 1881–1885*, Stockholm, 1920, p. 86.)

[3] Madame L. Hegermann-Lindencrone, *The Sunny Side of Diplomatic Life* (New York, 1914), pp. 100–101.

the years. He quoted as one example a Swede's assertion that Nora's extravagant tip to the porter of a crown, which he had merely intended to exemplify her carelessness with money, signified her desire to level the relationship between capitalist and worker; and told how another scholar had discovered a deep meaning in his choice of the name Makrina (which in Greek means far-sighted) for a character in *Emperor and Galilean*, whereas he had only used it because he had found the name in an old book and liked it.[1]

He also gave Paulsen some stern advice about writing. 'Fixing me with a glance over his gold spectacles, he said: "You mustn't walk around dreaming. Use your eyes. That is doubly necessary for anyone who wishes to become an author... Tell me", he asked suddenly, "What colour is the wallpaper in your room?"' Paulsen had to confess that he did not know. ' "You see!", cried Ibsen triumphantly, as always whenever he discovered anything which confirmed his suspicions. "I was right. You don't notice anything. Though how a human being with normal senses can live in a room without noticing the colour of the walls ... When I enter a strange house I note the tiniest detail, nothing escapes me. Yes", he added quietly, more to himself than to me. "I see everything"'.[2]

He gave proof of his visual memory that winter when a Norwegian lady named Fanny Rijs, on being presented to him at one of his own receptions, said: 'There is no need to introduce us. We danced together in Bergen.' Ibsen replied curtly (and untruthfully): 'I have never danced', and walked away into his study. But a few minutes later he emerged, said: 'You are right', described precisely what she had been wearing at the dance twenty-five years before, and even sketched a necklace she had been wearing.[3] When she left on 28 February, Ibsen gave her a signed photograph of himself bearing the inscription: 'Do not forget Rome.'

During the spring of 1881 Ibsen, still smarting under the treatment accorded to Sigurd, seriously pondered giving up his Norwegian citizenship. 'He [Sigurd] is intending to become naturalised here', he wrote to Johan Thoresen on 9 March. 'He speaks and writes French, German and Italian like a native, is well versed in both politics and economics, and so feels confident that he will be able to make a career without having to resort to Norway. The question is whether I too shall not feel occasioned to expatriate myself. There will be many advantages for me in becoming an Italian or German citizen, and now that the Ecclesiastical Department has dispossessed my son I don't know what further business I have up there. We are exceptionally contented here in Rome.' He was never in fact to make so final a break with Norway, thanks largely perhaps

---

[1] Paulsen, *Samliv med Ibsen*, I, pp. 75–76.

[2] *Ibid.*, pp. 21–22.

[3] Information from Professor Francis Bull.

to Suzannah's influence; but the mood expressed in this letter was shortly to find dramatic expression.

He had not, hitherto, been lucky in his translators, in any country, but he all but acquired what would have been a very interesting one that spring. Ludvig Josephson had, as we have seen, conceived the idea of staging *Love's Comedy* in Stockholm, and he approached no less a person than August Strindberg to translate it. Although Strindberg, now thirty-two, had written eight plays, only one of these, the historical drama *Master Olof*, ranks among his best; his great days as a dramatist still lay ahead of him. Josephson's suggestion tempted him. 'I have looked at Ibsen's *Love's Comedy*', he replied on 14 March. 'It will be a long and expensive job. If you want me to translate it, make me a formal offer and name a deadline, for I daren't risk attempting so big a task for nothing.'[1] Unfortunately Josephson could offer very little, and the project lapsed (it was to be eight years before *Love's Comedy* was seen in Sweden). One wonders what Strindberg, whose marriage to Siri von Essen was already begining to strain at the seams, would have made of this particular play, with its message that love and marriage are incompatible.

On 27 March Ibsen made a further attempt to have his pension increased, addressing his appeal on this occasion to H. E. Berner, editor for the past ten years of *Dagbladet* and now a newly-elected member of the Storthing. The letter, with its detailed documentation of the problems which faced a successful author in a small country a century ago, is worth quoting *in extenso*:

... *When some time ago the Storthing granted first Bjørnson and later myself an annual pension of 400 specie-dollars, this was generally regarded as a public recognition of and reward for our literary activity, and was as such gratefully accepted by us. The notion of copyright was then, as now, still largely disregarded in Scandinavia. Neither the government nor the Storthing had taken measures to insure Norwegian authors, least of all dramatists, against the arbitrary pilfering of any outsider who chose to pick up a pen. In other words the law did not permit us, like other citizens, to enjoy the fruits of our labours. The Christiania Theatre's practice was to pay a small fee for the right to perform a play in perpetuity. Thus, for The Vikings at Helgeland I received 30 specie-dollars [£8], with an intimation that if I was not satisfied with this sum they proposed to stage the play without paying any fee at all, as the law entitled them. The other theatres in Norway, and the touring companies, of course paid nothing. The same was true of the smaller theatres in Sweden and Denmark. Even the Royal Theatre in Stockholm, once, as you will probably recall, performed a play of Bjørnson without paying a farthing, although the author protested strenuously. Subsequently, perhaps as a result of the notice which that matter attracted,*

---

[1] *August Strindbergs brev*, ed. Torsten Eklund (Stockholm, 1948 ff.), II, p. 241.

the Royal Theatres of Stockholm and Copenhagen have rewarded us by paying whatever they felt inclined to, a token of progress which we were compelled to accept and be grateful for, since neither the government nor the Storthing had protected our literary interests by signing literary conventions with Sweden and Denmark.

Thus virtually all of Bjørnson's and my plays were taken from us, one after the other, without our being able to enjoy the financial fruits which are permitted without question to authors in other countries. I have only fully realised the extent of our loss since the copyright agreements with Sweden and Denmark were signed.[1] But for Bjørnson and myself these agreements have come too late, because during those earlier anarchic years our works were taken from us for nothing or, at the best, for very small sums.

But this is not all; indeed, for us it is the least of the matter. What has hit us far harder has been the absence of any copyright agreement between Norway and Germany or any other country outside Scandinavia. You will know that many of Bjørnson's and my books have been translated in Germany and that many of our plays are performed in the theatres there. But if people assume that this gratifying recognition brings us any considerable, or even trivial, financial reward, they are much mistaken. It is the translators or their publishers who reap the reward, and we Norwegian dramatists can do nothing about it. If we commission translations of our plays at our own expense we can be pretty sure that within a short time another translation, if not several, will appear and supplant our own.

It is, I appreciate, unthinkable that Norway should take steps to initiate a general international copyright agreement; or rather become a party to the agreement which already exists between most other European countries. As a good Norwegian I would not wish such a thing; for such an agreement would enormously increase the cost of every foreign book, scholarly or literary, which we might wish to make available to our public in translation. And this would block many of the sources of enlightenment to which Norway now has free access. Free? Yes, free for Norway, but not for Bjørnson or me. For it is we who, for many years, have paid, as we do today, the bulk of the duty on our country's imports of foreign literature. And this duty amounts to no small sum. I think I could with a good conscience declare that Bjørnson and I are the two most heavily taxed men in Norway . . .

The money which Bjørnson and I have received from the state bears no relation to the loss we have suffered and shall continue to suffer both at home and abroad. Could not the Storthing consider it both just and inexpensive to grant us reasonable com-

---

[1] These agreements came into force from 1 January 1878 (Sweden) and 1 January 1880 (Denmark). Similar agreements were made with Italy in 1884 and France in 1893, but Ibsen's copyright remained unprotected in other countries until Norway joined the Berne Convention in 1896.

T

pensation by increasing our pensions? . . . It is noteworthy that in our country edible game has become protected by law before authors. In our dealings with foreign countries we are still classed with beasts of prey. Anyone may hunt us without let or hindrance, and the worst is that we have to pay the cost of their ammunition . . . I would respectfully call to mind that when Nordenskiöld and Palander discovered the North-East passage¹ the Swedish Parliament granted them each an annual pension of 4,000 crowns [£222]. I permit myself to think that Bjørnson and I have, by our literary explorations, discovered something approximating to both North-East and North-West Passages, which may in the future be as much used by the Scandinavian peoples as those which Palander and Nordenskiöld have opened . . .

Berner promised to do his best in the matter, and it came before the Storthing a year later, with what success we shall see.

That spring of 1881 Ibsen spent a couple of days with Lorentz Dietrichson revisiting the country places they had explored together seventeen years earlier. They took the train to Frascati and Tusculum and rode on donkeys, as before, across to Grottaferrata and Castelgandolfo, this time without mishap. They spent a night at Albano and the next morning walked to Genzano, looking in at the café in which Ibsen had lived, and strolling down to Lake Nemi. In Olcanda all was unchanged except that the protrait of Pope Pius IX had been replaced by those of Victor Emmanuel, Cavour and Garibaldi. During this trip Ibsen, after bewailing the inability of governments to put big ideas into practice, suddenly broke off and said: 'People think I have changed my views as time has passed, but that is quite wrong; my development has been wholly consistent . . . I am jotting down a few notes which will show the world how precisely similar I am now to what I was when I first discovered myself.' Dietrichson comments that this seems to be evidence that Ibsen was already preparing the autobiography from which Hegel was so unhappily to dissuade him.² It may have been of this project that Ibsen informed Hegel on 22 March: 'I am writing a new book which will be ready in the summer . . . This work interests me much, and I feel convinced that it will also be received with interest by the public. But I won't for the moment tell you its theme; later, perhaps.' (But it may also have been *An Enemy of the People*, which he completed with unwonted speed the following year and may already have been in his thoughts.)

Meanwhile, John Paulsen had been running into trouble as an author; his latest novel had been refused by Hegel, and he seems to have become swollen-

---

¹ In 1878–1880, from the Atlantic to the Pacific.
² Dietrichson, I, p. 363.

headed. His relations with Ibsen had taken a marked turn for the worse. 'I am not surprised that you do not wish to publish it', Ibsen wrote to Hegel on 21 April. 'I am afraid Paulsen is falling more and more into the bad habit of over-rapid and slipshod composition. No properly prepared plan, no rounded, lifelike characters. But I've grown tired of warning him against this path which he has chosen to follow, as I see it bears no fruit and, besides, he takes it amiss. He has an immense and unmannerly confidence in himself.' Ibsen's doubts about Paulsen's character were shortly to receive painful confirmation.

On 18 June Ibsen informed Hegel: 'There has been a change in my literary plans for the summer. I have temporarily shelved the work I previously mentioned to you, and early this month embarked on a theme which has long occupied my thoughts and which at length forced itself so insistently upon me that I could no longer ignore it. I hope to be able to send you the manuscript by the middle of October. I'll tell you the title later; for the moment I shall merely say that I describe it as "a domestic drama in three acts". I need hardly add that this play has no kind of connection with *A Doll's House*.' This last remark was in reply to a letter from Hegel telling him that there was a rumour in Copenhagen that he was working on a sequel to that play.[1]

That month John Paulsen left Rome; he and Ibsen were never to meet again. On 28 June Ibsen moved with Suzannah and Sigurd to Sorrento on the west coast, where they stayed, as they had two years previously, at the Hotel Tramontano, and where Dietrichson and his family shortly joined them. The weather was tremendously hot. 'My wife suffers more than us from the heat, and especially the sirocco', he wrote to Camilla Collett that August, 'but she manages to survive with the help of a daily sea-bathe. I don't think you could have survived the summer down here. To walk is almost out of the question; one must just sit as still as possible.' Despite these conditions, he was able to write to Hegel on 30 September 'I take advantage of a free moment to tell you briefly that on the 23rd inst. I finished the first draft of my new play and on the 25th began my fair copy. The play is entitled *Ghosts: A Domestic Drama in Three Acts*. If possible you shall have the whole thing by the end of October.'

This 'fair copy' in fact took the form of a new draft, and as time was getting short if the book was to catch the Christmas sales Ibsen revised Act One (the draft of which he finished on 4 October) and posted off the fair copy of it to Hegel on 16 October before redrafting Acts Two and Three. 'The second act', he assured Hegel, 'which will be somewhat shorter you shall have within fourteen days, and the rest at the beginning of next month, so that the book

---

[1] Nielsen, II, p. 576.

will I hope be able to be in the bookshops in early December, which was the time *A Doll's House* appeared . . . I beg that the manuscript shall not be allowed to come into the hands of any unauthorised person.' Working fever-ishly against the clock he completed the draft of Act Two (which he had begun on 13 October) in seven days, and that of Act Three in four days. On 4 Novem-ber he posted off the fair copy of Act Two plus the first page of Act Three to Hegel, promising that 'the remainder will be sent to you with all speed from Rome, whither we return tomorrow'.

On 23 November, writing from Rome, he uttered a mild warning to Hegel. '*Ghosts* will probably cause alarm in some circles; but that can't be helped. If it didn't, there would have been no necessity for me to have written it.' He was already, he added in the same letter 'planning a new four-act comedy which I had thought about before but put aside to make way for *Ghosts*, which was obsessing me and monopolising my thoughts'.

Ghosts—the story of a woman who leaves her husband, is persuaded by the Pastor (whom she loves) to return home, does so, and bears a son who turns out to have inherited his father's syphilis—was duly published by Gyldendal, in an edition of ten thousand copies (two thousand more than *A Doll's House*) on 13 December 1881, and at once aroused a consternation and hostility beyond anything Ibsen had envisaged. At first he accepted this calmly; he knew there were small prospects of its being performed in either Scandinavia or Germany, but reckoned it would, like *Brand* and *Peer Gynt*, make its effect on the reading public. On 22 December he wrote to Ludwig Passarge: 'My new play has come out, and has created a violent commotion in the Scandina-vian press. Every day I receive letters and newspaper articles, some for, some against. A copy will be sent you very shortly; but I feel it is quite impossible that the play should be performed in any German theatre at this time; I hardly think they'll dare to stage it even in Scandinavia for some little while. Incident-ally, it has been printed in an edition of 10,000 copies and there is every prospect that a new edition will be required soon'—a forecast that was to prove sadly incorrect, though on the strength of it he had, two days earlier, asked Hegel to invest almost the whole proceeds of the first edition, six thousand crowns (£333) in gilt-edged securities at 4½ per cent.

Replying to a toast at the Scandinavian Club on 20 December, he remarked that Christmas, which to most people brought joy and peace, to him usually brought battle, since it was at this season that his books appeared; but that to him battle was a joy, and peace merely a breathing-space until he could take up the struggle anew. Nevertheless, when he added up his accounts for 1881, he must have hoped hard for that second edition, for he had earned barely half as much as in the previous year:

	crowns	£
9th edition of *Brand*	1,360	76
Fees from German League of Dramatists, 1st quarter	29	2
Fee from Thalia Theatre, Hamburg, for '*Nora*'	816	45
5th edition of *Peer Gynt*	1,320	73
Fees from German League of Dramatists, 2nd quarter	26	1
Fees for '*Nora*' in north German Theatres, via E. Lange	1,336	74
Fees from Bergen Theatre for various performances	240	13
1st edition of *Ghosts*	6,150	342
	11,277	626

However, on 2 January 1882 he wrote in buoyant mood to Hegel: 'The violent criticisms and insane attacks which people are levelling against *Ghosts* don't worry me in the least. I was expecting this. When *Love's Comedy* appeared there was just such an hysterical outcry in Norway as there is now. They moaned about *Peer Gynt* too, and *The Pillars of Society* and *A Doll's House*, just as much. The commotion will die away this time, as it did before.' Only as an afterthought did he add: 'One thing worries me a little when I think how big an edition you printed. Has all this fuss damaged the sales of the book?' Hegel replied on 10 January:

Dear Dr Ibsen,

. . . You ask: has all this to-do damaged the sales of the book? To this I must decidedly answer: Yes.

As you will know from the reviews, *Ghosts* has caused a great sensation and has been the literary event of the winter, like *A Doll's House* two years ago. This is only as one would expect. But, amazingly, there ensued almost at once great indignation at the circumstances which are portrayed in *Ghosts* and which people wish at all costs not to have in family literature. The effect of this became noticeable immediately. Of the large edition a not inconsiderable number of copies had been subscribed in advance, partly to the provinces, partly to Norway and Sweden.

From several of the booksellers outside Copenhagen, notably from Chr–a, Bergen and Stockholm, where the papers have openly opposed the sale of the book, I have already been informed that they could not find the expected sales for *Ghosts* and have therefore asked me to take back

T*

large quantities of the book, not merely those they had on sale or return, but also some that they took on the normal terms and which should not normally be credited. In view of the need to maintain a good relationship with my colleagues I felt it wisest to make them this concession. Here in Copenhagen the sales of *Ghosts* have been markedly smaller than those of your earlier books. And the whole business has had a damaging effect on *their* sales. I usually sell a not inconsiderable number of your works each Christmas, but this year the figures have been noticeably smaller.

I felt bound, my dear Herr Ibsen, to tell you this plainly . . .

Your most affectionate

Fr. Hegel.[1]

August Lindberg has described the scene in Stockholm on the day of publication. 'There was a rush to the bookshops. But the excitement vanished in silence. Absolute silence. The newspapers said nothing and the bookshops sent the book back to the publisher. It was contraband. Something which could not decently be discussed.'[2] And Alexander Kielland informed Georg Brandes that Cammermeyer, the leading bookshop in Christiania, had returned no less than five hundred copies to Gyldendal.[3] *Ghosts*, in short, was not a book to have about the house. It was not merely that it attacked some of the most sacred principles of the age, such as the sanctity of marriage (*A Doll's House* had done that), and the duty of a son to honour his father. Far worse, it referred unmistakably (if not by name) to venereal disease, defended free love, and suggested that under certain circumstances even incest might be justifiable. Even some of Ibsen's strongest supporters were antagonised. When Lindberg asked Ludvig Josephson, who had championed Ibsen's cause so ardently in Christiania, whether he would not consider presenting *Ghosts* at his theatre in Stockholm, Josephson refused point blank. 'The play', he told Lindberg, 'is one of the filthiest things ever written in Scandinavia.'[4] And Erik Bøgh reported to his board at the Royal Theatre, Copenhagen, that *Ghosts* was 'a repulsive pathological phenomenon which, by undermining the morality of our social order, threatens its foundations',[5] and advised its rejection, a recommendation with which the board concurred.

---

[1] Nielsen, II, pp. 355–356.

[2] Lindberg, p. 43.

[3] *Brandes Brevveksling*, IV, p. 336. Kielland added interestingly that he liked *Ghosts* 'less for its own sake than for the insight it gives me into this elegant, cautious, decorated, slightly snobbish person who, like Nora, has always had a secret desire to say: "Damn and blast!" in the midst of all his elegance—and has now acquired the courage.'

[4] Lindberg, p. 45.

[5] Agerholm, p. 279.

It was, however, in Norway itself that *Ghosts* was attacked most violently. Ibsen had expected the conservative papers to dislike it, but he was shocked to discover that the liberal press denounced it with even greater fervour. The left-wing *Oplandenes Avis* set the tone when it declared (21 December) that 'complete silence would, in our opinion, be the most fitting reception for such a work'. Despite this recommendation the reviewer went on to describe it as 'the most unpleasant book we have read for a long while', drawing some comfort from the fact that it was 'in our humble opinion at least, much worse written than the author's previous works'. An anonymous reviewer in *Dagbladet* (14 December) wrote: 'It is as though Ibsen had taken enjoyment in saying all the worst things he knew, and in saying them in the most outrageous way he could conceive.' The author of these words, Arne Garborg, had, ironically, just published a story entitled *The Freethinker*. The ageing Andreas Munch published a poem in *Morgenbladet* called *A Fallen Star*, likening Ibsen to a star which has allowed itself to be lured down into 'the region of mists', has there turned into a meteor which has buried itself in 'the black earth, swollen with corpses', and lies there giving off 'an evil stench of corruption'. An editorial in the same paper on 18 December concluded: 'The book has no place on the Christmas table of any Christian home.' Even such progressive writers as Jonas Lie and Alexander Keilland privately raised their eyebrows; and Henrik Jæger, who six years later was to write an admiring biography of Ibsen, lectured at Christiania University against the play, and toured the country repeating his opinions (which he later recanted).

A few bold spirits championed the play. Hans Jæger, later to be imprisoned for writing a supposedly pornographic novel, the young director Gunnar Heiberg, and those two formidable suffragettes Amalie Skram and Camilla Collett, all defended it in *Dagbladet*;[1] so did Bjørnson, who, despite, the recent bad friendship between him and Ibsen, praised it as 'free, bold and courageous'. 'That is like him', wrote Ibsen to Olof Skavlan on 24 January 1882. 'He has in truth a great, imperial spirit, and I shall never forget this.' And P. O. Schjøtt, the Professor of Greek at Christiania University, writing a year later in *Nyt Tidsskrift* (1882, pp. 100–104), compared the play to the ancient Greek dramas: 'When the greatest tragic and comic poets of Athens presented the political, ethical and religious ideas of their age, and even their champions, on the stage, someone no doubt denounced them and called their work tendentious. But posterity saw this as quite normal practice. When the ancient art of dramatic writing stood at its zenith, in that golden age, it was this realism or, if you will, this tendentiousness, which gave it its vitality and

---

[1] Einar Skavlan, *Gunnar Heiberg* (Oslo, 1960), p. 105.

character . . . We generalise thus with particular reference to Ibsen's latest play . . . For of all the modern dramas we have read, *Ghosts* comes closest to classical tragedy . . . When the dust of ignorant criticism has subsided, which we trust will happen soon, this play of Ibsen's, with its pure, bold contours, will stand not only as his noblest deed but as the greatest work of art which he, or indeed our whole dramatic literature, has produced.'

Schjøtt's last sentence was a reference to a review of the play by Georg Brandes who, in *Morgenbladet* (the Danish, not the Norwegian newspaper of that name), had declared it to be 'not the most perfect play he has written, but the noblest deed in his literary career'. Brandes was almost the only Dane to come out in the play's favour; his review delighted Ibsen, and re-established good relations between the two men.

In Rome, Ibsen read the various comments with increasing indignation. 'What is one to say of the attitude taken by the so-called liberal press?' he wrote to Brandes on 3 January 1882 (his first letter to Brandes for over five years). 'These leaders who talk and write of freedom and progress and at the same time let themselves be the slaves of the supposed opinions of their subscribers?' Three days later he wrote to the Danish writer Sophus Schandorph: 'I was prepared for some such commotion. If for nothing else, certain of our Norwegian reviewers have an undeniable talent for completely mis-understanding and misinterpreting the authors whose books they presume to judge.' After protesting that the views expressed in *Ghosts* were not necessarily his own ('In none of my plays is the author so totally detached and uncom-mitted as in this'[1]) he went on to deny that *Ghosts* advocated nihilism. 'The play is not concerned with advocating anything. It merely points to the fact that nihilism is fermenting beneath the surface in Norway as everywhere else. It is inevitable. A Pastor Manders will always incite some Mrs Alving into being. And she, simply because she is a woman, will, once she has started, go to the ultimate extreme.'

On 28 January he wrote to another Danish writer, Otto Borchsenius: 'It may well be that in certain respects this play is somewhat audacious. But I thought the time had come when a few boundary marks had to be shifted. And it was much easier for me, as an elder writer, to do this than for the many younger writers who might want to do something of the kind. I was prepared for a storm to break over me; but one can't run away from such things. That would

---

[1] This assertion was denounced by Strindberg in a letter to Edvard Brandes, 18 February 1882 ('Isn't Ibsen cowardly?'). But Strindberg admired the play, telling Brandes to thank his brother for the latter's defence of it, and even in 1884, when he had become violently hostile towards Ibsen, he admitted: 'But he has written *Ghosts*. I mustn't hate him.' (Letter to Bjørnson, 4 May 1884; *August Strindbergs brev*, II, p. 353, IV, p. 146.)

have been cowardice. What has most depressed me has been not the attacks themselves, but the lack of guts which has been revealed in the ranks of the so-called liberals in Norway. They are poor stuff with which to man the barricades.'

On 8 March he wrote a letter of warm thanks to Bjørnson 'for so openly and honourably standing forth in my defence at a time when I have been attacked from so many quarters. It was of course only what I would have expected from your bold warrior spirit . . . Rest assured that I shall never forget you. I have also noticed that during your stay in America you wrote kind words in my praise. Thank you for that too . . . I heard you were ill there, and when you were on your way home I read of storms at sea. Then I suddenly and vividly realised how immensely much you mean to me, as to all of us. I felt that if anything should happen to you it would be a great disaster for our land and I should lose all joy in creating.'

So far from discouraging him from further writing, the smell of battle stimulated Ibsen. On 16 March he informed Hegel that he was 'fully occupied with preparations for a new work. This time it will be a peaceful play, which cabinet ministers and wholesale merchants and their ladies will be able to read, and from which the theatres will not need to shrink . . . As far as *Ghosts* is concerned, comprehension will seep into the minds of the good people of our country, and that in the not too distant future. But all these fading and decrepit figures who have spat upon this work will one day bring upon their heads the crushing judgment of future literary historians . . . My book contains the future.'

The Christiania Theatre and the Royal Theatre in Stockholm followed the example of the Royal Theatre in Copenhagen and Nya Teatern in refusing to stage the play. On 20 May, however, *Ghosts* at last received its world premiere in, of all places, Chicago, where it was presented in the original language at the Aurora Turner Hall before an audience of Scandinavian immigrants with the Danish actress Helga von Bluhme as Mrs Alving, the other parts being taken by Danish and Norwegian amateurs. This production—the first on record of any Ibsen play in America—subsequently toured Minneapolis and other cities of the Middle West which contained large Scandinavian populations. But it was to be over a year before the play was performed in Europe, and even when the scandal had died down and it was being acted before respectful audiences it was thirteen years before a new edition was required. It remained a book not to be seen about the house.

But if *Ghosts* shocked the literary and theatrical establishment of Scandinavia, it made an immediate and stimulating impact on the young. Herman Bang, then aged twenty-five, and later to become a celebrated Danish novelist and one of Ibsen's most influential pioneers in France, describes how it excited his generation even before it became a subject of scandal. 'The play was distributed to the booksellers towards evening. The keenest buyers ran out in the dark to get it. That evening I visited a young actor who had just read Ghosts ... "This", he said, "is the greatest play our age will see." The debate had already started by the next morning. An extraordinary number of people seemed to have read the play that night ... One or two restless people who had nothing to lose, having no good name to be smeared by association with Ghosts, gave public readings. People flocked to the obscure places where these readings took place, out by the bridges, far into the suburbs. A group of unwanted actors determined to tour it. They wanted to act the play in the provinces.'[1]

But, Bang adds, 'good society knew its duty', and the project had to be abandoned. Nevertheless, it 'was performed semi-privately, I know not in what impossible places', and all but achieved a professional production in Copenhagen within weeks of publication, for Theodor Andersen, the head of the Casino Theatre, 'read it twenty times before finally rejecting it'.[2]

In Germany, once the play had been published (which did not happen until 1884), the same pattern was repeated. Bang was in Germany then, and tells of a performance of A Doll's House at Meiningen, with the celebrated actress Marie Ramlo as guest artist. The theatre was full of young students. 'Frau Ramlo was excellent, but it was not she who held their attention. The young people barely heard her. They read when the curtain was down, and they read when the curtain was up. They read furtively and amazed, as though fearful, read, as the book was passed secretly from hand to hand, a little, humble, yellow, paper-bound volume of a hundred pages bearing the title Gespenster [Ghosts]. What a strange evening when all those hundreds of young people read as one the play about the sins of their fathers, and when, as a drama about marriage was being acted behind the footlights, that other drama of parents and their children forced its way up from the auditorium on to the stage. They did not dare to read the book at home, and so they read it secretly here.'[3]

Bang adds that young actors and actresses used Ghosts as an audition piece long before it was allowed to be played in Germany (in 1886, and then only privately), and that 'young beginners acted the play secretly in suburban halls far out on the fringes of civilisation, as in Norway.'[4]

Ibsen's contemporaries saw Ghosts primarily as a play about physical illness, just as they had seen A Doll's House primarily as a play about women's rights.

---

[1] Herman Bang, Teatret (Copenhagen, 1892), pp. 239–240. Cf. also Skavlan, p. 105.
[2] Ibid., pp. 230–231.
[3] Ibid., p. 240.
[4] Ibid., p. 241.

With few exceptions, they failed to realise that the true subject of *Ghosts* is the devitalising effect of a dumb acceptance of convention. As Halvdan Koht has written: 'Oswald is branded with disease, not because his father was a beast, but because Mrs Alving had obeyed the immoral ethics of society'[1]—in other words, *Ghosts* is a play about ethical, not physical debility. The importance of waging war against the past, the need for each individual to find his or her own freedom, the danger of renouncing love in the name of duty—these are the real themes of *Ghosts*, as they are the themes of every play which Ibsen wrote from *A Doll's House* onwards. And the targets are the same as those which he had attacked in *A Doll's House* and, before that, in *The Pillars of Society*, and which he was to go on attacking until the end of his life—the hollowness of great reputations, provincialism of outlook, the narrow and inhibiting effect of small-town life, the suppression of individual freedom from within as well as from without, and the neglect of the significance of heredity—a problem much discussed among the Scandinavians in Rome, one of whom, the botanist J. P. Jacobsen, had translated Darwin's *Origin of Species* and *The Descent of Man* into Danish. Zola, of course, had hastened to exploit Darwin's thesis that man, like other animals, must adapt himself to the environment in which he lives; but Ibsen hated being compared with Zola, for whom he had a low regard. 'Zola', he once remarked, 'descends into the sewer to bathe in it; I, to cleanse it.'[2]

How much Ibsen had actually read of Zola is not clear. In 1882 he told William Archer he had read nothing, but in 1898 he told a Swedish journalist he had 'read much of him, though not his great cycle of novels', and described him as 'clearly and beyond doubt a great talent'. But this was during his seventieth birthday celebrations, when he was being polite about everybody. Zola's opinion of Ibsen seems to have been equally ambiguous. He was largely responsible for the first French production of him in 1891, by reminding Antoine of *Ghosts* (Antoine had thought of doing it, but had dropped the idea; Zola had read an essay by Jacques Saint-Cères in the *Revue de l'Art Dramatique* describing Ibsen as a naturalist, and felt he had found a fellow-warrior).[3] On the other hand, when asked his opinion of the influence of Ibsen on the French

---

[1] Koht, II, p. 118. In view of the oft-repeated complaint that syphilis cannot be inherited from one's father, it is worth pointing out that it can be inherited from one's mother, and that a woman can have syphilis without realising it or suffering any particular discomfort. In other words, and this is a far more frightening explanation of Oswald's illness than the usual one, Mrs Alving must have caught syphilis from her husband and passed it on to her son. Ibsen knew more about medicine than some of his critics.

[2] Erik Lie, *Jonas Lie, en livsskildring* (Oslo, 1933), p. 169, quoting Georg Pauli.

[3] Cf. Antoine's diaries, quoted by H. Gregersen, *Ibsen in Spain* (Cambridge, Mass., 1936), pp. 20–21.

stage (and of Tolstoy on the French novel), Zola is said to have replied that 'he did not attach much importance to the question, for he held that the ideas which were supposed to rain on Paris from the North were in reality French ones which had been disseminated by French writers and had come back to their place of origin, occasionally crystallised or intensified by the more sombre imagination of Scandinavian or Russian writers'.[1] The legend of Ibsen's supposed debt to Scribe, Dumas *fils*, George Sand and the rest died hard.

Ibsen never liked admitting that any of his plays owed a debt to any other writer, protesting that in any age writers tended to find similar themes. As Professor Francis Bull has remarked,[2] however, the similarities between *Ghosts* and a *conte* entitled *The Daughter* by the Norwegian writer Mauritz Hansen published half a century earlier are so striking that it is difficult not to believe that, consciously or unconsciously, Ibsen must have used the latter as a starting-point. *The Daughter* tells how a dissipated lieutenant-colonel, formidably named Hannibal Hedebrandt, has in his youth had an affair with his maid, Else. Then he meets a lady of his own station but, on discovering that Else is with child, marries her off to a caretaker. Else goes mad and dies, but her daughter Henriette grows up in the Hedebrandt household; she is repelled by her supposed father, the caretaker, who has a wooden leg. It is of course perfectly possible, and I think likely, that Ibsen had read this story in his youth and forgotten it, and that certain details had forced themselves up out of his unconscious—possibly assisted by his memories of his own illegitimate child by a servant-maid likewise named Else.

Manders, as has been noted, was immediately motivated by Ibsen's indignation at the Norwegian Ecclesiastical Department's treatment of his son. Regina was based on a maid whom the Ibsens had had in Munich; she was of Bavarian birth, but had spent some while in Paris, and incorporated various French expressions in the high German she used when speaking to Ibsen and Suzannah, though among her friends she talked the Bavarian dialect. Mrs Alving is not unlike a portrait of what Nora might have become had she decided to stay with her husband and children, and one wonders whether her creation may not have been partly inspired by that 'happy ending' which Ibsen had found himself compelled to write for *A Doll's House*. Like Nora, Mrs Alving is strangled by convention and a misplaced sense of duty. 'I *had* to write *Ghosts*', Ibsen told the Swedish Countess Sophie Adlersparre in a letter of 24 June 1882. 'I couldn't stop at *A Doll's House*; after Nora, I had to create Mrs Alving.' Viewed in this

---

[1] Cf. William Archer, *Ibsen as I Knew Him*, p. 8; *Aftonbladet*, Stockholm, 12 April 1898; Kela Nyholm, *Henrik Ibsen paa den franske scene, Ibsen-Årbok 1957–9*, p. 26; E. A. Vizetelly, *Emile Zola, Novelist and Reformer* (London, 1904), p. 389.

[2] *CE*, IX, p. 20.

context, Oswald's syphilis may be regarded as a symbol of the dead customs and traditions which stunt and cripple us and lay waste our life.

Ghosts has been described by many critics, following Schjøtt, as the most classically constructed of Ibsen's plays, not merely in its obedience to the Aristotelian unities but in the economy of its construction. That is not quite true; it is in fact, with *The Pillars of Society* and *An Enemy of the People* (and, though this may surprise some, *The Wild Duck*) one of the most cuttable plays he wrote. Manders in particular has a good deal of superfluous dialogue; his is much the longest part in the play, and represents one of the very few examples, if not indeed the only one, of Ibsen allowing his personal feelings to get out of hand to the extent of unbalancing his composition. It is particularly important in performance that he should be played straight, not as a caricature, and that he should be a handsome man; otherwise Mrs Alving's youthful infatuation with him becomes hard to believe. Nor should his verbosity and pomposity be exaggerated; he has not much more of either than many a modern bishop or politician.

In one important technical respect *Ghosts* anticipates the later plays, and that is in the density of its dialogue. *The Pillars of Society* and *A Doll's House* are both simply written (and comparatively easy to translate), because for most of the time the characters say what they mean. But in *Ghosts*, Mrs Alving and Manders especially spend much of the time circling round a subject to which they dread referring directly, and at these moments the dialogue is oblique, sometimes even opaque. This double-density dialogue, when the characters say one thing and mean another, was to be one of Ibsen's most important contributions to the technique of prose drama. He knew that when people talk about something concerning which they feel a sense of guilt, they cease to speak directly and instead talk evasively and with circumlocution; and actors, when they are playing these lines, have to speak the text but act the sub-text, the unspoken thoughts between the lines. One of the greatest problems that faces a translator of Ibsen is to convey this meaning behind the meaning; if this is not indicated (as Ibsen himself indicates it) it is practically impossible for an actor to convey that sense of guilt and evasion from which almost all of Ibsen's major characters suffer, and which is so often at crises the mainspring of their actions, or their failure to act.

Historically, *Ghosts* occupies a position of immense importance. Julius Hoffory remarked in 1888 that much of its effect on Ibsen's contemporaries was due to the fact that here was a play comparable to those of Aeschylus and Sophocles, but about modern people;[1] a fact easily forgotten by us, to whom it

---

[1] *Tilskueren* (Copenhagen, 1888), pp. 61–70.

is as much a costume play as the *Agamemnon*. *Ghosts* was the first great tragedy
written about middle-class people in plain, everyday prose. *Danton's Death* and
Woyzeck are composed in a high-flown prose which frequently, and splendidly,
overlaps the frontier of poetry; and while other playwrights had attempted to
do what Ibsen achieved in *Ghosts*, none had succeeded. Time has not dulled
its impact (though it sometimes, in England and America at any rate, suffers
from being publicised as 'the play which shocked our grandfathers'). Indeed, it
gains enormously by not having, as so often in the last century, a declamatory
and melodramatic Mrs Alving. Ibsen's plays needed, and helped to nurture, a
new kind of player with the strength of restraint, life-size, not Wagnerian.
Bernardt and Henry Irving rejected his works; Duse embraced them.

In March 1934 James Joyce saw a performance of *Ghosts* in Paris. The fact
that one of Captain Alving's children was a wreck and the other (Regina)
healthy intrigued him, and the following month inspired him to one of his
wittiest poems:

Epilogue to Ibsen's 'Ghosts'

Dear quick, whose conscience buried deep
The grim old grouser has been salving,
Permit one spectre more to peep.
I am the ghost of Captain Alving.

Silenced and smothered by my past
Like the lewd knight in dirty linen
I struggle forth to swell the cast
And air a long-suppressed opinion.

For muddling weddings into wakes
No fool could vie with Pastor Manders.
I, though a dab at ducks and drakes,
Let gooseys serve or sauce their ganders.

My spouse bore me a blighted boy,
Our slavey pupped a bouncing bitch.
Paternity, thy name is joy
When the wise sire knows which is which.

Both swear I am that self-same man
By whom their infants were begotten.
Explain, fate, if you care and can
Why one is sound and one is rotten.

Olaf may plod his stony path
And live as chastely as Susanna
Yet pick up in some Turkish bath
His *quantum est* of *Pox Romana*,

While Haakon hikes up primrose way,
Spreeing and gleeing while he goes,
To smirk upon his latter day
Without a pimple on his nose.

I give it up I am afraid
But if I loafed and found it fun
Remember how a coyclad maid
Knows how to take it out of one.

The more I dither on and drink
My midnight bowl of spirit punch
The firmlier I feel and think
Friend Manders came too oft to lunch.

Since scuttling ship Vikings like me
Reck not to whom the blame is laid,
Y.M.C.A., V.D., T.B.,
Or Harbourmaster of Port-Said.

Blame all and none and take to task
The harlot's lure, the swain's desire.
Heal by all means but hardly ask
Did this man sin or did his sire.

The shack's ablaze. That canting scamp,
The carpenter, has dished the parson.
Now had they kept their powder damp
Like me there would have been no arson.

Nay, more, were I not all I was,
Weak, wanton, waster out and out,
There would have been no world's applause
And damn all to write home about.

THIRTEEN

𝕏 An Enemy of the People

(1882)

DURING THE WINTER of 1881–1882, when the hubbub about *Ghosts* was at its height, Ibsen met for the first time his energetic new Scottish champion. Young William Archer had been ordered south for his health, and after walking from Cannes to Leghorn he proceeded by train to Rome. One of his first objects there was, naturally, to secure an introduction to the author whose work he so admired, and he described the meeting in a letter to his brother Charles, written in December 1881:

'The great event has come off, satisfactorily, but not in the manner I expected ... I had been about a quarter of an hour there [at the Scandinavian Club], and was standing close to the door, when it opened and in walked unmistakably the great Henrik. My photograph is very good as far as the face is concerned, but it gives you the idea of broader shoulders and a fuller chest than he really has. He is of middle height, rather under than over—at any rate in talking to him I feel noticeably taller. [Archer stood around six feet.] ... He went around for a while talking to different people, and gave you the impression, which I was prepared for, of extreme quietness. The red ribbon which excited young [*sic*] Bjørnson's contempt was very prominent in his buttonhole. After a while I got Professor Ravnkilde [the Danish composer and Chairman of the Club] to introduce me to him. I saw at once that he did not connect my name with *Samfundets Støtter* [*The Pillars of Society*], so after a little I told him about it. He had heard of the production, but not my name, and took my rather lame excuses for not having got his permission very readily ... He invited me to call at his house, which I shall do some day this week; and besides, I shall see him again at the [Club], when I hope to get a little more under the surface, if it is at all possible ... He does not read of any of the French dramatists, and moreover he hardly ever goes to the theatre—and small blame to him in Italy, say I, though he says there are some very good Italian actors, besides the famous ones. Altogether, the interview was a success. Though I can't say that L's description of him as a *spidsborger* [*petit bourgeois*] is quite justified, he certainly is not the man you would imagine to have written Aase's death-scene and the fourth act of *Brand* . . . At first sight there is an absence of anything Titanic about him . . . However, for the present "the old min's friendly", and that's the main point.'[1]

A few weeks later Archer wrote to J. M. Robertson that he was seeing Ibsen 'almost every day at a café which he and I both frequent for an afternoon glass of vermouth, and I have a yarn with him occasionally'.[2] This was the Café Nazionale at the corner of the Corso and the Via della Mercede. Ibsen must have liked Archer, for he invited him to his home, which Archer found 'comfortable, yet comfortless . . . well furnished, but with no air of home about it . . . His writing room was very bare and painfully orderly.'[3] When Archer left Rome on 4 March Ibsen gave him an inscribed photograph; and when he returned in April, 'the old min was not only friendly but effusive'.[4] Archer wrote an article entitled *Henrik Ibsen at home in the Via Capo le Case* and offered it to Edmund Yates, the editor of *The World* (a periodical of which Archer was to be the dramatic critic for twenty-one years); but Yates (who had once been the occasion of a quarrel between Dickens and Thackeray) rejected it, it was never published and, sadly, it has not survived among Archer's papers.

A Danish scholar, Harald Høffding, also met Ibsen for the first time that winter. 'He looked almost like a boatswain; broad and big-boned, brown in the face, he sat motionless and with half-closed eyes.' When he met him again ten years later Høffding received a very different impression of, 'an elegant little man. *À deux*', he added, 'Ibsen was very loquacious, though he avoided any discussion of his writings.'[5] Georg Pauli confirms this last point; whenever anyone tried to probe Ibsen about his plays, Pauli says he would reply with a question, such as: 'How long have you been in Rome, madam?'—'Did you have a good journey?' etc.[6] And Fritz von Dardel, whom he had met at the Vienna Exhibition and who was now in Rome, confirms Høffding's impression of the new darkness of Ibsen's complexion, though he implies another cause than sun. 'He has fattened', noted Dardel in his diary, 'and has developed a high facial colour. To any query why he did not have his son educated in Norway, he replied: "Because he can have a pleasanter life almost anywhere else." '[7]

---

[1] Charles Archer, pp. 101–102.
[2] *Ibid.*, p. 104.
[3] William Archer, *Ibsen as I Knew Him*, p. 7.
[4] Charles Archer, p. 113.
[5] Harald Høffding, *Erindringer* (Copenhagen, 1928), pp. 159–161.
[6] Pauli, pp. 115–116.
[7] Fritz von Dardel, *Dagboksanteckningar, 1881–5*, p. 86.

On 18 February 1882, Ibsen had written a second letter to H. E. Berner, the Member of Parliament whom he had asked the previous March to try to get his and Bjørnson's pensions raised. Berner had replied that April asking for fuller details of the losses Ibsen had incurred through the absence of copyright protection. Ibsen, strangely and, as it turned out, perhaps fatally, delayed replying for ten months; but his letter gives some interesting details and underlines his predicament:

. . . *In Finland many, indeed most of my plays have been translated and played in Swedish as well as Finnish.*

In Russia I know for sure that at any rate The League of Youth *has been translated and played. I learn from newspaper notices that the same is to be true of* A Doll's House.[1]

The last-named play has also been translated into Polish and played in Warsaw. Some years ago a translation of my volume of poems appeared there too, but since this was much cut by the Russian censor a completely new edition was arranged, printed and published in Cracow, i.e. on Austrian soil.

The Vikings at Helgeland *has been translated into and played in Hungarian. I hear the same is true of* A Doll's House, *or anyway a production is being considered.*

In England there exist two translations of the last-named play.[2] The Pillars of Society *has also been translated into English and performed in London.*

It can be stated with fair certainty that there exist in various countries translations of my plays which have not come to my knowledge. Naturally I have received nothing for any of the above-mentioned translations and performances.

Regarding my literary affairs in Germany, I shall permit myself the following brief summary.

The Vikings at Helgeland *was translated at my expense by Emma Klingenfeld, and printed and published likewise at my expense, and without my receiving any payment, by Theodor Ackermann in Munich, who as agent also takes fifty per cent of the income from copies sold. The German booksellers dare not publish Norwegian plays in the normal ways since thanks to the lack of any copyright agreement they cannot be protected against other translations appearing in competition.*

Lady Inger of Østraat *has been translated and published on the same terms as* The Vikings at Helgeland.

The Pillars of Society *likewise.*

---

[1] Ibsen's information was out-of-date. Helena Modjeska had already played *A Doll's House* in St Petersburg (in Polish) the previous November. She played it in Warsaw in February 1882, the month Ibsen wrote this letter.

[2] Weber's unfortunate version, and a slightly (but not much) better one by Henrietta Frances Lord, published in London early in 1882.

This play has besides been translated by Wilhelm Lange in Berlin, who on his own account has had it performed at many German theatres and has also published it through Ph. Reclam in Leipzig in his 'Universalbibliothek'. Lange's translation sells at 2 pfennigs, whereas mine, which is decently produced, costs 2 reichsmarks and therefore enjoys only a small sale. Hr. Emil Jonas has also published an 'adaptation' of the play, which likewise is printed in a bargain edition and is played in many places in Germany.

The League of Youth has been translated by Adolf Strodtman in Berlin and published by Duncker there. This publication has nothing to do with me and of course brings me nothing.

Another translation of this play has been published by W. Lange and similarly brings me nothing.

The Pretenders has been translated by Adolf Strodtman and published, as has The League of Youth. All performing fees for these go exclusively to the translator . . .

Moreover, Ibsen adds, many German theatres will not act his plays because he cannot grant them exclusive rights, so that they cannot be sure that it will not be staged simultaneously or even earlier at another theatre in the same town. For the same reason, such theatres as do accept them dare not risk spending as much as they might on decor, etc., because they cannot expect so many performances. As regards Scandinavia, he reckons to have lost 3,000 crowns on *The League of Youth* and *The Vikings at Helgeland* in Sweden, because he got only *ex gratia* payments instead of what he would have received had Norway been a signatory of the copyright pact. By contrast, as a result of the agreement with Denmark, he had received 9,000 crowns from the Royal Theatre in Copenhagen for *A Doll's House*, whereas from *The Pillars of Society* and *The Vikings at Helgeland* he got only 2,000 crowns apiece, and from *The League of Youth* and *The Pretenders* only 1,200 crowns each, although all these four plays had had about as many performances as *A Doll's House*. In all, he reckons to have lost about 21,600 crowns (£1,200) in Danish performing fees alone prior to the signing of the agreement, 'Think', he concludes, 'what Bjørnson and I could have got had an agreement been in force with Germany, which has a hundred and fifty theatres!'

But his letter was too late. By the time Berner received it he had, on 1 February, put his motion before the Storthing, and they had rejected it.

On 2 June 1882, a fortnight after the Chicago premiere of *Ghosts*, there had occurred the first American production in English of an Ibsen play, though he might have had difficulty in recognising it as his. The place was Milwaukee and the play *A Doll's House*, re-entitled *The Child Wife*, and freely adapted from the German by a schoolmaster named William M. Lawrence. Lawrence set the play in England, introducing an Irish widow to give the play some humour, and of course using the happy ending. In the second act one of Nora's (or Eva's, as Lawrence called her) children sang a pretty song, which the audience enjoyed so much that she had to repeat it. 'Love is the theme', noted one reviewer, 'yet not a line of the play is impure.' Another critic named Lawrence as the author, while a third referred to the *play* as 'Henry Ibsen'.[1]

Meanwhile, during that spring and early summer of 1882, while the storm over *Ghosts* still raged, Ibsen went ahead with his new play, which progressed with unwonted speed. No working notes or preliminary draft has survived, so that we do not know, as we do for most of his plays, how long he took to write each act, or what alterations he made from his original conception; but on 21 June he was able to inform Hegel: 'Yesterday I completed my new dramatic work. It is entitled *An Enemy of the People*, and is in five acts. I am still a little uncertain whether to call it a comedy or simply a play; it has much of the character of a comedy, but there is also a serious basic theme.' At the beginning of August he left Rome for Gossensass, whence on 9 September he posted the fair copy of the final act to Hegel. 'It has been fun', he wrote, 'working on this play, and I feel a sense of emptiness and deprivation at being parted from it. Dr Stockmann and I got on most excellently; we agree about so many things; but the Doctor has a more muddled head on his shoulders than I have, and has besides certain characteristics which will permit people to tolerate things from his lips which they might not accept so readily had they issued from mine. If you have begun to read the manuscript, I think you will share this opinion.'

The speed with which Ibsen completed *An Enemy of the People*, without the usual eighteen months of cud-chewing ('He has never been so quick before!' commented Georg Brandes to Alexander Kielland on 30 June)[2] suggests that this must have been the work he had conceived and pondered before putting it aside for *Ghosts*, as described in his letters to Hegel of 12 November 1880 and 22 March 1881. Moreover, Lorentz Dietrichson and Kristofer Janson both record earlier conversations with Ibsen in which he expressed many of the opinions which he was to put into Dr Stockmann's mouth. On New Year's Eve 1880, Janson noted in his diary: 'Today Ibsen and I discussed French politics, especially the expulsion of the monks from their monasteries. Ibsen deplored this greatly, and said: "Haven't I always said that you republicans are the worst tyrants of all? You don't respect individual freedom. Republicanism is the form of government in which individual freedom has the least chance of being respected . . . What is the majority? The ignorant mass. Intelligence

---

[1] Einar Haugen, *Ibsen i Amerika*, in *Edda*, 1935, pp. 553 ff.
[2] *Brandes Brevveksling*, IV, p. 345.

always belongs to the minority. How many of the majority do you think are entitled to hold any opinion? The only people I have any real sympathy with are the socialists and nihilists. They want something wholeheartedly and are consistent." '[1] And Dietrichson recalled: 'The ideas which he expressed in *An Enemy of the People* were already fully developed by the spring of 1881 and were aired in almost every conversation we had at that time.'[2]

The reception of *Ghosts* in Norway had brought Ibsen's distrust of popular opinion and contemporary liberalism to the boil. 'What is one to say of the attitude taken by the so-called liberal press?' he had written to Georg Brandes on 3 January 1882. 'These leaders who talk and write of freedom and progress, and at the same time allow themselves to be the slaves of the supposed opinions of their subscribers? I become more and more convinced that there is something demoralising about involving oneself in politics and attaching oneself to a party. Under no circumstances will I ever link myself with any party which has the majority behind it. Bjørnson says: "The majority is always right." As a practising politician I suppose he has to say that. But I say: "The minority is always right." I am of course not thinking of the minority of reactionaries who have been left astern by the big central party which we call liberal; I mean the minority which forges ahead in territory which the majority has not yet reached. I believe that he is right who is most closely attuned to the future ... For me freedom is the first condition of life, and the highest. At home people don't bother much about freedom but only about freedoms—a few more or a few less, according to the party standpoint. I feel most painfully affected by this vulgarity, this plebeianism in our public attitude. In the course of their undeniably worthy efforts to turn our country into a democratic community, people have unwittingly gone a good way towards turning us into a mob community. The aristocracy of the intellect seems to be in short supply in Norway.'[3]

Later the same month (24 January) he had written on similar lines to Olaf Skavlan: 'I myself am responsible for what I write, and I alone. I cannot possibly embarrass any party, for I belong to none. I want to act as a lone *franc-tireur* in the outposts, and operate on my own ... Is it only in the political field that men are to be allowed to work for freedom in Norway? Is it not first

---

[1] Janson, pp. 78–80.

[2] Dietrichson, I, p. 362.

[3] Several of the phrases Ibsen used in this letter recur in *An Enemy of the People*. 'When my new play reaches you', he wrote to Brandes on 21 September 1882, shortly after finishing it, 'you will perhaps be able to understand what interest and, I may add, fun it has given me to recall the many scattered and casual remarks I have made in my letters to you.' Didrik Grønvold recalls that Ibsen had spoken to him of the necessity of having an aristocracy to educate a nation as early as 1877 in Munich (*Diktere og musikere*, p. 12).

and foremost man's spirit that needs to be set free? Such spiritual slaves as we are cannot even use the freedom we already have. Norway is a free country inhabited by serfs.' These words, like those written to Brandes, are precisely in the mood and manner of Dr Stockmann.

An Enemy of the People tells the story of a doctor at a small spa who discovers that the Baths, on which the livelihood of the town depends, are contaminated. At first the locals praise him as a public benefactor, but when they learn that the Baths will have to be closed for several years and their income affected, they turn against him and, when he calls a meeting to put his views to them, brand him as an enemy of the people. In this famous fourth act, Dr Stockmann utters many of the opinions which Ibsen himself had been expressing in Rome:

'I can't stand politicians! I've had all I can take of them! They're like goats in a plantation of young trees! They destroy everything! . . .'

'The most dangerous enemies of truth and freedom are the majority! Yes, the solid, liberal, bloody majority—they're the ones we have to fear! . . . Who form the majority in any country? The wise, or the fools? I think we'd all have to agree that the fools are in a terrifying, overwhelming majority all over the world! But in the name of God it can't be right that the fools should rule the wise! Yes, yes, you can shout me down. But you can't say I'm wrong! The majority has the power, unfortunately—but the majority is not right! The ones who are right are a few isolated individuals like me. The minority is always right! . . .'

'I'm not so forgiving as a certain person. I don't say: "I forgive ye, for ye know not what ye do!" '

Dr Stockmann's first reaction as his daughter is sacked, his patients refuse to employ him and the mob breaks his windows is to take his wife and children away; but he finally decides to stay and try to re-educate the townspeople, beginning with the lowest and poorest:

DR STOCKMANN: . . . I'm going to experiment with mongrels for once. They've good heads on them sometimes.

EILIF: But what shall we do when we've become free men and aristocrats?

DR STOCKMANN: Then, my boys, you'll chase all those damned politicians into the Atlantic Ocean!

MRS STOCKMANN: Let's hope it won't be the politicians who'll chase you out, Thomas.

DR STOCKMANN: Are you quite mad, Catherine? Chase me out? Now, when I am the strongest man in town?

MRS STOCKMANN: The strongest—now?

DR STOCKMANN: Yes! I'll go further! I am one of the strongest men in the whole world . . . Hush! You mustn't talk about it yet. But I've made a great discovery!

MRS STOCKMANN: Not again!

DR STOCKMANN: Yes—yes! (*Gathers them round him and whispers to them.*) The fact is, you see, that the strongest man in the world is he who stands most alone.

The plot of *An Enemy of the People* had its origin in two actual incidents. Alfred Meisner, a young German poet whom Ibsen knew in Munich, had told him how, when his father had been medical officer at the spa of Teiplitz in the eighteen-thirties, there had occurred an outbreak of cholera which the Doctor felt it his duty to make known publicly. As a result the season was ruined and the citizens of Teiplitz became so enraged that they stoned the Doctor's house and forced him to flee the town.

Then there had been the case in Norway of a chemist named Harald Thaulow. For nearly ten years Thaulow had furiously attacked the Christiania Steam Kitchens for neglecting their duty towards the city's poor. He had delivered a violent speech on the subject in 1874, during Ibsen's visit to Norway; and on 23 February 1881, only a fortnight before he died, Thaulow had attempted to read a prepared speech at the annual general meeting of the Steam Kitchens. The chairman of the meeting tried to prevent him from speaking, and eventually the public forced him, amid commotion, to withdraw. Ibsen read a report of this meeting in *Aftenposten* (24 February), just at the time when his indignation at the reception of *Ghosts* was reaching its climax, and he must have recognised in the eccentric old chemist a spirit very kindred to its own. The newspaper account is worth quoting:

THAULOW: I will not stop, you have no right to stop me, Mr Chairman. (*Continues.*) Point number ten—

CONSUL HEFYTE: Mr Thaulow must be stopped!

THAULOW *continues. Several of the public show their displeasure by walking about the hall.* THE CHAIRMAN *asks the meeting whether they recognise his right to bar* MR THAULOW *from the floor. Unanimous 'Ayes'.* THE CHAIRMAN *again asks* MR THAULOW *to stop reading.*

THAULOW: I will not be silenced.

THE CHAIRMAN: In that case, I shall—

THAULOW: I'll keep it quite short. (*Reads on.*)

CONSUL HEFTYE: Is he to be allowed to continue?

THAULOW (*continues reading*): The glorious achievements of the Christiania
　　　　　Steam Kitchens—I'll soon be through.
CONSUL HEFTYE: If this goes on the meeting can't continue.
CHAIRMAN:　　I regret that I must interrupt Mr Thaulow. You have not
　　　　　the floor—
THAULOW *reads on*.
CONSUL HEFTYE: Be quiet, or you'll be thrown out.
THAULOW:　　Oh, very well.
THAULOW *sits down at last. After the* CHAIRMAN *had read his report for some
　　　　　minutes*—
THAULOW:　　... It's too much. It's no use trying to oppose the
　　　　　mob—
CONSUL HEFTYE: Did the Chairman hear Mr Thaulow refer to us as the
　　　　　mob? ...
At length MR THAULOW *left the meeting in a rage, saying*: I'll have no more
　　　　　to do with you. I won't cast my pearls into the sand. This
　　　　　is a damned insult being inflicted on a free people in a free
　　　　　society. Now I'll go! Stand in the dunce's corner and be
　　　　　ashamed of yourselves!

As with *The Pillars of Society*, an English Member of Parliament may also
have contributed something to the play. Charles Bradlaugh, having narrowly
escaped imprisonment for his part in a pamphlet advocating birth control (he
had actually been sentenced, but had escaped on appeal) had been elected
Radical M.P. for Northampton in 1880, but had been barred from taking his
seat on the ground that, since he was a confessed free-thinker, the oath would
not bind him. New elections were held in Northampton, and he was returned
each time, but was still excluded; in 1881, he was forcibly removed from the
House by ten policemen. It was not until 1886 that a new Speaker granted
him the right to take the oath and sit. 'You should hear Ibsen on Bradlaugh—he
has the most vivid sympathy for him', wrote William Archer to his brother
Charles on 14 March 1882, when Ibsen was about to start writing *An Enemy of
the People*; and Bradlaugh has an obvious deal in common with Dr Stockmann.
So, it has often been pointed out, do Bjørnson and Jonas Lie, both intellectually confused, warm-hearted, eloquent and impatient men, with strong
family feelings and an infinite capacity for moral indignation. But, as Ibsen
hinted in his letter to Hegel of 9 September 1882, he himself was probably the
chief model for the character, at any rate in Act Four; and it is worth remembering that the house in Skien in which Ibsen had been born had been called
Stockmannsgården.

After posting the final pages to Hegel on 9 September Ibsen remained for a month in Gossensass, staying, as he was to do on future occasions, at the friendly Gröbner family hotel. While there he received, and granted, a request from America for the right to translate and publish *The Pillars of Society*, *A Doll's House* and *Ghosts*. The request came from Rasmus B. Anderson, Professor of Scandinavian Languages at the University of Wisconsin, who that year published a review of *Brand* in the *Literary World* and an essay on Ibsen in *The American*, the first articles about him to appear in America apart from Bjørnson's panegyric. Anderson was to supervise the project, and Ibsen, in his reply of 14 September, begged him to see that 'the language of the translation should be kept as close as possible to ordinary everyday speech; all the turns of phrase and expressions which belong only to books should most carefully be avoided in dramatic works, especially mine, which aim to produce in the reader or spectator a feeling that he is, during the reading or performance, witnessing a slice of real life'. It was advice that many of his translators, recent as well as contemporary, would have done well to heed. But these translations, if completed, never appeared—fortunately, since the translator was that William M. Lawrence who had been responsible for the travestied version of *A Doll's House* produced in Milwaukee. Henrietta Frances Lord's version of *A Doll's House* was published by Dutton's of New York this year; *The Pillars of Society* and *An Enemy of the People* had to wait until 1888.

On 9 October (the snow must have come later than usual to Gossensass that year) Ibsen left Gossensass and moved south to the little town of Brixen, where he put up at the Hotel Elefant, 'the best hotel in the Tyrol', as he described it to Hegel on 28 October. He had intended to stay there only briefly, but heavy floods cut the roads and railways to the south, and it was not until 24 November that he was able to return to Rome.

When he got there he found an unpleasant surprise awaiting him. John Paulsen had published with Gyldendal a novel called *The Pehrsen Family*, and one can only suppose that Frederik Hegel had (as with *Brand*) not read the manuscript before sending it to press, or in proof. The book deals with a middle-aged couple and their only son. The father, a self-made tradesman, is short, domineering, emotionally buttoned-up, contemptuous of his country, and obsessed by a secret passion to gain a medal, an end towards which he has done some careful lobbying. He has a drunken old father of whom he is ashamed, and walks with his hands behind his back. As a young man, he had been very poor and taken refuge in alcohol, and there had been a whip-round among his acquaintances to help him out. His wife, an avid novel-reader whose 'weak health had been broken in the struggle with this hard man', had seen him through this crisis; the lower he had sunk, the higher she had risen; Paulsen

v

calls her 'Murillo's Madonna', the painting named by Ibsen in his poem *In the Gallery*. He becomes prosperous and tries to be aristocratic (Paulsen uses the adjective *fornem* which had begun to recur somewhat frequently in Ibsen's letters and conversation, and which is held up as an ideal by Dr Stockmann in *An Enemy of the People*). But the humiliations which Pehrsen suffered in youth have left him with a feeling of inferiority from which he cannot escape. The son dreams of a diplomatic career, and the family emigrates to Rome (of the social life of which Paulsen paints a lively picture). The book has Paulsen's usual virtues and defects; it is extremely readable (even today), written with an eye for detail and a sense of atmosphere, and ends the way his books usually end, in rubbishy and unconvincing melodrama.

It seems inconceivable that Paulsen did not intend to portray the Ibsens, or that he could have been unconscious that his readers would assume them to be the originals; it also seems extraordinary that he could have wished to libel a man whom he genuinely admired and who had been particularly kind to him. Yet perhaps Paulsen was being no more naïve than Ibsen had been in assuming that Bjørnson would not be offended by *The League of Youth*. He wrote Ibsen a letter assuring him that he had intended no harm, to which Ibsen replied with an open card addressed care of the Scandinavian Club and bearing the one word 'Scoundrel!' with his signature. And that was the end of that friendship.

An Enemy of the People was published on 28 November 1882, in an edition (despite the calamitous sales of *Ghosts*) of ten thousand copies. Its reception was mixed. Not surprisingly, Dr Stockmann's hard remarks about political parties offended all the reviewers who belonged to either; a contemporary cartoon (in *Vikingen*, on 9 December) showed Ibsen chastising first the Liberals to the delight of the Tories, then the Tories to the delight of the Liberals, and finally, in the person of Dr Stockmann, both together. Henrik Jæger, fresh from lecturing against *Ghosts* round the country, declared in *Aftenposten* (4, 5 and 6 December) that *An Enemy of the People* was 'personally the most likeable, psychologically the most interesting, and aesthetically the weakest of Ibsen's plays'. Arne Garborg, in *Nyt Tidsskrift* (1882, pp. 571–581) praised its technique but complained that 'there is a great deal of violent swearing', and that the public meeting in Act Four, which evidently nettled him, was 'rather detached and distant, almost as though portrayed from some other age but in a modern setting'. Erik Vullum in *Dagbladet* (29 and 30 November and 1 December) objected that, just as Bjørnson had been going round the country 'and even in America', holding meetings to proclaim his convictions about truth and justice, so 'now Ibsen comes and does exactly the same; he holds public meetings from town to town, and the public has to pay to attend them'.

Danish liberal circles were very cool. Edvard Brandes, greatly piqued, began his review in *Dansk Morgenbladet* (7 December) by calling it 'a disappointment', sharply criticised several of Dr Stockmann's remarks, and ended by characterising the play as 'a mere dramatised newspaper article written in answer to some poor newspaper scribblings [i.e., the attacks upon *Ghosts*] which weren't worth a ha'porth of gunpowder, let alone a literary reply from a great author'. Strindberg, whose political feelings were equally fervent, also disliked it. 'I begin to hate Ibsen after *An Enemy of the People*', he wrote to Bjørnson on 4 May 1884. 'There's something insufferably *aesthetic* about him' (the modern word would be 'uncommitted'). Georg Brandes did not review it, though he later described it as 'one of his keenest and wittiest plays'.[1]

Much the most percipient review came from Erik Bøgh who, however wrong he may have been about *Ghosts*, saw what Ibsen was aiming at. In *Dagens Nyheder*[2] (5 December), Bøgh wrote: 'Henrik Ibsen is incontestably the writer who . . . least bothers himself with private causes. He has never pleaded the cause of any social class, any religious faith or any party, political or aesthetic; still less has he, like the French theatrical advocates, defended any of the Seven Deadly Sins and sought to move hearts and evoke tears on behalf of any penitent Magdalene or interesting criminal. He has other issues on his brief. He is now, once and for all, the attorney of ideas, and this task he performs without pity or mercy, without respect for Right or Left, and with no compliments to the jurors or public gallery . . . Those who know the play only through newspaper accounts will ask: "But how can an audience's attention be held for an entire evening by a debate which rages for three acts about a drainage system, in the fourth act makes fun of demagogy, and in the fifth is finished?" My answer would be: "It is not possible—for anyone except Ibsen. He has so wrought this masterpiece that no one will deny it, or at any rate no one who knows anything about the theatre." But Heaven preserve us from those who would imitate him without his unique gifts; for the success which this miraculously interesting theatrical debate will have on the stage will certainly result in a multitude of newspaper articles composed in dialogue.'

Bøgh also, with a fellow-craftsman's percipience, praised Ibsen's ability to 'treat a genuinely tragic theme with no trace of tragic apparatus, no pathos, employing everyday circumstances with everyday people speaking everyday prose . . . presenting his hero not merely without an idealised costume but without any pretence at an idealised personality'.

The theatres seized eagerly upon the play. The Christiania Theatre and the Royal Theatres of Copenhagen and Stockholm, all of which had rejected

---

[1] Georg Brandes, *Henrik Ibsen* (Copenhagen, 1898), p. 144.
[2] Reprinted in *Dit og Dat af 1882* (Copenhagen, 1883), pp. 228–239.

Ghosts as unfit for public presentation, immediately acquired production rights of *An Enemy of the People*, apparently unembarrassed by the fact that its theme was the unworthiness of those who 'do not dare'. Hans Schrøder, the director of the Christiania Theatre, telegraphed Ibsen for permission to give the first public performance of the play, and Ibsen agreed, stinging them for a lump payment of 4,000 crowns (£222); he had let them have *A Doll's House* for 2,500 crowns (£139). During December he wrote Schrøder three letters which have only recently come to light[1] and which are indispensable reading to any director attempting to stage the play:

Rome, 14 December 1882
Permit me to address to you a few lines concerning the forthcoming production of An Enemy of the People. *It is not my intention or wish to attempt to influence in* absentio *either the staging or the casting; but the expression of certain feelings which I hold regarding various aspects of the play can do no harm.*

I trust I may assume that Mrs Wolf will play Mrs Stockmann . . . If for the role of Hovstad you have an otherwise suitable actor of not too heroic build, that is the kind of man you should choose. Hovstad is the son of poor people, has grown up in a dirty home on wretched and inadequate food, has frozen and toiled horribly throughout his childhood, and subsequently, as a poverty-stricken young man, has had to undergo considerable privation. Such living conditions leave their mark not only on a man's spirit but also on his outward appearance. Men of heroic exterior are an exception among the plebs. Whatever the circumstances Hovstad must always wear a depressed appearance, somewhat shrunken and stooping, and uncertain in his movements; all, of course, portrayed with complete naturalism.

Billing's lines are so worded that they require an east-coast and not e.g. a Bergen dialect. He is, essentially,. an east-coast character.

Captain Horster has been ridiculously misunderstood by a Danish critic. He characterises Horster as an old man, Dr Stockmann's old friend, etc. This is, of course, utterly wrong. Horster is a young man, one of the young people whose healthy appetite delights the Doctor, though he is an infrequent visitor at the house because he dislikes the company of Hovstad and Billing. Already in Act One, Horster's interest in Petra must subtly and delicately be indicated, and during the brief exchanges between him and her in Act Five we must sense that they stand at the threshold of a deep and passionate relationship.

Both the boys must be carefully instructed so that the difference in their characters is clearly established. And I must beg that in Act Four every possible actor at your disposal be used. The stage director must here enjoin the greatest possible naturalism and

---

[1] Øyvind Anker, *Henrik Ibsens brevveksling med Christiania Theater, 1878–1899*, pp. 25–31.

strictly forbid any caricaturing or exaggeration. The more realistic characters you can work into the crowd the better.

Throughout the play the stage director must inexorably insist that none of the players alters his or her lines. They must be spoken exactly as they stand in the text. A lively tempo is desirable. When I was last at the Christiania Theatre the speech seemed to me to be very slow.

But above all, truthfulness to nature—the illusion that everything is real and that one is sitting and watching something that is actually taking place in real life. An Enemy of the People is not easy to stage. It demands exceptionally well-drilled ensemble playing, i.e. protracted and meticulously supervised rehearsals. But I rely upon the good-will of all concerned . . .

Ten days later, on Christmas Eve, Ibsen had occasion to write again to Schrøder:

Morgenbladet has published an announcement about the casting for An Enemy of the People, *in consequence of which I must further inconvenience you with a few lines. I see that Gundersen is to play the Mayor. This actor's appearance hardly suggests a man who cannot bear to eat hot food in the evening, has a bad stomach and an uncertain digestion, and lives on weak tea. Nor is it well suited to a man who is characterised as neat, refined and fastidious. But these shortcomings can partly be countered by the right clothes and make-up. Mr Gundersen must therefore pay careful attention to these two points. Nor does Mr Reimers' physique fit such a temperament as Dr Stockmann's; hot-headed people are in general more slightly built. The same advice accordingly applies to Mr Reimers as that which I have suggested for Mr Gundersen. He must make himself as thin and small as possible.*

On 31 December Ibsen wrote again:

I fear I must once again trouble you with a few lines. From your kind letter which reached me yesterday I gather it is intended to have both the boys in my play acted by girls. This has somewhat disturbed me, since it seems to imply that sufficient attention has not been paid to the spirit in which this play was written and in which it requires to be staged. To allow boys' parts to be taken by women may sometimes be excusable in operetta, vaudeville, or the so-called romantic drama; for in these the prime requirement is unqualified illusion; every member of the audience is fully conscious throughout the evening that he is merely sitting in a theatre and watching a theatrical performance. But this should not be the case when An Enemy of the People *is being acted. The spectator must feel as though he were invisibly present in Dr Stockmann's living-room; everything here must seem real; the two boys included. Consequently they cannot be played by actresses dressed up in wigs and stays; their feminine figures will not be able to be concealed by their costume of shirt and trousers, and they will never make any spectator believe that he is looking at real schoolboys from some small town. How in any case can a grown woman make herself look like a ten year old child? Both parts must therefore be played by children, at worst by a couple of small girls whose figures are not yet fully developed; and then damn the corsets and let them have big boys' boots on their legs. They must also, of course, be taught the way boys behave.*

It is stated in the play that at the public meeting Dr Stockmann is to be dressed in black; but his clothes must not be new or elegant, and his white cravat should sit a little crooked.

The prospect of increased performance fees, and of a normal sale for the book, must have comforted Ibsen, for 1882 had been an even worse year financially than 1881. Apart from Gyldendal's advance on *An Enemy of the People*, and the reprint of *Poems*, he had earned only 1,130 crowns (£62):

	Crowns	£
Remainder of fee for *A Doll's House* from August Rasmussen (Danish touring rights)	200	11
Royalties for *Nora* at Vienna Stadttheater (4th quarter, 1881)	213	12
Fee for *Catiline* at Nya Teatern, Stockholm	400	22
Royalties for *Nora* at Munich Hoftheater (3rd and 4th quarters, 1881)	187	10
Fees, etc. from German League of Dramatists	47	3
Further fees, etc. from German League of Dramatists	29	1
Unspecified royalties from Munich Hoftheater	54	3
4th edition of *Poems*	975	54
1st edition of *An Enemy of the People*	8,400	467
	10,505	583

Yet, although by the beginning of the year his share holdings had amounted to 66,000 crowns (£3,667), he nevertheless asked Hegel on 2 December to buy him a further 4,000 crowns' (£222) worth of securities. Few writers can ever have saved so high a proportion of what they earned.

An Enemy of the People is less frequently performed today than most of Ibsen's mature plays, for two principal reasons. One is, simply, the size of the cast. A crowd costs money, and without a crowd the great fourth act loses much of its impact (and a small crowd is almost worse than no crowd at all). The other problem is ideological. Some of the opinions expressed by Dr Stockmann, especially his demand for 'aristocrats', contempt for the masses, and assertion that 'the minority is always right' strike an illiberal note in modern ears. On these points Ibsen was in fact expressing a commonly shared attitude; Mill, Tocqueville, Dickens and most liberal thinkers of the time distrusted the tyranny of the commonplace majority. 'Those whose opinions go by the name of public opinion . . . are always a mass, that is to say, collective mediocrity', wrote Mill in his great essay *On Liberty*. 'No government by a democracy or a numerous aristocracy, either in its political acts or in the opinions, qualities, and tone of mind which it fosters, ever did or could rise above mediocrity, except in so far as the sovereign Many have let themselves be guided (which in their best times they always have done) by the counsels and influence of a more highly gifted and instructed One or Few. The initiation of all wise or noble things comes and must come from individuals; generally at first from some one individual.' That is precisely Dr Stockmann's message. But it is an unfashionable viewpoint to put forward in an age of universal suffrage.

The play has, too, suffered worse than most from the dead hand of academic criticism. The kind of commentator that dismisses *Emperor and Galilean* as 'stone-cold', *Brand* as 'ambiguous' and *Little Eyolf* as 'a falling-off' (to quote from a recent and embarrassing English book intended as a vindication of Ibsen) has tended to reject *An Enemy of the People* as 'thin'. It lacks, indeed, the extra density and overtones of Ibsen's later works; but there are precious few other plays outside the Greeks, Shakespeare and Chekhov with which it need fear comparison. The truths it expresses have not dated, and are not likely to as long as there are town councils and politicians. Even adequately performed, it is one of the most accessible and compulsive of Ibsen's plays; and Dr Stockmann is one of the half-dozen greatest male parts he wrote.

Of all the roles that Konstantin Stanislavsky acted, by any author, this was his favourite, and when he acted it in Petrograd in 1905 for the Moscow Arts Theatre it was the scene of a remarkable demonstration. Stanislavsky has described the occasion in his autobiography:

'In that time of political unrest—it was but a little while before the first revolution—the feeling of protest was very strong in all spheres of society. They waited for the hero who could tell the truth strongly and bravely in the very teeth of the government. It is not to be wondered at that the image of Dr Stockmann became popular at once in Moscow, and especially so in Petrograd. *An Enemy of the People* became the favourite play of the revolutionists, notwithstanding the fact that Stockmann himself despised the solid majority and believed in individuals to whom he could entrust the conduct of life. But Stockmann protested, Stockmann told the truth, and that was considered enough.

'On the day of the well-known massacre in Kazansky Square, *An Enemy of the People* was on the boards of our theatre. The average run of spectators that night was from the intelligentsia, the professors and learned men of Petrograd. I remember that the stalls were filled almost entirely with grey heads. Thanks to the sad events of the day, the audience was very excited and answered even the slightest hints about liberty in every word of Stockmann's protest. In the most unexpected places in the play the thunder of applause would break in on the performance . . . The atmosphere in the theatre was such that we expected arrests at any minute and a stop to the performance. Censors, who sat at all the performances of *An Enemy of the People* and saw to it that I, who played Dr Stockmann, should use only the censored text, and raised trouble over every syllable that was not admitted by the censorship, were on this evening even more watchful than on other occasions. I had to be doubly careful. When the text of a role is cut and re-cut many times it is not hard to make a mistake and say too much or too little.

'In the last act of the play Dr Stockmann, putting into order his room which has been stoned by the crowd, finds in the general chaos his black coat,[1] in which he appeared at the meeting the day before. Seeing a rent in the cloth, Stockmann says to his wife: "One must never put on a new coat when one goes to fight for freedom and truth."

'The spectators in the theatre connected this sentence with the massacre in Kazansky Square, when more than one new coat must have been torn in the name of freedom and truth. Unexpectedly, my words aroused such a pandemonium that it was necessary to stop the performance, into which a real mob scene was interpolated by impromptu. There had taken place the unification of the actor and the spectators, who took on themselves the role of chief actor in the theatre, that same mob action of which so much is said by the theoreticians of art. The entire audience rose from its seats and threw itself towards the footlights. Thanks to the fact that the stage was very low and there was no orchestra before it, I saw hundreds of hands stretched towards me, all of which I was forced to shake. The younger people in the audience jumped on to the stage and embraced Dr Stockmann. It was not easy to establish order and to continue with the play. That evening I found out through my own experience what power the theatre could exercise.'[2]

---

[1] More accurately, his trousers.

[2] Konstantin Stanislavsky, *My Life in Art*, translated by J. J. Robbins (London 1924), pp. 378–379. Stanislavsky based his physical appearance in the role on Rimsky-Korsakov, and borrowed several gestures and characteristics from Gorki.

There will always, somewhere in the world, be a Kazansky Square;[1] and the historical importance of *An Enemy of the People* lies, as Erik Bøgh realised, in that it is, except for *Danton's Death*, which no-one then knew about, the first political debate which succeeds in remaining a great play. It possesses, too, a wit and lightness which people do not usually associate with Ibsen, though he had both qualities at his command, as *Peer Gynt* and *The League of Youth* bear witness. It is the most Shavian of Ibsen's plays; and the last act is one of his finest. What, one might ask on finishing Act Four, *can* he write that will not seem an anti-climax after this? Yet when one has read or seen that final act, one wonders how else one could possibly have supposed that he would end the play—the surest test of dramatic inevitability.

Some months after the publication of *An Enemy of the People* Georg Brandes wrote to Ibsen apparently (the letter is lost) rebuking him for isolationism and not putting his shoulder to the progressive wheel. Ibsen replied (12 June 1883): 'You are of course right when you say that we must all try to spread our opinions. But I firmly believe that an intellectual pioneer can never gather a majority around him. In ten years the majority may have reached the point where Dr Stockmann stood when the people held their meeting. But during those ten years the Doctor has not stood stationary; he is still at least ten years ahead of the others. The majority, the masses, the mob, will never catch him up; he can never rally them behind him. I myself feel a similarly unrelenting compulsion to keep pressing forward. A crowd now stands where I stood when I wrote my earlier books. But I myself am there no longer, I am somewhere else—far ahead of them—or so I hope.'

To the end of his literary career, which spanned fifty years, Ibsen was to keep moving relentlessly forward, never repeating the pattern of an earlier success. Just as, fifteen years previously, he had abandoned the epic form of poetic drama which had established him, so now he was to abandon the type of (to use a loose term) sociological drama which was to spread his fame throughout the western world, and with which his name is still principally and misleadingly linked. Having exposed the hollowness of a certain kind of left-wing politician in *The League of Youth*, he had gone on to expose the equal hollowness of their right-wing counterparts in *The Pillars of Society*; having questioned the sanctity of marriage in *A Doll's House*, he had questioned

---

[1] When it was staged in Paris at the time of the Dreyfus affair everyone identified Stockmann with Emile Zola (Lugné-Poe, p. 88). Its first performance there became linked with riots in the city, and it was deliberately chosen for the first Ibsen production in Spain, at the Teatre de Novetats in Barcelona on 14 April 1893, to help 'organised opposition to the established order in government and industry' (Gregersen, pp. 53–54.)

it yet further, together with several other equally sacred cows, in *Ghosts*. Then he had returned to the field of politics, broadening his sights so as to include the ordinary voter in his line of fire. *An Enemy of the People* is an attack, not merely on those who lead people by the nose, but on those who allow themselves to be thus led. These four plays, for all their differences, shared one theme in common: the necessity of discovering who one really is and of trying to become that person. In his next play, he was to question even this belief.

Select Bibliography

AGERHOLM, Edvard. *Henrik Ibsen og Det Kongelige Teater*, in *Gads Danske Magasin* (Copenhagen, 1910–1911).

ANKER, Øyvind. *Christiania Theater's Repertoire, 1827–1899* (Oslo,[1] 1956).

ANKER, Øyvind. *Henrik Ibsens brevveksling med Christiania theater, 1878–1899* (Oslo, 1965).

ANDERSEN, Annette. *Ibsen in America*, in *Scandinavian Studies and Notes* (Menaska, Wis., 1935–1937).

ANDERSEN, Hans Christian. *Brevveksling med Edvard og Henriette Collin*, ed. C. Behrend and H. Topsøe-Jensen, I–VI (Copenhagen, 1933–1937).

ANDERSEN, Hans Christian. *Dagbøger og Breve, 1868–1875*, ed. Jonas Collin (Copenhagen, 1906).

ARCHER, Charles. *William Archer* (London, 1931).

ARCHER, William. *Ibsen as I Knew Him*, in *Monthly Review* (London, 1906).

ARCHER, William. Introductions to *The Collected Works of Henrik Ibsen*, revised and edited by William Archer, I–XII (London, 1906 ff.).

BANG, Herman. *Teatret* (Copenhagen, 1892).

BERGGRAV, Eivind, and BULL, Francis. *Ibsens sjelelige kriser* (Oslo, 1937).

BERGMAN, Gösta M. *Den moderna teaterns genombrott, 1890–1925* (Stockholm, 1966).

BERGSØE, Vilhelm. *Henrik Ibsen paa Ischia og 'Fra Piazza del Popolo'* (Copenhagen & Christiania, 1907).

BJØRNSON, Bjørn. *Bare ungdom* (Oslo, 1934).

BJØRNSON, Bjørn. *Fra barndommens dage* (Christiania, 1922).

BJØRNSON, Bjørnstjerne. *Gro-tid (brev fra aarene 1857–1870)*, ed. Halvdan Koht, I, II (Christiania, 1912).

BJØRNSON, Bjørnstjerne. *Brytnings-aar (brev fra aarene 1871–1878)*, ed. Halvdan Koht, I, II (Christiania, 1921).

BJØRNSON, Bjørnstjerne. *Kamp-tid (brev fra aarene 1879–1884)*, ed. Halvdan Koht I, II (Oslo, 1932).

BJØRNSON, Bjørnstjerne. *Breve til Karoline, 1858–1907*, ed. Dagny Bjørnson-Sautreau (Oslo, 1957).

BJØRNSON, Bjørnstjerne. *Brevveksling med danske, 1875–1910*, ed. Øyvind Anker, Francis Bull and Torben Nielsen, I–III (Copenhagen, 1953).

---

[1] Christiania was renamed Oslo in 1925.

BJØRNSON, Bjørnstjerne. *Brevveksling med svenske, 1858–1909*, ed. Øyvind Anker, Francis Bull and Örjan Lindberger, I–III (Copenhagen, 1960–1961).

BLANC, T. *Christiania theaters historie, 1827–1877* (Christiania, 1899).

BRANDES, Edvard. *Litterære Tendenser* (Copenhagen, 1968).

BRANDES, Edvard. *Om Teater* (Copenhagen, 1947).

BRANDES, Georg, and BRANDES, Edvard. *Brevveksling med nordiske Forfattere og Videnskabsmænd*, I–VIII, ed. Morten Borup, Francis Bull and John Landquist (Copenhagen, 1939–1942).

BRANDES, Georg. *Henrik Ibsen* (Copenhagen, 1898).

BRANDES, Georg. *Levned*, I–III (Copenhagen, 1905–1908).

BREDSDORFF, Elias. *Sir Edmund Gosse's Correspondence with Scandinavian Writers* (Copenhagen, 1960).

BULL, Francis. *Essays i utvalg* (Oslo, 1964).

BULL, Francis. *Henrik Ibsen* in *Norsk litteratur-historie*, ed. Francis Bull, Frederik Paasche, A. H. Winsnes and Philip Houm, IV (Oslo, 1960).

BULL, Francis. Introductions to *Peer Gynt* and *Ghosts* in *C.E.* (*Henrik Ibsen, samlede verker, hundreårsutgave*), ed. Halvdan Koht, Francis Bull and Didrik Arup Seip (Oslo, 1928–1958).

BULL, Francis. *Nordisk kunsterliv i Rom* (Oslo, 1960).

BULL, Francis. *Tradisjoner og minner* (Oslo, 1945).

CHESNAIS, P. G. la. Introductions to *Œuvres complètes d'Henrik Ibsen, traduites par P. G. la Chesnais*, I–XVI (Paris, 1914–1945).

DARDEL, Fritz von. *Dagboksanteckningar, 1873–1876* (Stockholm, 1916).

DARDEL, Fritz von. *Dagboksanteckningar, 1881–1885* (Stockholm, 1920).

DERRY, T. K. *A Short History of Norway* (London, 1957).

DIETRICHSON, Lorentz. *Svundne tider, I–IV* (Christiania, 1894–1917).

DUVE, Arne, *Symbolikken i Henrik Ibsens skuespill* (Oslo, 1945).

ELLER, W. H. *Ibsen in Germany, 1870–1900* (Boston, 1918).

FENGER, Henning. *Georg Brandes Læreaar* (Copenhagen, 1955).

FENGER, Henning. *Ibsen og Georg Brandes indtil 1872*, in *Edda* (Oslo, 1964).

GEORGE, David E. R., *Henrik Ibsen in Deutschland: Rezeption und Revision* (Göttingen, 1968).

GOSSE, Edmund. *Ibsen* (London, 1907).

GOSSE, Edmund. *Two Visits to Denmark, 1872, 1874* (London, 1911).

GRAN, Gerhard. *Henrik Ibsen: liv og verker*, I, II (Christiania, 1918).

GRAN, Gerhard, ed. *Henrik Ibsen: festskrift i anledning af hans 70de fødselsdag* (Bergen, 1898).

GRANVILLE BARKER, Harley. *The Coming of Ibsen* in *The Eighteen-Eighties*, ed. Walter de la Mare (Cambridge, 1930).

GREGERSEN, H. *Ibsen in Spain* (Cambridge, Mass., 1936).

GRØNVOLD, Didrik. *Diktere og musikere* (Oslo, 1945).

GRØNVOLD, Marcus. *Fra Ulrikken til Alperne* (Oslo, 1925).

HALVORSEN, J. B. *Henrik Ibsen* in *Norsk forfatter-lexicon, 1814–1880*, III (Christiania, 1892).

HAMRE, Kari. *Clemens Petersen og hans forhold til norsk litteratur i aarene 1856–1869* (Oslo, 1945).

HEIBERG, Gunnar. *Ibsen og Bjørnson paa scenen* (Christiania, 1918).

HEIBERG, Gunnar. *Salt og sukker* (Christiania, 1924).

HEIBERG, Johanne Luise. *Et Liv gjennemlivet i Erindringer*, III (Copenhagen, 1892).

IBSEN, Bergliot. *De tre* (Oslo, 1948).

IBSEN, Henrik. *Samlede verker, hundreårsutgave*, I–XXI, ed. Halvdan Koht, Francis Bull and Didrik Arup Seip (Oslo, 1928–1958). [*C.E.*]

IBSEN, Henrik. *Efterladte skrifter*, ed. Halvdan Koht and Julius Elias, I–III (Christiania and Copenhagen, 1909).

JÆGER, Henrik. *Henrik Ibsen: et livsbillede* (Christiania, 1888).

JANSON, Kristofer. *Hvad jeg har oplevet* (Christiania, 1913).

JOSEPHSON, Ludvig. *Ett och annat om Henrik Ibsen och Kristiania teater* (Stockholm, 1898).

KINCK, B. M. *Henrik Ibsen og Laura Kieler*, in *Edda*, 1935.

KNORRING, Oscar von. *Två månader i Egypten* (Stockholm, 1873).

KNUDTZON, Frederik G. *Ungdomsdage* (Copenhagen, 1927).

KOHT, Halvdan. *Henrik Ibsen: eit diktarliv*, I, II (revised edition, Oslo, 1954).

KOHT, Halvdan. Introductions to *Brand, The League of Youth, Emperor and Galilean, The Pillars of Society, A Doll's House* and *An Enemy of the People* in *C.E.*

KOMMANDANTVOLD, K. M. *Ibsen og Sverige* (Oslo, 1956).

LAMM, Martin. *Det moderna dramat* (Stockholm, 1948).

LIE, Erik. *Erindringer fra et dikterhjem* (Oslo, 1928).

LIE, Erik. *Jonas Lie, oplevelser, fortalt af Erik Lie* (Christiania and Copenhagen, 1908).

LINDBERG, Per. *August Lindberg* (Stockholm, 1943).

LINDSTRÖM, Göran. *Strindberg contra Ibsen* in *Ibsen-Årbok, 1955–1956* (Skien, 1956).

LUGNÉ-POE, Aurélien. *Ibsen* (Paris, 1936).

MCFARLANE, J. W., ed. *The Oxford Ibsen*, IV–VI (London, 1960–1966).

MEYER, Michael. Introductions to and Stage Histories of *The Pretenders, Brand, Peer Gynt, The Pillars of Society, A Doll's House, Ghosts* and *An Enemy of the People*, translated by Michael Meyer (London, 1960–1966).

MIDBØE, Hans. *Streiflys over Ibsen* (Oslo, 1960).

NÆRUP, Carl. *Jonas Lie og hanssamtidige* (Christiania, 1915).

NIELSEN, L. C. *Frederik V. Hegel: et Mindeskrift*, I, II (Copenhagen, 1909).

NYHOLM, Kela. *Henrik Ibsen paa den franske scene*, in *Ibsen-Årbok, 1957–1959* (Skien, 1959).

OLLÉN, Gunnar. *Ibsens dramatik* (Stockholm, 1955).

ØSTVEDT, Einar. *Henrik Ibsen* (Oslo, 1968).

ØSTVEDT, Einar. *Henrik Ibsen og la bella Italia* (Skien, 1965).

PAULI, Georg. *Mina romerska år* (Stockholm, 1924).

PAULSEN, John. *Mine Erindringer* (Copenhagen, 1900).

PAULSEN, John. *Nye Erindringer* (Copenhagen, 1901).

PAULSEN, John. *Erindringer. Siste Samling* (Copenhagen, 1903).

PAULSEN, John. *Samliv med Ibsen* (Copenhagen and Christiania, 1906).

PAULSEN, John. *Samliv med Ibsen, 2den Samling* (Copenhagen and Christiania, 1913).

PETTERSEN, Hjalmar. *Henrik Ibsen 1828–1928, bedømt af Samtid og Eftertid* (Oslo, 1928).

SCHINDLER, Peter, *En Ungdom* (Copenhagen, 1942).

SEIP, Didrik Arup. Introduction to *Poems* in *C.E.*

SHAW, George Bernard. *Our Theatre in the Nineties* (revised edition, London, 1954), I–III.

SHAW, George Bernard. *The Quintessence of Ibsenism* (3rd edition, London, 1922).

SKAVLAN, Einar. *Gunnar Heiberg* (Oslo, 1960).

SPRINCHORN, Evert, ed. *Ibsen, Letters and Speeches* (New York, 1964).

STANISLAVSKY, Konstantin. *My Life in Art*, transl. J. J. Robbins (London, 1924).

STRINDBERG, August. *August Strindbergs brev*, ed. Torsten Eklund, I–XI (Stockholm, 1948 ff.).

STRINDBERG, August. *Konstakademiens utställning, 1877*, in *Kulturhistoriske studier* (Stockholm, 1881).

STRINDBERG, August. *Den litterära reaktionen i Sverige sedan 1865*, in *Tilskueren* (Copenhagen, 1886).

TEDFORD, Ingrid. *Ibsen Bibliography, 1928–1957* (Oslo, 1961).

TENNANT, P. F. D., *Ibsen's Dramatic Technique* (Cambridge, 1948).

THORESEN, Magdalene. *Breve, 1855–1901*, ed. J. Clausen and P. F. Rist (Copenhagen, 1919).

THORESEN, Magdalene. *Om Henrik Ibsen og hans hustru*, in *Juleroser* (Copenhagen, 1901).

VISTED, Kristofer. *Henrik Ibsen i karikaturen*, in *Boken om bøger*, II (Oslo, 1927).

ZUCKER, A. E. *Ibsen, the Master Builder* (London, 1929).

NEWSPAPERS AND PERIODICALS

Academy, Aftenbladet, Aftenposten, Aftonbladet (Stockholm), *Bergens-posten, Bergens Tidende, Dagbladet* (Christiania), *Dagbladet* (Copenhagen), *Dansk Maanedsskrift, Dølen, Edda, Fædrelandet, Folkets Avis, Fortnightly Review, Illustreret Nyhedsblad* (Christiania), *Illustreret Tidende* (Copenhagen), *Illustrated London News, London Figaro, Morgenbladet* (Christiania), *Morgenbladet* (Copenhagen), *Ny Illustrerad Tidning* (Stockholm), *Nyt Tidsskrift, Ord och Bild, Pall Mall Gazette, St James's Magazine, Samtiden, Scribner's Monthly Magazine, Spectator, Tilskueren, Vikingen.*

INDEX